The Synoptic Problem
A Bibliography, 1716–1988

New Gospel Studies 4

The Synoptic Problem
A Bibliography, 1716–1988

*
**

compiled and edited by

Thomas Richmond Willis Longstaff

and

Page A. Thomas

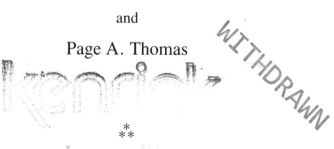

Kenrick

seminary library

Charles L. Souvay Memorial

*
**

MERCER

PEETERS

Ref
016.226
L857A

90701

ISBN 0-86554-321-6

The Synoptic Problem
A Bibliography, 1716–1988

Copyright © 1988
Mercer University Press, Macon GA 31207
All rights reserved
Printed in the United States of America

*
**

The paper used in this publication meets the minimum requirements
of American National Standard for Information Sciences—
Permanence of Paper for Printed Library Materials, ANSI Z39.48-1984.

*
**

Library of Congress Cataloging-in-Publication Data
Longstaff, Thomas R. W.
    The synoptic problem : a bibliography, 1716–1988 / compiled and edited
by Thomas Richmond Willis Longstaff and Page A. Thomas.
    xxviii + 232 pp. 6 × 9″ (15 × 23cm) — (New gospel studies ; 4)
    Includes indexes.
    ISBN 0-86554-321-6 (alk. paper)
    1. Synoptic problem—Bibliography.
2. Bible. N.T. Gospels—Bibliography.
I. Thomas, Page A. (Page Allison), 1936–
II. Title. III. Series.
Z7772.M1L66   1988
[BS2555.2]
016.226′066—dc19   88-21575
                                                                        CIP

Contents

Dedication

To Cynthia, Sarah, Anna, and William,
my nuclear family.
—Thomas R. W. Longstaff

To Caryetta, my wife.
—Page A. Thomas

Foreword

The time span from 1716 to 1988, a period of 272 years, can be divided into three periods, each dominated by a different solution to the synoptic problem. Until 1790 the view that the Gospels were composed in the canonical order Matthew, Mark, Luke, John held sway in virtually all the universities of Christendom. The period between 1790 and 1870, though featuring a plethora of experimental solutions to the synoptic problem, was nonetheless dominated by the view that the Gospels were probably composed in the sequence Matthew, Luke, Mark, John. The cornerstone of this reigning hypothesis, a solution more widely held in German universities than any other hypothesis, was the theory that Mark wrote third and composed his Gospel with a knowledge of the texts of both Matthew and Luke. The period of 1870 until 1970 was characterized by an as yet unexplained consensus within the world of liberal Protestant theological scholarship that Mark was the first gospel to have been written, and that Matthew and Luke independently copied Mark and a second source called "Q" which was made up primarily of sayings of Jesus. Since 1970, among experts, the solution to the Synoptic Problem has increasingly come to be regarded as an open question.

If one wishes to challenge this periodization of the history of the Synoptic Problem, the place to begin is with this bibliography. For within the covers of this volume one can find bibliographical references to most if not all the literature that bears on this question. Thus, for example, if one turns to the volume edited by Bernard Orchard and Thomas R. W. Longstaff, *J. J. Griesbach, Synoptic and Text-Critical Studies, 1776–1976* (Cambridge University Press, 1978), one will find on pages 176-81 a selected bibliography compiled by Frans Neirynck and Frans Van Segbroeck entitled "The Griesbach Hypothesis: a bibliography." The view that Mark was composed third in order and made use of both Matthew and Luke was first demonstrated by Johann

Jacob Griesbach in his famous *Commentatio* in 1789–1790. From that date onward, this view, according to the bibliography compiled by Neirynck and Segbroeck, gradually gained adherents until it reached a peak of academic acceptance during the decade 1830–1840. Reaction to the revolutionary social and theological implications of David Friedrich Strauss's *Das Leben Jesu* (1835–1836) appears to have adversely affected the academic popularity of this view. Why? To answer this question we need to see Strauss in relationship to his teacher Ferdinand Christian Baur. Baur, along with certain other scholars of the so-called Tübingen School which Baur headed, was among those scholars who had adopted the view that Mark was third.

The Tübingen School as a whole dated the Gospels after the eyewitness period. This shook the foundations and rattled the bell towers of conservative theology and further undermined the already threatened authority of "crown and altar." Strauss was the most brilliant star in that constellation of younger scholars standing in close relationship to Baur. He agreed with Baur both in dating the Gospels late and in accepting what had come to be known as the "Griesbach hypothesis." In some circles, it should be noted, this hypothesis was actually referred to as the "Tübingen hypothesis," in spite of the fact that some members of the school advocated solutions to the source question other than that of Griesbach.[1] Thus the reaction against Strauss and the Tübingen School that may have adversely affected further acceptance of the Griesbach solution, in part at least, was linked to the dangerously late date (second century) given to the Gospels in that school. In any case, according to the data drawn from the Neirynck-Segbroeck bibliography, publication of works advocating or assuming the Griesbach solution began to taper off during the decade 1840–1850. But in time the academic popularity of this hypothesis in Germany appears to have regained strength, if one may judge from the increase in publication during 1860–1870 over that of the previous decade. According to the Neirynck-Segbroeck bibliography the publication of books and articles presupposing the Griesbach hypothesis began to fall off again after the decade 1860–1870, and ceased entirely in Germany after 1890. Thus while reaction to Strauss may account for some adverse spin-off effects against the Griesbach hypothesis in the decade or so following the Strauss tempest, it is clear that the eventual demise of this hypothesis in Germany was not due to sociological and theological reaction against the Tübingen school. This hypothesis remained academically strong in both Protestant and

---

[1]See Reginald H. Fuller, "Baur Versus Hilgenfeld: A Forgotten Chapter in the Debate on the Synoptic Problem," NTS 24 (1978): 355- 70.

Roman Catholic universities in Germany up until the establishment of the Second Reich in 1870.

It is important to note that the Griesbach Hypothesis, while it originated in minds formed by the Protestant ethos, was not in and of itself a theory that favored the Protestant cause vis-à-vis Roman Catholicism. It was in due time adopted on critical grounds by some of the best Roman Catholic minds in Germany. In this regard one thinks especially of the Roman Catholic church historian Johannes Josef Döllinger.[2]

Before we dig more deeply into the history of the Synoptic Problem and especially the history of the eventual demise of the nineteenth- century Griesbach Hypothesis, it will be necessary to engage in more research into the political, sociological, and theological profile of adherents of the various nineteenth-century solutions of the Synoptic Problem. Until now it has been regarded as undesirable for the sake of academic and ecumenical theology to make any reference to the confessional stance of given scholars. But with the kind of historical investigation now called for, such academic proprieties must give way to realistic sociological analysis. So, while the Neirynck-Segbroeck bibliography will be a sine qua non for the student of the history of nineteenth-century criticism, it should be regarded as only a preliminary tool useful for the making of general observations. These general observations can be verified and/or corrected only by further research. The point is that the Neirynck-Segbroeck bibliography is the place to go to begin this further research. And what is the case in microcosm with regard to this specialized bibliography of sixty-five items, is ipso facto the case in macrocosm with the larger bibliography of approximately 1,967 titles not including the different editions and translations compiled by Longstaff and Thomas. It also is no more and no less than a preliminary yet indispensable tool for further research.

The title of this volume suggests that it will contain most if not all scholarly books and articles on the Synoptic Problem. And in the narrow sense of what is signified by ''Synoptic Problem,'' Longstaff and Thomas have given the reader a reasonably complete listing of such works. Certainly most if not all works that are known to have had any influence on the history of the academic discussion of the Synoptic Problem will be found listed alphabetically under the names of the authors. But the task of identifying such work is not complete, and doubtless scores if not hundreds of writings of this kind may yet be included. This is not to speak of the additional literature that will be

---

[2]After 1870 Döllinger became a founding member of the Old Catholic Church after being unable to accept the decrees of Vatican I.

unearthed in due time, as we broaden our inquiry to include the social history of the German universities during the nineteenth century, and as we investigate ideological factors involved in the calling of German university professors during the Second Reich.

As Longstaff and Thomas note, this bibliography is not limited to works on the Synoptic Problem in any "narrow sense." It includes works related to the wider question of the sources. It also includes works by critics who are utilizing (rather than arguing for) one theory or another. Thus, for example, many works in which the authors are utilizing the "Q" hypothesis have been included even though these works may not shed any light on the Synoptic Problem per se.

Some recent works have been added to this bibliography where authors have attempted to treat the text of one or more of the evangelists without assuming a particular source theory. In other cases, outstanding books about Jesus written since 1980, showing little or no methodological dependence on the two-document hypothesis, have been included. This is because these works illuminate some of the indirect effects of contemporary discussion of the Synoptic Problem.[3]

This bibliography is presented as a research instrument for the study of the "Synoptic Problem" in its widest possible context. The range of topics touched upon in this bibliography includes text criticism, synopsis making, source criticism, form criticism, and redaction criticism, as well as works that make clear the importance of the Synoptic Problem for understanding the so-called "historical" Jesus, and the question of canon. In this way the Synoptic Problem can be seen as important for Christian theology. Its importance for church history remains obscure, though not without interest.

Longstaff and Thomas have been at great pains to produce a state-of-the-art bibliography that is "user friendly." Their preface is must reading, for it states in detail how they have proceeded to achieve these ends and explicates by a judicious use of disclaimers the limits of this bibliography as a research volume, without defining in any excessively limiting way its possibilities as a research tool. The inclusion of the OCLC numbers for each entry is especially to be noted.

For the reader uninitiated into the mysteries of the Synoptic Problem and bewildered by its manifold complexity it is recommended that she or he begin with the volume of classical essays on the Synoptic Problem collected and

---

[3]See Bruce Chilton, "Silver Blaze Rides Again: Two Recent Historical Approaches to Jesus." (279B)

edited by Arthur J. Bellinzoni, Jr., Joseph B. Tyson, and William O. Walker, Jr.—*The Two-Source Hypothesis: A Critical Appraisal* (Macon GA: Mercer University Press, 1985). From these essays taken as a set it is possible to recognize that the contemporary discussion proceeds from criticism of Streeter's fundamental solution of the Synoptic Problem worked out in great detail in his book *The Four Gospels: A Study of Origins* (London: Macmillan, 1924).

For the reader interested in the history of the Synoptic Problem in its formative period and place, that is, Germany 1784 (Lessing) to 1863 (Holtzmann), it is recommended that he or she begin with Hans-Herbert Stoldt's *Geschichte und Kritik der Marcus-hypothese* (Göttingen: Vandenhoeck und Ruprecht, 1977; translated and edited by Donald L. Niewyk as *History and Criticism of the Marcan Hypothesis,* Macon GA: Mercer University Press, 1980). In studying the history of the Synoptic Problem, the "Date-of-Publication/Writing Index" in this volume will be of great value in enabling the reader to keep track of chronological developments, and in seeing each work within both its immediate and larger historical contexts.

Specialists will be surprised how much more there is to learn about given topics through use of the "Keyword Index" in this volume. For example, on the topic of the so-called "minor agreements," one can quickly learn that there are over a dozen works on this topic listed in the "Keyword Index." For each of these works there is a concise heading, so that under the heading "Minor Agreements of Matthew and Luke against Mark" one is referred immediately to an essay listed in the bibliography by Albert Fuchs which examines the treatment of these agreements by S. McLaughlin. With this bibliographical data in view, the inquiring reader is in a position to browse meaningfully in two ways. On the one hand, one will notice immediately the titles of some further studies Fuchs has contributed (one or more of these contain further treatment of this topic, including Fuchs's own solution for the problem of explaining these agreements). And on the other hand, one can turn to the name S. McLaughlin in the bibliography to get the bibliographical data on his work treating these agreements. In this way the "Keyword Index" provides a comprehensive guide to the interrelated character of this corpus of literature on the Synoptic Problem, will speed up and facilitate research, and thus significantly enhance the value of this bibliography. Each researcher possessing a copy of this volume has the opportunity of supplementing and correcting this "Keyword Index" in accordance with his or her own research agenda. The compilers welcome the colleagueship of such scholars in the perfecting of this bibliography.

What is inevitably missing in a book of this genre is any indication of the grandeur of the research for truth that has inspired the scholarship here documented and indexed. There is no explanation offered for the incredible amount of labor that has been expended and continues to be expended in the effort to resolve the Synoptic Problem. And yet, who will be able to thumb through these pages, so laboriously and so painstakingly compiled and edited by Longstaff and Thomas, and not be able to surmise something of the importance of what is at stake in all this investigation and reinvestigation of the relationships among the Gospels? This new tool for research is a sign, not of the past, but of the future. It represents a watershed on the continent of Gospel studies. What happens now is in the hands of the hardy and the true.

Dallas, Texas   *William R. Farmer*
July 1988

Preface

This bibliography had its origin in a Ph.D. dissertation project of Thomas R. W. Longstaff which he completed at Columbia University and Union Theological Seminary in New York between the years 1966 and 1972. At the completion of the project a sizable bibliography had been amassed (far greater in scope than the bibliography printed in the published version of that thesis[1]) which was shared with a number of others who were working on questions related to the sources of and relationships between the synoptic gospels.

In 1970, at the request of Professor William R. Farmer, photocopies of the working bibliography (which at that time included approximately 525 entries) were prepared for private use by members of the Society of Biblical Literature's seminar on the ''Sequence of the Gospels.'' In 1971 a supplement was issued, adding another sixty-five titles to the list.

From 1972 until 1983 the ''working bibliography'' had been kept reasonably up-to-date by adding new titles as they appeared in print or from other works citing older titles not included in the ''working bibliography.''

In 1983 Mercer University Press suggested that the bibliography be included in the New Gospel Studies series. The bibliography was revised and new titles added from *New Testament Abstracts* as well as from the bibliographies published in the most important books and articles on the synoptic problem. By the summer of 1985 an exhaustive and comprehensive list of resources available to researchers interested in the questions of synoptic origins and relationships had been compiled.

After an initial examination of the bibliography by Dr. James Dunkly, librarian of the Episcopal Divinity School/Weston School of Theology in

---

[1]Thomas R. W. Longstaff, *Evidence of Conflation in Mark? A Study in the Synoptic Problem*, SBLDS 28 (Missoula MT: Scholars Press, 1977).

Cambridge, Massachusetts, it was decided that each entry would be verified as to its completeness and accuracy. To accomplish this, each entry was re-keyed into the database management system "Pro-Cite" produced by Personal Bibliographic Software, Inc., 412 Longshore Drive, Ann Arbor, Michigan 48106, on a Tandy 1000HD for sorting and indexing purposes and transferred to the word processing system "Scripsit 1000" for editing.

Most entries, except those marked with one or two asterisks (* or **—see the list of sigla), have been verified against the original work or against a second or third citation of the work. A conscious effort has been made to be as thorough and accurate as possible in the citations and to include within the citations all pertinent data needed for citing and locating a particular title for research purposes. A major bibliography of this size is only as complete and accurate as its predecessors are, as no one person can be expected to have read and indexed *all* the material on a particular subject, especially one as complicated and diverse as the Synoptic Problem.

The following database and printed indexes and abstracts have been used for verification and accuracy.

1. OCLC. On line Data Base (Ohio College Library Center). Dublin, Ohio.
2. *Catholic Periodical and Literature Index*. Haverford PA: Catholic Library Association, 1968–   .
3. *Elenchus bibliographicus*. Louvain: Peeters [etc.], 1924–   .
4. *Elenchus bibliographicus biblicus*. Rome: Pontifical Biblical Institute Press, 1968–1977/1978.
5. *Elenchus bibliographicus biblicus of Biblica*. Rome: Pontifical Biblical Institute Press, 1979–   .
6. *Index to Religious Periodical Literature*. Chicago: American Theological Library Association, 1949/1952–1976.
7. *International Zeitschriftenschau für Bibelwissenschaft und Grenzgebiete = International Review of Biblical Studies = Revue Internationale des Etudes Bibliques*. Düsseldorf: Patmos Verlag [etc.], 1951/1952–   .
8. *National Union Catalog, Pre-1956 Imprints. Cumulative Author Lists.* 1958–   .
9. *New Testament Abstracts*. Cambridge MA: Weston School of Theology, 1956–   .
10. *Religious Index One. Periodicals*. Chicago: American Theological Library Association, 1977–   .

The bibliographies on Q prepared by Frans Neirynck and Frans Van Segbroeck, David M. Scholer, and John S. Kloppenborg also have been consulted.

It must be recognized that no such bibliography will ever be complete. It is always possible to add a few more titles of new (or overlooked) publications. It is also likely (perhaps certain) that some users of this volume will find that a particular book or article, considered by them of great importance, has been omitted. Current technology, however, makes this inevitable characteristic of a printed bibliography less problematic than in earlier years. This bibliography is maintained as a computer data base. In July 1987 the sorted and indexed data was transferred from a personal computer database to the composition computer system at Mercer University Press. Between July 1987 and July 1988, approximately 200 entries were added to the existing 1,747. Rather than have an addendum or renumber, which would have required resorting and reindexing, these additional entries were added to existing numbers as A, B, C, and so forth (for example, 175B). These new entries are included in the Date Index and Keyword Index. It will be possible to continue to add titles (as they are published or noted) and to provide users with supplements at reasonable intervals. Accordingly, users of this volume are encouraged to suggest titles for addition (or even for deletion as irrelevant). Such suggestions may be addressed to either of the compilers or to Mercer University Press.

This bibliography includes the major works (books and reviews; articles in journals and collected essays; dissertations; unpublished material) not only with reference to the synoptic problem, but with reference to the wider question of the sources of and interrelationships among the synoptic gospels. A number of works are included which, while not dealing with the issues directly, are relevant and have been cited in the literature. Many of the books in the bibliography themselves contain excellent bibliographies. The most important of these have the notation ''Includes bibl.''

This bibliography is divided into three sections: (1) Author/title index; (2) date of publication/writing index (author and entry number listed); and (3) keyword index with entry numbers.

(1) Author/title index. This index includes the usual author/editor statement, title statement, and edition and publication statement. To this has been added any information regarding reprints, microforms, later editions, and translations and/or original title, thereby providing the user with a printing history of the text. Book reviews are listed with the book citation, with a ''see reference'' from the reviewer, for example: Nineham, Dennis E. 1977. As reviewer see Farmer, William R., _Synoptic Problem_. Most books listed include an OCLC access number or _NUC Pre-1956_ identification number and a library holding code from OCLC or NUC. Brief notes, such as ''A revision

of the author's thesis," "In German, French, or English," "Originally issued as," and so forth are included. It is hoped that these additions to the usual bibliographic information will make this a very "user-friendly" bibliography.

(2) Date-of-publication/writing index. This index includes the date of the first edition or date of the original text.

(3) Keyword index. The question of how to index a bibliography of this size and make it useful for the user has plagued the authors from the very beginning. Since none of us had read all of the approximately 1,967 titles, and many of the titles were not self-explanatory, we decided to use the keyword approach rather than a strict subject index. Words or terms from the titles serve as the basic terms in the index, along with preselected categories (such as "Augustinian Hypothesis," "Two-Document Hypothesis," "Two-Gospel (Griesbach) Hypothesis," "Q," "Verbal Agreement," and so forth). A Scripture index of texts mentioned in the titles is included as part of the keyword index. This is, as far as we can determine, the first attempt to include a "subject" index to a major bibliography; therefore, suggestions would be appreciated.

Thomas R. W. Longstaff   *Page A. Thomas*
Waterville, Maine   Dallas, Texas
July 1988   July 1988

Acknowledgments

It is customary, expected, and especially appropriate here to acknowledge the efforts of those whose assistance has made the completion of this work possible. In this spirit, and with genuine gratitude, I would like to express appreciation to:

Arthur Nagle, my student research assistant at Colby College in 1983–1984, who spent many long hours reading through issues of *New Testament Abstracts* and even longer hours at a computer terminal entering many of the titles which appear in this work. Without his cheerful diligence the work might not have progressed as far as it did in those early years. Certainly without his assistance the work would have been even more tedious than together we found it to be.

Colby College, its trustees, administration, and faculty, whose support of my professional activities has always been exceptional. In this instance the cooperation of Jonathan Allen and the staff of the Computer Services Department were invaluable.

The Massachusetts Institute of Technology, and especially to Steven Lerman and the staff of Project Athena. My work on this project reached its conclusion while I was a visiting scholar at the Center for Materials Research in Archaeology and Ethnology and in the Program in Science, Technology, and Society at "The Institute." The resources of Project Athena, a computer network compatible with the computing facilities at Colby College, made it possible for me to work without inconvenience, interruption, or the need to learn a "new system."

James Dunkly and the staff at the library at the Episcopal Divinity School/Weston School of Theology in Cambridge, Massachusetts. The combination of an excellent library and a cordial and cooperative staff made the checking and rechecking of minutiae far more pleasant than it might have been.

Page A. Thomas, who shared the burden of completing the project with me. He not only completed the detailed work remaining, but "polished" the bibliography, and provided structure and the indexes, and supplemented it with notations of recently published works (as well as adding earlier titles which had been overlooked).

William R. Farmer, for his friendship and support through nearly twenty-five years. Although my interests have shifted, Bill's friendship has remained constant. Without his support this project would never have been attempted or completed.

Cynthia, Sarah, Anna, and William, my nuclear family, whose tolerance and unselfish support of my diverse endeavors is largely responsible for the completion of many of them. I claim as my own responsibility those which remain unfinished. To them I dedicate my part in this bibliography.

Waterville, Maine   *Thomas R. W. Longstaff*
16 May 1988

In the same spirit of genuine gratitude, I would like to express appreciation to:

John D. Zimmerman, Allen Clayton, and Robert Lee Williams for reading the manuscript and "galley proofs" and catching, I hope, all those little typographical mishaps that have plagued the most careful scholars and printers since the beginning of printing.

Linda Umoh, who spent her free time at the American Theological Library Convention in Berkeley, California, researching unverified entries in the Graduate Theological Union Library and for making valuable suggestions as to structure, style, and so forth.

William R. Farmer, who was responsible for bringing Thomas R. W. Longstaff and me together for the completion of this bibliography. I value his friendship and the support he has given me since my days as a student in Perkins in the late 1950s and as a member of the Bridwell Library Staff since that time to the present.

Bridwell Library, Perkins School of Theology, Southern Methodist University, Dallas, Texas, where I have had the freedom to pursue my own interests in the fields of Old and New Testament Studies and Archaeology. The resources here have been invaluable in completing this project.

Decherd Turner, who introduced me to the study of bibliography by inviting me to join the staff of Bridwell Library in 1961. He tutored me for almost twenty years in the ways of the bibliophiles and I will ever be grateful for his patience, guidance, and gentle ways.

Caryetta, my wife, who has endured my unorthodox pursuits and bibliographic habits, and the sound of the printer until wee hours in the morning. Without her assistance the updating of the indexes would never have been completed on time. To her my part in this bibliography is dedicated.

Dallas, Texas   *Page A. Thomas*
2 July 1988

Sample Entries

Example 1

768A [1]Kähler, Martin. [2]*The So-Called Historical Jesus and the Historic, Biblical Christ.* [3]Trans., ed., and with an intro. by Carl E. Braaten; foreword by Paul J. Tillich. [4]Philadelphia: [5]Fortress Press, [6]1964. [7](Seminary Editions.) 1977. [8]153pp. [9](Fortress Texts in Modern Theology.) 1988 (to be published in November 1988). [10]Translation of the first and second essays in *Der sogenannte historische Jesus und der geschichtliche, biblische Christus.* [11]2. erw. und erläuterte Aufl. Leipzig: George Böhme, 1896. 206pp. [12]Neu hrsg. von E. Wolf, 2. erweiterte Aufl. [13](Theologische Bücherei 2.) München: C. Kaiser, 1965. [14]4. Aufl. 1969. 126pp. [15]Microfiche of 1896 printing. Chicago: American Theological Library Association, 1985. (ATLA Monograph Preservation Program. ATLA Fiche 1985-1824.)

OCLC: 17042 ISB; 5169125 WAU; 17983215 (announced for November 1988); 9141308 CFT; 6163029 TJC; 1426482 TOL; 17493464 TJC.

---

[1]Author. [2]Title. [3]Other title page information.
[4]Place of publication. [5]Publisher. [6]Date of publication.
[7]Series statement of 1977 printing. [8]Extent of work.
[9]Series statement of 1988 printing (announced). [10]Translation statement.
[11]Edition and publication statements of the 1896 edition.
[12]New German edition, with new editor.
[13]Series statement of German edition.
[14]Fourth German edition. [15]Microform.

Example 2

865 Lambrecht, Jan. [1]*Parables of Jesus: Insight and Challenge.* Trans. from the Dutch by René Van de Walle, and Christopher Begg. Bangalore, India: Theological Publications in India, 1978. 346pp. [2]*Once More Astonished: The Parables of Jesus.* New York: Crossroad, 1981. 245pp. [3]Trans. of *Terwijl hij tot ons sprak: Parabels van Jesus.* Met een voorwoord van A. J. Simonis en P. Schruers. Amsterdam: Lanoo/Tielt, 1976. 296pp. [4]French. *Tandis qu'il nous parlait: Introduction aux paraboles.* Traduit par Soeur Marie Claes; préface de A. L. Descamps. Paris: Éditions Lethielleux; à Namur: Culture et Vérité, 1980. 302pp. (Le Sycamore.)
OCLC: 456070 ISS; 7573057 ISB; 3467618 BWE; 9221901 BWE

[1]English title published in 1978.
[2]English title re-issued under new title in 1981.
[3]Original Dutch title published in 1976.
[4]French translation published in 1980.

Example 3

898 Léon-Dufour, Xavier. [1]*The Gospels and the Jesus of History.* Trans. from the French, ed. by John McHugh. New York: Image Books, 1968. 312pp. [2]London: Collins, 1968. 288pp. [3]New York: Image Books, 1970. [4]Trans. of *Les Évangiles et l'histoire de Jésus.* Paris: Éditions de Seuil, 1963. 525pp. [5]German. *Die Évangelien und der historische Jesus.* Aschaffenburg: Paul Pattloch, 1966. 599pp. [6]Spanish. *Los evangelios y la historia de Jesus.* Traducción castellana por Pedro Darnell. Barcelona: Editorial Estela, 1966. 457pp. (Coleccíon theologia 3.) [7]Includes bibl.
OCLC: 12998940 TCT; 462477 CSU; 387510 ATO; 7788044 TJC; 13846166 CLU.

[1]English title, New York printing, 1968.
[2]English title, London printing, 1968.
[3]English title, New York printing, 1970.
[4]Original French title, 1963.
[5]German translation, 1966.
[6]Spanish translation, 1966.
[7]Includes bibliography.

Abbreviations

BZ   *Biblische Zeitschrift* (Paderborn)
CBG   *Collationes Brugenses et Gandavenses* (Gent)
CBQ   *Catholic Biblical Quarterly* (Washington)
CCER   *Cahiers du cercle Ernest-Renan (Paris)*
ChrC   *Christian Century* (Chicago)
ChrSR   *Christian Scholar Review* (Wenham MA)
ChrTo   *Christianity Today* (Carol Stream IL)
CleR   *Clergy Review* (London)
ColVlaamTs   *Collationes. Vlaams Tydschrift voor Theologie en Pastoraal* (Gent)
Communio   *Communio* (Sevillia)
CoTh   *Collectanea theologica* (Warszawa)
CQR   *Church Quarterly Review* (London)
CrNSt   *Cristianesimo nella Storia* (Bologna)
CThM   *Concordia Theological Monthly* (St. Louis MO)
CThQ   *Concordia Theological Quarterly* (St. Louis MO)
CTJ   *Calvin Theological Journal* (Grand Rapids MI)
CTM   *Currents in Theology and Mission* (Chicago)
DBS   *Dictionnaire de la Bible. Supplément* (Paris)
DeBiM   *Deltion biblikōn meletōn* (Athens)
Direction   *Direction*
DR   *Downside Review* (Bath)
DrewG   *Drew Gateway* (Madison NJ)
DT(P)   *Divus Thomas* (Piacenza)
DTT   *Dansk Teologisch Tidsskrift* (Copenhagen)
EE   *Estudios ecclesiásticos* (Madrid)
EeV   *Esprit et Vie* (Langres)
Encounter   *Encounter: Creative Theological Scholarship* (Indianapolis IN)
EQ   *Evangelical Quarterly* (London)
EstBib   *Estudios Biblicos* (Madrid)
ET   *Expository Times* (Birmingham)
EThL   *Ephemerides Theologicae Lovanienses* (Louvain/Leuven)
ETR   *Études théologiques et religieuses* (Montpellier)
EvTh   *Evangelische Theologie* (München)
Exp   *Expositor* (London)
Forum   *Forum* (Donner MT)
Gr   *Gregorianum. Commentarii de re theologica et philosophica* (Rome)
GThT   *Gereformeerd theologisch tijdschrift* (Amsterdam)
HibJ   *Hibbert Journal. A Quarterly Review of Religion, Theology, and Philosophy* (London)
HThR   *Harvard Theological Review* (Cambridge MA)
HThS   *Harvard Theological Studies* (Cambridge MA)
HUCA   *Hebrew Union College Annual* (Cincinnati)
IBiS   *Irish Biblical Studies* (Belfast)

Interp *Interpretation* (Richmond VA)
Interpreter *Interpreter* (London)
IThQ *Irish Theological Quarterly* (Marynooth)
JAAR *Journal of the American Academy of Religion* (Atlanta GA)
JBL *Journal of Biblical Literature* (Atlanta GA)
JBR *Journal of Bible and Religion* (Boston MA)
JBW *Jahrbücher der biblischen Wissenschaft* (Göttingen)
JDTh *Jahrbücher für deutsche Theologie* (Stuttgart)
JETS *Journal of the Evangelical Theological Society* (Wheaton IL)
JPTh *Jahrbücher für protestantische Theologie* (Braunschweig)
JR *Journal of Religion* (Chicago)
JSNT *Journal for the Study of the New Testament* (Sheffield)
JTC *Journal of Theology and the Church* (New York)
JThS *Journal of Theological Studies* (Oxford)
JTSA *Journal of Theology for Southern Africa* (Braamfontein, Transvaal)
Kairos *Kairos. Zeitschrift für Religionswissenschaft und Theologie* (Salzburg)
LiBi *Linguistica Biblica* (Bonn)
LoS *Life of the Spirit* (London)
LQ *Lutheran Quarterly* (Gettysburg)
LQHR *London Quarterly and Holborn Review* (London)
LThJ *Lutheran Theological Journal* (Adelaide, Australia)
LThK *Lexikon für Theologie und Kirche* (Freiburg)
LTP *Laval théologique et philosophique* (Québec)
MCM *Modern Churchman* (Oxford)
NBl *New Blackfriars* (London)
NKZ *Neue kirchliche Zeitschrift* (Erlangen)
NovT *Novum Testamentum* (Leiden)
NovTSup Supplements to NovT (Leiden)
NRTh *Nouvelle revue théologique* (Louvain/Leuven)
NTS *New Testament Studies* (Cambridge)
NTT *Norsk teologish tidsskrift* (Oslo)
PerspRS *Perspectives in Religious Studies* (Macon GA)
PSThJ *Perkins School of Theology Journal* (Dallas)
RAp *Revue apologétique* (Paris)
RB *Revue biblique* (Jerusalem)
RelLife *Religion in Life* (Nashville)
RelStB *Religious Study Bulletin* (Calgary, Alberta)
RelStR *Religious Studies Review* (Hanover PA)
RelStT *Religious Study and Theology* (Formerly *Religious Study Bulletin*) (Calgary, Alberta)
ResQ *Restoration Quarterly* (Abilene TX)
RevQ *Revue de Qumran* (Paris)
RGG *Religion in Geschichte und Gegenwart* (Tübingen)

RHPR *Revue d'histoire et de philosophie Religieuses* (Strasbourg)
RHR *Revue de l'historie des Religions* (Paris)
RivBib *Rivista biblica* (Rome)
RJ *Reformed Journal* (Grand Rapids MI)
RSPhTh *Revue des sciences philosophiques et théologiques* (Paris)
RSR *Recherches de science religieuse* (Paris)
RThPh *Revue de théologie et de philosophie* (Lausanne)
RTh(P) *Nouvelle revue de théologie*
RTL *Revue théologique de Louvain* (Louvain/Leuven)
RTR *Reformed Theological Review* (Melbourne)
SacDot *Sacra dottrina* (Bologna)
Salm *Salmanticensis* (Salamanca)
SBLDS Society of Biblical Literature Dissertation Series
SBLSPS Society of Biblical Literature Seminar Papers Series
SCnt *The Second Century. A Journal of Early Christian Studies* (Abilene TX)
Scrip *Scripture. Quarterly of the Catholic Biblical Association* (Edinburgh)
SEÅ *Svensk Exegetisk Årsbok* (Uppsala)
Semeia *Semeia* (Missoula MT, etc.)
SJTh *Scottish Journal of Theology* (Edinburgh)
SNTSMS Society for New Testament Studies Monograph Series
StEv *Studia Evangelica* (Berlin)
StNTSU *Studien zum Neuen Testament und seiner Umwelt* (Linz)
StPat *Studia Patavina* (Padua)
StTh *Studia Theologica* (Lund)
SvTK *Svensk Teologisk Kvartalskrift* (Lund)
TeItSett *Teologia It. Sett*
Th *Theology. A Journal of Historic Christianity* (London)
ThBe *Theologische Beiträge* (Wuppertal)
ThBl *Theologische Blätter* (Leipzig)
Themelios *Themelios.* An International Journal for Theological Studies (Middlesex)
Theol(A) *Theologia* (Athens)
ThG *Theologie der Gegenwart* (Leipzig)
ThJb(T) *Theologische Jahrbücher* (Tübingen)
ThLZ *Theologische Literaturzeitung* (Leipzig)
ThPh *Theologie und Philosophie* (Frankfurt)
ThQ *Theologische Quartalschrift* (Tübingen)
ThR *Theologische Rundschau* (Tübingen)
ThRv *Theologische Revue* (Münster)
ThStKr *Theologische Studien und Kritiken* (Hamburg)
ThSt *Theological Studies* (New York)
ThT *Theologisch tijdschrift* (Leiden)
ThTo *Theology Today* (Princeton NJ)
ThZ *Theologische Zeitschrift* (Basel)

TRE *Theologische Realenzyklopädie* (Berlin)
TTh *Tijdschrift voor theologie* (Nijmegen)
TThZ *Trierer Theologische Zeitschrift* (Trier)
TVers *Theologische Versuche* (Berlin)
TynB *Tyndale Bulletin* (London)
TZTh *Tübingen Zeitschrift für Theologie*
USQR *Union Theological Seminary Quarterly Review* (New York)
VetChr *Vetera Christianorum* (Bari)
Way *Way* (formerly *Way of St. Francis* and *Way—Catholic Viewpoints*) (San Francisco)
WThJ *Westminster Theological Journal* (Philadelphia)
ZKTh *Zeitschrift für katholische Theologie* (Wien)
ZKWL *Zeitschrift für kirchliche Wissenschaft und kirchliches Leben* (Leipzig)
ZNW *Zeitschrift für die Neutestamentliche Wissenschaft* (Berlin)
ZRGG *Zeitschrift für Religions- und Geistesgeschichte* (Köln)
ZTh *Zeitschrift für Theologie* (Freiberg)
ZThK *Zeitschrift für Theologie und Kirche* (Tübingen)
ZThK.B *Zeitschrift für Theologie und Kirche*. Beiheft (Tübingen)
ZWTh *Zeitschrift für Wissenschaftliche Theologie* (Jena)

Other Abbreviations and Signs

Aufl *Auflage* (edition)

bibl bibliography

(CR) critical review

ET English translation

NUC *National Union Catalog, Pre-1956 Imprints* (*see* below)

OCLC Registered trademark of OCLC Computer Library Center, Inc., Dublin, Ohio 43017 (*see* below)

pt part

(R) review

Rpt reprint

* Indicates a citation that has *not* been verified with the original source or with a second bibliography.

** Indicates a citation, not verified, with incorrect or missing data—that is, citation is *known to be incorrect* as printed.

Symbols for holding libraries following OCLC access numbers are listed in the *OCLC Participating Institutions, Arranged by OCLC Symbol* directory. Symbols for holding libraries following NUC numbers are listed in the front and back of each volume of the *National Union Catalog, Pre-1956 Imprints* printed catalog.

The Synoptic Problem
A Bibliography, 1716–1988

1 Abbott, E. A. *Clue: A Guide through Greek to Hebrew Scripture.* London: Black, 1900. 157pp. (Abbott, E. A. *Diatessarica* pt 1.)
OCLC: 1019583 ISB.

2 _____. *The Corrections of Mark Adopted by Matthew and Luke.* London: Black, 1901, 334pp. (Abbott, E. A. *Diatessarica* pt 2.)
OCLC: 3464297 ISB.

3 _____. *Diatessarica.* 10 pts. London: Black, 1901–1917.

4 _____. *The Fourfold Gospel.* 5 vols. Cambridge: University Press, 1913–1917. (Abbott, E. A. *Diatessarica* pt 10.)
OCLC: 3926958 EXC.

5 _____. "Gospels." In *Encyclopaedia Britannica.* 9th ed. 10:789-843. Edinburgh, 1879.

6 _____, and W. G. Rushbrook. *The Common Tradition of the Synoptic Gospels: In the Text of the Revised Version.* London: Macmillan, 1884. 156pp.
OCLC: 4687243 ISB.

7 Abel, Ernest L. "Who Wrote Matthew?" NTS 17 (1971): 138-52.

8 Abrahams, Israel. *Studies in Pharisaism and the Gospels.* Cambridge: University Press, 1917. 1st series. Microfiche. Louisville KY: Lost Cause Press, 1977. 178pp.
Originally intended as vol. 3 of C. G. Montefiore's *The Synoptic Gospels.* London: Macmillan, 1909.
OCLC: 1944162 ISB; 4305127 ISB.

9 _____. *Studies in Pharisaism and the Gospels.* With a Prolegomenon by Morton S. Enslin. New York: Ktav, 1967. 1st and 2nd series. 2 vols. in 1. (Library of Biblical Studies.)
OCLC: 383576 ITD.

10 Achtemeier, Paul J. "The Lucan Perspective on the Miracles of Jesus: A Preliminary Sketch." JBL 94 (1975): 547-62.

11 _____. "The Origin and Function of the Pre-Marcan Miracle Catenae." JBL 91 (1972): 198-221.

12 _____. "Toward the Isolation of Pre-Markan Miracle Catenae." JBL 89 (1970): 265-91.

13A Addis, W. E. "The Criticism of the Hexateuch Compared with that of the Synoptic Gospels." In *Studies in the Synoptic Problem*, by Members of the University of Oxford, W. Sanday, ed., 364-86. Oxford: Clarendon Press, 1911. Microfiche. Louisville KY: Lost Cause Press, 1977. OCLC: 753275 ISB; 4045911 ISB.

13B Agnew, Peter W. "The Two-Gospel Hypothesis and a Biographical Genre for the Gospels." In *New Synoptic Studies: The Cambridge Gospel Conference and Beyond,* William R. Farmer, ed., 481-99. Macon GA: Mercer University Press, 1983. OCLC: 9783753 ISB.

14 Akagi, Tai. "The Literary Development of the Coptic Gospel of Thomas." Ph.D. diss., Western Reserve University, 1965. 406 leaves. Microfilm. Ann Arbor MI: University Microfilms, 1966. NUC: 67-77780 CBPac.

15 Aland, Kurt, ed. *Synopsis Quattuor Evangeliorum. Locis parallelis evangeliorum apocryphorum et patrum adhibitis edidit Kurt Aland. Editio decima et recognita ad textum editionum* [26]*Nestle-Aland et* [3]*Greek New Testament aptata.* 13th ed. rev. Stuttgart: Württembergische Bibelanstalt, 1985. xxxiii + 590pp. 9th ed. newly rev. 1976. 4th ed. rev. 1967. 1st ed. 1963.
Prefatory matter in German, Latin, and English; text in Greek. The 1st ed. of Aland's synopsis (1963) employed the then-current edition of Nestle's text (Nestle-Aland 25th, 1963); with the 9th ed. of the synopsis (1976) the text was conformed to the 26th ed. of Nestle-Aland's *Novum Testamentum graece* (subsequently published in 1979); and with the 13th ed. of the synopsis the critical apparatus was conformed to that of Nestle-Aland 26th. OCLC: 5313480 OCA.

16 Albertz, Martin. *Die Botschaft des Neuen Testaments.* 1/1: *Die Entstehung des Evangeliums.* Zollikon Zürich: Evangelischer Verlag, 1947. OCLC: 4517152 ISB.

17 _____. *Die Synoptischen Streitgespräche: Ein Beitrag zur Formengeschichte des Urchristentums.* Berlin: Trowitzsch und Sohn, 1921. 166pp. OCLC: 1212959 BMC.

18 Albright, W. F., and C. S. Mann. *Matthew: Introduction, Translation, and Notes.* Garden City: Doubleday, 1971. 366pp. (Anchor Bible 26.) OCLC: 200174 ISB.

19A Aletti, Jean Noël. "Problème synoptique et théorie des permutations." RSR 60 (1972): 575-94.

19B Alexander, Philip S. "Midrash and the Gospels." In *Synoptic Studies: The Ampleforth Conferences of 1982 and 1983*, C. M. Tuckett, ed., 1-18. Sheffield: JSOT Press, 1984. (JSNT Supplement Series 7.) OCLC: 12451599 ISB.

19C _____. "Rabbinic Biography and the Biography of Jesus: A Survey of the Evidence." In *Synoptic Studies: The Ampleforth Conferences of 1982 and 1983*, C. M. Tuckett, ed., 19-50. Sheffield: JSOT Press, 1984. (JSNT Supplement Series 7.) OCLC: 12451599 ISB.

20 Allen, Willoughby C. "The Aramaic Background of the Gospels." In *Studies in the Synoptic Problem*, by Members of the University of Oxford, W. Sanday, ed., 287-312. Oxford: Clarendon Press, 1911. Microfilm. Louisville KY: Lost Cause Press, 1977. OCLC: 753275 ISB; 4045911 ISB.

21 _____. "The Aramaic Element in St. Mark." ET 13 (1901–1902): 328-30.

22 _____. "The Book of Sayings used by the Editor of the First Gospel." In *Studies in the Synoptic Problem*, by Members of the University of Oxford, W. Sanday, ed., 235-86. Oxford: Clarendon Press, 1911. Microfiche. Louisville KY: Lost Cause Press, 1977. OCLC: 753275 ISB; 4045911 ISB.

23 _____. *A Critical and Exegetical Commentary on the Gospel According to St. Matthew*. Edinburgh: T. & T. Clark, 1907. New York: C. Scribner's, 1907. 3rd ed. Edinburgh, 1912. New York, 1925. 338pp. Includes bibl. OCLC: 2584392 BCT; 355252 ISB; 882993 BHA; 7510700 ZYU.

24 _____. "A Criticism of the Two Document Theory of the Synoptic Gospels." *Interpreter* 10 (1914): 375-81.

25 _____. "Did St. Matthew and St. Luke use the Logia?" ET 11 (1899–1900): 424-26.

26 _____. "The Original Language of the Gospel According to St. Mark." Exp 6th ser. 1 (1900): 436-43.

27A Amann, É. *Le Protévangile de Jacques et ses ramaniements Latins*. Paris: Letouzey, 1910. 378pp. (Documents pour servir à l'étude des origines chrétiennes: Les Apocryphes du Nouveau Testament.) OCLC: 918968 CLU, COI.

27B Ammon, Christoph Friedrich von. *Dissertatio de Luca emendatore Matthaei*. Erlangen, 1805.*

28A Amore, R. C. *Two Masters, One Message. The Lives and Teachings of Gautama and Jesus*. Nashville: Abingdon Press, 1978. 208pp. Includes bibl. OCLC: 3447238 ISB.

28B Anger, Rudolf. *Ratio, qua loci Veteris Testamenti in Evangelio Matthaei laudantur, quid valeat ad illustrandam huius evangelii originem.* 3 vols. Leipzig: Litteris Edelmanni, Typogr. Universit., 1861–1862.
Issued as 3 "Programmschriften" of the Universität Leipzig for 1861–1862.
OCLC: 9769437 EMT.

29 Arai, S. "Das Gleichnis vom verlorenen Schaf—Eine traditionsgeschichte Untersuchung." AJBI 2 (1976): 111-37.

30 Argyle, A. W. "Agreements Between Matthew and Luke." ET 73 (1961–1962): 19-21.

31 _____. "An Alleged Semitism." ET 67 (1955–1956): 247.

32 _____. "An Alleged Semitism." ET 80 (1968–1969): 285-86.

33 _____. "Evidence for the View that St. Luke Used St. Matthew's Gospel." JBL 83 (1964): 390-96.
Reissued in *The Two-Source Hypothesis: A Critical Appraisal,* A. J. Bellinzoni, Jr., ed., 371-79. Macon GA: Mercer University Press, 1985.
OCLC: 11599674 ISB.

34 _____. *The Gospel According to Matthew.* Cambridge; New York: Cambridge University Press, 1963. 227pp. (Cambridge Bible Commentary: New English Bible.)
OCLC: 10401106 ISB.

35 _____. "The Greek of Luke and Acts." NTS 20 (1974): 441-45.

36 _____. "M and the Pauline Epistles." ET 81 (1969–1970): 340-42.

37 _____. "The Methods of the Evangelists and the Q Hypothesis." Th 67 (1964): 156-57.

38 _____. "Parallels Between the Pauline Epistles and Q." ET 60 (1948–1949): 318-20.

39 _____. "Paul and Q." ET 62 (1950–1951): 157.

40 _____. "Scripture Quotations in Q Material." ET 65 (1953–1954): 285-86.

41 Aune, David E. "Christian Prophecy and the Sayings of Jesus: An Index of Synoptic Pericopae Ostensibly Influenced by Early Christian Prophets." In *Society of Biblical Literature 1975 Seminar Papers,* George MacRae, ed., 2:131-42. Missoula MT: Scholars Press, 1975.

42 _____. *Prophecy in Early Christianity and the Ancient Mediterranean World.* Grand Rapids MI: Eerdmans, 1983. 522pp. Includes bibl.
OCLC: 9555379 ISB.

43 _____, ed. *Studies in New Testament and Early Christian Literature: Essays in Honor of Allen P. Wikgren.* Leiden: Brill, 1972. 274pp. (NovTSup 33.)
OCLC: 707874 ISB.

44   Ayles, H. H. B. "Origin and Date of the First Gospel." *Interpreter* 12 (1916): 170-77.

45   Baarda, T. "Markus 14,11: *epeggeilanto.*" GTht 73 (1973): 65-75.

46   ———, A. F. J. Klijn, and W. C. van Unnik, eds. *Miscellanea Neotestamentica.* Leiden: Brill, 1978. Vol. 1. (NovTSup 47.)
English, French, German, or Greek.
OCLC: 4359572 ISB.

47   Bacon, Benjamin W. *The Beginnings of Gospel Story: A Historico-Critical Inquiry into the Sources and Structure of the Gospel According to Mark. With exposition, notes upon the text, for English readers.* New Haven: Yale University Press, 1909. 238pp. (The Modern Commentary.)
OCLC: 338551 ISB.

48   ———. *The Gospel of Mark: Its Composition and Date.* New Haven: Yale University Press, 1925. 340pp.
OCLC: 1442446 ISB.

49   ———. *Is Mark a Roman Gospel?* Cambridge MA: Harvard University Press, 1919. New York: Kraus Reprint, 1969. 106pp. (Harvard Theological Studies 7.)
OCLC: 541435 ISB; 3551999 MFM.

50   ———. *The Making of the New Testament.* New York: Holt, 1912. London: T. Butterworth, 1912. 256pp. (Home University Library of Modern Knowledge 50.) Includes bibl.
OCLC: 713372 YMM; 4131158 MBS.

51   ———. "The Nature and Design of Q, the Second Synoptic Source." HibJ 22 (1923-1924): 674-88.

52   ———. *Studies in Matthew.* New York: Holt, 1930. London: Constable, 1930. 533pp.
Trans. of Matthew in pt. 3, pp. 163-335.
OCLC: 386448 ISB.

53   ———. "A Turning Point in Synoptic Criticism." HThR 1 (1908): 48-69.

54   Badcock, F. J. "The Date and Authorship of Q." CQR 132 (1941): 197-209.

55A   Badham, F. P. *St. Mark's Indebtedness to St. Matthew.* London: T. Fisher Unwin, 1897. New York: E. R. Herrick, 1897. 131pp.
OCLC: 4173981 ACL.

55B   Baird, William. "Luke's Use of Matthew: Griesbach Revisited." PSThJ 40/3 (1987): 35-38.

56   Bajard, J. "La structure de la péricope de Nazareth en Lc IV, 16-30. Propositions pour une lecture plus cohérente." EThL 45 (1969): 165-71.

57 Baker, Alfred. "Form and the Gospels." DRev 88 (1970): 14-26.

58A Balch, D. L. "Backgrounds of 1 Cor vii: Ascetical Words of the Lord in Q; Moses as an Ascetic θεῖος ἀνήρ in II Cor iii." NTS 18 (1972): 351-64.

58B Balch, D. L. "Comparing Literary Patterns in Luke and Lucian." PSThJ 40/2 (1987): 39-42.
A critical response to *The Death of Jesus* by Joseph B. Tyson. First read at a colloquy on New Critical Approaches in Synoptic Studies, held at Southern Methodist University, fall semester, 1986.

59 Balz, Horst R. *Methodische Probleme der neutestamentlichen Christologie.* Neukirchen: Neukirchen Verlag, 1967. 310pp. (Wissenschaftliche Monographien zum Alten und Neuen Testament 25.)
Based on the author's thesis, Universität Erlangen-Nürnberg, Erlangen. OCLC: 996407 ISB.

60 Bammel, Ernst. "The Baptist in Early Christian Tradition." NTS 18 (1971): 95-128.

61 _____. "Das Ende von Q." In *Verborum Veritas: Festschrift für Gustav Stählin zum 70. Geburtstag,* Otto Böcher and Klaus Haacker, eds., 39-50. Wuppertal: Theologischer Verlag Brockhaus, 1970.
OCLC: 3136383 KAT.

62 _____. "Papias." RGG 5 (1961): 47-48.

63 Banks, Robert. *Jesus and the Law in the Synoptic Tradition.* Cambridge; New York: Cambridge University Press, 1975. 310pp. (SNTSMS 28.)
A revision of the author's thesis, Cambridge, 1969.
OCLC: 1504695 ISB.

64 Barbour, R. S. *Traditio-Historical Criticism of the Gospels: Some Comments on Current Methods.* London: SPCK, 1972. 54pp. (Studies in Creative Criticism 4.)
OCLC: 628943 ICU.

65 Barclay, Robert. *The First Three Gospels.* Philadelphia: Westminster, 1966. London: SCM, 1966. 317pp. Includes bibl.
Based on a series of articles entitled "The Making and Meaning of the Gospels" which appeared in the *British Weekly.*
OCLC: 383220 WSU; 3138405 MBS.

66 Baring-Gould, S. *The Lost and Hostile Gospels: An Essay on the Toledoth Jeschu, and the Petrine and Pauline Gospels of the First Three Centuries of which Fragments Remain.* London: Williams and Norgate, 1874. 305pp.
OCLC: 5291181 STS.

67 Barnett, Albert E. *The New Testament: Its Making and Meaning.* Rev. New York: Abingdon Press, 1958. 304pp. Includes bibl.
OCLC: 382550 WSU.

68   Barr, Allan. *A Diagram of Synoptic Relationships: In Four Colours.* Edinburgh: T. & T. Clark, 1938. 7 folded pp.
OCLC: 826548 ISB.

69A   _____. "The Use and Disposal of the Marcan Source in Luke's Passion Narrative." ET 55 (1943–1944): 227-31.

69B   Barr, James. "The Miracles." In *Jesus and Man's Hope,* Donald G. Miller and Dikran Y. Hadidian, eds., 2:305-10. Pittsburgh: Pittsburgh Theological Seminary, 1971. (Perspective 2.)
OCLC: 142572 ISB.

70   Barrett, C. K. *The Gospel According to St. John: An Intro. with Commentary and Notes on the Greek Text.* New York: Macmillan, 1955. 531pp. London: SPCK, 1955. 1960. 2nd ed. Philadelphia: Westminster, 1978. 638pp.
OCLC: 1417156 BPS; 421166 ISB; 3381486 OKO.

71   _____. *The Holy Spirit and the Gospel Tradition.* London: SPCK, 1966. 176pp. Spanish. *El Espíritu Santo en la tradición sinóptica.* Salamanca: Secretariado Trinitario 1978. 275pp. (Koinonia 8.)
OCLC: 824541 IVD; 11902407 EBS.

72   _____. "The House of Prayer and the Den of Thieves." In *Jesus und Paulus: Festschrift für Werner Georg Kümmel zum 70. Geburtstag,* E. Earle Ellis and Erich Grässer, eds., 13-20. Göttingen: Vandenhoeck & Ruprecht, 1975.
OCLC: 1623299 ISB.

73   _____. "Q: A Re-examination." ET 54 (1942-1943): 320-23.
Reissued in *The Two-Source Hypothesis: A Critical Appraisal,* A. J. Bellinzoni, Jr., ed., 259-68. Macon GA: Mercer University Press, 1985.
OCLC: 11599674 ISB.

74   Barth, Fritz. *Einleitung in das Neue Testament.* Gütersloh: Bertelsmann, 1908. 488pp. 2nd ed. 1911. 467pp. 3rd ed. 1914. 490pp. 4th and 5th eds. 1921. 494pp.
OCLC: 4479989 IND; 9296822 EXG; 8116714; 6541630 ISB.

75   Barth, Gerhard. "Matthew's Understanding of the Law." In *Tradition and Interpretation in Matthew,* by Günther Bornkamm, Gerhard Barth, and H. J. Held; trans. by Percy Scott, 58-164. Philadelphia: Westminster, 1963. (New Testament Library.)
OCLC: 383441 ISB.

76   Bartlet, J. Vernon. "The Sources of St. Luke's Gospel." In *Studies in the Synoptic Problem,* by Members of the University of Oxford, W. Sanday, ed., 315-63. Oxford: Clarendon Press, 1911. Microfiche. Louisville KY: Lost Cause Press, 1977.
OCLC: 753275 ISB; 4045911 ISB.

77   Bartsch, H. W. "Eine bisher übersehene Zitierung des LXX in Mark 4,30." ThZ 15 (1959): 126-28.

78 Bauer, Bruno. *Kritik der Evangelien und Geschichte ihres Ursprungs.* Berlin: Hempel, 1851–1852. Aalen: Scientia Verlag, 1983. 4 vols. in 2 OCLC: 11079079 EYW.

79 Baur, Ferdinand C. "Rezension von C. H. Weisses Evangelische Geschichte." In *Jahrbücher für wissenschaftliche Kritik* (1839): 161ff. Review of (1674). OCLC: 6993771 BTI.

80 _____. *Kritische Untersuchungen über die kanonischen Evangelien, ihr Verhältniss zu einander, ihren Charakter und Ursprung.* Tübingen: L. F. Fues, 1847. 626pp. OCLC: 2832696 ISB.

81A _____. *Das Markusevangelium: nach seinem Ursprung und Charakter, nebst einem Anhang über das Evangelium Marcions.* Tübingen: L. F. Fues, 1851. 226pp. OCLC: 2704633 VTS.

81B _____. "Rückblick auf die neuesten Untersuchungen über das Markusevangelium." ThJb(T) 12 (1853): 54-93.

81C _____. "Der Ursprung und Character des Lukasevangeliums, mit Rücksicht auf die neuesten Untersuchungen." ThJb(T) 5 (1846): 453-615.

82 Bea, A. *The Study of the Synoptic Gospels: New Approaches and Outlooks.* English version ed. Joseph Fitzmyer. London: Chapman; New York: Harper & Row, 1965. Trans. of *La storicita del Vangeli.* 95pp. OCLC: 2649135 DAY; 387548 ISB.

83 Beardslee, William A. *Literary Criticism of the New Testament.* Philadelphia: Fortress Press, 1970. 86pp. (Guide to Biblical Scholarship: New Testament Series.) OCLC: 52774 ISB.

84 _____. "The Motif of Fulfillment in the Eschatology of the Synoptic Gospels." In *Transitions in Biblical Scholarship*, J. Coert Rylaarsdam, ed., 171-91. Chicago: University of Chicago Press, 1968. (Essays in Divinity 6.) OCLC: 192574 ISB.

85 _____. "The Wisdom Tradition and the Synoptic Gospels." JAAR 35 (1967): 231-40.

86 Beare, Francis Wright. *The Earliest Records of Jesus: A Companion to The Synopsis of the First Three Gospels, by Albert Huck.* New York: Abingdon Press, 1962. Oxford: Blackwell, 1962. 1964. 254pp. Includes bibl. OCLC: 383661 ISB; 2577285 EZN; 5581116 ODC.

87 _____. *The Gospel According to Matthew.* Cambridge MA: Harper & Row, 1981. Oxford: Blackwell, 1981. 254pp. Includes bibl. OCLC: 9321951 LLU; 7967574 IDK.

88 _____. "The Mission of the Disciples and the Mission Charge: Matthew 10 and Parallels." JBL 89 (1970): 1-13.

89 _____. "On the Synoptic Problem: A New Documentary Theory." AThR Suppl. Ser 3 (1974): 15-28.

---- Bearnaert, P. Mourlon. *See* Dideberg, Dany. (374).

---- _____. *See* Lafontaine, R. (854).

90 Beasley-Murray, George Raymond. *Jesus and the Kingdom of God.* Grand Rapids MI: Eerdmans; Exeter: Paternoster, 1986. 446pp. Includes bibl. OCLC: 12669482 ISB.

91 Beauvery, R. "La Guérison d'un aveugle à Bethsaïde (Mc 8, 22-26.)" NRTh 90 (1968): 1,083-91.

92 Bellinzoni, Arthur J. "Extra-Canonical Literature and the Synoptic Problem." In *Jesus, the Gospels, and the Church,* E. P. Sanders, ed., 3-15. Macon GA: Mercer University Press, 1987. OCLC: 16130939 ISB.

93 _____. *The Sayings of Jesus in the Writings of Justin Martyr.* Leiden: Brill, 1967. 157pp. (NovTSup 17.) OCLC: 383283 ISB.

94 _____, ed. *The Two-Source Hypothesis: A Critical Appraisal.* Macon GA: Mercer University Press, 1985. x + 486pp. OCLC: 11599674 ISB.

95 Belser, Johannes. *Einleitung in das Neue Testament.* Freiburg i. Br.: B. Herder, 1901. 2., verm. und verb. Aufl. 1905. OCLC: 6384329 CUF; 376829 ISB.

96 Benoit, Pierre. 1960. As reviewer see Solanges, Bruno de. *Synopse* (1457).

97 _____. *L'Evangile selon Saint Matthieu.* Paris: Editions du Cerf, 1950. 2nd ed. rev. 1953. 1961. 181pp. 3rd ed. 1963. 171pp. (La Sainte Bible.) OCL: 7356595 ISB; 4542508 KKA: 6475956 BXM.

98 Benoit, Pierre, and M.-É. Boismard. *Synopse des quatre Evangiles en français: avec parallèles des apocryphes et des Pères.* Paris: Editions du Cerf, 1965–1977. 3 vols. 2. éd., rev. et corrigée par P. Sandevoir. 1972. 2 vols. Includes bibl. OCLC: 1620274 TJC; 5640735 ISB. Reviews: Sanders, E. P. JBL 94 (1975): 128-32; vol. 2. Murphy-O'Connor, J. RB 79 (1972): 431-35.

99 Berg, P. "Die Quellen des Lukasevangeliums." NKZ 21 (1910): 282-313, 337-52.

100 Berger, K. *Die Gesetzesauslegung Jesu: ihr historischer Hintergrund im Judentum und im Alten Testament.* Neukirchen: Neukirchener Verlag, 1972– . (Wissenschaftliche Monographien zum Alten und Neuen Testament 40.) OCLC: 490814 ISB.

101 Bergsma, J., ed. *De Levens van Jezus in het Middelnederlandsch.* Leiden: A. W. Sijthoff, 1895–1898. 288pp. (Bibliotheek van Middelnederlandsch letterkunde 54, 55, 61.) Issued in parts. No More Published. OCLC: 4533192 CLE.

102 Bertram, Georg. *Neues Testament und historische Methode: Bedeutung und Grenzen historischer Aufgaben in der neutestamentlichen Forschung.* Tübingen: J. C. B. Mohr (Paul Siebeck), 1928. 46pp. (Sammlung gemeinverständlicher Vorträge und Schriften aus dem Gebiet der Theologie und Religionsgeschichte 134.) OCLC: 13730700 ISB.

103 Best, Ernest. "The Commentators and the Gospels." ET 79 (1967–1968): 260-64.

104 _____. "An Early Sayings Collection." NovT 18 (1976): 1-16.

105 _____. "Mark's Preservation of the Tradition." In *L'Evangile selon Marc: tradition et rédaction,* M. Sabbe, et al., eds., 21-34. Louvain: University Press, 1974. (BEThL 34.) OCLC: 2345456 ISB.

106 _____. *The Temptation and the Passion: the Markan Soteriology.* Cambridge: University Press, 1965. 221pp. (SNTSMS 2.) OCLC: 392379 ISB.

107 Betz, Hans Dieter. "Eine Episode im Jüngsten Gericht (Mt 7, 21-23)." ZThK 78 (1981): 1-30. Reissued in his *Studien zur Bergpredigt,* 111-40. Tübingen: Mohr, 1985. (OCLC: 13952860 GTX.) ET: "An Episode in the Last Judgment (Matt. 7:21-23.)" In his *Essays on the Sermon on the Mount,* 125-57. 1985.

108 _____. *Essays on the Sermon on the Mount.* Philadelphia: Fortress Press, 1985. 170pp. Trans. of *Studien zur Bergpredigt.* Tübingen: J. C. B. Mohr (Paul Siebeck), 1985. 154pp. OCLC: 10779510 ISB; 13952860 GTX.

109 _____. "Die hermeneutischen Prinzipien in der Bergpredigt (Mt. 5,17-20.)" In *Verifikationen: Festschrift für Gerhard Ebeling zum 70. Geburtstag,* E. Jüngel, J. Wallmann, W. Werbeck, eds., 27-41. Tübingen: J. C. B. Mohr (Paul Siebeck), 1982. Reissued in his *Studien zur Bergpredigt,* 34-48. ET: "The Hermeneutical Principles of the Sermon on the Mount (Mt 5:17-20)" JTSA 42 (1983), 17-28; *Essays on the Sermon on the Mount,* 37-53, 1985. OCLC: 9118622 ISB.

110 _____. "Kosmogonie und Ethik in der Bergpredigt." ZThK 81 (1984): 139-71.

111 Betz, Otto. "The Dichotomized Servant and the End of Judas Iscariot." RevQ 5 (1964): 43-58.

112 Beyer, Klaus. "Semitische Syntax im Neuen Testament." Vol. 1:1, *Satzlehre*. Göttingen: Vandenhoeck & Ruprecht, 1962. (Studien zur Umwelt des Neuen Testaments 1.)
OCLC: 6546085 TJC.

113 Beyschlag, Willibald. "Die apostolische Spruchsammlung und unsere vier Evangelien." ThStKr 54 (1881): 565-636.

114 ———. "Zu dem vorstehenden Aufsatz von D. B. Weiss: 'Zur Evangelienfrage'." ThStKr 56 (1883): 594-602.

115A Biggs, H. "The Q Debate since 1955." *Themelios* 6 (1981): 18-28.

115B Bijlefeld, William A. "The Relation of the Gospels to Islamic Culture and Religion." In *Jesus and Man's Hope*, Donald G. Miller and Dikran Y. Hadidian, eds., 2:273-85. Pittsburgh: Pittsburgh Theological Seminary, 1971. (Perspective 2.)
OCLC: 142572 ISB.

116 Binder, H. "Von Markus zu den Grossevangelien." ThZ 35 (1979): 283-89.

117 Bindley, T. H. "Papias and the Matthaean Oracles." CQR 84 (1917): 31-43.

118 Birkeland, Harris. *The Language of Jesus*. Oslo: I kommisjon hos Jacob Dybwad, 1954. 40pp. (Avhandlinger utg. av det Norske videnskapsakademi i Oslo. II. Hist. filos. klasse 1954, no. 1.)
OCLC: 3343750 GUA.

119 Bjerkelund, C. J. "En tradisjons- og redaksjonshistorisk analyse av perikopene om tempelrendelsen." NTT 69 (1968): 206-18.

120 Black, Matthew. *An Aramaic Approach to the Gospels and Acts*. Oxford: Clarendon Press, 1946. 250pp. 2nd ed. 1954. 304pp. 3rd ed. 1967. 359pp.
An expansion of four lectures delivered in the spring of 1940 to the New Testament classes of Glasgow University and Trinity College. Submitted in ms. as a thesis for the degree of D. Litt. at the University of Glasgow, awarded in 1944.
OCLC: 345114 ISB; 2334686 ISB; 383212 IYU.

121 ———. " 'Not Peace but a Sword': Matt 10,34ff; Luke 12,51ff." In *Jesus and the Politics of His Day*, E. Bammel and C. F. D. Moule, eds., 287-94. Cambridge; New York: Cambridge University Press, 1984.
OCLC: 8927740 ISB.

122 ———. "The Problem of the Aramaic Element in the Gospels." ET 59 (1947–1948): 171-76.

123 ———. "The Son of Man Passion Sayings in the Gospel Tradition." ZNW 60 (1969): 1-8.

124 Bleek, Friedrich. *Beiträge zur Einleitung und Auslegung der heiligen Schrift*. Bd. 1. *Beiträge zur Evangelien Kritik*. Berlin: C. Trimer, 1846. 284pp. No more published.
NUC: UTS.

125 _____. *Einleitung in das Neue Testament.* Berlin: Reimer, 1862. 799pp. 2nd ed. 1866. 1st and 2nd editions edited and revised by his son Johannes F. Bleek. 3rd ed. 1875. 924pp. 4th ed. 1886. 1,035pp. 3rd and 4th editions reedited and further revised by W. Mangold.
OCLC: 7147780 CFT; 11373464 EWF; 6547648 STS.

126 _____. *An Introduction to the New Testament.* Edinburgh: T. & T. Clark, 1869–1870. 2 vols. 1874–1876. 1876–1877. 1883. (Clark's Foreign Theological Library.)
ET by William Urwich based on 2nd ed. of *Einleitung in das Neue Testament.*
OCLC: 6698964 ISB; 4576956 CLE; 17628767 VUT; 4060132 CFT.

127 _____. *Synoptische Erklärung der drei ersten Evangelien.* Leipzig: W. Engelmann, 1862. 2 vols. Published posthumously by Heinrich Holtzmann.
OCLC: 7140842 CFT.

128 Bligh, J. "The Gerasene Demoniac and the Resurrection of Christ." CBQ 31 (1969): 383-90.

129 _____. "Matching Passages in the Gospels." *Way* 8 (1968): 306-17.

130 _____. "Matching Passages, 2: St. Matthew's Passion Narrative." *Way* 9 (1969): 59-73.

131 _____. "Matching Passages, 3: The Resurrection Narratives." *Way* 9 (1969): 148-61.

132 _____. "Matching Passages, 4: The Sermon on the Mount." *Way* 9 (1969): 234-42.

133 _____. "Matching Passages, 5: The Sermon on the Mount—II." *Way* 9 (1969): 321-30.

134 Blinzler, Joseph von. "Die literarische Eigenart des sogenannten Reiseberichts im Lukasevangelium." In *Synoptische Studien: Alfred Wikenhauser zum siebzigsten Geburtstag am 22. Februar 1953 dargebracht von Freunden, Kollegen und Schülern,* J. Schmidt and A. Vögtle, eds., 20-52. München: Karl Zink Verlag, 1953.
OCLC: 6765909 ISB.

135A Blomberg, Craig L. "When is a Parallel Really a Parallel? A Test Case: The Lucan Parables." WThJ 46 (1984): 78-103.

135B Bloomfield, Samuel Thomas. *Hē Kainē Diathēkē. The Greek Testament with English Notes.* London: J. Smith for J. G. & F. Rivington, 1832. 2 vols. 3rd ed. 1839. 6th ed. 1845.
OCLC: 11739860 EXC.

135C _____. *Recensio synoptica annotationis sacrae, Being a Critical Digest and Synoptical Arrangement of the Most Important Annotations on the New Testament, Exegetical, Philological and Doctrinal.* Vol. 2. London: C. and J. Rivington, 1826.
OCLC: 2899284 BCT.

136 Bocher, O. "Lukas und Johannes der Täufer." StNTSU 4 (1979): 24-44.

137 Boismard, M.-É. 1973. As reviewer see Solanges, Bruno de. *Synopse* (1457).

138 _____. "Évangile des Ébionites et problème synoptique (Mc, 1, 2-6 et par.)" RB 73 (1966): 321-52.

139 _____. "La guérison du lépreux (Mc 1,40-45 et par.)" Salm 28 (1981): 283-91.

140 _____. "The Two-Source Theory at an Impasse." NTS 26 (1979): 1-17.

---- _____. *See* Benoit, Pierre. (98).

141 _____, David L. Dungan, William R. Farmer, and Frans Neirynck, eds. *Proceedings of the Jerusalem Symposium on the Interrelations of the Gospels.* Louvain: Peeters; Macon GA: Mercer University Press, forthcoming.

142 Bolton, W. J. *The Evidences of Christianity as Exhibited in the Writings of Its Apologists Down to Augustine: An Essay.* Cambridge: Macmillan, 1853. 302pp. Boston: Gould and Lincoln, 1854. 302pp. New York: R. Carter, 1854. 230pp. Photocopy: Ann Arbor MI: University Microfilms, 1978.
OCLC: 4750638 KAT; 4419824 AKC; 5186332 IPL.

143 Boman, Thorlief. *Die Jesus-Überlieferung im Licht der neueren Volkskunde.* Göttingen: Vandenhoeck & Ruprecht, 1967. 259pp. Includes bibl.
OCLC: 740555 WIT.

144 Bonnard, Pierre. "La Tradition dans le Nouveau Testament." RHPR 40 (1960): 20-30.

145 Bonsirven, Joseph. *Les Enseignements de Jésus-Christ.* Quatrième éd. Paris: Beauchesne, 1946. 511pp.
OCLC: 820560 BWE.

146A Borchert, Gerald Leo. "An Analysis of the Literary Arrangement and Theological Views in the Coptic Gnostic Gospel of Philip." Th.D. diss., Princeton Theological Seminary, 1967. Microfilm: Ann Arbor MI: University Microfilms, 1968.
NUC 69-133133: PLT; PPULC.

146B Borg, Marcus J. *Conflict, Holiness & Politics in the Teachings of Jesus.* New York; Toronto: Edwin Mellen Press, 1984. ix + 397pp. (Studies in the Bible and Early Christianity 5.)
Revision of thesis (doctoral), Oxford University, 1972.
OCLC: 10754066 ISB.

147 Borgen, Peder, "John and the Synoptics in the Passion Narrative." NTS 5 (1958–1959): 246-59.

148 Boring, M. Eugene. "Christian Prophecy and Matt 10:23: A Test Exegesis." In *Society of Biblical Literature 1976 Seminar Papers,* George MacRea, ed., 127-34. Missoula MT: Scholars Press, 1976.

149 _____. "Christian Prophecy and Matthew 23:34-36: A Test Exegesis." In *Society of Biblical Literature 1977 Seminar Papers,* Paul J. Achtemeier, ed., 117-26. Missoula MT: Scholars Press, 1977.

150 _____. "Christian Prophecy and the Sayings of Jesus. The State of the Question." NTS 29 (1983): 104-12.

151 _____. "Christian Prophecy in Q." In *Sayings of the Risen Jesus: Christian Prophecy in the Synoptic Tradition,* by M. Eugene Boring, 137-83. Cambridge; New York: Cambridge University Press, 1982. (SNTSMS 46.)
OCLC: 7978129 ISB.

152 _____. "How Can We Identify Oracles of Christian Prophets in the Synoptic Tradition? Mark 3:28-29 as a Test Case." JBL 91 (1972): 501-21.

153 _____. "The Paucity of Sayings in Mark: A Hypothesis." In *Society of Biblical Literature 1977 Seminar Papers,* Paul J. Achtemeier, ed., 371-77. Missoula MT: Scholars Press, 1977.

154 _____. "The Unforgivable Sin Logion Mark III 28-29/Matt XII 31-32/ Luke XII 10: Formal Analysis and History of the Tradition." NovT 18 (1976): 258-79.

155 _____. "What Are We Looking For? Toward a Definition of the Term 'Christian Prophet'." In *Society of Biblical Literature 1973 Seminar Papers,* George MacRae, ed., 2:142-54. Cambridge MA: Society of Biblical Literature, 1973.

156 Bornkamm, Günther. "The Authority to 'Bind' and 'Loose' in the Church in Matthew's Gospel: The Problem of Sources in Matthew's Gospel." In *Jesus and Man's Hope,* D. G. Buttrick, ed., 1:37-50. Pittsburgh: Pittsburgh Theological Seminary, 1970. (Perspective 1.)
OCLC: 142572 ISB.

157 _____. *Bibel, das Neue Testament: Eine Einführung in seine Schriften in Rahmen der Geschichte des Urchristentums.* Stuttgart; Berlin: Kreuz-Verlag, 1971. 176pp. (Themen der Theologie 9.) ET: *The New Testament: A Guide to Its Writings,* trans. Reginald H. Fuller and Ilse Fuller. Philadelphia: Fortress Press, 1973. viii + 166pp. Includes bibl.
OCLC: 284301 DRB; 692446 ISB.

158 _____. "Das Doppelgebot der Liebe." In *Neutestamentliche Studien für Rudolf Bultmann zu seinem 70. Geburtstag am 20. August 1954,* Walter Eltester, ed., 85-93. Berlin: A. Töpelmann, 1954. (Beihefte zur Zeitschrift für die neutestamentliche Wissenschaft und die Kunde der Älteren Kirche 21.)
OCLC: 1305018 ISB.

159 _____. "Evangelien, Synoptische." In RGG 3rd ed., 2:754-66. Tübingen: J. C. B. Mohr (Paul Siebeck), 1958.

160 _____. *Jesus of Nazareth*. Trans. Irene McLuskey and Fraser McLuskey with James M. Robinson. New York: Harper, 1960. London: Hodder and Stoughton, 1960. 239pp. Trans. of *Jesus von Nazareth*. 4th and 5th eds. Stuttgart: W. Kohlhammer, 1960. 216pp. Includes bibl. OCLC: 316834 ISB; 8343045 BCT; 9673184 WTS.

161 _____, Gerhard Barth, and Heinz Joachim Held. *Tradition and Interpretation in Matthew*. Trans. Percy Scott. Philadelphia: Westminster, 1963; London: SCM, 1963. 1972. 307pp. (New Testament Library.) Trans. of *Überlieferung und Auslegung im Matthäusevangelium*. Neukirchen: Neukirchen Verlag, 1960. 304pp. 1975. 326pp. (Wissenschaftliche Monographien zum Alten und Neuen Testament 1.) Includes bibl. OCLC: 3643585 BHA; 1017900 YNG; 812759 ISB; 4975775 DRU.

162 Bosold, Iris. *Pazifismus und prophetische Provokation: das Grussverbot Lk 10,4b und sein historischer Kontext*. Stuttgart: Katholisches Bibelwerk, 1978. 98pp. (Stuttgarter Bibelstudien 90.) Includes bibl. OCLC: 4581545 ISB.

163 Bousset, Wilhelm. *Die Evangeliencitate Justins des Märtyrers in ihrem Wert für die Evangelienkritik*. Göttingen: Vandenhoeck & Ruprecht, 1891. 127pp. OCLC: 303280 ISB.

164 _____. "Wellhausens Evangelienkritik." ThR 9 (1906): 1-14, 43-51.

165 Bouttier, Michel. "Les paraboles du maitre dans les tradition synoptique." ETR 48 (1973): 175-95.

166 Bovon, François. *Introduction aux Évangiles synoptiques*. Genèva: Centrale universitaire des polycopiés, 1970. 85 leaves. OCLC: 948388 IDK.

167 Bowman, John. *The Gospel of Mark: The New Christian Jewish Passover Haggadah*. Leiden: Brill, 1965. 392pp. (Studia Post-Biblical 8.) Includes bibl. OCLC: 392262 ISB.

168 Bradby, E. L. "In Defense of Q." ET 68 (1956–1957): 315-18. Reissued in *The Two-Source Hypothesis: A Critical Appraisal*, A. J. Bellinzoni, Jr., ed., 287-93. Macon GA: Mercer University Press, 1985. OCLC: 11599674 ISB

169 Brandenburger, Egon. *Markus 13 und die Apokalyptik*. Göttingen: Vandenhoeck & Ruprecht, 1984. 182pp. (Forschungen zur Religion und Literatur des Alten und Neuen Testaments 134.) OCLC: 11329114 ISB.

170 Branscomb, B. Harvie. *The Gospel of Mark.* London: Hodder and Stoughton; New York: Harper, 1937. 314pp. (Moffatt New Testament Commentary 2.) Includes bibl.
OCLC: 384928 ISB; 8385392 MOD.

171 Brekelmans, C., et al. *Questions disputées d'Ancien Testament; méthode et théologie.* Louvain: University Press, 1974. 202pp. (BEThL 33.) French, English, or German.
OCLC: 1121484.

172 Briggs, Charles A. "The Use of the Logia of Matthew in the Gospel of Mark." JBL 23 (1904): 191-210.

173 Briggs, R. C. *Interpreting the Gospels: An Introduction to Methods and Issues in the Study of the Synoptic Gospels.* Nashville: Abingdon Press, 1969. 188pp. Rev. ed. *Interpreting the New Testament: An Introduction to Methods and Issues in the Study of the New Testament.* Nashville: Abingdon Press, 1973. 288pp.
OCLC: 13257 ISB; 804929 ISB.

174 Briscoe, Hollie L. "A Comparison of the Parables of the Gospel According to Thomas and the Synoptic Gospels." Th.D. diss: Southwestern Baptist Theological Seminary, 1965. 231 leaves. Photocopy. Ann Arbor MI: University Microfilms, 1970?.
NUC: NcD.

175A Broadribb, D. "Proto Luke." BibR 4 (1968): 7-26.

175B Broadus, John Albert. *A Harmony of the Gospels in the Revised Version. With New Helps for Historical Study.* New York: Hodder & Stoughton; George H. Doran, 1893. New 8th ed., rev. and enlarged by A. T. Robertson. 1903. xvii + 290pp.
"A List of the Principal Harmonies of the Gospels (Compiled Partly from Clark's Historical Sketch)," 279-80.
OCLC: (3rd ed. 1903) 4187916 MOE; 5573749 IND.

176 Broer, Ingo. *Freiheit vom Gesetz und Radikalisierung des Gesetzes: Ein Beitrag zur Theologie des Evangelisten Matthäus.* Stuttgart: Katholisches Bibelwerk, 1980. 144pp. (Stuttgarter Bibelstudien 98.)
OCLC: 7620362 ISB.

177 _____. *Friede durch Gewaltversicht? Vier Abhandlungen zu Friedensproblematik und Bergpredigt.* Stuttgart: Katholisches Bibelwerk, 1984.*

178 _____. *Die Seligpreisungen der Bergpredigt: Studien zu ihrer Überlieferung und Interpretation.* Königstein/Ts.: P. Hanstein, 1986. 110pp. (BBB 61.) Includes bibl.
OCLC: 14718261 ISB.

179 Brogan, W. J. (1971). As reviewer see Suggs, M. Jack, *Wisdom* (1522).

180 Brown, David. "The Synoptic Problem." ET 6 (1895): 272-74.

181 Brown, J. P. "An Early Revision of the Gospel of Mark." JBL 78 (1959): 215-27.

182 _____. "The Form of 'Q' Known to Matthew." NTS 8 (1961–1962): 27-42.

183A _____. "Mark as Witness to an Edited form of Q." JBL 80 (1961): 29-44.

183B Brown, Raymond E. "The Gospel of John." In *Jesus and Man's Hope*, Donald G. Miller and Dikran Y. Hadidian, eds., 2:349-51. Pittsburgh: Pittsburgh Theological Seminary, 1971. (Perspective 2.)
OCLC: 142572 ISB.

---- _____. *See* Thils, Gustave (1562).

184A Bruce, Alexander Balmain. "Concerning the Three Gospels." In *1. The Synoptic Gospels* [by A. B. Bruce and] *2. The Gospel of St. John* [by Marcus Dods], vol. 1 of *The Expositor's Greek Testament*, W. Robertson Nicoll, ed., 3-26. New York: Dodd, Mead, 1897.
OCLC: 6192151 OKG.

184B _____. *With Open Face: or, Jesus Mirrored in Matthew, Mark, and Luke*. New York: Scribner's, 1896. 257pp. London: Hodder and Stoughton, 1896. 332pp.
Nine of the chapters first appeared in the *Expositor* in 1896. The last four chapters appear here for the first time.
OCLC: 2313982 TLM; 4221357 ACL.

185A Buchanan, George Wesley. "Has the Griesbach Hypothesis been Falsified?" JBL 93 (1974): 550-72.

185B _____. *Jesus, the King and His Kingdom*. Macon GA: Mercer University Press, 1984. xix + 347pp.
OCLC: 10207341 ISB.

185C _____. "Matthean Beatitudes and Traditional Promises." In *New Synoptic Studies: The Cambridge Gospel Conference and Beyond*, William R. Farmer, ed., 161-84. Macon GA: Mercer University Press, 1983.
OCLC: 9783753 ISB.

186 Buchler, A. "The Law of Purification in Mark vii. 1-23." ET 21 (1909–1910): 34-40.

187 Buckley, Eric R. *An Introduction to the Synoptic Problem*. London: Arnold, 1912. 292pp.
OCLC: 3494286 ISB.

188 Bultmann, Rudolf. "Die Frage der Echtheit vom Mt. 16:17-19." ThBl 20 (1941): 265-79.

189 _____. *The History of the Synoptic Tradition*. Trans. John Marsh. Oxford: Basil Blackwell; New York: Harper & Row, 1963. viii + 456pp. Rev. ed. 1968. viii + 462pp. Trans. of *Die Geschichte der synoptischen Tradition*. 3rd ed. rev. Göttingen: Vandenhoeck & Ruprecht, 1958 (^{2}1931, ^{1}1921).
OCLC: 487642 ISB; 324607 IAU.

190 _____. "The New Approach to the Synoptic Problem." JR 6 (1926): 337-62.
Reissued in *Existence and Faith. Shorter Writings of Rudolf Bultmann,* trans. Schubert M. Ogden, 35-54. New York: Meridian Books, 1960; London: Hodder & Stoughton, 1961; Cleveland: World, 1965; London: Collins, 1973.
OCLC: 387259 ISB; 6208707 WTS; 4298590 OKO; 10486536 BMU.

191 _____. *Theology of the New Testament.* Trans. Kendrick Grobel. 2 vols. New York: Charles Scribner's, 1951–1955; London: SCM, 1952–1955. 2 vols. in 1: New York: Charles Scribner's; London: SCM; New York: Harper & Row, 1965. (Scribner Studies in Contemporary Theology.) Trans. of *Theologie des Neuen Testaments.* Tübingen: J. C. B. Mohr (Paul Siebeck), 1948. 1953. 9. Aufl., durchgesehen und ergänzt von Otto Merk. 1984.
OCLC: 7833602 BCT; 2740646 BWE; 8500297 IBQ; 13568218; 12596551 BHA.

192 _____. "Was lässt die Spruchquelle über die Urgemeinde erkennen." *Oldenburgisches Kirchenblatt* 19 (1913): 35-37, 41-44.

193 _____, and Karl Kundsin. *Form Criticism: A New Method of New Testament Research,* by Rudolf Bultmann, and *Primitive Christianity in the Light of Gospel Research,* by Karl Kundsin, trans. by F. C. Grant. Chicago; New York: Willett, Clark, 1934. New York: Harper Torchbooks, 1962. Trans. of *Die Erforschung der synoptischen Evangelien* and *Das Urchristentum im Lichte der Evangelienforschung,* which were published as volumes 1 and 2 of the series, Aus der Welt der Religion, neutestamentliche Reihe. 161pp.
OCLC: 1520580 ISB; 4365131 MBS.

194 Bundy, Walter E. *Jesus and the First Three Gospels: An Introduction to the Synoptic Tradition.* Cambridge MA: Harvard University Press, 1955. 598pp.
OCLC: 602149 ISB.

195 Burchard, Christoph. "Das doppelte Liebesgebot in der frühen christlichen Überlieferung." In *Der Ruf Jesu und die Antwort der Gemeinde: exegetische Untersuchungen Joachim Jeremias zum 70. Geburtstag gewidmet von seinen Schülern,* Eduard Lohse, Christoph Burchard, and Berndt Schaller, eds., 39-62. Göttingen: Vandenhoeck & Ruprecht, 1970.
OCLC: 4089580 ISB.

196 Burgon, John W. *The Last Twelve Verses of the Gospel According to S. Mark Vindicated Against Recent Critical Objectors and Established.* Oxford: Parker, 1871. 334pp. Grand Rapids MI: Associated Publishers and Authors, 1970?. 379pp. Intro. by Edward F. Hills, 17-67.
OCLC: 3049150 BSC.

197 Burkill, T. Alec. "Which Came First?" ChrC 81 (1964): 1430. Review of *The Synoptic Problem* by William R. Farmer (458).

198 Burkitt, Francis C. 1923. As reviewer see Jameson, H. G. *Origin* (746).

199 _____. 1925: As reviewer see Streeter, B. H. *Four Gospels* (1510).

200 _____. *The Earliest Sources for the Life of Jesus.* Boston: Houghton Mifflin, 1910. 131pp. New and rev. ed. London: Constable; New York: Dutton, 1922. 130pp. Includes bibl.
OCLC: 3149061 MBS; 4669269 ISB.

201 _____, ed. *Evangelion da-Mepharreshe: The Curetonian Version of the Four Gospels, with the Readings of the Sinai Palimpsest and the Early Syriac Patristic Evidence.* Cambridge: University Press, 1904. 2 vols. Microfilm: Chicago: University of Chicago, Joseph Regenstein Library, Dept. of Photoduplication for the ATLA Microtext Project, 1976?.
OCLC: 8262774 BAN; 2639584 ISB (original in the Yale Divinity School Library).

202 _____. *The Gospel History and Its Transmission.* Edinburgh: T. & T. Clark, 1906. 359pp.
Ten lectures, delivered at the Passmore Edwards Settlement in London as the Jowett Lectures for 1906.
OCLC: 3268216 YAH.

203 _____. "Gospels." In *Encyclopaedia of Religion and Ethics,* James Hastings, ed., 6:335-46. 1913.

204 _____. "Tatian's Diatessaron and the Dutch Harmonies." JThS 25 (1923–1924): 113-30.

205 _____. *Two Lectures on the Gospels.* London; New York: Macmillan, 1901. 94pp.
OCLC: 3381853 ISB.

206 Burney, Charles F. *The Poetry of Our Lord: An Examination of the Formal Elements of Hebrew Poetry in the Discourses of Jesus Christ.* Oxford: Clarendon Press, 1925. 182pp. Photocopy: Ann Arbor MI: University Microfilms, 1978.
OCLC: 593124 ISB; 4292462 NJR.

207 Burton, Ernest Dewitt. "Some Phases in the Synoptic Problem." JBL 31 (1912): 95-113.

208 _____. *Some Principles of Literary Criticism and Their Application to the Synoptic Problem.* Chicago: University of Chicago Press, 1904. 72pp. Rpt from vol. 5 of the Decennial Publications of the University of Chicago.
OCLC: 5174538 ISB.

209A Busch, Friedrich. *Zum Verständnis der synoptischen Eschatologie: Markus 13 neue Untersucht.* Gütersloh: C. Bertelsmann, 1938. 157pp. (Neutestamentliche Forschungen 4. Reihe, 2. Heft.) Includes bibl.
Inaug. Diss., Kiel, 1938.
NUC: ICRL; MH.

209B Büsching, Anton Friedrich. *Die vier Evangelisten mit ihren eigenen Wor-*
ten zusammengesetzt vom neuen verdeutschet auch mit hinlänglichen
Erklärungen versehen. Hamburg: F. C. Ritter, 1766.
NUC: CtY-D; MH-AH; CtY.

210 Buse, Ivor. "St. John and 'The First Synoptic Pericope'." NovT 3 (1959):
57-61.

211 Bussby, Frederick. "Is Q an Aramaic Document?" ET 65 (1953–1954):
272-75.

212 Busse, Ulrich. *Die Wunder des Propheten Jesus: Die Rezeption, Kom-*
position und Interpretation der Wundertradition im Evangelium des Lu-
kas. Stuttgart: Verlag Katholisches Bibelwerk, 1977. 512pp. (Forschung
zur Bibel 24.) Includes bibl.
A revision and abridgement of the author's thesis, Münster, 1976, presented under the title "'Ιησοῦς εὐεργετῶν."
OCLC: 3283208 RCE.

213 Bussmann, W. *Synoptische Studien.* 3 vols. in 1. Halle: Buchhandlung des
Waisenhauses, 1925–1931. Includes bibl.
OCLC: 10088819 MBB.

214 Butler, B. C. "The Historical Setting of St. Matthew's Gospel." DR 66
(1948): 127-38.

215 _____. "M. Vaganay and the 'Community Discourse'." NTS 1 (1955):
283-90.

216 _____. "Notes on the Synoptic Problem." JThS 4 (1953): 24-27.

217 _____. *The Originality of St. Matthew: A Critique of the Two-Docu-*
ment Hypothesis. Cambridge: Cambridge University Press, 1951. 178pp.
Pages 62-71 are reissued in *The Two-Source Hypothesis: A Critical Ap-*
praisal, Arthur J. Bellinzoni, Jr., ed., 133-42. Macon GA: Mercer University Press, 1985.
OCLC: 3926916 ISB; 11599674 ISB.
Review: Farrer, Austin M. JThS 3 (1952): 102-106.

218 _____. "St. Luke's Debt to St. Matthew." HThR 32 (1939): 237-308.

219 _____. "St. Paul's Knowledge and Use of St. Matthew." DR 60 (1948):
363-83.

220 _____. "The Synoptic Problem." In *A New Catholic Commentary on*
Holy Scriptures, Bernard Orchard, gen. ed., 815-21. London; Edin-
burgh: Nelson, 1969.
Reissued in *The Two-Source Hypothesis. A Critical Appraisal,* Arthur J.
Bellinzoni, Jr., ed., 97-118. Macon GA: Mercer University Press, 1985.
OCLC: 60440 ISB; 11599674 ISB.

221 _____. "The Synoptic Problem Again." DR 73 (1954): 24-46.

222 Buttrick, David G., ed. *Jesus and Man's Hope.* Vol. 1. Pittsburgh: Pittsburgh Theological Seminary, 1970. (Perspective 1.)
Vol. 1 of 2-vol. collection of written contributions to The Pittsburgh Festival of the Gospels, hosted by the Pittsburgh Theological Seminary on its 175th anniversary celebration, 6-10 April 1970. *See* Miller, Donald G., for vol. 2.
OCLC: 142572 ISB.

223 Cadbury, Henry J. "Between Jesus and the Gospels." HThR 16 (1923): 81-92.

224 _____. "Four Features of Lucan Style." In *Studies in Luke-Acts: Essays Presented in Honor of Paul Schubert,* Leander E. Keck and J. Louis Martyn, eds., 87-102. Nashville: Abingdon Press, 1966.
OCLC: 392394 ISB.

225 _____. "Lexical Notes on Luke-Acts IV: On Direct Quotation with Some Uses of ὅτι and εἰ." JBL 48 (1929): 412-25.

226 _____. *The Making of Luke-Acts.* New York: Macmillan, 1927. 385pp.
OCLC: 2709946 ISB.

227 _____. *The Style and Literary Method of Luke.* Cambridge MA: Harvard University Press, 1920. Rpt: New York, Kraus, 1969. 205pp. (Harvard Theological Studies 6.)
Submitted as a Ph.D. diss. at Harvard University in 1913.
OCLC: 3477949 MRN.

228 Cadoux, Arthur T. *The Sources of the Second Gospel.* London: J. Clarke; New York: Macmillan, 1935. 296pp.
OCLC: 2855886 MBS; 8391946 ISB.

229 Cain, Marvin F. "A Comparison of the Parallel Passages in Matthew and Mark." Ph.D. diss. in progress under the direction of W. D. Davies, Duke University, 1967.*

230 Caird, George B. "Shake off the Dust from Your Feet (Mk 6:11.)" ET 81 (1969–1970): 40-43.

231 _____. "The Study of the Gospels. I. Source Criticism." ET 87 (1975–1976): 99-104.

232 Cambier, J., Lucien Cerfaux, et al. *La formation des Evangiles: problème synoptique et Formgeschichte.* Bruges: Desclée de Brouwer, 1957. 222pp. (Recherches Bibliques 2.)
OCLC: 2038719 ISB.

233 Cameron, Peter Scott. *Violence and the Kingdom: The Interpretation of Matthew 11:12.* Frankfurt; Bern; New York: Peter Lang, 1984. 310pp. (Arbeiten zum Neuen Testament und Judentum 5.) Includes bibl.
OCLC: 11239677 ISB.

234 Cameron, Ronald. "Gos. Thom. 46, 78 and Their Q Parallels (7:28, 24-25.)" In *AAR/SBL Abstracts 1984,* K. H. Richards and J. B. Wiggins, eds., 224. Chico CA: Scholars Press, 1984.

235 _____. *Sayings Traditions in the Apocryphon of James.* Philadelphia: Fortress Press, 1984. The author's diss. (Ph.D), Harvard University, 1983. Microfiche. Ann Arbor MI: University Microfilms International, 1984. Photocopy. 1984. 205 leaves. (Harvard Theological Studies 34.) OCLC: 11157452 ISB; 12084643 HLS; 12001586 BHA; 11360652 EMT.

236 Campbell, D. B. J. *The Synoptic Gospels: A Commentary for Teachers and Students.* Foreword by Adam Fox. London: Murray, 1966. New York: Seabury, 1969. (Seabury Paperback.) 166pp. OCLC: 2164497 TSW; 29166 ISB.

237 Campenhausen, Hans, von. *The Formation of the Christian Bible.* Trans. J. A. Baker. Philadelphia: Fortress Press; London: A. & C. Black, 1972. Philadelphia: Fortress Press, 1977. 342pp. Trans. of *Die Entstehung der christlichen Bibel.* Tübingen: J. C. B. Mohr (Paul Siebeck), 1968. 393pp. (Beiträge zur historischen Theologie 39.) French. *La formation de la bible chrétienne.* Version française par Denise Appia et Max Dominice. Neuchâtel: Delachaux et Niestlé, 1971. (Le monde de la Bible.) 307pp. OCLC: 5502344; 3241953 ISB; 3655573 CRC; 767815 BWE.

238 Cantwell, L. "The Parentage of Jesus: Mt 1:18-21." NovT 24 (1983): 304-15.

239 Carlston, Charles E. "On Q and the Cross." In *Scripture, Tradition and Interpretation: Essays Presented to Everett F. Harrison,* W. W. Gasque and W. S. LaSor, eds., 27-33. Grand Rapids MI: Eerdmans, 1978. OCLC: 3311627 ISB.

240 _____. "A Positive Criterion of Authenticity." BR 7 (1962): 33-44.

241 _____. "The Things that Defile (Mark vii, 14) and the Law in Matthew and Mark." NTS 15 (1968–1969): 75-96.

242 _____. "Wisdom and Eschatology in Q." In *Logia. Les Paroles de Jésus = The Sayings of Jesus: Mémorial Joseph Coppens,* Joël Delobel, ed., 101-19. Leuven: University Press and Peeters, 1982. (BEThL 59.) OCLC: 9450792 ISB; 11043145 ICU.

243 Carlston, Charles E., and D. Norlin. "Once More—Statistics and Q." HThR 64 (1971): 59-78.

244 Carmignac, Jean. *The Birth of the Synoptic Gospels.* Trans. Michael J. Wrenn. Chicago: Franciscan Herald Press, 1986. French. *La naissance des Evangiles Synoptiques.* Paris: O.E.I.L., 1984. 102pp. 2. éd., avec réponse aux critiques. 1984. 118pp. 3. éd., avec réponse aux critiques. 1984. 119pp. OCLC: 13333496 EMT; 12432987 VYF; 11767068 VYN; 12129253 DAY.

245 _____. *Recherches sur le "Notre Père."* Paris: Letouzey & Ané, 1969. 608pp. Includes bibl. OCLC: 932719 DAY.

246 _____. "Studies in the Hebrew Background of the Synoptic Gospels." In *Annual of the Swedish Theological Institute* 7:64-93. 1968–1969.

247 _____. *Die vier Evangelien: ins Hebräische übersetzt von Franz Delitzsch (1877–1890–1902.)* Intro. par Jean Carmignac; kritischer Apparat der zwölf Auflagen von Hubert Klein. Turnhout, Belgique: Brépols, 1984. lxiv + 206, 206pp. (Traductions hébraïques des Evangiles 4.)
Text in Hebrew; intro. matter in English, French, and German. Rpt of the text of the 1889 ed. with new intro. and critical apparatus.
OCLC: 12337332 NDD.

248 Carpenter, J. E. *The Bible in the Nineteenth Century: Eight Lectures.* New York; Bombay: Longmans, Green, 1903. 512pp.
Lectures delivered in various towns in England, Scotland, and Wales, during the years 1900–1903. Includes: The First Three Gospels, The Fourth Gospel, The Bible and the Church.
OCLC: 3235845 ISB.

249 _____. *The First Three Gospels: Their Origin and Relations.* 2nd ed. Boston: American Unitarian Association, 1890. 410pp. 3rd ed. London: P. Green, 1904. 350pp. 4th ed. London: Lindsey Press, 1906. 401pp.
OCLC: 9979400 TLC; 3212116 WEL; 6457173 RCE.

250 Carrington, Philip. *According to Mark: A Running Commentary on the Oldest Gospel.* Cambridge: University Press, 1960. 384pp.
OCLC: 383166 ISB.

251 Carruth, Shawn. "Ears to Hear: Sayings of Jesus in 'Q' and the Gospel of Thomas." BiTod 21 (1983): 89-95.

252 Cartlidge, David R., and David L. Dungan, eds. *Documents for the Study of the Gospels.* Cleveland: Collins, 1980. Philadelphia: Fortress Press, 1980. 1981. 298pp.
OCLC: 10194063 RBN; 5448951 ISB; 10276707 EXO.

253 Cassels, Walter Richard. *The Gospel according to Peter: A Study.* London: Longmans, Green, 1894. 139pp.
OCLC: 6418247 GZM.

254 Cassian, Evéque. "The Interrelation of the Gospels: Matthew-Luke-John." In *Studia Evangelica.* Papers presented to the International Congress on The Four Gospels in 1957 held at Christ Church, Oxford, 1957, Kurt Aland, F. L. Cross, et al., eds., 129-47. Berlin: Akademie-Verlag, 1959. (Texte und Untersuchungen 73.)
OCLC: 1637245 ISB; 13641309 BZM.

255 _____. "Luke after Matthew, but before John." In *Studia Evangelica.* Papers presented to the International Congress on the Four Gospels in 1957 held at Christ Church, Oxford, 1957, Kurt Aland, F. L. Cross, et al., eds., 142-47. Berlin: Akademie-Verlag, 1959. (Texte und Untersuchungen 73.)
OCLC: 1637245 ISB; 13641309 BZM.

256 Castor, George Dewitt. ''The Relation of Mark to the Source Q.'' JBL 31 (1912): 82-91.

257 Catchpole, D. R. ''The Angelic Son of Man in Luke 12:8.'' NovT 24 (1982): 255-65.

258 ———. ''The Answer of Jesus to Caiaphas (Matt. xxvi. 64).'' NTS 17 (1971): 213-26.

259 ———. ''On Doing Violence to the Kingdom.'' JTSA 25 (1978): 50-61.

260 ———. ''On Doing Violence to the Kingdom (Mt 11,12/Lc 16,16.)'' IBiS 3 (1981): 77-92.

261 ———. ''Q and 'The Friend at Midnight' (Luke xi. 5-8/9.)'' JThS 34 (1983): 407-24.

262 ———. ''The Ravens, the Lilies and the Q Hypothesis: A Form-Critical Perspective on the Source-Critical Problem.'' StNTSU 6-7 (1981–1982): 77-87.

263 ———. ''Reproof and Reconciliation in the Q Community: A Study of the Tradition-History of Mt. 18,15-17,21-22/Lk 17,3-4.'' StNTSU 8 (1983): 79-90.

264 ———. ''The Son of Man's Search for Faith (Luke xviii 8b.)'' NovT 19 (1977): 81-104.

265 ———. ''The Synoptic Divorce Material as a Tradition-Historical Problem.'' BJRL 57 (1974): 92-127.

266 ———. ''Tradition History.'' In *New Testament Interpretation: Essays on Principles and Methods*, I. H. Marshall, ed., 165-80. Grand Rapids MI: Eerdmans; Exeter: Paternoster Press, 1977.
OCLC: 3034272 ISB; 3751115 GTX.

267 Causse, M. ''Réflexions sur le probléme synoptique.'' ETR 55 (1980): 113-19.
Review article of B. Orchard and T. R. W. Longstaff, eds., *J. J. Griesbach* (1151).

268 Cave, C. H. ''Lazarus and the Lukan Deuteronomy.'' NTS 15 (1968–1969): 319-25.

269 Cerfaux, Lucien. *The Four Gospels, an Historical Introduction: The Oral Tradition; Matthew, Mark, Luke, and John; the Apocryphal Gospels.* Trans. Patrick Hepburne-Scott, with an intro. by Leonard Johnston. Westminster MD: Newman Press, 1960. London: Darton, Longman & Todd, 1960. 145pp. Trans. of *Le voix vivante de l'évangile au début de l'Eglise.* Tournai; Paris: Casterman, 1946. 189pp. (Collection Lovanium.) 2. éd. 1956. 157pp. (Bible et vie chrétienne.) Paris: Editions de Maredsous, 1958. 159pp.
OCLC: 387477 ISB; 819499 BAN; 7370065 IDJ; 7370025 IDJ; 13564869 JFS; 17636612 ZSJ.

270 _____. *Jésus aux origins de la tradition: Matériaux pour l'histoire evangélique.* Pref. de A. L. Descamps. Paris: Desclée de Brouwer, 1968. 303pp. (Pour une histoire de Jésus 3.) Includes bibl.
OCLC: 728072 DAY.

271 _____. "L'utilisation de la source Q par Luc. Introduction du séminaire." In *L'Evangile de Luc: Problèmes littéraires et théologiques: mémorial Lucien Cerfaux,* Frans Neirynck, ed., 61-69. Gembloux: J. Duculot, 1973. (BEThL 32.)
OCLC: 763098 ISB.

272 _____. "Le problème synoptique: À propos d'un livre récent." NRTh 76 (1954): 494-505.

273 Chapman, John. *The Four Gospels.* New York: Sheed and Ward, 1944. 85pp. London: Sheed and Ward, 1944. 64pp.
OCLC: 387488 ISB; 9039162 MOG.

274 _____. *Matthew, Mark, and Luke: A Study in the Order and Interrelation of the Synoptic Gospels.* Ed. with an intro. and some additional matter by John M. T. Barton. London: Longmans, Green, 1937. 312pp.
OCLC: 899225 BWE.

275 _____. "The Order of the Gospels in the Parent of Codex Bezae." ZNW 6 (1905): 339-46.

276 _____. "St. Irenaeus on the Dates of the Gospels." JThS 6 (1904–1905): 563-69.

277 _____. "Zacharias, Slain between the Temple and the Altar." JThS 13 (1912): 398-410.**

278 Cherry, R. Stephen. "Agreements between Matthew and Luke." ET 74 (1962–1963): 63.

279A Chilton, Bruce. "The Gospel according to Thomas as a Source of Jesus' Teaching." In *The Jesus Tradition Outside the Gospels,* D. Wenham, ed., 155-75. Sheffield: JSOT Press, 1985. (Gospel Perspectives 5.)
OCLC: 12509903 AZS.

279B _____. "Silver Blaze Rides Again: Two Recent Historical Approaches to Jesus." *Reflections. Yale Divinity School Journal* (Winter 1987): 8-11.

280 Christ, Felix. *Jesus Sophia. Die Sophia-Christologie bei den Synoptikern.* Zürich: Zwingli-Verlag, 1970. 196pp. (Abhandlungen zur Theologie des Alten und Neuen Testaments 57.) Includes bibl.
An abridgement of the author's thesis, Basel.
OCLC: 3819936 ISB.
Review: Frankemölle, Hubert. ThRv 68 (1972): 114-15.

281 Cladder, Herman J. *Zur Literaturgeschichte der Evangelien.* 1. reihe. *Unsere Evangelien. Akademische Vorträge.* Freiburg: Herder, 1919. 262pp.
OCLC: 8707747 SOI; 843217 PCJ.

282 Clark. A. C. *The Descent of Manuscripts.* Oxford: Clarendon Press, 1918. Rpt: Oxford: Clarendon Press; New York: Oxford University Press, 1969. 464pp.
Discusses the transmission of the texts of Cicero and Plato.
OCLC: 1946904 CIN; 8810577 MRT.

283A _____. *The Primitive Text of the Gospels and Acts.* Oxford: Clarendon Press, 1914. 112pp.
OCLC: 2487293 BUF.

283B Clausen, Henrik Nicolai. *Quatuor Evangeliorum tabulae synopticae.* Copenhagen: Hauniae, 1829.
NUC: MH-AH.

284 Cohu, John Rougier. *The Gospels in the Light of Modern Research.* Oxford: Parker; London: Simpkin, Marshall, 1909.
OCLC: 4140391 ACL.

285 Collins, Raymond F. "The Sayings Source." In his *Introduction to the New Testament,* 130-33. London: SCM Press, 1983. Garden City NY: Doubleday, 1983.
OCLC: 14571794 EQE; 8627719 ISB.

286A Collison, J. G. F. "Eschatology in the Gospel of Luke." In *New Synoptic Studies: The Cambridge Gospel Conference and Beyond,* William R. Farmer, ed., 363-71. Macon GA: Mercer University Press, 1983.
OCLC: 9783753 ISB.

286B _____. "Linguistic Usages in the Gospel of Luke." Ph.D. diss., Southern Methodist University, 1977. 375 leaves. Photocopy. Ann Arbor MI: University Microfilms International, 1984. Microfilm. 1978. Includes bibl.
OCLC: 4238105 ISB; 11219780 ISB, DWT; 13950080 GTX.

286C _____. "Linguistic Usages in the Gospel of Luke." In *New Synoptic Studies: The Cambridge Gospel Conference and Beyond,* William R. Farmer, ed., 245-60. Macon GA: Mercer University Press, 1983.
Abstract of thesis (286B).
OCLC: 9783753 ISB.

286D Combrink, H. J. B., et al. *Die sinoptiese evangelies en handelinge: inleiding en teologie.* A. B. du Toit, ed. Pretoria: NG Kerkboekhandel, 1980. 281pp. (Handleiding by die Nuwe Testament 4.) ET: *The Synoptic Gospels and Acts: Introduction and Theology.* Trans. D. Roy Briggs. Pretoria, 1983. 2nd ed. 1985. (Guide to the New Testament 4.)
OCLC: 7698796 WTS; 9865219 ISB; 17011871 TSW.

286E Connick, C. Milo. "The Records (Matthew, Mark, Luke)." In his *The New Testament. An Introduction to Its History, Literature, and Thought,* 71-103. Encino; Belmont CA: Dickenson Pub. Co., 1972. 2nd ed. 1978.
Esp. "The Synoptic Problem," 90-93.
OCLC: 320630 ICU; 3016699 OKG.

287 Connolly, Hugh. "The Appeal to Aramaic Sources of Our Gospels." DR 66 (1948): 25-37.

288 Connolly, R. H. "A Side-Light on the Methods of Tatian." JThS 12 (1910–1911): 268-73.

289 _____. "Syriacisms in St. Luke." JThS 37 (1936): 374-85.

290 Conybeare, F. C. "An Armenian Diatessaron?" JThS 25 (1923–1924): 232-45.

291 Conzelmann, Hans. "Literaturbericht zu den synoptischen Evangelien." ThR 37 (1972): 220-72.

292 _____. "Literaturbericht zu den synoptischen Evangelien (Fortsetzung.)" ThR 43 (1978): 3-51.

293 _____. "Literaturbericht zu den synoptischen Evangelien (Nachtrag.)" ThR 43 (1978): 321-27.

294 _____. "Present and Future in the Synoptic Tradition." JTC 5 (1968): 26-44.

295 _____. *The Theology of St. Luke*. Trans. Geoffrey Buswell. New York: Harper, 1961. Philadelphia: Fortress Press, 1982. 255pp. Trans. of *Die Mitte der Zeit: Studien zur Theologie des Lukas*. Tübingen. J. C. B. Mohr (Paul Siebeck), 1954. 210pp. 6. Aufl. unveränderter Nachdruck der 4. verb. und erg. Aufl. Tübingen: Mohr, 1977. 242pp. (Beiträge zur historischen Theologie 17.) Includes bibl.
OCLC: 3930118 ISB; 3573694 VA@; 383168 OCL; 8280640 IYU.

296 _____. "Zur Methode der Leben-Jesu-Forschung: Rudolf Bultmann zum 75. Geburtstag." ZThK.B 56 (1959): 2-13.

297 _____, and Andreas Lindemann. *Arbeitsbuch zum Neuen Testament*. Tübingen: J. C. B. Mohr (Paul Siebeck), 1975. 440 pp. 7. verbesserte und ergänzte Aufl. Tübingen: Mohr, 1983. 458pp. (Uni-Taschenbücher 52.)
OCLC: 2210539 ISB; 10647586 SNN.

298 Cook, M. J. "Interpreting 'Pro-Jewish' Passages in Matthew." HUCA 54 (1983): 135-46.

299 Cooper, John Charles. "Logia." In *The Dictionary of Bible and Religion*, W. H. Gentz, ed., 622-23. Nashville: Abingdon Press, 1986.
OCLC: 12215045 ISB.

300A _____. "Q (Quelle)." In *The Dictionary of Bible and Religion*, W. H. Gentz, ed., 862. Nashville: Abingdon Press, 1986.
OCLC: 12215045 ISB.

300B _____. "Synoptic Gospels." In *The Dictionary of Bible and Religion*, W. H. Gentz, ed., 1,012-13. Nashville: Abingdon Press, 1986.
OCLC: 12215045 ISB.

301A Cope, O. Lamar. ''The Argument Revolves: The Pivotal Evidence for Marcan Priority Is Reversing Itself.'' In *New Synoptic Studies: The Cambridge Gospel Conference and Beyond,* William R. Farmer, ed., 143-59. Macon GA: Mercer University Press, 1983.
OCLC: 9783753 ISB.

301B _____. ''The Death of John the Baptist in the Gospel of Matthew, or The Case of the Confusing Conjunction.'' CBQ 38 (1976): 515-19.

302 _____. ''The Earliest Gospel Was the 'Signs Gospel.' '' In *Jesus, the Gospels, and the Church,* E. P. Sanders, ed., 17-24. Macon GA: Mercer University Press, 1987.
OCLC: 16130939 ISB.

303 _____. *Matthew, a Scribe Trained for the Kingdom of Heaven.* Washington: Catholic Biblical Association of America, 1976. 142pp. (Catholic Biblical Quarterly Monograph Series 5.) Includes bibl.
Originally presented as the author's thesis, Union Theological Seminary, 1971.
OCLC: 2136509 ISB.

304 Coppens, Joseph. *Le Fils de l'homme néotestamentaire.* Vol. 3. *La relève apocalyptique du messianisme royal.* Leuven: University Press, 1981. 197pp. (BEThL 55.) Includes bibl.
OCLC: 9969623 ISB.

305 _____. *Le messianisme et sa relève prophétique: les anticipations vétérotestamentaires: leur accomplissement en Jésus.* Gembloux: J. Duculot, 1974. 273pp. (BEThL 38.)
OCLC: 1738100 PTS.

306 _____. *La relève apocalyptique du messianisme royal.* Leuven: University Press, 1979–1983. 3 vols. (BEThL 50, 55, 61.)
OCLC: 8386696 DTM.

307A _____, and Luc Dequeker. *Le fils l'homme et les saints du tres-haut en Daniel, VII: Dans les Apocryphes et dans le Nouveau Testament.* 2. éd. augm. Louvain: Publications universitaires de Louvain, 1961. 108pp. (ALBO ser 3. fasc. 23.) Includes bibl.
OCLC: 3389840 ISB.

307B Corley, Bruce C., ed. *Colloquy on New Testament Studies: A Time for Reappraisal and Fresh Approaches.* Macon GA: Mercer University Press, 1983. xiv + 368pp.
Esp. pt. 2, ''Seminar on the Synoptic Problem,'' 29-194.
Edited-for-publication papers and dialogue transcripts of the Colloquy on New Testament Studies, Southwestern Baptist Theological Seminary, Fort Worth, Texas, 5 November 1980.
OCLC: 9489011 ISB

308 Correns, Dietrich. "Jona und Salomo." In *Wort in der Zeit neutesta-mentliche Studien: Festgabe für Carl H. Rengstorf,* W. Haubeck and M. Bachmann, eds., 86-94. Leiden: Brill, 1980.
OCLC: 7463668 ISB.

309 Couchoud, P. L. "L'évangile de Marc a-t-il été écrit en Latin?" RHR 94 (1926): 161-92.

310 Courcier, J. "L'analyse ordinale des évangiles synoptiques." RSPhTh 58 (1974): 619-30.

311 Cowper, B. Harris, trans. *The Apocryphal Gospels and Other Documents Relating to the History of Christ.* Trans. from the originals in Greek, Latin, Syriac, etc., with notes, scriptural references, and prolegomena by B. Harris Cowper. London: William and Norgate, 1867. 456pp. 6th ed. London: Nutt, 1897. 7th ed. London: Nutt, 1910. Microfilm: Chicago: University of Chicago. Joseph Regenstein Library, for the ATLA Bd. of Microtext, 1975.
OCLC: 13363420 KAT; 2956214 ICU; 6728487 ISB.

312 Cranfield, C. E. B. *The Gospel according to Saint Mark: An Introduction and Commentary.* Cambridge: University Press, 1959. 479pp. Rpt with rev. additional supplementary notes. Cambridge: Cambridge University Press, 1977. 503pp. (Cambridge Greek Testament Commentary.) Includes bibl.
Greek and English.
OCLC: 6722212 VYN; 8460336 ITC.

313 Crawford, Barry S. "Near Expectation in the Sayings of Jesus." JBL 100 (1982): 225-44.

314 Credner, K. A. *Einleitung in das neue Testament.* Halle: Verlag der Buchhandlung des Waisenhauses, 1836. 2 vols.
NUC: ICU.

315 Creed, John M. *The Gospel According to St. Luke: The Greek Text, with introduction, notes, and indices.* London: Macmillan, 1930. 340pp. Rpt: London: Macmillan; New York: St. Martin's Press, 1960. London; New York, 1969. Includes bibl.
OCLC: 8378592 BCT; 1061515 SNN.

316 _____. "L and the Structure of the Lucan Gospel: A Study of the Proto-Luke Hypothesis." ET 46 (1934–1935): 101-107.

317 _____. "The Supposed 'Proto-Lucan' Narrative of the Trial Before Pilate: A Rejoinder." ET 46 (1934–1935): 378-79.

318 Cribbs, F. L. "St. Luke and the Johannine Tradition." JBL 90 (1971): 422-50.

---- Cross, Frank Leslie. *See* Huck, Albert (728).

319 Crossan, John D. *In Fragments: The Aphorisms of Jesus.* "Appendix 2: Sequence of Q Presumed in this Book," 342-45. San Francisco: Harper & Row, 1983.
OCLC: 9557479 ISB.
Reviews: Fuller, R. H. AThR 66 (1984): 310-11; Howard, C. D. ChrSR 14 (1984/1985): 93-94; Kelber, W. H. JBL 104 (1985): 716-19; Praeder, S. M. CBQ 46 (1984): 784-85; Sabourin, L. RelStT 5/2 (1985): 105-106; Williams, J. A. RelStR 11 (1985): 73.

320 _____. "Mark and the Relatives of Jesus." NovT 15 (1973): 81-113.

321 _____. "Parable and Example in the Teaching of Jesus." NTS 18 (1972): 285-307.

322 _____. "Redaction and Citation in Mark 11:9-10 and 11:17." BR 17 (1972): 33-50.

323 _____. "The Seed Parables of Jesus." JBL 92 (1973): 244-66.

324 _____. "The Servant Parables of Jesus." *Semeia* 1 (1974): 17-62.

325 Crum, John Macleod Campbell. "The Document Q." HibJ 24 (1925–1926): 346-49, 537-62.

326 _____. "Mark and 'Q'." Th 12 (1926): 275-82, 350-56.

327 _____. *The Original Jerusalem Gospel: Being Essays on the Document Q.* London: Constable, 1927. New York: Macmillan, 1927. 190pp.
OCLC: 6070405 ISB; 7029863 EYR.

328 Cullmann, Oscar. "Les récentes études sur la formation de la tradition évangélique." RHPR 5 (1925): 459-77.

329 Curtis, K. P. G. "In Support of Q." ET 84 (1972–1973): 309-10.

330 Curtis, Philip. "The Biblical Work of Doctor Farrer." Th 73 (1970): 292-301.

331 Dalman, Gustaf H. *The Words of Jesus Considered in Light of Post-Biblical Jewish Writings and the Aramaic Language.* I. *Introduction and Fundamental Ideas.* Authorized English version by D. M. Kay. Edinburgh: T. & T. Clark, 1902. 350pp. Microfilm. Ann Arbor MI: University Microfilms International, 1973. Rpt: Minneapolis: Klock & Klock Christian Pub., 1981.
The "Messianic texts," which form an appendix to the German text, *Die Worte Jesu* (1898; 2nd ed. 1930; rpt 1965), have not been included in the English edition.
OCLC: 1937516 VDB; 7793690 MOU; 8153015 IGR; German ed.: 3391166 RSC; 11109502 ITC; 6690284 ISB.

332 Dalmau, E. M. *See* Martinez Dalmau, Eduardo.

333 Dalpadado, J. K. *Reading the Gospel: A Guide to Readers and Teachers.* Boston: St. Paul Editions, 1976. 310pp. (Contemporary New Testament Series.) Includes bibl.
OCLC: 1974124 IVD.

334 Dambricourt, Georges. *Les Traditions du Pentateuque et les Evangiles synoptiques*. Paris: Spes, 1966. 299pp.
OCLC: 13846120 CLU.

335 Danner, Dan G. ''The 'Q' Document and the Words of Jesus. A Review of Theodore R. Rosché, 'The Words of Jesus and the Future of the 'Q' Hypothesis.' '' ResQ 26 (1983): 193-201.

336 Daube, David. *The New Testament and Rabbinic Judaism*. London: University of London, Athlone Press, 1956. New York: Arno Press, 1973. Salem NH: Ayer Co., 1984. 460pp. (Jordan Lectures in Comparative Religion 2. Jewish People: History, Religion, Literature.)
OCLC: 5526313 CFT; 1284724 ISB; 667000; 10796770 DAY.

337 _____. ''Temple Tax.'' In *Jesus, the Gospels, and the Church*, E. P. Sanders, ed., 121-34. Macon GA: Mercer University Press, 1987.
OCLC: 16130939 ISB

338 _____. ''Zukunftsmusik: Some Desirable Lines of Exploration in the New Testament.'' BJRL 68 (1985): 53-75.

339 Dauer, Anton. *Johannes und Lukas: Untersuchungen zu den johanneisch-lukanischen Parallelperikopen Joh 4, 46-54/Lk 7, 1-10-Joh 12, 1-8/Lk 7, 36-50; 10, 38-42-Joh 20, 19-29/Lk 24, 36-49*. Würzburg: Echter Verlag, 1984. 505pp. (Forschung zur Bibel 50.) Includes bibl.
See esp. pp. 76-116 (Lk 7, 1-10 par.)
OCLC: 11415155 ISB.

340 Dausch, Petrus. *Die synoptische Frage*. Münster: Aschendorff, 1914. 44pp. (Biblische Zeitfragen 7. Folge, 4. Hft.)
NUC: ICU; NjPT.

341 Dautzenberg, G. ''Zur Stellung des Markusevangeliums in der Geschichte der urchristlichen Theologie.'' *Kairos* 18 (1976): 282-91.

342A Davidson, Samuel. *The Four Gospels*. Vol. 1 of his *An Introduction to the New Testament: Containing an Examination of the Most Important Questions Relating to the Authority, Interpretation, and Integrity of the Canonical Books, with Reference to the Latest Inquiries*. 3 vols. London: Bagster, 1848-1851.
OCLC: 1113331 ISB.

342B _____. *An Introduction to the Study of the New Testament: Critical, Exegetical, and Theological*. Vol. 2. London: Longmans, Green, 1868. 2nd ed., rev. and improved. 1882. 3rd ed., rev. and improved. London: Kegan Paul, Trench, Trübner, 1894.
OCLC: 8177873 ISB; 1113367 ISB.

343 Davies, David. ''The Position of Adverbs in Luke.'' In *Studies in New Testament Language and Text: Essays in Honour of George D. Kilpatrick on the Occasion of his Sixty-Fifth Birthday*, J. K. Elliott, ed., 106-21. Leiden: Brill, 1976. (NovTSup 44.)
OCLC: 2370190 IVD; 2161596 ISB.

344 Davies, William D. *Christian Origins and Judaism.* Philadelphia: Westminster Press, 1962. London: Darton, Longman & Todd, 1962. 261pp. OCLC: 759621 ISB; 3226240 BHA.

345 _____. "Reflections on a Scandinavian Approach to 'The Gospel Tradition'." In *Neotestamentica et Patristica: eine Freundesgabe Hernn Prof. Dr. Oscar Cullmann zu seinem 60. Geburtstag überreicht,* A. N. Wilder, ed., 14-34. Leiden: Brill, 1962. (NovTSup 6.) OCLC: 384272 ISB.

346 _____. *The Setting of the Sermon on the Mount.* Cambridge: Cambridge University Press, 1964. 1966. 546pp. Includes bibl. OCLC: 336409 ISB.

347A Davis, Charles T. "Mark: The Petrine Gospel." In *New Synoptic Studies: The Cambridge Gospel Conference and Beyond,* William R. Farmer, ed., 441-66. Macon GA: Mercer University Press, 1983. OCLC: 9783753 ISB.

347B _____. "Tradition and Redaction in Matthew 1:18-2:23." JBL 90 (1971): 404-21.

348 Davis, Joseph L. "The Literary History and Theory of the Parabolic Material in Mark 4 in Relation to the Gospel as a Whole." Ph.D. diss., Union Theological Seminary in Virginia, 1966.

349 Dehandschutter, Boudewijn. "L'évangile de Thomas comme collection de paroles de Jésus." In *Logia. Les paroles de Jésus = The Sayings of Jesus: Mémorial Joseph Coppens,* Joël Delobel, ed., 507-15. Leuven: University Press and Peeters, 1982. (BEThL 59.) OCLC: 9450792 ISB; 11045145 UTS.

350A Deiss, L., ed. and trans. *Synopse de Matthieu, Marc, et Luce avec les parallèles de Jean.* Paris: Desclée de Brouwer, 1964. 2 vols. Nouv. éd. Paris, 1975. 308pp. (Connaitre la Bible.) Includes bibl. OCLC: 7356550 IDJ: 2374010 PTS.

350B Delitzsch, Franz. *Das Matthaeus-evangelium.* T. 1 of his *Neue Untersuchungen über Entstehung und Anlage der kanonischen Evangelien.* Leipzig: Dörffling u. Franke, 1853. 112pp. No more published. NUC: ICU; CtY; MH; PPPD; NjPT.

351 Delling, Gerhard. "Johann Jakob Griesbach. Seine Zeit, sein Leben, sein Werk." ThZ 33 (1977): 81-99. ET: "Johann Jakob Griesbach: His Life, Work, and Times," trans. Ronald Walls. In *J. J. Griesbach: Synoptic and Text-Critical Studies, 1776–1976,* Bernard Orchard and Thomas R. W. Longstaff, eds., 5-21. Cambridge; New York: Cambridge University Press, 1978. (SNTSMS 34.) First prepared for delivery at the Griesbach Colloquy in 1976 in Münster. OCLC: (ET) 3541663 ISB.

352 Delobel, Joël, ed. *Logia. Les paroles de Jésus = The Sayings of Jesus: Mémorial Joseph Coppens.* Leuven: University Press and Peeters, 1982. 647pp. (BEThL 59.) Includes bibl.
English, French, or German.
OCLC: 9450792 ISB: 11043145 ICU.
Reviews: Catchpole, D. R. JSNT 22 (1984): 110-12; Epp, E. J. JBL 103 (1984): 494-95; Focant, C. RTL 15 (1984): 99-102; Kloppenborg, J. S. CBQ 46 (1984): 381-83.

353 Delorme, J. "Bibliographie pratique sur les évangiles Synoptiques." AmiCl 78 (1968): 43-44.

354 DelVerme, Marcello. "I 'guai' di Matteo e Luca e le decime dei farisei (Mt. 23,23; Lc. 11,42.)" RB 32 (1984): 273-314.

---- Demeester, H. *See* Lindemans, Jean. (918).

355 Denaux, Adelbert. "Kleine inleiding op het Marcusevangelie." CBG 16 (1970): 309-41.

356 _____. "Het Lucasevangelie: traditiegeschiedenis en opbouw." ColVlaamTS 18 (1972): 3-25.

357A _____. "Der Spruch von den zwei Wegen im Rahmen des Epilogs der Bergpredigt (Mt. 7, 13-14 par. Lk. 13, 23-24.) Tradition und Redaktion." In *Logia. Les paroles de Jésus = The Sayings of Jesus: Mémorial Joseph Coppens,* Joël Delobel, ed., 305-35. Leuven: University Press and Peeters, 1982. (BEThL 59.)
OCLC: 9450792 ISB; 11043145 UTS.

357B _____, and Marc Vervenne. *Synopsis van de eerste drie evangeliën.* Leuven: Vlaamse Bijbelstichting; Turnhout: Brepols, 1986. lxv + 332pp.
Dutch synopsis with Dutch translation of the Synoptic Gospels based on the Greek of Nestle-Aland 26th ed., with minimal textual apparatus.

358 Denker, J. "La fuente de los logia (Q)." RivB 47 (1985): 185-206.

---- Dequeker, Luc. *See* Coppens, Joseph. (307A).

359 Dermience, Alice "La péricope de la Cananéenne (Mt 15, 21-28.) Rédaction et théologie." EThL 58 (1982): 25-49.

360 Descamps, A. "Progrès et continuité das le critique des évangiles et des Actes." RTL 1 (1970): 5-44.

361 Devisch, M. "Le document Q, source de Matthieu: problématique actuelle." In *L'Evangile selon Matthieu: rédaction et théologie,* M. Didier, ed., 71-97. Gembloux: J. Duculot, 1972. (BEThL 29.)
OCLC: 785508 ISB.

362 _____. "De Geschiedenis van de Quelle-hypothese. 1. Van J. G. Eichhorn tot B. H. Streeter; 2. De recente exegese." Thesis, Leuven, 1975.

363 _____. "La relation entre l'évangile de Marc et le document Q." In *L'Evangile selon Marc: tradition et rédaction,* M. Sabbe, et al., eds., 59-91. Louvain: University Press, 1974. (BEThL 34.)
OCLC: 2345456 ISB.

364 _____. "La source dite des Logia et ses problèmes." EThL 51 (1975): 82-89.

365 DeWette, Wilhelm Martin Leberecht. *Kurze Erklärung der Evangelien des Lukas und Markus.* Leipzig: Weidmann, 1836. 2nd ed. 1839. 3rd ed. 1846. 4th ed. edited by H. Messner. 1857. (Kurzgefasstes exegetisches Handbuch zum Neuen Testament 1/2.)
OCLC: (3rd ed.) 17425354 ITC.

366 _____. *Lehrbuch der historisch-kritischen Einleitung in die kanonischen Bücher des Neuen Testaments.* Berlin: G. Reimer, 1826. 2nd ed. 1830. 3rd ed. 1834. 4th ed. 1842. 5th ed. 1848. 6th ed. edited by Hermann Messner and Gottlieb Lünemann. 1860. 432pp. (His *Lehrbuch der historisch-kritischen Einleitung in die Bibel Alten und Neuen Testaments* 2.) ET: *An Historical-critical Introduction to the Canonical Books of the New Testament.* Trans. from the 5th, improved and enl. ed. by Frederick Frothingham. Boston: Crosby, Nichols, 1858. 388pp.
OCLC: (6th ed.) 4244925 ISB; (ET) 6381262 ISB.

367 Dewey, Joanna. *Markan Public Debate: Literary Technique, Concentric Structure and Theology in Mark 2:1-3:6.* Chico, Calif.: Scholars Press, 1979. 227pp. (SBLDS 48.) Includes bibl.
Originally presented as the author's thesis, Graduate Theological Union, 1977.
OCLC: 5170416; (copy of dissertation) 4255213 ISB; (microfiche) 10294067 BCT.

368 Dibelius, Martin. *Die Botschaft von Jesus Christus: Die alte Überlieferung der Gemeinde in Geschichten. Sprüchen und Reden wiederhergestellt und verdeutscht.* Tübingen: J. C. B. Mohr (Paul Siebeck), 1935. 169pp.
OCLC: 6254382 ISB.

369 _____. *A Fresh Approach to the New Testament and Early Christian Literature.* London: Ivor Nicholson & Watson, 1937. Westport CT: Greenwood Press, 1979. 280pp. (International Library of Christian Knowledge.) Includes bibl.
OCLC: 9913084 IAY; 4593395 IWU.

370 _____. *From Tradition to Gospel.* Trans. from the revised 2nd ed. of *Die Formgeschichte des Evangeliums* in collaboration with the author by Bertram Lee Woolf. London: Ivor Robinson and Watson, 1934. New York: Charles Scribner's, 1965. (Scribner's Library.) Greenwood SC: Attic Press, 1982. (Library of Theological Translations.) 311pp.
OCLC: 2146317 ISB; 287632 DNU; 9599944 VVN; (German 1919) 6255024 WTS; (German 1971) 3945192 KAT.

371 _____. "Papias." RGG 4 (1930): 892-93.

372 _____. "The Structure and Literary Character of the Gospels." HThR 20 (1927): 151-70.

373 _____. *Die urchristliche "Überlieferung von Johannes dem Täufer."* Göttingen: Vandenhoeck & Ruprecht, 1911. 150pp. (Forschungen zur Religion und Literatur des Alten und Neuen Testaments 15.) OCLC: 4904828 ISB.

374 Dideberg, Dany, and P. Mourlon Beernaert. " 'Jésus vint en Galilée.' Essai sur la structure de Marc 1, 21-45." NRTh 98 (1976): 306-23.

375A Didier, M., ed. *L'Evangile selon Matthieu: redaction et théologie.* Gembloux: J. Duculot, 1970. 428pp. (BEThL 29.) English, French, or German. OCLC: 785508 ISB.

375B Dillistone, F. W. "The Gospels in the Faith and Life of the Church: A Historical Perspective." In *Jesus and Man's Hope,* Donald G. Miller and Dikran Y. Hadidian, eds., 2:141-49. Pittsburgh: Pittsburgh Theological Seminary, 1971. (Perspective 2.) OCLC: 142572 ISB.

376 Dillon, R. J. "Early Christian Experience in the Gospel Sayings." BiTod 21 (1983): 83-88.

377 Dodd, Charles H. "The Framework of the Gospel Narrative." ET 43 (1931–1932): 396-400. Reissued in his *New Testament Studies,* 1-11. Manchester: Manchester University Press, 1953. New York: Charles. Scribner's, 1954. Rpt with corrections 1967. OCLC: 4644418 ISB; 2787094 WOO; 2125999 AZS.

378 _____. *The Parables of the Kingdom.* Rev. ed. New York: Scribner's, 1961. London: Nisbet, 1961. 176pp. London: Collins, 1961. 160pp. (Fontana Books.) Previous eds.: London: James Nisbet, [1]1935, [2]1936, [3]1936, [4]1948. Spanish. *Las parábolas del reino.* Madrid: Ediciones Cristiandad, 1974. 196pp. (Epifania: el libro de bosillo Cristiandad 6.) Based on a course of Shaffer Lectures given in the Divinity School, Yale University, 1935. OCLC: 372244 ISB; 9347909 EYR; 5763488 BCT; 5812888 IDK.

379 _____. "Present Tendencies in the Criticism of the Gospels." ET 43 (1931–1932): 246-51.

380 Doeve, Jan Willem. "La rôle de la tradition orale dans la composition des évangiles synoptiques." In *La formation des évangiles: Problème synoptique et Formgeschichte,* J. Cambier, et al., eds., 70-84. Bruxelles: Desclée de Brouwer, 1957. (Recherches Bibliques 2.) OCLC: 2038719 ISB.

381A _____. "Some Notes with Reference to 'ta logia tou theou' in Romans III 2." In *Studia Paulina in honorem Johannis de Zwaan septuagenarii,* J. N. Sevensten and W. C. van Unnik, eds., 111-23. Haarlem: Erven F. Bohn, 1953. OCLC: 3678193 ISB.

381B Döllinger, Johann Joseph Ignaz von. *Christentum und Kirche in der Zeit der Grundlegung.* Regensburg: G. J. Manz, 1860. 480pp. 2nd ed. 1868. 484pp.
NUC: ICU; NNUT. OCLC: 2313624 LLM.

382 Donahue, J. R. *Are You the Christ? The Trial Narrative in the Gospel of Mark.* Missoula MT: Published by Society of Biblical Literature for the Seminar on Mark, 1973. 269pp. (SBLDS 10.) Includes bibl.
Originally presented as the author's thesis, University of Chicago, 1972.
OCLC: 790501 ISB.

383 Doresse, Jean. *The Secret Books of the Egyptian Gnostics: An Introduction to the Gnostic Coptic Manuscripts Discovered at Chenoboskion.* Trans. Philip Mairet, with an English translation and critical evaluation of the Gospel according to Thomas. London: Hollis & Carter, 1960. 445pp. New York: Viking Press, 1960. New York: AMS Press, 1972. New York: Inner Traditions International, 1986. Trans. of *Les livres secrets des gnostiques d'Egypte. I. Introductio aux écrits gnostiques coptes découverts à Khénoboskion.* Paris: Plon, 1958. Monaco: Rocher, 1984. 374pp. (Gnose.)
The Gospel of Thomas translated into English from the French by Leonard Johnston.
OCLC: 1222867 WLU; 5452836 ISB; 282102 ATO; 13525388 DTM; 4172375 ISB; 13124006 CGU.

384 Doudna, John C. *The Greek of the Gospel of Mark.* Philadelphia: Society of Biblical Literature and Exegesis, 1961. 136pp. (Journal of Biblical Literature Monograph Series 12.) Includes bibl.
OCLC: 3231826 ISB.

385A Downing, F. G. "Compositional Conventions and the Synoptic Problem." JBL 107 (March 1988): 69-85.

385B _____. "Contemporary Analogies to the Gospels and Acts: 'Genres' or 'Motifs'?" In *Synoptic Studies: The Ampleforth Conferences of 1982 and 1983,* C. M. Tuckett, ed., 51-65. Sheffield: JSOT Press, 1984. (JSNT Supplement Series 7.)
OCLC: 12451599 ISB.

385C _____. "Quite Like Q. A Genre for 'Q': The 'Lives' of Cynic Philosophers." Bib 69 (1988): 196-225.

385D _____. "Redaction Criticism: Josephus' *Antiquities* and the Synoptic Gospels (II)." JSNT 9 (1980): 29-48.

386 _____. "Towards the Rehabilitation of Q." NTS 11 (1964–1965): 169-81.
Reissued in *The Two-Source Hypothesis: A Critical Appraisal,* A. J. Bellinzoni, Jr., ed., 269-85. Macon GA: Mercer University Press, 1985.
OCLC: 11599674 ISB.

387A Drury, John. *Tradition and Design in Luke's Gospel: A Study in Early Christian Historiography.* Atlanta: John Knox Press, 1977. 207pp. Includes bibl.
OCLC: 10035145 NPL.

387B Dschulnigg, Peter. *Sprache, Redaktion und Intention des Markus-evangeliums: Eigentümlichkeiten der Sprache des Markus-evangeliums und ihre Bedeutung für die Redaktionskritik.* Stuttgart: Katholisches Bibelwerk, 1984. xv + 771pp. (Stuttgarter Biblische Beiträge 11.)
Originally presented as the author's doctoral thesis, Universität Luzern, winter semester 1983–1984.
OCLC: 12941222 ISB.

388A Dungan, David L. "Albert Schweitzer's Disillusionment with the Historical Reconstruction of the Life of Jesus." PSThJ 29 (1976): 27-48.

388B _____. "Critique of the Q Hypothesis." In *The Two-Source Hypothesis: A Critical Appraisal,* A. J. Bellinzoni, Jr., ed., 427-33. Macon GA: Mercer University Press, 1985.
OCLC: 11599674 ISB.

388C _____. "The Cultural Background of the Use of the Term 'Canon' in Early Christianity." In *Aufstieg und Niedergang der römischen Welt,* II.26, W. Haase and H. Temporini, eds. Berlin: Walter de Gruyter, 1989 (forthcoming).

389A _____, ed. *Documents for the Study of the Gospels.* 1980. *See* Cartlidge, David R. (252).

389B _____. "A Griesbach Perspective on the Argument from Order." In *Synoptic Studies: The Ampleforth Conferences of 1982 and 1983,* C. M. Tuckett, ed., 67-74. Sheffield: JSOT Press, 1984. (JSNT Supplement Series 7.)
OCLC: 12451599 ISB.

390 _____. "Jesus and Violence." In *Jesus, the Gospels, and the Church,* E. P. Sanders, ed., 135-62. Macon GA: Mercer University Press, 1987.
OCLC: 16130939 ISB.

391A _____. "Mark—The Abridgement of Matthew and Luke." In *Jesus and Man's Hope,* D. G. Buttrick, ed., 1:51-97. Pittsburgh: Pittsburgh Theological Seminary, 1970. (Perspective 1.)
Pages 54-74 are reissued in *The Two-Source Hypothesis: A Critical Appraisal,* Arthur J. Bellinzoni, Jr., ed., 143-61. Macon GA: Mercer University Press, 1985.
OCLC: 142572 ISB; 11599674 ISB.

391B _____. ''The Purpose and Provenance of the Gospel of Mark according to the 'Two-Gospel' (Griesbach) Hypothesis.'' In *Colloquy on New Testament Studies: A Time for Reappraisal and Fresh Approaches*, Bruce C. Corley, ed., 133-56. Macon GA: Mercer University Press, 1983.

A revision of an earlier form of a paper on the same topic with slightly different title: ''The Purpose and Provenance of the Gospel of Mark according to the Two-Gospel (Owen-Griesbach) Hypothesis.'' In *New Synoptic Studies: The Cambridge Gospel Conference and Beyond*, William R. Farmer, ed., 411-40. Macon GA: Mercer University Press, 1983.

OCLC: 9489011 ISB; 9783753 ISB.

392 _____. ''Reactionary Trends in the Gospel Producing Activity of the Early Church: Marcion, Tatian, Mark.'' In *L'Evangile selon Marc: tradition et rédaction,* M. Sabbe, et al., eds., 179-202. Louvain: University Press, 1974. (BEThL 34.)

OCLC: 2345456 ISB.

393A _____. *The Sayings of Jesus in the Churches of Paul: The Use of the Synoptic Tradition in the Regulation of Early Church Life.* Philadelphia: Fortress Press, 1971. Oxford: Blackwell, 1971. 180pp. Includes bibl.

OCLC: 210523 ISB; 267671 PTE.

393B _____, et al., eds. *Proceedings of the Jerusalem Symposium.* See Boismard, M.-É., David L. Dungan, William R. Farmer, and Frans Neirynck, eds. (141).

393C _____. ''Synopses of the Future.'' Bib 66 (1985): 457-92.

393D _____. ''Theory of Synopsis Construction.'' Bib 61 (1980): 305-29.

394 Dunn, James D. G. ''Mark 2.1-3.6: A Bridge Between Jesus and Paul on the Question of the Law.'' NTS 30 (1984): 395-415.

395 _____. ''Prophetic 'I'—Sayings and the Jesus Tradition. The Importance of Testing Prophetic Utterances within Early Christianity.'' NTS 24 (1977): 175-98.

396 Dupont, Jacques. 1970: As reviewer see Lambrecht, Jan. *Marcus* (863).

397 _____. *Les Béatitudes.* Nouv. éd. entièrement refondue. Bruges: Abbaye de Saint-André, 1958–1973. Paris: J. Gabalda, 1969–1973. 3 vols. (Études bibliques.)

Contents: 1. Le problème littéraire: les deux versions du Sermon sur la montagne et des Béatitudes; 2. La bonne nouvelle; 3. Les Evangélistes.

OCLC: 876673 BHA; 2304963 DCU.

398 _____. ''Dieu ou Mammon (Mt 6, 24; Lc 16, 13.)'' CristStor 5 (1984): 441-61.

Reissued in his *Études,* 551-67. 1985.

399 _____. *Études sur les évangiles synoptiques.* Présentées par F. Neirynck. Leuven: University Press and Peeters, 1985. 2 vols. 1,210pp. (BEThL 70 A-B.)

OCLC: 12652984 ISB.

400 _____. ''Gesù Messia dei poveri, Messia povero.'' In *Seguire Gesù povero (Parola e Storia),* by J. Dupont, A. G. Hamman, and G. Miccoli, 7-87. Magnano: Communità di Base, 1984. French. ''Jésus Messie des pauvres. Messie pauvre.'' In his *Études,* 86-130. 1985.
OCLC: (French) 12652984 ISB.

401 _____. ''La parabole du maître qui rentre dans la nuit (Mc. 13, 34-36.)'' In *Mélanges bibliques en hommage au R. P. Béda Rigaux,* A. Descamps, ed., 89-116. Gembloux: J. Duculot, 1970.
OCLC: 506223 ISB.

402 _____. *Les tentations de Jésus au désert.* Paris: Desclée de Brouwer, 1968. 152pp. (Studia neotestamentica 4.) German. *Die Versuchung Jesu in der Wüste.* Stuttgart: Verlag Katholisches Bibelwerk, 1969. 132pp. (Stuttgarter Bibelstudien 37.) Includes bibl.
OCLC: 744897 CMC; 6082040 CUF.

403 _____. ''La transmission des paroles de Jésus sur la lampe et la mesure dans Marc 4, 21-25 et dans la tradition Q.'' In *Logia. Les paroles de Jésus = The Sayings of Jesus: Mémorial Joseph Coppens,* Joël Delobel, ed., 201-36. Leuven: University Press and Peeters, 1982. (BEThL 59.)
Reissued in his *Études,* 259-94. 1985.
OCLC: 9450792 ISB; 11043145 UTS.

404 _____, et al. *Jésus aux origines de la christologie.* Leuven: University Press, 1975. 375pp. (BEThL 40.)
English, French, or German.
OCLC: 2374459 ISB.

405 Duthoit, R. ''Une nouvelle synopse des évangiles.'' NRTh 82 (1960): 247-68.

406 Dyer, Charles H. ''Do the Synoptics Depend on Each Other?'' BS 138 (1981): 230-45.

407 Easton, Burton S. ''The First Evangelic Tradition.'' JBL 50 (1931): 148-55.

408 _____. *The Gospel According to St. Luke: A Critical and Exegetical Commentary.* New York: Scribner's, 1926. Edinburgh: T. & T. Clark, 1926. 367pp. Microform. Ann Arbor MI: University Microfilms International, 1981. Includes bibl.
OCLC: 2928658 ISB; 4139487 BCT; 7802511 MOU.

409 _____. *The Gospel Before the Gospels.* New York: Scribner's, 1928. 170pp. Includes bibl.
Lectures given on the Bishop Paddock Foundation, at the General Theological Seminary, New York City, in December 1927, as the series for 1927–1928.
OCLC: 1744778 VA@.

410 _____. ''Linguistic Evidence for the Lucan Source L.'' JBL 29 (1910): 139-80.

411 Edersheim, Alfred. *The Life and Times of Jesus the Messiah.* 2 vols. 8th ed., rev. New York; London; Bombay: Longmans, Green, 1905. 3rd ed. 1886. 2nd ed. 1884. 1st ed. 1883. New American Edition. Grand Rapids MI: Eerdmans, 1956. xxxv + 695pp. and xii + 828pp. 2 vols. in 1. Grand Rapids MI: Associated Publishers and Authors, 1971. 1,178pp. One-volume edition, 1977. Includes bibl.
OCLC: 7676112 KAT; 3194198 GWC; 4749582 CBC.

412 _____. "On a New Theory of the Origin and Composition of the Synoptic Gospels Proposed by G. Wetzel." In *Studia Biblica: Essays on Biblical Archaeology and Criticism, and Kindred Subjects,* 1:75-88. Oxford: Clarendon Press, 1885.
OCLC: 3785218 ISB.

413 Edwards, Richard A. "An Approach to a Theology of Q." JR 51 (1971): 247-69.

414 _____. "Christian Prophecy and the Q Tradition." In *Society of Biblical Literature 1976 Seminar Papers,* George MacRae, ed., 119-26. Missoula MT: Scholars Press, 1976.

415 _____. *A Concordance to Q.* Missoula MT: Scholars Press, 1975. 186pp. (Sources for Biblical Study 7.)
Text in Greek.
OCLC: 1256867 ISB.
Review: Jones, D. L. CBQ 39 (1977): 147-48.

416 _____. "The Eschatological Correlative as a *Gattung* in the New Testament." ZNW 60 (1969): 9-20.

417 _____. "Matthew's Use of Q in Chapter Eleven." In *Logia. Les paroles de Jésus = The Sayings of Jesus: Mémorial Joseph Coppens,* Joël Delobel, ed., 257-75. Leuven: University Press and Peeters, 1982. (BEThL 59.)
OCLC: 9450792 ISB; 11043145 UTS.

418 _____. "A New Approach to the Gospel of Mark." LQ 22 (1970): 330-35.

419 _____. *The Sign of Jonah in the Theology of the Evangelists and Q.* Naperville IL: Alec R. Allenson, 1971. London: SCM Press, 1971. 122pp. (Studies in Biblical Theology 2nd ser. 18.) Includes bibl.
OCLC: 163480; 540393 ISB.

420 _____. *A Theology of Q: Eschatology, Prophecy, and Wisdom.* Philadelphia: Fortress Press, 1976. 173pp. Includes bibl.
OCLC: 2002951 ISB.
Reviews: Kingsbury, J. D. Interp 31 (1977): 318-20; Sabourin, L. BibThB 6 (1976): 295-98; Smith, D. M. JAAR 45 (1977): 372-74; Topel, L. J. CBQ 39 (1977): 148-50.

421 Eichhorn, Johann Gottfried. *Einleitung in das Neue Testament.* 5 vols. Leipzig: Weidmann, 1804–1827. 2nd ed. 6 vols. in 4. 1811–1835.
Vols. 2 and 3 have added t.p. J. G. Eichhorn's *Kritische Schriften.* 6er-7er Band; vol. 4 has half title *Allgemeine Einleitung in das Neue Testament.*
OCLC: 6000289 ISB.

422 ———. "Über die drei ersten Evangelien." His ABBL 5:759-996. Leipzig: Weidmann, 1794.

423 Eijl, Edmond J. M. van, ed. *Facultas S. Theologiae Lovaniensis, 1432–1797; bijdragen tot haar geschiedenis = Contributions to Its History = contributions à son histoire.* Leuven: University Press, 1977. 569pp. (BEThl 45.) Includes bibl.
OCLC: 6280129 ISB.

424 Elliott, J. Keith. "Nouns with Diminutive Endings in the New Testament." NovT 12 (1970): 391-98.

425 ———. "The Synoptic Problem and the Laws of Tradition: A Cautionary Note." ET 82 (1970–1971): 148-52.

426 ———. "The Use of ἕτερος in the New Testament." ZNW 60 (1969): 140-41.

427 Ellis, E. Earle "Gospel Criticism: A Perspective on the State of the Art." In *Das Evangelium und die Evangelien: Vorträge vom Tübinger Symposium 1982,* P. Stuhlmacher, ed., 27-54. Tübingen: J. C. B. Mohr (Paul Siebeck), 1983. (Wissenschaftliche Untersuchungen zum Neuen Testament 28.)
OCLC: 10371104 ISB.

428 Emmet, Cyril W. "Professor Harnack on the Second Source of the First and Third Gospel." ET 19 (1907–1908): 297-300, 358-63.

429 Enchiridion Biblicum. *Enchiridion Biblicum: Documenta Ecclesiastica Sacram Scripturam Spectantia Auctoritate Pontificiae Commissionis de Re Biblica Edita.* Rome: Librariam Vaticanam, 1927. 194pp. Ed. 2. aucta et recognita. Naples: M. d'Auria Pontificius Editor, 1954. 279pp. Rome: Librariam Vaticanam, 1961. 194pp. Naples: M. D'Auria Pontificius Editor, 1965. 284pp.
OCLC: 5942165; 807988 BWE; 2489066 DAY; 8320709 UTS.

430 Enslin, Morton Scott. *Christian Beginnings.* New York: Harper & Brothers, 1938. ix + 533pp. 2 vols. Rpt: New York: Harper & Row, 1956 (Harper Torchbooks: Cloister Library TB 6).
Contents: pt. 1, The Background; pt. 2, The Beginning of the Gospel Story; pt. 3. The Literature of the Christian Movement.
Esp. "The Synoptic Problem," 426-36.
OCLC: 8527823 ISB; 3135917 (pts. 1 & 2) OCO; 9625966 (pts. 1 & 2, 1965 printing) CNO; 6260777 (pt. 3) KSW.

431 ———. "Luke and Matthew: Compilers or Authors?" ANRW 25/3 (1985): 2358-88.

432 Eppstein, Victor. "The Historicity of the Gospel Account of the Cleansing of the Temple." ZNW 55 (1964): 42-58.

433 Ernst, Josef. *Anfänge der Christologie.* Stuttgart: KBW Verlag, 1972. 173pp. (Stuttgarter Bibelstudien 57.) Includes bibl.
OCLC: 560684 ISB.

434 Etcheverria, R. Trevijano. "La multiplicacion de los panes (Mc. 6, 30-46; 8, 1-10 y par.)" Burg 15 (1974): 435-65.

435 Evans. C. F. "The Central Section of St. Luke's Gospel." In *Studies in the Gospels: Essays in Memory of R. H. Lightfoot,* D. E. Nineham, ed., 37-53. Oxford: Blackwell, 1955.
OCLC: 2394516 ISB.

436 Evans, Owen E. "Synoptic Criticism Since Streeter." ET 72 (1960–1961): 295-99.

437A _____. "The Unforgivable Sin." ET 68 (1956–1957): 240-44.

437B Evanson, Edward. *The Dissonance of the Four Generally Received Evangelists, and the Evidence of Their Respective Authenticity.* Ipswich: G. Jermyn, 1792. 289pp.
OCLC: 7952846 LTS.

438 Ewald, Heinrich. *Die drei ersten Evangelien.* Göttingen: Vandenhoeck & Ruprecht, 1850.*

439 _____. "Ursprung und Wesen der Evangelien." JBW 1 (1848): 113-54; 2 (1849): 180-224; 3 (1850): 140-77.

440 Ewald, Paul. *Das Hauptproblem der Evangelienfrage und der Weg zu seiner Lösung: Eine akademische Vorlesung nebst Exkursen.* Leipzig: J. C. Hinrichs, 1890. 256pp.
OCLC: 4564445 IND.

441A Farmer, William R. "Appendix. A Response to Joseph Fitzmyer's Defense of the 'Two-Document' Hypothesis." In *New Synoptic Studies: The Cambridge Gospel Conference and Beyond,* William R. Farmer, ed., 501-23. Macon GA: Mercer University Press, 1983.
OCLC: 9783753 ISB.

441B _____. "Basic Affirmation with Some Demurrals: A Response to Roland Mushat Frye." In *The Relationships among the Gospels: An Interdisciplinary Dialogue,* William O. Walker, Jr., ed., 303-22. San Antonio: Trinity University Press, 1978. (Trinity University Monograph Series in Religion 5.)
OCLC: 4365624 ISB.

441C _____. "Certain Results Reached by Sir John C. Hawkins and C. F. Burney Which Make More Sense If Luke Knew Matthew, and Mark Knew Matthew and Luke." In *Synoptic Studies: The Ampleforth Conferences of 1982 and 1983,* C. M. Tuckett, ed., 75-98. Sheffield: JSOT Press, 1984. (JSNT Supplement Series 7.)
OCLC: 12451599 ISB.

441D _____. "The Church's Stake in the Question of 'Q'." PSThJ 39/3 (1986): 9-19.

441E _____. "Critical Reflections on Werner George Kümmel's *History of New Testament Research.*" PSThJ 34/1 (1980): 41-48.

442A _____. "A Fresh Approach to Q." In *Christianity, Judaism, and Other Greco-Roman Cults: Studies for Morton Smith at Sixty,* J. Neusner, ed., 1:39-50. Leiden: Brill, 1975. (Studies in Judaism in Late Antiquity 12.) Reissued in *The Two-Source Hypothesis: A Critical Appraisal,* A. J. Bellinzoni, Jr., ed., 397-408. Macon GA: Mercer University Press, 1985. OCLC: 1578493 ISB; 11599674 ISB.

442B _____. "The Genesis of the Colloquium." In *J. J. Griesbach, Synoptic and Text-Critical Studies, 1776–1976,* Bernard Orchard and Thomas R. W. Longstaff, eds., 1-4. Cambridge; New York: Cambridge University Press, 1978. OCLC: 3541663 ISB.

442C _____. "The Gospel of Mark." In *Jesus and Man's Hope,* Donald G. Miller and Dikran Y. Hadidian, eds., 2:343-44. Pittsburgh: Pittsburgh Theological Seminary, 1971. (Perspective 2.) OCLC: 142572 ISB.

443 _____. "An Historical Essay on the Humanity of Jesus Christ." In *Christian History and Interpretation: Studies presented to John Knox,* William R. Farmer, C. F. D. Moule, and R. R. Niebuhr, eds., 101-26. Cambridge: Cambridge University Press, 1967. OCLC: 377866 ISB.

444A _____. "The Import of the Two-Gospel Hypothesis." CThQ 48 (1984): 55-59.

444B _____. "Introduction." In *History and Criticism of the Marcan Hypothesis,* by Hans-Herbert Stoldt. Trans. and ed. Donald L. Niewyk from *Geschichte und Kritik der Markushypothese.* Göttingen: Vandenhoeck und Ruprecht, 1977 (1497). Macon GA: Mercer University Press; Edinburgh: T. & T. Clark, 1980. OCLC: 6847895 ISB; 3330200 ISB.

444C _____. "Introduction." In *New Synoptic Studies: The Cambridge Gospel Conference and Beyond,* William R. Farmer, ed., vii-xli. Macon GA: Mercer University Press, 1983. Contents: (1) In Retrospect. (2) Cambridge (England) 1979: pt. 1. The Patristic Evidence; pt. 2. Further Evidence for the Posteriority of Mark and for the Early Character of Matthean Tradition in Relation to Luke and Mark; pt. 3. New Methodological Approaches; pt. 4. Papers Assuming the Two-Gospel (Griesbach) Hypothesis; pt. 5. Papers Exploring a Paradigm Shift in Gospel Studies. Appendix: Response to Joseph A. Fitzmyer's defense of Streeter's arguments for the priority of Mark and the existence of 'Q.' OCLC: 9783753 ISB.

444D _____. "Introduction" to, and editor of, Pt. 2: "Seminar on the Synoptic Problem." In *Colloquy on New Testament Studies: A Time for Reappraisal and Fresh Approaches,* ed. with intro. by Bruce Corley, 29-194. Macon GA: Mercer University Press, 1983.

William R. Farmer introduced and moderated the program: "History and Development of Mark's Gospel," Helmut Koester; Seminar Dialogue with Helmut Koester; "The Late Secondary Redaction of Mark's Gospel and the Griesbach Hypothesis: A Response to Helmut Koester," David Peabody; "The Purpose and Provenance of the Gospel of Mark according to the 'Two-Gospel' (Griesbach) Hypothesis," David Dungan; Seminar Dialogue with David Dungan; "The Roman Provenance of 1 Peter and the Gospel of Mark: A Response to David Dungan." John H. Elliott.

OCLC: 9489011 ISB.

445A _____. "Is Streeter's Fundamental Solution to the Synoptic Problem Still Valid?" In *The New Testament Age: Essays in Honor of Bo Reicke,* William C. Weinrich, ed., 1:147-64. 2 vols. Macon GA: Mercer University Press, 1984.

OCLC: 10458733 ISB.

445B _____. *Jesus and the Gospel: Tradition, Scripture, and Canon.* Philadelphia: Fortress Press, 1982. xiv + 300pp.

OCLC: 7925180 ISB.

Reviews: Foster, Durwood. PSThJ 40/3 (1987): 51-54; Meyer, Ben F. SCnt 5/3 (1985-1986): 165-71.

445C _____, ed. "John Drury, Allan McNicol, William O. Walker, Jr., and Denis Farkasfalvy in Discussion." PSThJ 40/3 (1987): 22-24.

446 _____. "Kritik der Markushypothese." ThZ 34 (1978); 172-74.

A review of Hans-Herbert Stoldt's *History and Criticism of the Marcan Hypothesis* (1497).

447 _____. "The Lachmann Fallacy." NTS 14 (1967–1968): 441-43.

448A _____. *The Last Twelve Verses of Mark.* Cambridge; New York: Cambridge University Press, 1974. (SNTSMS 25.)

OCLC: 980076 ISB.

448B _____. "Luke's Use of Matthew: A Christological Inquiry." PSThJ 40/3 (1987): 39-50.

449A _____. "Modern Developments of Griesbach's Hypothesis." NTS 23 (1977): 275-95.

449B _____, ed. *New Synoptic Studies: The Cambridge Gospel Conference and Beyond.* Macon GA: Mercer University Press, 1983. xli + 533pp.

OCLC: 9783753 ISB.

450A _____. "Notes on a Literary and Form-Critical Analysis of Some of the Synoptic Material Peculiar to Luke." NTS 8 (1961–1962): 301-16.

450B   _____. *Occasional Notes on Some Points of Interest in New Testament Studies.* Macon GA: Mercer University Press, 1980.

The preface indicates Farmer's perception of the state of Gospel Studies in August 1980. Two notes are important for the Synoptic Problem: "A Note on the Ideological Background of the Marcan Hypothesis," 1-6; "Notes for a Compositional Analysis on the Griesbach Hypothesis of the Empty Tomb Stories in the Synoptic Gospels," 7-14.
OCLC: 7291166 BWE.

450C   _____. "The Patristic Evidence Reexamined: A Response to George Kennedy." In *New Synoptic Studies: The Cambridge Gospel Conference and Beyond,* William R. Farmer, ed., 3-15. Macon GA: Mercer University Press, 1983.
OCLC: 9783753 ISB.

450D   _____. "The Post-Sectarian Character of Matthew and Its Post-War Setting in Syria." PerspRS 3 (1976): 235-47.

450E   _____. "Preface." PSThJ 33/4 (1980): 1-2.

The entire issue is devoted to the theme "A Time for Reappraisal and Fresh Approaches."

451   _____. "The Present State of the Synoptic Problem." PSThJ 32/1 (1978): 1-7.

452   _____. "The Problem of Christian Origins: A Programmatic Essay." In *Studies in the History and Text of the New Testament in Honor of Kenneth Willis Clark,* Boyd L. Daniels and M. Jack Suggs, eds., 81-88. Salt Lake City: University of Utah Press, 1967. (Studies and Documents 29.)
OCLC: 430040 ISB.

453A   _____, et al., eds. *Proceedings of the Jerusalem Symposium.* See Boismard, M.-É., David L. Dungan, William R. Farmer, and Frans Neirynck, eds. (141).

453B   _____. " 'Q': State of the Question." BibTh 3 (1986): 202-20.

Korean translation by Lee Jong-Yun of paper read to Korean New Testament Society, summer 1985.

453C   _____. "Redaction Criticism and the Synoptic Problem." In *The Society of Biblical Literature 1971 Seminar Papers,* 28-31. Atlanta: Society of Biblical Literature, 1971.

453D   _____. "Reply to Michael Goulder." In *Synoptic Studies: The Ampleforth Conferences of 1982 and 1983,* C. M. Tuckett, ed., 105-109. Sheffield: JSOT Press, 1984. (JSNT Supplement Series 7.)
OCLC: 12451599 ISB.

454   _____. "A Response to Joseph Fitzmyer's Defense of the 'Two-Document' Hypothesis." In *New Synoptic Studies: The Cambridge Gospel Conference and Beyond,* William R. Farmer, ed., 501-23. Macon GA: Mercer University Press, 1983. "Fitzmyer's Defense of 'Q,' " 517-23.
OCLC: 9783753 ISB.

455 _____. "A Response to Robert Morgenthaler's *Statistische Synopse*." Bib 54 (1973): 417-33.

456 _____. "A 'Skeleton in the Closet' of Gospel Research." BR 6 (1961): 18-42.

457A _____. "Some Thoughts on the Provenance of Matthew." In *The Teacher's Yoke: Studies in Memory of Henry Trantham*, E. Jerry Vardaman and James Leo Garrett, Jr., eds., 109-16. Waco TX: Baylor University Press, 1964.
OCLC: 1184657 ISB.

457B _____. "Source Criticism: Some Comments on the Present Situation." USQR 42/1-2 (1988): 49-57.
An invited contribution to the "Biblical Jubilee: 'What Was, Is, and Shall Be,' " as a part of the Sesquicentennial Celebration of Union Theological Seminary, New York, 8-9 April 1987.

457C _____. "The Stoldt-Conzelmann Controversy: A Review Article." PerspRS 7 (1980): 152-62.

458 _____. *The Synoptic Problem: A Critical Analysis*. New York: Macmillan, 1964. Rpt with corrections. Dillsboro NC: Western North Carolina Press [Macon GA: Mercer University Press], 1976. xi + 308pp.
Pages 199-232 are reissued in *The Two-Source Hypothesis: A Critical Appraisal*, Arthur J. Bellinzoni, Jr., ed., 163-97. Macon GA: Mercer University Press, 1985.
OCLC: 383208 ISB; 7720818 ICW; 2486493 DCU; 11599674 ISB.
Reviews: Burkill, T. Alec. ChrC 81 (1964): 1430; Nineham, D. E. JThS 28 (1977): 548-49; Schmithals, W. ThLZ 92 (1967): 424-25; Snape, H. C. MCM 9 (1966): 184-91.

459 _____. "The Synoptic Problem: A Glimpse into the Continuing Discussion." Unpublished paper, 1968.

460 _____. "The Synoptic Problem: The Inadequacies of the Generally Accepted Solution." PSThJ 33/4 (1980): 20-27.

461 _____. "The Synoptic Problem and the Contemporary Theological Chaos." ChrC 83 (1966): 1204-1206.

462 _____. *Synopticon: The Verbal Agreement Between the Greek Texts of Matthew, Mark and Luke Contextually Exhibited*. London; New York: Cambridge University Press, 1969. 229pp.
OCLC: 55843 ISB.

463 _____. "Timeless Truth and Apostolic Faith." PSThJ 37/3 (1984): 7-11.

464 _____. "The Two-Document Hypothesis as a Methodological Criterion in Synoptic Research." AThR 48 (1966): 380-96.

465 Farrer, Austin M. 1952. As reviewer see Butler, B. C. *Originality of St. Matthew* (217).

466 _____. "On Dispensing with Q." In *Studies in the Gospels: Essays in Memory of R. H. Lightfoot,* Dennis E. Nineham, ed., 55-88. Oxford: Basil Blackwell, 1955.
Reissued in *The Two-Source Hypothesis: A Critical Appraisal,* Arthur J. Bellinzoni, Jr., ed., 321-56. Macon GA: Mercer University Press, 1985.
OCLC: 2394516 ISB; 11599674 ISB.

467 _____. "Q." Th 59 (1956): 247-48.

468 _____. *St. Matthew and St. Mark.* Westminster, Eng.: Dacre Press, 1954. 236pp. (Edward Cadbury Lectures 1953-1954.)
OCLC: 1070370 ISB.

469 _____. *A Study in St. Mark.* New York: Oxford University Press, 1952. 398pp.
OCLC: 3510631 TLM.

470 Fee, Gordon D. "Modern Text Criticism and the Synoptic Problem." In *J. J. Griesbach, Synoptic and Text-Critical Studies, 1776–1976,* Bernard Orchard and Thomas R. W. Longstaff, eds., 154-69. Cambridge: Cambridge University Press, 1978. (SNTSMS 34.)
OCLC: 3541663 ISB.

471 _____. "A Text-Critical Look at the Synoptic Problem." NovT 22 (1980): 12-28.

472 Feine, Paul. *Eine vorkanonische Überlieferung des Lukas in Evangelium und Apostelgeschichte: Eine Untersuchung.* Gotha: F. A. Perthes, 1891. 252pp.
OCLC: 3599319 ISB.

473 Fenton, John C. *The Gospel of St. Matthew.* Baltimore; Harmondsworth: Penguin Books, 1963. (Pelican New Testament Commentaries.) *Saint Matthew.* Philadelphia: Westminster Press, 1978. 487pp. (Westminster Pelican Commentaries.)
OCLC: 1578581 ISB; 3089095 IYU.

474 Fernandez, Enrique López. "Nueva solución al problema sinoptico. La teoría de Antonio Gaboury: hipótesis, argumentos y crítica." EstBib 30 (1971): 313-43.

475 Feuillet, A. "Évangiles synoptiques. Vue d'ensemble sur l'histoire de leur exégèse." EeV 86 (1976): 641-46.

476A Filson, Floyd Vivian. *A Commentary on the Gospel According to St. Matthew.* London: A. & C. Black, 1960. 2nd ed. 1971. 319pp. (Black's New Testament Commentaries.)
OCLC: 1005371 ISB; 622813 ISB.

476B _____. "The Literary Relations Among the Gospels." In *The Interpreter's One-Volume Commentary on the Bible,* Charles M. Laymon, ed., 1,129-35. Nashville; New York: Abingdon Press, 1971. *Interpreter's Concise Commentary: The Gospels.* 1983.
OCLC: 155546 ISB; 9197605 OKG.

477A Findlay, Adam F. *Byways in Early Christian Literature: Studies in the Uncanonical Gospels and Acts.* Edinburgh: T. & T. Clark, 1923. vii + 354pp. (Kerr Lectures 1920-1921.)
OCLC: 346663 ISB.

477B Fiorenza, Elisabeth Schüssler. "Apokalypsis and Propheteia. The Book of Revelation in the Context of Early Christian Prophecy." In *L'Apocalypse johannique et l'apocalyptique dans le Nouveau Testament,* J. Lambrecht, ed., 105-28. Gembloux: J. Duculot, 1980. (BEThL 53.)
OCLC: 7010075 ISB; 8220789 AZS.

---- Fischer, Karl Martin. *See* Schenke, Hans-Martin (1335).

478 Fitzmyer, Joseph A. *Essays on the Semitic Background of the New Testament.* Missoula MT: Scholars Press, 1974. 524pp. (SBL Sources for Biblical Study 5.)
OCLC: 1057128 ISB.

479A _____. *The Gospel According to Luke. Introduction, translation and notes.* 2 vols. Garden City NY: Doubleday, 1981–1985. (Anchor Bible 28, 28A.)
OCLC: 6918343 ISB.

479B _____. "Judaic Studies and the Gospels: The Seminar." In *The Relationships among the Gospels: An Interdisciplinary Dialogue,* William O. Walker, Jr., ed., 237-58. San Antonio: Trinity University Press, 1978. (Trinity University Monograph Series in Religion 5.)
OCLC: 4365624 ISB.

480 _____. "Luke's Use of Q." In *The Two-Source Hypothesis: A Critical Appraisal,* Arthur J. Bellinzoni, Jr., ed., 245-57. Macon GA: Mercer University Press, 1985.

481 _____. "The Matthean Divorce Texts and Some New Palestinian Evidence." ThSt 37 (1976): 197-226.

482 _____. "Memory and Manuscript: The Origins and Transmission of the Gospel Tradition." ThSt 23 (1962): 442-57.
A Review of Birger Gerhardsson's *Memory and Manuscript* (525).

483 _____. "The Priority of Mark and the 'Q' Source in Luke." In *Jesus and Man's Hope,* D. G. Buttrick, ed., 1:131-70. Pittsburgh: Pittsburgh Theological Seminary, 1970. (Perspective 1.)
Reissued in *To Advance the Gospel: New Testament Studies,* by Joseph A. Fitzmyer, 3-40. New York: Crossroad, 1981. Pages 134-47 and 164-66 are reissued in *The Two-Source Hypothesis: A Critical Appraisal,* Arthur J. Bellinzoni, Jr., ed., 37-52. Macon GA: Mercer University Press, 1985.
OCLC: 142572 ISB; 11599674 ISB.

_____. *To Advance the Gospel: New Testament Studies.* New York: Crossroad, 1981. 265pp.
OCLC: 7168538 ISB.

485 _____. "The Use of 'Agein' and 'Pherein' in the Synoptic Gospels." *Festschrift to Honour F. Wilbur Gingrich, Lexicographer, Scholar, Teacher, and Committed Christian Layman,* Eugene H. Barth and Ronald E. Cocroft, eds., 147-60. Leiden: Brill, 1972.
OCLC: 531495 ISB.

486 Fleddermann, Harry. "The Beginning of Q [Lk 3:7-9, 16-17.]" In *Society of Biblical Literature 1985 Seminar Papers,* K. H. Richards, ed., 153-59. Chico CA: Scholars Press, 1985. (SBLSPS 24.)

487 _____. "The Discipleship Discourse (Mark 9:33-50)." CBQ 43 (1981): 57-75.

488 _____. "John and the Coming One (Matt 3:11-12 ‖ Luke 3:16-17.)" In *Society of Biblical Literature 1984 Seminar Papers,* K. H. Richards, ed., 377-84. Chico CA: Scholars Press, 1984. (SBLSPS 23.)

---- Flusser, David. *See* Lowe, M. (956).

489 Foakes-Jackson, Frederick John, and Kirsopp Lake. *The Beginnings of Christianity.* 5 vols. London: Macmillan, 1920–1933. Grand Rapids MI: Baker, 1965, 1979.
OCLC: 3874655 CFT; 3677701 CSM; 5211973 COI.

490 Fonseca, Aloisius Gonzaga da. *Quaestio synoptica.* Rome: Pontifico Instituto Biblico, 1952. Editio tertia. 1952. 224pp. (Institutiones Biblicae, series altera.)
OCLC: 175707 PCJ.

491 Foster, L. A. "The 'Q' Myth in Synoptic Studies." BETS 7 (1964): 111-19.

492 Frankemölle, H. 1972. As Reviewer see Christ, Felix. *Jesus Sophia* (280).

493 _____. "Amtskritik in Matthäus-Evangelium?" Bib 54 (1973): 247-62.

494 Freudenberg, J. "Die synoptische Weherede: Tradition und Redaktion in Mt 23 par." Diss., University of Münster, 1972.*

495 Freudenberger, R. "Zum Text der zweiten Vaterunserbitte." NTS 15 (1968–1969): 419-32.

496 Frey, Louis. *Analyse ordinale des évangiles synoptiques.* Paris: Mouton, 1972. 383pp. (Mathematiques et sciences de l'homme 11.) Includes bibl.
OCLC: 723638.

497 Fritzsche, Karl Friedrich August. *Evangelium Matthaei.* Recensuit et cum commentariis perpetuis edidit C. F. A. Fritzsche. Lipsiae: Sumptibus Frederici Fleischeri, 1826. 872pp. (Fritzsche, K. F. A. *Quatuor N. T. Evangelia* 1.)
Text in Greek; other matter in Latin.
OCLC: 9343467 WTS.

498 _____. *Evangelium Marci.* Recensuit et cum commentariis perpetuis
     edidit C. F. A. Fritzsche. Lipsiae: Sumptibus Frederici Fleischeri, 1830.
     805pp. (Fritzsche, K. F. A. *Quatuor N. T. Evangelia* 2.)
     Text in Greek; other matter in Latin.
     NUC: CtY-D; MH.

499 Frizzi, Giuseppe. "Carattere originale e relevanza degli 'apostoli inviati'
     in Q/Lc. 11, 49-51; 13, 34-35/Mt. 23, 34-36.37-39." RivBib 21 (1973):
     401-12.

500A _____. "L'Opostolos delle tradizioni sinottiche (Mc, Q, Mt, Lc, et
      Atti.)" RivBib 22 (1974): 3-37.*

500B Frye, Roland Mushat. "A Literary Perspective for the Criticism of the
      Gospels." In *Jesus and Man's Hope,* Donald G. Miller and Dikran Y.
      Hadidian, eds., 2:193-221. Pittsburgh: Pittsburgh Theological Semi-
      nary, 1971. (Perspective 2.)
      OCLC: 142572 ISB.

500C _____. "The Synoptic Problems and Analogies in Other Literatures."
      In *The Relationships among the Gospels: An Interdisciplinary Dia-
      logue,* William O. Walker, Jr., ed., 261-302. San Antonio: Trinity Uni-
      versity Press, 1978. (Trinity University Monograph Series in Religion
      5.)
      OCLC: 4365624 ISB.

501 Fuchs, Albert. "Die Behandlung der mt/lk Übereinstimmungen gegen Mk
     durch S. McLoughlin und ihre Bedeutung für die synoptische Frage."
     In *Probleme der Forschung,* Albert Fuchs, ed., 24-57. München: H.
     Wien, 1978. (Studien zum Neuen Testament und seiner Umwelt. Serie
     A, 3.)
     OCLC: 13954741 DTM.

502 _____. *Die Entwicklung der Beelzebulkontroverse bei den Synoptikern:
     traditionsgeschichtliche und redaktionsgeschichtliche Untersuchung von
     Mk 3, 22-27 und Parallelen, verbunden mit der Rückfrage nach Jesus.*
     Linz: Studien zum Neuen Testament und seiner Umwelt, 1980. 179pp.
     (Studien zum Neuen Testament und seiner Umwelt, Serie B, 5.) In-
     cludes bibl.
     OCLC: 6961376 DRU.

503 _____. "Entwicklungsgeschichtliche Studie zu Mk 1, 29-31 par Mt 8,
     14-15 par Lk 4, 38-39." StNTSU 6-7 (1981–1982): 21-76.

504 _____. *Sprachliche Untersuchungen zu Matthäus und Lukas: Ein Bei-
     trag zur Quellenkritik: die Blindenheilung, Mt 9, 27-31: das Zeugnis der
     Christen in der Verfolgung, Lk 21, 14-15.* Rome: Biblical Institute Press,
     1971. 217pp. (Analecta biblica 49.) Includes bibl.
     A revision of the author's thesis, Salzburg, 1968.
     OCLC: 272228 ISB.
     Review: Goulder, M. D. JThS 23 (1972): 197-200.

505 _____. "Die Überschneidungen von Mk und 'Q' nach B. H. Streeter und E. P. Sanders und ihre wahre Bedeutung (Mk 1, 1-8 par.)" In *Wort in der Zeit: neutestamentliche Studien. Festgabe für Karl Heinrich Rengstorf zum 75. Geburtstag,* Wilfrid Haubeck and Michael Bachmann, eds., 28-81. Leiden: Brill, 1980.
OCLC: 7463668 ISB; 7361667 STS.

506 _____. "Versuchung Jesu." StNTSU 9 (1984): 95-159.

507 _____. "Die Wiederbelebung der Griesbachhypothese oder Wissenschaft auf dem Holzweg." StNTSU 5 (1980): 139-49.

508A Fuller, Reginald H. "Baur Versus Hilgenfeld: A Forgotten Chapter in the Debate on the Synoptic Problem." NTS 24 (1978): 355-70.

508B _____. "Classics and the Gospels: The Seminar." In *The Relationships among the Gospels: An Interdisciplinary Dialogue,* William O. Walker, Jr., ed., 173-92. San Antonio: Trinity University Press, 1978. (Trinity University Monograph Series in Religion 5.)
OCLC: 4365624 ISB.

509 _____. "Das Doppelgebot der Liebe: Ein Testfall für die Echtheitskriterien der Worte Jesu." In *Jesus Christus in Historie und Theologie: Neutestamentliche Festschrift für Hans Conzelmann zum 60. Geburtstag,* G. Strecker, ed., 317-29. Tübingen: J. C. B. Mohr (Paul Siebeck), 1975.
ET: "The Double Commandment of Love: A Test Case for the Criteria of Authenticity." In *Essays on the Love Commandment,* trans. Reginald H. Fuller and Ilse Fuller, 41-56. Philadelphia: Fortress Press, 1978.
OCLC: 2120453 ISB; 4076205 ISB.

510 _____. "Die neuere Diskussion über das synoptische Problem." ThZ 34 (1978): 129-48.

511 _____. *The New Testament in Current Study.* New York: Scribner's, 1962. viii + 147pp. Rev. ed. London: SCM, 1963. viii + 159pp.
Esp. "Synoptic Studies," 70-85.
Journal update: "The New Testament in Current Study." PerspRS 1/2 (1974): 108-24 ("Synoptic Studies: The Rise of Redaction Criticism," 117-18).
OCLC: 378193 ISB; 3027719 BPS.

512 _____, E. P. Sanders, and Thomas R. W. Longstaff. "The Synoptic Problem: After Ten Years [book reviews.]" PSThJ 28/2 (1975): 63-74.

513A Funk, Robert W. "The Looking-Glass Tree Is for the Birds. Ezekiel 17:22-24; Mark 4:30-32." Interp 27 (1973): 3-9.

513B _____, ed. *New Gospel Parallels.* 2 vols. Philadelphia: Fortress Press, 1985. xx + 492pp., xx + 396pp.
Vol. 1. *The Synoptic Gospels.* Vol. 2. *John and the Other Gospels.* Like Swanson (1528B) before him, Funk avoids the problem of assuming an original common order of parallel pericopes by the expedient of printing *each* gospel successively as the "lead gospel" in separate parts of the synopsis (see David L. Dungan, p. 474 in 393C).
OCLC: 11915771 ISB.

513C _____. "The Parables." In *Jesus and Man's Hope,* Donald G. Miller and Dikran Y. Hadidian, eds., 2:287-303. Pittsburgh: Pittsburgh Theological Seminary, 1971. (Perspective 2.)
OCLC: 142572 ISB.

513D Furnish, Victor P. "Griesbach Hypothesis." In *The Interpreter's Dictionary of the Bible,* Supplementary Volume, Keith Crim, gen. ed., Victor P. Furnish, NT ed., 381. Nashville: Abingdon Press, 1976.

514A Fusco, Vittorio. "L'accord mineur Mt 13, 11a/Lc 8, 10a contre Mc 4, 11a." In *Logia. Les paroles de Jésus = The Sayings of Jesus: Mémorial Joseph Coppens,* Joël Delobel, ed., 355-61. Leuven: University Press and Peeters, 1982. (BEThL 59.)
OCLC: 9450792 ISB; 11043145 CLU.

514B Gamba, Giuseppe Giov. "A Further Reexamination of Evidence from the Early Tradition." In *New Synoptic Studies: The Cambridge Gospel Conference and Beyond,* William R. Farmer, ed., 17-35. Macon GA: Mercer University Press, 1983.
OCLC: 9783753 ISB.

515 Gaboury, Antonio. 1972. As reviewer see Schramm, T. *Markus-Stoff* (1385).

516 _____. *La structure des évangiles synoptiques: la Structure-type à l'origine des synoptiques.* Leiden: Brill, 1970. 228pp. (NovTSup 22.)
A revision of the author's thesis, Commissio Pontificia de Re Biblica, 1962.
OCLC: 254420 ISB.
Review: Montague, G. T. CBQ 34 (1972): 76-78.

517 Gamber, Klaus. *Jesus-Worte: Eine vorkanonische Logiensammlung im Lukas-Evangelium.* Regensburg: F. Pustet, 1983. 98pp. (Studia Patristica et Liturgica. Beiheft 9.)
OCLC: 10318037 IND.

518 Gander, Georges. *La notion primitive d'église, d'après l'évangile selon Matthieu, chapitre 16, versets 18 et 19.* Aix-en-Provence: Faculté libre de théologie protestante, 1966. 143pp.
OCLC: 8470966 TJC.

519 Gardner-Smith, Percival. *Saint John and the Synoptic Gospels.* Cambridge: Cambridge University Press, 1938. 100pp.
OCLC: 2414944 ISB.

KENRICK SEMINARY LIBRARY
5200 GLENNON DRIVE
ST. LOUIS, MISSOURI 63119

520 Gast, Frederick. "Synoptic Problem." In *Jerome Biblical Commentary,* Raymond E. Brown, Joseph A. Fitzmyer, and Ronald E. Murphy, eds., 2:1-6. New York: Prentice-Hall, 1968. London: G. Chapman, 1969. OCLC: 355447 ISB; 13656457 VCB.

521 Gaston, Lloyd. *Horae Synopticae Electronicae: Word Statistics of the Synoptic Gospels.* Missoula MT: Society of Biblical Literature, 1973. 101pp. (SBL Sources for Biblical Study 3.) OCLC: 947637 ISB. Review: Sparks, H. F. D. JThS 26 (1975): 146-49.

522 _____. "Sondergut und Markusstoff in Luk. 21." ThZ 16 (1960): 161-72.

---- Geden, Alfred S. *See* Moulton, William F. (1074).

523 Geiger, Ruthild. *Die lukanischen Endzeitreden: Studien zur Eschatologie des Lukas-Evangeliums.* Bern: Herbert Lang, 1973. 277pp. (Europäische Hochschulschriften: Reihe 23, Theologie 16.) Includes bibl. OCLC: 830267 BHA.

524 Gerhardsson, Birger. "Agape and Imitation of Christ." In *Jesus, the Gospels, and the Church,* E. P. Sanders, ed., 163-76. Macon GA: Mercer University Press, 1987. OCLC: 16130939 ISB.

525A _____. *Memory and Manuscript: Oral Tradition and Written Transmission in Rabbinic Judaism and Early Christianity.* Trans. Eric J. Sharpe. Lund: C. W. K. Gleerup, 1964. 379pp. (Acta Seminarii Neotestamentici Upsaliensis 22.) Includes bibl. Diss., Uppsala. OCLC: 1061433 ISB; 11515666 CDS.

525B _____. *The Origins of the Gospel Traditions.* Philadelphia: Fortress Press, 1979. London: SCM Press, 1979. 95pp. Includes bibl. Trans. of "Evangeliernas förhistoria," lectures given in March 1976 at Holzhausen, Germany. OCLC: 4495683 ISB; 14965078.

526 _____. "The Parable of the Sower and Its Interpretation." NTS 14 (1967–1968): 165-93.

527 _____. *Tradition and Transmission in Early Christianity.* Lund: C. W. K. Gleerup, 1964. 47pp. (Coniectanea Neotestamentica 20.) OCLC: 337971 ISB.

528A Gersdorf, Christoph Gotthelf. *Beiträge zur Sprach-Characteristik der Schriftsteller des Neuen Testaments: Eine Sammlung meist neuer Bemerkungen.* Ersten Theil (no more published). Leipzig: Weidmann, 1816. 579pp. OCLC: 10131894 ISB.

528B Gfrörer, August Friedrich. *Die heilige Sage.* Stuttgart: C. Schweizerbart, 1838. 3 pts. in 1 vol. (His *Geschichte des Urchristentums* 2.) OCLC: 6880203 CLE.

529 Gieseler, Johann Carl Ludwig. *Historisch-kritischer Versuch über die Entstehung und die frühesten Schicksale der schriftlichen Evangelien.* Leipzig: W. Englemann, 1818. 203pp. OCLC: 4266701 ISB.

530 Gilbert, George H. "The Jesus of 'Q'—The Oldest Source in the Gospels." HibJ 10 (1911–1912): 533-42.

531 Gilmour, S. MacLean. "A Critical Re-examination of Proto-Luke." JBL 67 (1948): 143-52.

532 _____. "The Gospel According to St. Luke: Introduction and Exegesis." In *The Interpreter's Bible,* George A. Buttrick, ed., 8:3-434. Nashville: Abingdon Press, 1952. OCLC: 346303 WSU; 355416 ISB.

533 Glasson, T. F. "Did Matthew and Luke use a 'Western' Text of Mark?" ET 55 (1943–1944): 180-84.

534 _____. "Did Matthew and Luke use a 'Western' Text of Mark?" ET 77 (1965–1966): 120-21.

535 _____. "An Early Revision of the Gospel of Mark." JBL 85 (1966): 231-33.

536 Glickman, Steven Craig. "The Temptation Account in Matthew and Luke." Diss., University of Basel, 1983. 539 leaves. Photocopy: Dallas TX: J. B. Swift Pub. Co., 1983. OCLC: 10517986 DTM.

537 Glombitza, Otto. "Die Titel διδάσκαλος und ἐπιστάτης für Jesus bei Lukas." ZNW 49 (1958): 275-78.

538 Glover, Richard. "Patristic Quotations and Gospel Sources." NTS 31 (1985): 234-51.

539 Gnilka, Joachim. *Das Evangelium nach Markus.* Zürich: Benziger, 1978– 1979. 2 vols. (Evangelisch-katholischer Kommentar zum N.T. 2.) Contents: 1. Teil. Mk 1–8,26; 2. Teil. Mk 8,27–16,20. OCLC: 5286680 ICU.

540 _____. "Synoptiker, II, 2a. Theologie der Spruchquelle." LThK 9 (1964): 1245-46.

541 Godet, Frédérick Louis. *A Commentary on the Gospel of St. Luke.* Trans. from the 2nd French ed. by E. W. Shalders & M. D. Cusin. Edinburgh: T. & T. Clark, 1887. (Clark's Foreign Theological Library 45-46.) 4th ed. 1890. 2 vols. With a preface and notes to the American ed. by John Hall. New York: Funk & Wagnalls, 1894. Microfiche. Pastor's Resource Services, 1971. Chattanooga TN: Expositor's Microfilm Library, 1978? *Commentary on Luke.* Grand Rapids MI: Kregel Publications, 1981. (Kregel Reprint Library.) 574pp. Trans. of Commentaire sur l'Evangile de saint Luc. OCLC: 13746274 MCB; 6281622 MOG; 12123164 INA; 7557044 IMC; 6962321 TBI; 6339873 CDC; 7945165 DTM.

542 _____. *Introduction to the New Testament*. Trans. from the French by William Affleck. Edinburgh: T. & T. Clark, 1894–1899. 2 vols. (no more published).
Contents: 1. Particular introduction, The Epistles of St. Paul; 2. The Collection of the Four Gospels and the Gospel of St. Matthew.
OCLC: 11236664 SBI; Microfiche (ATL) 3493101.

543 Goguel, Maurice. *Introduction au Nouveau Testament*. Paris: Ernest Leroux, 1922–1926. 4 vols. in 5 (no more published). (Bibliothèque historique des religions.)
Contents: 1. Les évangiles synoptiques; 2. Le quatrième évangile; 3. Le livre des actes; 4. (2 vols.) Les épitres pauliniennes.
OCLC: 9660313 UTS; Microfilm (ATL) 4597938.

544 _____. "Luke and Mark: With a Discussion of Streeter's Theory." HThR 26 (1933): 1-55.

545 _____. "Une nouvelle école de critique évangélique: La 'Form- und traditionsgeschichtliche Schule'." RHR 94 (1926): 114-60.

---- Gooch, P. *See* Richardson, Peter. (1244).

546 Goodenough, Erwin R. "A Reply [to R. P. Casey's 'Professor Goodenough and the Fourth Gospel' (535-42)]." JBL 64 (1945): 543-44.

547 Goodspeed, Edgar J. *The Formation of the New Testament*. Chicago: University of Chicago Press, 1926. Midway Reprint, 1974. 209pp. Includes bibl.
OCLC: 1494816 ISB; 2887379 AJB.

548 _____. *A History of Early Christian Literature*. Chicago: University of Chicago Press, 1942. 324pp. Rev. and enl. by Robert M. Grant. 1966. 214pp.
OCLC: 1167936 ISB; 304245 ISB.

549 _____. *An Introduction to the New Testament*. Chicago: University of Chicago Press, 1937. 362pp. Spanish. *Introducción al Nuevo Testamento*. Prólogo de Juan M. Norris. Traducción del inglés por Adam F. Soso. México, D. F.: Casa Unida de Publicaciones, 1948. 271pp. (Bibliotheca de Cultura Evangelica.)
OCLC: 386367 ISB; 13730945 ISB.

550 _____. *Matthew, Apostle and Evangelist*. Philadelphia: Winston, 1959. 166pp.
OCLC: 391249 ISB.

551 Goodwin, W. W. *A Greek Grammar*. New ed. London: Macmillan, 1894. New York: St. Martin's Press, 1977. 451pp. Rev. by Charles Burton Gulick. Boston: Ginn, 1930. (College Classical Series.) New Rochelle NY: Caratzas, 1981. 457pp. New York: St. Martin's Press, 1981. 451pp.
OCLC: 3222031 MOU; 5159854 CLA; 8272587 TMA; 9966785 CRP.

552 Gould, Ezra Palmer. *A Critical and Exegetical Commentary on the Gospel According to St. Mark.* Edinburgh: T. & T. Clark, 1896. New York: Scribner's, 1896. 1922. 8th impression. 1948. 1961. Microfiche. Pastor's Resource Services, 1971. Edinburgh: T. & T. Clark, 1969. lvii + 317pp. (ICC 27.)
OCLC: 6908076 TBI; 950442 ISB; 10168075 DRP; 2043248 ATO; 9611069 CNO; 6731941 CDC; 845776 BPS.

553 Goulder, M. D. 1969. As reviewer see Wrege, Hans T. *Die Überlieferungsgeschichte der Bergpredigt* (1725).

554 ———. 1972. As reviewer see Fuchs, Albert. *Sprachliche* (504).

555 ———. *The Evangelists' Calendar: A Lectionary Explanation of the Development of Scripture.* London: SPCK, 1978. 334pp. (Speaker's Lectures in Biblical Studies 1972.)
OCLC: 4714576 ISB.

556 ———. "Farrer on Q." Th 83 (1980): 190-95.

557 ———. "A House Built on Sand." In *Alternative Approaches to New Testament Study,* A. E. Harvey, ed., 1-24. London: SPCK, 1985.
OCLC: 12524651 ISB.

558 ———. "Mark xvi. 1-8 and Parallels." NTS 24 (1978): 235-40.

559 ———. *Midrash and Lection in Matthew.* London: SPCK, 1974. 528pp. (Speaker's Lectures in Biblical Studies 1969–1971.) Includes bibl.
OCLC: 1130240 ISB.

560A ———. "On Putting Q to the Test." NTS 24 (1978): 218-34.

560B ———. "The Order of a Crank." In *Synoptic Studies: The Ampleforth Conferences of 1982 and 1983,* C. M. Tuckett, ed., 111-30. Sheffield: JSOT Press, 1984. (JSNT Supplement Series 7.)
OCLC: 12451599 ISB.

560C ———. "Some Observations on Professor Farmer's 'Certain Results . . .'." In *Synoptic Studies: The Ampleforth Conferences of 1982 and 1983,* C. M. Tuckett, ed., 99-104. Sheffield: JSOT Press, 1984. (JSNT Supplement Series 7.)
OCLC: 12451599 ISB.

561 Graffin, R., ed. *Patrologia Syriaca, complectens opera omnia ss. patrum, doctorum scriptorumque catholicorum, quibus accedunt aliorum a catholicorum auctorum scripta quae ad res ecclesiasticas pertinent, quotquot syriace supersunt, secundum codices praesertim londinenses, parisienses.* Paris: Firmin-Didot et socii, 1894.
Syriac and Latin in parallel columns.
OCLC: 610430 ISB.

562 Gransden, Antonia. *Historical Writing in England.* 2 vols. London: Routledge and Kegan Paul, 1974–1982. Ithaca NY: Cornell University Press, 1974–1982.
OCLC: 3090957; 1120971.

563 Grant, Frederick C. "The Contents of Q." A section in his *The Gospel of Matthew*, vol. 1, *Chapters 1-13:52 in the King James Verison, with Introduction and Critical Notes*, 12-13. New York: Harper & Brothers; London: Eyre and Spottiswoode, 1955. (Harper's Annotated Bible Series 10.)
OCLC: 4277715 OKO.

564 _____. *The Earliest Gospel*. New York: Abingdon Press, 1943. 270pp. (Cole Lectures 1943.)
OCLC: 269537 WSU; An Apex Book 3990421 ISB.

565 _____. *The Gospels: Their Origin and Their Growth*. New York: Harper, 1957. London: Faber & Faber, 1957. New York: Octagon Books, 1983. 216pp. Includes bibl.
OCLC: 383451 ISB; 3500698 MBS; Photocopy (University Microfilms) 13469392 RBN; 9785309 IDA.

566 _____. *The Growth of the Gospels*. New York: Abingdon Press, 1933. 226pp.
OCLC: 4040293 ISB.

567 _____. "Was There a Document Q?" RelLife 21 (1941–1942): 35-44.

568A Grant, Robert M. *The Earliest Lives of Jesus*. London: SPCK, 1961. New York: Harper, 1961. 134pp. Includes bibl.
Includes Origen's exegetical writings on the Gospels, 124-26.
OCLC: 3019145 ISB; 227695 HEI.

568B _____. "The Gospels." In his *A Historical Introduction to the New Testament*, 105-18. New York; Evanston: Harper & Row, 1963. 448pp.
Esp. "Probabilities about the Gospels," 107-13; "Q for Quelle," 113-16; "The Synoptic Problem," 117-18.

569 _____. *The Secret Sayings of Jesus,* by Robert M. Grant in collaboration with David Noel Freedman. With an English translation of the Gospel of Thomas by William R. Schoedel. Garden City NY: Doubleday, 1960. 206pp. London: Collins, 1960. (Fontana Books 69R.) 192pp. Includes bibl.
OCLC: 942353 ISB; 2232811 YAH; Dolphin Book 3575049 ICA.

570 Grässer, Erich. *Das Problem der Parusieverzögerung in den synoptischen Evangelien und in der Apostelgeschichte*. Berlin: A. Töpelmann, 1957. 234pp. 2. berichtigte und erweiterte Aufl. 1960. 256pp. 3., durch. e. ausführl. Einl. u. e. Literaturverz. erg. Aufl. Berlin; New York, 1977. 257pp. (Beihefte zur Zeitschrift für die neutestamentliche Wissenschaft und die Kunde der älteren Kirche 22.) Includes bibl.
Originally presented as the author's thesis, Marburg, 1955.
OCLC: 8905216 CFT; 4122881 KAT; 4133887 DTM.

571 Gratz, Petrus Alois. *Neuer Versuch, die Entstehung der drey ersten Evangelien zu erklären*. Tübingen: L. F. Fues, 1812. 262pp. (His *Kritische Schriften* 1.)
NUC: NjPT; NNUT.

572 Green, H. Benedict. "The Credibility of Luke's Transformation of Matthew." In *Synoptic Studies: The Ampleforth Conferences of 1982 and 1983*, C. M. Tuckett, ed., 131-55. Sheffield: JSOT Press, 1984. (JSNT Supplement Series 7.)
OCLC: 12451599 ISB.

573 _____. "Matthew 12, 22-50 and Parallels: An Alternative to Matthaean Conflation." In *Synoptic Studies: The Ampleforth Conferences of 1982 and 1983*, C. M. Tuckett, ed., 157-76. Sheffield: JSOT Press, 1984. (JSNT Supplement Series 7.)
OCLC: 12451599 ISB.

574 Greenlee, J. H. "*INA* Clauses and Related Expressions." BTr 6 (1955): 12-16.

575 Cancelled.

576A Greeven, Heinrich, ed. *Albert Huck. Synopse der drei ersten Evangelien mit Beigabe der johanneischen Parallelstellen.* 13. Auflage, völlig neu bearbeitet von Heinrich Greeven. [*Synopsis of the First Three Gospels with the Addition of the Johannine Parallels.* 13th ed., fundamentally rev. by Heinrich Greeven.] Tübingen: J. C. B. Mohr (Paul Siebeck), 1981. xli + 298pp. + 1 Abkürzungen und Zeichen [Abbreviations and Symbols] card.
A "fundamental revision" of Huck-Lietzmann (728) based on a "new recension" of the Greek text that departs from the Nestle-Aland and other editions. Text in Greek with German/English headings; preface and introduction in German and English in parallel columns; index of pericopes in German/English.
OCLC: 8115171 ICU.

576B _____. "Erwägungen zur synoptischen Textkritik." NTS 6 (1959–1960): 281-96.

576C _____. "The Gospel Synopsis from 1776 to the Present Day." In *J. J. Griesbach, Synoptic and Text-Critical Studies, 1776–1976*, Bernard Orchard and Thomas R. W. Longstaff, eds., 22-49. Cambridge; New York: Cambridge University Press, 1978. (SNTSMS 34.)
First delivered at the Griesbach Colloquy in 1976 in Münster.
OCLC: 3541663 ISB.

577 Gregory, J. B. *The Oracles ascribed to Matthew by Papias of Hierapolis: A Contribution to the Criticism of the New Testament. With appendices on the Authorship of the* De Vita Contemplativa, *the Date of the Crucifixion, and the Date of the Martyrdom of Polycarp.* London: Longmans, Green, 1894. 274pp.
OCLC: 2823264 BCT.

578A Grelot, P. *Evangiles et tradition apostolique: Réflexions sur un certain "Christ hébreu."* Paris: Cerf, 1984. 197pp. (Apologique.)
Response to C. Tresmontant's *Le Christ hébreu.* Paris, 1983.
OCLC: 11269542 ISB.

578B Greswell, Edward. *Dissertations upon the Principles and Arrangement of a Harmony of the Gospels*. 2nd ed. Oxford: University Press, 1837. 4 vols.
OCLC: 11423083 GCL.

579 Griesbach, Johann J. *Commentatio qua Marci Evangelium totum e Matthaei et Lucae commentariis decerptum esse monstratur*. Jena: J. C. G. Goepferdt, 1789–1790. ET: "A Demonstration that Mark Was Written After Matthew and Luke," trans. Bernard Orchard. In *J. J. Griesbach, Synoptic and Text-Critical Studies, 1776–1976*, Bernard Orchard and Thomas R. W. Longstaff, eds., 103-35. Latin text reprinted on pp. 74-102. Cambridge; New York: Cambridge University Press, 1978. (SNTSMS 34.)
OCLC: 3541663 ISB.

580A _____. *Commentarius criticus in textum Graecum Novi Testamenti*. 2 pts. Jena: J. C. G. Goepferdt, 1798–1811.

580B _____. "Επιμετρον ad commentarium criticum in Matthaei Textum." In *Commentarius Criticus in Textum Graecum Novi Testamenti*. Particula 2, 45-64. Jena: J. C. G. Goepferdt, 1811.

581 _____. *Inquisitio in fontes, unde Evangelistae suas de resurrectione Domini narrationes hauserint*. Jena: J. C. G. Goepferdt, 1783. Rpt in *J. J. Griesbachii Opuscula academica*, J. P. Gabler, ed., 2:241-56. Jena: F. Frommanni, 1825.
OCLC: 9876654 ISB.

582 _____, ed. *Synopsis Evangeliorum Matthaei, Marci et Lucae una cum iis Joannis pericopis: Quae historiam passionis et resurrectionis Jesu Christi complectuntur*. Ed. 2. emendatior et auctior. Halae Saxonum: Jo. Jac. Curtii Haeredes, 1797. 331pp.
Intro. matter in Latin; text in Greek.
OCLC: 3821677 MBS.

583 Grigsby, Bruce. "Compositional Hypotheses for the Lucan 'Magnificat'—Tensions for the Evangelical." EQ 56 (1984): 159-72.

584 Grintz, Jehoshua M. "Hebrew as the Spoken and Written Language in the Last Days of the Second Temple." JBL 79 (1960): 32-47.

585 Grobel, Kendrick. *Formgeschichte und synoptische Quellenanalyse*. Göttingen: Vandenhoeck & Ruprecht, 1937. 130pp. (Forschungen zur Religion und Literatur des Alten und Neuen Testaments, N. F. 35.) Includes bibl.
OCLC: 3856859 ISB.

586 Grundmann, Walter. *Das Evangelium nach Lukas*. 2., neubearb. Aufl. Berlin: Evangelische Verlagsanstalt, 1961. 10. Aufl. 1984. 457pp. (Theologischer Handkommentar zum Neuen Testament 3.) Includes bibl.
"Eine völlige Neubearbeitung der 1934 erschienenen ersten Auflage von Friedrich Hauck."
OCLC: 976065 ISB; 13030720 HGS; 13048317 FQG.

587 _____. *Das Evangelium nach Markus*. Berlin: Evangelische Verlagsanstalt, 1959. 3. Aufl. 1965. 1968. 5. Aufl. 1971. 347pp. 8. Aufl.
1980. 460pp. (Theologischer Handkommentar zum Neuen Testament
2.)
OCLC: 7677188 IHT; 9075857 AUU; 11459100 GCL; 10575653 EXN.

588 _____. *Das Evangelium nach Matthäus*. Berlin: Evangelische Verlag-
sanstalt, 1968. 2. Aufl. 1971. 3. Aufl. 1972. 4. Aufl. 1975. 580pp.
(Theologischer Handkommentar zum Neuen Testament 1.)
OCLC: 1014911 ISB; 2472601 BCT; 1114387 BAN; 6714208 DRU.

589 _____. ''Die Sammlung der Jesusworte in der Spruchquelle. Der Inhalt
der Spruchquelle. 'Lehre der Weisheit' in der Spruchquelle.'' In *Die
frühe Christenheit und ihre Schriften: Umwelt, Entstehung und Eigenart der neutestamentlichen Bücher*, by W. Grundmann, with a foreword
by Klaus Haacker, 67-73. Stuttgart: Calwer, 1983. (Calwer Paperback.)
OCLC: 11251546 ISB.

590 _____. ''Weisheit im Horizont des Reiches Gottes: eine Studie zur Verkündigung Jesu nach der Spruchüberlieferung Q.'' In *Die Kirche des
Anfangs: Festschrift für Heinz Schürmann zum 65. Geburtstag*, Rudolf
Schnackenburg, Josef Ernst, and Joachim Wanke, eds., 175-99. Leipzig: St.-Benno-Verlag, 1977. Freiburg: Herder, 1978. (Erfurter theologische Studien 38.)
OCLC: 4079038 GTX.

591 Guelich, Robert A. ''The Matthean Beatitudes: 'Entrance-Requirements'
or Eschatological Blessings?'' JBL 95 (1976): 415-34.

592 Guillaumont, A., ed. and trans. *The Gospel According to Thomas*. Coptic
text established and translated by A. Guillaumont, et al. Leiden: Brill;
London: Collins, 1959. New York: Harper & Row, 1959. San Fran-
cisco: Harper & Row, 1984. 62pp. Includes bibl.
Coptic and English on facing pages.
OCLC: 9790140 MAA; 269623 UTS; 10429934 ISB.

593 Gundry, Robert H. ''LMṬLYM: 1 Q Isaiah *a* 50,6 and Mark 14,65.'' RevQ
2 (1959–1960): 559-67.

594 _____. ''The Language Milieu of First-Century Palestine. Its Bearing
on the Authenticity of the Gospel Tradition.'' JBL 83 (1964): 404-408.

595A _____. *Matthew: A Commentary on his Literary and Theological Art*.
Grand Rapids MI: Eerdmans, 1982. 652pp. Includes bibl.
OCLC: 7733821 ISB.

595B Gustafson, James M. ''The Relation of the Gospels to the Moral Life.''
In *Jesus and Man's Hope*, Donald G. Miller and Dikran Y. Hadidian,
eds. 2:103-17. Pittsburgh: Pittsburgh Theological Seminary, 1971.
(Perspective 2.)
OCLC: 142572 ISB.

595C Gustafson, Robert K. "Source Criticism." In *Mercer Dictionary of the Bible,* Watson E. Mills, gen. ed. Macon GA: Mercer University Press, forthcoming. Includes bibl.

596A Guthrie, Donald. *New Testament Introduction.* 1. *Gospels and Acts.* London: Tyndale Press, 1965. 380pp. 3rd ed. rev. in 1 vol. *New Testament Introduction.* Downers Grove IL: Inter-Varsity Press, 1970. 1971. 1,054pp.
OCLC: 5671751 ISB; 9277153 KKS; 541841 DAY.

596B _____. "Synoptic Gospels." In *The New International Dictionary of the Christian Church,* J. D. Douglas, et al., eds., 947-48. Grand Rapids MI: Zondervan, 1974.

597 Güttgemanns, E. "Die synoptische Frage im Lichte der modernen Sprach- und Literaturwissenschaft, 1." LiBi 29-30 (1973): 2-40.

598 Guy, Harold A. *A Critical Introduction to the Gospels.* London: Macmillan; New York: St. Martin's Press, 1955. 152pp.
OCLC: 972637 ISB.

599 _____. *The Gospel of Mark.* London: Macmillan; New York: St. Martin's Press, 1968. 191pp.
OCLC: 392301 DTM.

600 _____. *The Synoptic Gospels.* London: Macmillan; New York: St. Martin's Press, 1960. 183pp.
OCLC: 1840990 ISB.

601 Haacker, K. "Ehescheidung und Wiederverheiratung im Neuen Testament." ThQ 151 (1971): 28-38.

602 Hadas, Moses, and Morton Smith. *Heroes and Gods: Spiritual Biographies in Antiquity.* New York: Harper & Row, 1965. London: Routledge and Kegan Paul, 1965. (Religious Perspectives 13.) Freeport NY: Books for Libraries Press, 1970. 266pp. (Essay Index Reprint Series.)
OCLC: 167676 ISB; 1169311 BCT; 109491 IGA.

---- Hadidian, Dikran Y. *See* Miller, Donald G. (1051D).

603 Hadorn, Wilhelm. *Die Entstehung des Markus-Evangeliums.* Gütersloh: C. Bertelsmann, 1898. (BFChTh II, 4.)*

604 Haenchen, Ernst. "Johannische Probleme." ZThK 56 (1959): 19-54.

605 _____. "Matthäus 23." ZThK 48 (1951): 38-63.

606 _____. *Der Weg Jesu: Eine Erklärung des Markus-Evangeliums und der kanonischen Parallelen.* Berlin: A. Töpelmann, 1966. (Sammlung Töpelmann. 2. Reihe, Bd. 6.) 2., durchgeschene und verb. Aufl. Berlin: De Gruyter, 1968. 594pp. (De Gruyter Lehrbuch.)
OCLC: 5250663 OKG; 682438 ISB.

607 Hahn, Ferdinand. "Das Gleichnis von der Einladung zum Festmahl." In *Verborum veritas: Festschrift für Gustav Stählin zum 70. Geburtstag*, Otto Böcher and Klaus Haacker, eds., 51-82. Wuppertal: Theologischer Verlag Brockhaus, 1970. OCLC: 3136383 KAT.

608 _____. "Jesu Wort vom bergeversetzenden Glauben." ZNW 76 (1985): 149-69.

609 _____. *Mission in the New Testament*. Trans. Frank Clarke. Naperville IL: Alec R. Allenson, 1965. London: SCM Press, 1965. 184pp. (Studies in Biblical Theology 47.) Trans. of *Das Verständnis der Mission im Neuen Testament*. Neukirchen-Vluyn: Neukirchener Verlag des Erziehungsvereins, 1963. 2 Aufl. 1965. 168pp. (Wissenschaftliche Monographien zum Alten und Neuen Testament 13.)
Originally presented as the author's Habilitationsschrift, Heidelberg.
OCLC: 6084353 ISB; 7643326 IDI; 357862 ATO; 2532691 ISB.

610 _____. *The Titles of Jesus in Christology: Their History in Early Christianity*. Trans. Harold Knight and George Ogg. New York: World, 1969. London: Lutterworth Press, 1969. 442pp. (Lutterworth Library.) Trans. of *Christologische Hoheitstitel: Ihre Geschichte im frühen Christentum*. Göttingen: Vandenhoeck & Ruprecht, 1963. 1964. 3. unveränderte Aufl. 1966. 4. unveränderte Aufl. 1974. 415pp. (Forschungen zur Religion und Literatur des Alten und Neuen Testaments. Der ganzen Reihe 83.)
Based on thesis, Heidelberg, entitled "Anfänge christologischer Traditionen".
OCLC: 5258797 ISB; 3907932 CSM; 9522939 MUU; 4869648 DRU; 24150; 72005 ISB.

611 _____. "Die Worte vom Licht Lk 11, 33-36." In *Orientierung an Jesus: Zur Theologie der Synoptiker: Für Josef Schmid*, Paul Hoffmann, Norbert Brox, and Wilhelm Pesch, eds., 107-38. Freiburg: Herder, 1973. OCLC: 786219 ISB.

612 Haik, Paul S. "The Argument of the Gospel of Luke." Th.D. diss., Dallas Theological Seminary, 1965. 381 leaves. Microfilm. Dallas TX: Microfilm Service & Sales, [1970?]. OCLC: 10226399 CBC.

613 Hamann, H. P. "Saint Luke, the First New Testament Commentator." LThJ 13 (1979): 15-21.

614 _____. "Sic et Non: Are We So Sure of Matthean Dependence on Mark?" CThM 41 (1970): 462-69.

615 Hamerton-Kelly, Robert. 1971. As reviewer see Suggs, M. Jack. *Wisdom* (1522).

616 Hammond, C. E. *Outlines of Textual Criticism Applied to the New Testament*. Oxford: Clarendon Press, 1872. 138pp. 3rd ed., rev. 1880. 156pp. 4th ed. rev. 1884. 5th ed., rev. 1890. 160pp. 6th ed., rev. 1902. 179pp. (Clarendon Press Series.)
OCLC: 505642 ANC; 2795923 MBS; 3393937 BZM; 2822174 MBS; 4116306 ACL.

617 Hare, Douglas R. A. *The Theme of Jewish Persecution of Christians in the Gospel According to St. Matthew*. Cambridge: Cambridge University Press, 1967. 204pp. (SNTSMS 6.) Includes bibl.
OCLC: 414254 ISB.

618 Harnack, Adolf von. *Bruchstücke des Evangeliums und der Apokalypse des Petrus*. 2., verbesserte und erweiterte Aufl. Leipzig: J. C. Hinrichs, 1893. 78pp. (Texte und Untersuchungen zur Geschichte der altchristlichen Literatur 9.2.)
A preliminary edition appeared in the *Sitzungsberichte* of the Akademie der Wissenschaften, Berlin, 3 and 10 Nov. 1892.
Texts in Greek; translations and commentaries in German.
OCLC: 2015783 PKT.

619 _____. *The Date of the Acts and of the Synoptic Gospels*. Trans. J. R. Wilkerson. London: Williams & Norgate, 1911. New York: Putnam, 1911. 162pp. (His *New Testament Studies* 4.) Trans. of *Neue Untersuchungen zur Apostelgeschichte und zur Abfassungszeit der synoptischen Evangelien*. Leipzig: J. C. Hinrichs, 1911. 114pp. (His *Beiträge zur Einleitung in das Neue Testament* 4.)
OCLC: 9908036 WTS; 5026432 CLE; 3945169 ISB; 8780789 CFT.

620 _____. *Geschichte der altchristlichen Litterature bis Eusebius*. Leipzig: J. C. Hinrichs, 1893. 1897–1904. 2. erw. Aufl., mit einem Vorwort von Kurt Aland. 2 vols. in 4. 1958. Rpt: Leipzig: Zentralantiquariat der Deutschen Demokratischen Republic, 1968.
Contents: 1. T. Die Überlieferung und der Bestand. Bearb. unter Mitwirkung von Erwin Preuschen; 2. T. Die Chronologie: 1. Bd. Bis Irenäus. Nebst einleitenden Untersuchungen. 2. Bd. Von Irenaeus bis Eusebius.
OCLC: 6778038 CLE; 2603345 TEU; 4847052 CFT; 4721826 ISB; 2919827 YU#; 782797 DAY.

621 _____. *Luke the Physician, the Author of the Third Gospel and the Acts of the Apostles*. Trans. J. R. Wilkinson, ed. W. D. Morrison. London: Williams & Norgate; New York: G. P. Putnam's Sons, 1907. 2nd ed. 1911. 231pp. (His *New Testament Studies* 1. Crown Theological Library 20.)
OCLC: 2694099 ISB; 9628163 UTS; 8573166 PLF; 4599504 IAT; 6867827 SDN.

622 _____. *Marcion: Das Evangelium vom fremden Gott, eine Monographie zur Geschichte der Grundlegung der katholischen Kirche.* Leipzig: J. C. Hinrichs, 1921. 265, 357pp. 2. verb. und verm. Aufl. 1924. Rpt of the 2nd ed.: Darmstadt: Wissenschaftlichen Buchgesellschaft, 1960. 235, 455pp. (Texte und Untersuchungen zur Geschichte der altchristlichen Literatur 45. 3. Reihe 15.)
OCLC: 547296 ISB; 4964885 BHA; 1325963 BXM.

623 _____. *The Origin of the New Testament and the Most Important Consequences of the New Creation.* Trans. J. R. Wilkinson. New York: Macmillan, 1925. 1974. 229pp. (His *New Testament Studies* 6.) Trans. of *Die Entstehung des Neuen Testaments und die wichtigsten Folgen der neuen Schöpfung.* Leipzig: J. C. Hinrichs, 1914. 152pp. (His *Beiträge zur Einleitung in das Neue Testament* 6.)
OCLC: 2327061 TSM; 3533047 AZU; 3057431 FUG.

624 _____. *The Sayings of Jesus: The Second Source of St. Matthew and St. Luke.* Trans. J. R. Wilkinson. London: Williams & Norgate, 1908. New York: Putnam, 1908. 316pp. (His *New Testament Studies* 2.) Trans. of *Sprüche und Reden Jesu: Die Zweite Quelle des Matthäus und Lukas.* Leipzig: J. C. Hinrichs, 1907. 219pp. (His *Beiträge zur Einleitung in das Neue Testament* 2.)
OCLC: 6123810 PLT; 4443020 IGR.
Review of German ed.: Burkitt, F. C. JThS 8 (1906/1907): 454-59.

625 _____. *Untersuchungen zu den Schriften des Lukas.* Leipzig: J. C. Hinrichs, 1908.
A one vol. ed. of vols. 1-3 of his *Beiträge zur Einleitung in das Neue Testament.* 1906–1908. ET: *New Testament Studies.* Vols. 1-6. London; New York, 1907–1925.
NUC: MH; ICU; NcD.

626 Harrington, Wilfrid. *The Gospel According to St. Luke: A Commentary.* Westminster MD.: Newman Press, 1967. London: G. Chapman, 1968. 297pp. Includes bibl.
OCLC: 873538 TSW; 129067 ATO.

627 Harris, J. Rendel. *The Diatessaron of Tatian: A Preliminary Study.* London: C. J. Clay, 1890. 68pp.
OCLC: 4140409 ISB.

628 _____. *Four Lectures on the Western Text of the New Testament.* London: C. J. Clay, 1894. 96pp.
OCLC: 981707 CIN.

629 _____. *A Popular Account of the Newly-Recovered Gospel of Peter.* London: Hodder and Stoughton, 1893. 97pp.
OCLC: 2166710 EXN.

630 Hartman, L. "Dop, ande och barnaskap. Nagra traditionshistoriska överväganden till Mk 1:9-11 par." SEÅ 37-38 (1972–1973): 88-106.

631 _____. *Prophecy Interpreted: The Formation of Some Jewish Apocalyptic Texts and of the Eschatological Discourse Mark 13 par.* Lund: Gleerup, 1966. Microfilm. Library of Congress: Photoduplication Service, 1985. 299pp. (Coniectanea Biblica. New Testament Series 1.) Includes bibl.
OCLC: 40842 ISB; 13019714 CUY.

632 Hasel, Gerhard F. 1969. As reviewer see Hengel, Martin. *Nachfolge und Charisma* (654).

633 Hasenfratz, H.-P. *Die Rede von der Auferstehung Jesu Christi: Ein methodologischer Versuch.* Bonn: Linguistica Biblica, 1975. 271pp. (Forum theologiae linguisticae 10.) Includes bibl.
Originally presented as the author's thesis, Zürich, 1974.
OCLC: 2492654 TJC.

634 Hasert, Christian Adolf [Philosphotos Alethias]. *Die Evangelien: ihr Geist, ihr Verfasser und ihr Verhältnis zu einander: Ein Beitrag zur Lösung der kritischen Fragen über die Entstehung derselben.* Leipzig: Otto Wigand, 1845. 2nd ed. 1852.
NUC: NjPT; ICU; MB.

635 Hasler, Victor. *Amen: Redaktionsgeschichtliche Untersuchung zur Einführungsformel der Herrenworte "Wahrlich ich sage euch."* Zürich; Stuttgart: Gotthelf-Verlag, 1969. 207pp. Includes bibl.
Issued also as Habilitationsschrift, Bern, 1966.
OCLC: 190959 DTM.

636 Haupt, Walther. *Worte Jesu und Gemeindeüberlieferung: Eine Untersuchung zur Quellengeschichte der Synopse.* Leipzig: J. C. Hinrichs, 1913. 263pp. (Untersuchungen zum Neuen Testament 3.)
OCLC: 10167729 ISB.

637 Havener, Ivan. "Jesus in the Gospel Sayings." BiTod 21 (1983): 77-82.

638 _____. *Q, the Sayings of Jesus. With a reconstruction of Q by Athanasius Polag.* Wilmington DE: M. Glazier, 1987. 176pp. (Good News Studies 19.)
OCLC: 15105348 ISB.

639 Hawkins, John C. *Horae synopticae. Contributions to the Study of the Synoptic Problem.* Oxford: Clarendon Press, 1899. 183pp. 2nd rev. and suppl. 1909. Rpt: 1968. Grand Rapids MI: Baker, 1968. 223pp.
OCLC: 624935 UTS; 1006739 BAN; 4896326 ISB; 1261288 CSU; 192708 MAL.

640 _____. "Probabilities as to the So-Called Double Tradition of St. Matthew and St. Luke." In *Studies in the Synoptic Problem,* by Members of the University of Oxford, W. Sanday, ed., 95-138. Oxford: Clarendon Press, 1911. Microfiche. Louisville KY: Lost Cause Press, 1977.
OCLC: 753275 ISB; 4045911 ISB.

641 _____. "Some Internal Evidence for the Use of the Logia in the First and Third Gospels." ET 12 (1900–1901): 72-76, 139.

642 _____. "Three Limitations to St. Luke's Use of St. Mark's Gospel." In *Studies in the Synoptic Problem,* by Members of the University of Oxford. W. Sanday, ed., 27-94. Oxford: Clarendon Press, 1911. Microfiche. Louisville KY: Lost Cause Press, 1977.
OCLC: 753275 ISB; 4045911 ISB.

643 Hawthorne, Gerald F. "Christian Prophecy and the Sayings of Jesus: Evidence of and Criteria for." In *Society of Biblical Literature 1975 Seminar Papers,* George MacRae, ed., 2:105-29. Missoula MT: Scholars Press, 1975.

644 Headlam, Arthur C. "The Dates of the New Testament Books." In *Criticism of the New Testament,* by W. Sanday, et al., 45-207. London: John Murray, 1902. New York: Scribner's, 1902. 2nd ed. 1903. Microfiche. Chicago: American Theological Library Association, 1985. ATLA monograph preservation program, ATLA fiche 1985–0777. (St. Margaret's Lectures 1902.)
OCLC: 2822666 MNM; 4107994 ISB; 15624846 CBC.

645 _____. *The Life and Teaching of Jesus the Christ.* New York; London: Oxford University Press, 1923. 336pp. 2nd ed. London: J. Murray, 1927. 3rd ed. 1936. 4th ed. 1940. 338pp.
A considerable part of this book was delivered as lectures first in the University of Oxford and then in King's College, London.
OCLC: 2795916 ISB; 9090322 KKU; 6140581 TJC; 4716535 EXB.

646 _____. *The Miracles of the New Testament.* New York: Scribner's, 1915. London: John Murray, 1923. 361pp. (Morehouse Lectures 1914.)
OCLC: 1658652 IYU; 910777 TOL.

647 Heard, Richard G. "The AΠOMNHMONEYMATA in Papias, Justin and Irenaeus." NTS 1 (1954): 122-29.

648 _____. "Papias' Quotations from the New Testament." NTS 1 (1954): 130-34.

649 Hedrick, Charles W. "What is a Gospel? Geography, Time, and Narrative Structure." PerspRS 10 (1983): 255-68.

650 Heinrici, C. F. Georg. *Die Bergpredigt (Matth. 5-7, Luk. 6, 20-49).* Leipzig: A. Edelmann, 1899. 81pp. *Die Bergpredigt (Matth. 5-7, Luk. 6, 20-49). Quellenkritisch und begriffsgeschichtlich untersucht.* Leipzig: Dürr, 1900. 2 vols in 1. (His *Beiträge zur Geschichte und Erklärung des Neuen Testaments* 2.) *Die Bergpredigt (Matth. 5-7, Luk. 6, 20-49). Begriffsgeschichtlich untersucht.* Leipzig: A. Edelmann, 1905. 98pp. (Zur Feier des Reformationsfestes und des Übergangs des Rectorats.)
NUC: TxFCT; NjPT; IEG; GEU-T; MH.

651 _____. *Der litterarische Charakter der neutestamentlichen Schriften.* Leipzig: Dürr, 1908. 127pp.
NUC: ICU; NjPT; NcD.

652 Held, H. J. "Matthew as Interpreter of the Miracle Stories." In *Tradition and Interpretation in Matthew,* by Günther Bornkamm, Gerhard Barth, and H. J. Held; trans. Percy Scott, 165-299. Philadelphia: Westminster Press, 1963. (New Testament Library.)
OCLC: 383441 ISB.

653 Helmbold, Heinrich. *Vorsynoptische Evangelien.* Stuttgart: E. Klotz, 1953. 110pp.
OCLC: 2978941 ISB.

654 Hengel, Martin. *The Charismatic Leader and His Followers.* Trans. James C. G. Greig, ed. John Riches. Edinburgh: T. & T. Clark, 1981. New York: Crossroad, 1981. 111pp. (Studies of the New Testament and Its World.) Trans. of *Nachfolge und Charisma: Eine exegetisch- religionsgeschichtliche Studie zu Mt. 8, 21f. und Jesu Ruf in die Nachfolge.* Berlin: A. Töpelmann, 1968. 116pp. (Beiheft zur Zeitschrift für die neutestamentliche Wissenschaft und die Kunde der älteren Kirche 34.)
A revision of the author's lecture delivered before the Evangelisch-Theologische Fakultät, Universität Tübingen, 25 Jan. 1967.
OCLC: 3808354 ISB; 8015934 VYF; 7577778 ICU.
Review of German: Hasel, Gerhard F. *BibOr* 26 (1969): 262-64.

655 _____. *Judaism and Hellenism: Studies in Their Encounter in Palestine during the Early Hellenistic Period.* 2 vols. Trans. John Bowden. Philadelphia: Fortress; London: SCM Press, 1974. Philadelphia: Fortress Press, 1981. Trans. of *Judentum und Hellenismus: Studien zu ihrer Begegnung unter besonderer Berücksichtigung Palästinas bis zur Mitte des 2. Jh. v. Chr.* (Wissenschaftliche Untersuchungen zum Neuen Testament 10.) Tübingen: J. C. B. Mohr, 1969. 692pp. 2., durchges. u. erg. Aufl. 1973. 693pp.
A revision of the author's Habilitationsschrift, Tübingen, 1966.
OCLC: 221006 ISB; 785330 BWE; 1161541 ISB; 1226042; 7179344.

656 Hennecke, Edgar, ed. *New Testament Aporcypha.* 2 vols. Ed. Wilhelm Schneemelcher; trans. A. J. B. Higgins and others; ET ed. R. McL. Wilson. Philadelphia: Westminster, 1963–1966. London: SCM Press, 1963–1966. Trans. of *Neutestamentliche Apokryphen.* 3rd ed. Tübingen: Mohr, 1959–1964. 4th ed. 1968. 668pp.
Original German edition ed. Edgar Hennecke. Tübingen: J. C. B. Mohr, 1904. 2nd ed., 1924.
OCLC: 246330; 7531530 ISB; 1718847 VJA; (vol. 2, 1975) 2219200 ATO; 976081 ISB; 976072 BHA; 4310000 NAM; 4581923 CLE.

657 Herbst, Karl. *Was wollte Jesus selbst? Vorkirchliche Jesusworte in den Evangelien I-II.* 2 vols. Düsseldorf: Patmos-Verlag, 1979–1981.
OCLC: 6377693 TJC.

658 Herder, Johann Gottfried. "Regel der Zusammenstimmung unser Evangelien, aus ihrer Entstehung und Ordnung." In his *Sammtliche Werke zur Religion und Theologie*, 17:169-232. Stuttgart; Tübingen: J. G. Cotta Buchhandlung, 1830.
OCLC: 3924888 IUP.

659 _____. *Vom Erlöser der Menschen, nach unsern drei ersten Evangelien.* Riga: J. F. Hartknoch, 1796. (His *Christliche Schriften* 2.)
OCLC: 6872908 IAY.

660 _____. *Von Gottes Sohn, der Welt Heiland, nach Johannes Evangelium. Nebst einer Regel der Zusammenstimmung unserer Evangelien aus ihrer Entstehung und Ordnung.* Riga: J. F. Hartknoch, 1797. (His *Christliche Schriften* 3.)
OCLC: 6872908 IAY.

661 Hertwig, Otto Robert. *Tabellen zur Einleitung ins Neue Testament.* Berlin: G. W. F. Müller, 1849. 55pp.
OCLC: 16089721 ISB.

662 Heylen, V., ed. *Mislukt huwelijk en echtscheiding. Een milti-disciplinaire verkenning,* 127-42. Leuven: University Press, 1972.**

663 Hickling, Colin J. A. "The Plurality of 'Q'." In *Logia. Les paroles de Jésus = The Sayings of Jesus: Mémorial Joseph Coppens,* Joël Delobel, ed., 425-29. Leuven: University Press and Peeters, 1982. (BEThL 59.)
OCLC: 9450792 ISB; 11043145 ICU.

664 Higgins, Angus J. B. "Luke 1-2 in Tatian's *Diatessaron.*" JBL 103 (1984): 193-222.

665 _____. " 'Menschensohn' oder 'ich' in Q: Lk 12, 8-9/Mt 10, 32-33?" In *Jesus und der Menschensohn. Für Anton Vögtle,* Rudolf Pesch and Rudolf Schnackenburg, eds., 117-23. Freiburg im Breisgau: Herder, 1975.
OCLC: 2318718 IUC.

666 _____. *The Son of Man in the Teaching of Jesus.* Cambridge; New York: Cambridge University Press, 1980. 177pp. (SNTSMS 39.) Includes bibl.
OCLC: 5990553 ISB.

667 Hilgenfeld, Adolf. *Die Evangelien, nach ihrer Entstehung und geistlichen Bedeutung.* Leipzig: S. Hirzel, 1854. 355pp.
OCLC: 13024317 DRB.

668A _____. "Die Evangelien-Forschung nach ihrem Verlaufe und gegenwartigen Stände." ZWTh 4 (1861): 1-71, 137-204.

668B _____. "Die Evangelien-Frage und seine neueste Behandlung von Weisse, Volkmar, und Meyer." ThJb(T) (1860): 381-440, 498-532.**
[ThJb(T) ceased pub. in 1857.]

669 _____. "Die Evangelien und die geschichtliche Gestalt Jesu." ZWTh 6 (1863): 311-40.

670 _____. *Historisch-kritische Einleitung in das Neue Testament.* Leipzig: Fues's Verlag (R. Reisland), 1875. 828pp.
OCLC: 6740408 ISB.

671 _____. *Der Kanon und die Kritik des Neuen Testaments: In ihrer geschichtlichen Ausbildung und Gestaltung, nebst Herstellung und Beleuchtung des muratorischen Bruckstückes.* Halle: C. E. M. Pfeffer, 1863. 240pp.
OCLC: 8978261 ISB.

672 _____. *Das Markus-evangelium, nach seiner Composition, seiner Stellung in der Evangelien-literatur, seinem Ursprung und Charakter.* Leipzig: Breitkopf und Härtel, 1850. 132pp.
NUC: NjPT; ICU; MH; MB.

673 _____. "Neue Untersuchung über das Markus-Evangelium, mit Ruchsicht auf Dr. Baur's Darstellung." ThJb(T) 11 (1852): 102-32, 259-93.

674 _____. "Die neueste Evangelienforschung." ZWTh 20 (1877): 1-48.

675 _____. "Papias über Marcus und Matthäus." ZWTh 22 (1879): 1-18.

676 _____. "Papias von Hierapolis und die neueste Evangelienforschung." ZWTh 29 (1886): 257-91.

677 _____. "Die synoptische zweiquellen-Theorie in neuester Fassung." ZWTh 36 (1893): 1-56.

678 Hill, David. *New Testament Prophecy.* London: Marshall, Morgan & Scott, 1979. (Marshall's Theological Library.) Atlanta: John Knox Press, 1979. 241pp. (New Foundations Theological Library.) Includes bibl.
OCLC: 5170492 ISB; 5864638 BHA.

679 _____. "On the Evidence for the Creative Role of Christian Prophets." NTS 20 (1973–1974): 262-74.

680 Hill, J. Hamlyn, ed. and trans. *The Earliest Life of Christ Ever Compiled from the Four Gospels, being the Diatessaron of Tatian (circ. A.D. 160.) Literally translated from the Arabic version and containing the four Gospels woven into one story,* with an introduction and notes by J. Hamlyn Hill. Edinburgh: T. & T. Clark, 1894. 379pp. 2nd ed., abridged. 1910. 224pp.
OCLC: 626663 KSU; 3686038 ISB.

681 Hirsch, Emmanuel. "Fragestellung und Verfahren meiner Frühgeschichte des Evangeliums." ZNW 41 (1942): 106-24.

682 _____. *Frühgeschichte des Evangeliums.* 2., verm. Aufg. Tübingen: J. C. B. Mohr, 1951. 2 vols.
Includes the German text of Mark.
OCLC: 6766043 TJC.

683 Hobbs, Edward C. "A Quarter-Century Without 'Q.' " PSThJ 33/4 (1980): 10-19.

684 _____. "The Theological Price of Abandoning the Q-Hypothesis." In *AAR/SBL Abstracts 1984,* K. H. Richards and J. B. Wiggins, eds., 206. Chico CA: Scholars Press, 1984.

685 Hobson, A. A. *The Diatessaron of Tatian and the Synoptic Problem. Being an Investigation of the Diatessaron for the Light which It Throws Upon the Solution of the Problem of the Origin of the Synoptic Gospels.* Chicago: University of Chicago Press, 1904. 81pp. (Historical and Linguistic Studies in Literature Related to the New Testament, issued under the direction of the Department of Biblical and Patristic Studies, University of Chicago. 2nd series. Linguistic and Exegetical Studies 1/3.) OCLC: 2625897 BCT.

686 Hodgson, Robert. "On the *Gattung* of Q: A Dialogue with James M. Robinson." Bib 66 (1985): 73-95.

687 Hoffmann, Paul. 1975. As reviewer see Schulz, Siegfried. *Q* (1395).

688 _____. 1972. As Reviewer see Wrege, Hans-Theo. *Die Überlieferungsgeschichte* (1725).

689 _____. "Die Anfänge der Theologie in der Logienquelle." In *Gestalt und Anspruch des Neuen Testaments,* Josef Schreiner and Gerhard Dautzenberg, eds., 134-52. Würzburg: Echter Verlag, 1969. Includes bibl.
OCLC: 5300658 TJC.

690 _____. "Die bessere Gerechtigkeit. Auslegung der Bergpredigt III (Mt 5, 17-37)." BiLe 10 (1969): 175-89.

691 _____. "Jesusverkündigung in der Logienquelle." In *Jesus in den Evangelien: Ein Symposion mit Josef Blinzler, et al.,* Wilhelm Pesch, ed., 50-70. Stuttgart: Verlag Katholisches Bibelwerk, 1970. (Stuttgarter Bibelstudien 45.)
OCLC: 308189 CWR.

692 _____. "Lk 10, 5-11 in der Instruktionsreden der Logienquelle." In *Evangelisch-Katholischer Kommentar zum Neuen Testament,* A. Resch, ed., 3:37-53. Neukirchen: Neukirchener Verlag; Zürich: Benzinger Verlag, 1971.
OCLC: 826763 BWE.

693 _____. "Die Offenbarung des Sohnes. Die apokalyptischen Voraussetzungen und ihre Verarbeitung im Q-Logion Mt 11, 27 par Lk 10, 22." *Kairos* 12 (1970): 270-88.

694 _____. "Πάντες ἐργάται ἀδικίας: Redaktion und Tradition in Lc 13, 22-30." ZNW 58 (1967): 188-214.

695 _____. *Studien zur Theologie der Logienquelle.* Münster: Verlag As-
chendorff, 1972. 2., durchges. u. verb. Aufl. 1975. 357pp. 3. durchges.
Aufl. mit einem bibliographischen Nachtrag über die Literatur von 1970
bis 1981. 1982. 366pp. (Neutestamentliche Abhandlungen. N. F. 8.)
Includes bibl.
A revision of the author's Habilitationsschrift, Münster, 1968.
OCLC: 1089785 ISB; 2467164; 11017117 GZQ.
Reviews: Aune, D. E. CBQ 35 (1973): 93-95; Edwards, R. A. JBL 92
(1973): 606-608.

696 _____. "Tradition und Situation: Zur 'Verbindlichkeit' des Gebots der
Feindesliebe in der synoptischen Überlieferung und in der gegenwärtigen Friedensdiskussion." In *Ethik im Neuen Testament,* K. Kertelge,
ed., 50-117. Freiberg: Herder, 1984. (Quaestiones disputatae 102.)
OCLC: 11725122 ISB.

697 _____. "Die Überlieferungsgeschichte der Bergpredigt." ThRv 68
(1972): 115-17.

698 _____. "Die Versuchungsgeschichte in der Logienquelle: zur Ausern-
andersetzung der Judenchristen mit dem politischen Messianismus." BZ
13 (1969): 207-23.

699 Hoffmann, R. A. *Das Marcusevangelium und seine Quellen.* Königsberg: Thomas und Oppermann, 1904. 644pp.
OCLC: 15874102 IXT.

700 Hoffmann, R. Joseph. "Q." In his *Jesus Outside the Gospels,* 86-97.
Buffalo NY: Prometheus Books, 1984.
OCLC: 11394320 ISB.

701 Holcombe, John J. *Historic Relation of the Gospels.* London: 1899.**

702 Holdsworth, William W. *Gospel Origins: A Study in the Synoptic Prob-
lem.* New York: Scribner's, 1913. London: Duckworth, 1913. 211pp.
(Studies in Theology.) Includes bibl.
OCLC: 1832451 ISB; 4101396 ACL.

703 Holst, R. "Reexamining Mk 3:28f. and Its Parallels." ZNW 63 (1972):
122-24.

704 _____. "The Temptation of Jesus." ET 82 (1970–1971): 343-44.

705 Holsten, Karl C. J. *Die Drei Ursprünglichen noch Ungeschriebenen
Evangelien, zur synoptischen Frage.* Karlsruhe; Leipzig: H. Reuther,
1883. 79pp. Microfiche. Beltsville MD: NCR Corporation for the
American Theological Library Association Board of Microtext, 1977.
(ATLA F0003.)
OCLC: 13024331 DRB; 3288497.

706 _____. *Die synoptischen Evangelien nach der Form ihres Inhaltes: Für das Studium der synoptischen Frage dargestellt und erläutert.* Heidelberg: Karl Groos, 1885. 213pp. Photocopy. Durham NC: Duke University Library Photographic Services, 1984? Microfiche. Beltsville MD: NCR Corporation for the American Theological Library Association Board of Microtext, 1978. (ATLA F4402.)
OCLC: 6630995 NDD; 11325085 NDD; 4347019.

707 Holtzmann, Heinrich J. 1881. As reviewer *see* Simons, E. (1440)

708 _____. *Lehrbuch der historisch-kritischen Einleitung in das Neue Testament.* Freiburg: J. C. B. Mohr (Paul Siebeck), 1885. 2. verb. und verm. Aufl. 1886. 560pp. 3. verb. und verm. Aufl. 1892. 508pp. (Sammlung theologischer Lehrbücher.)
OCLC: 4579984 VTS; 8086024 TJC.

709 _____. *Lehrbuch der neutestamentlichen Theologie.* Freiburg; Leipzig: J. C. B. Mohr (Paul Siebeck), 1897. 2. neu bearb. Aufl., hrsg. von A. Jülicher und W. Bauer. 1911. 2 vols. (Sammlung theologischer Lehrbücher.) Includes bibl.
OCLC: 3752978 STS; 3085198 ISB.

710 _____. "Ein Marcus-Kontroverse in ihrer heutigen Gestalt." ARG 10 (1906): 18-40.

711 _____. *Die Synoptiker.* Freiburg: J. C. B. Mohr (Paul Siebeck), 1889. 3. gänzlich umgearb. Aufl. Tübingen: J. C. B. Mohr (Paul Siebeck), 1901. 429pp. (Hand-Commentar zum Neuen Testament 1/1.) Includes bibl.
OCLC: 1037968 OSU.

712 _____. *Die synoptischen Evangelien: Ihr Ursprung und geschichtlicher Charakter.* Leipzig: W. Engelmann, 1863. 514pp.
OCLC: 2975885 BSC.

713 _____. "Umschau auf dem Gebiete der neutestamentlichen Kritik. I. Die Evangelien." JPTh 1 (1875): 583-635.

714 _____. "Zur synoptischen Frage." JPTh 4 (1878): 145-88, 328-82, 533-68.

715 Honey, T. E. Floyd. "Did Mark Use Q?" JBL 62 (1943): 319-31.

716 Honoré, A. M. "A Statistical Study of the Synoptic Problem." NovT 10 (1968): 95-147.

717 Hooker, Morna Dorothy. "Christology and Methodology." NTS 17 (1971): 480-87.

718 _____. *The Message of Mark.* London: Epworth Press, 1983. 135pp.
OCLC: 10410652 OKO.

719A Horn, Friedrich Wilhelm. *Glaube und Handeln in der Theologie des Lu-kas.* Göttingen: Vandenhoeck & Ruprecht, 1983. 400pp. (Göttinger Theologische Arbeiten 26.) Includes bibl.
Originally presented as the author's thesis (doctoral), George-August-Universität, Göttingen, 1981.
OCLC: 9562712 ISB.

719B Horsley, Richard A. *Jesus and the Spiral of Violence: Popular Jewish Resistance in Roman Palestine.* San Francisco: Harper & Row, 1987. 355pp. Includes bibl.
OCLC: 15053050 ISB.

---- Hort, J. A. *See* Westcott, Brooke F. (1695).

720 Hoskyns, Edwin C., and Noel Davey. *The Riddle of the New Testament.* New York: Harcourt, Brace, 1931. 322pp. London: Faber & Faber, 1931. 1936. 1947. 1949. 1958. ^{3}1964. 238pp. Includes bibl.
"The Synoptic Problem," 76-82.
OCLC: 4066674 IOI; 263644 ISB; 4863599 DRB.

721A Howard, George, ed. and trans. *The Gospel of Matthew according to a Primitive Hebrew Text.* Macon GA: Mercer University Press, 1987. 228pp.
Hebrew text of Matthew, extracted from Shem Ṭov ben Yitshak Ibn Shaprut's *Evan boḥan,* presented with English translation and commentary.
OCLC: 16352448 ISB.

721B _____. "Stylistic Inversion and the Synoptic Tradition." JBL 97 (1978): 375-89.

721C Howard, Virgil, trans. "Reflections on Legitimacy and Limits of Theological Criticism." PSThJ 33/4 (1980): 49-54.
ET of a response made by Hans-Herbert Stoldt to Hans Conzelmann (1498). Howard prefaces his translation with a critical introduction to point at issue.

722 Howard, W. F. "The Origin of the Symbol 'Q.' " ET 50 (1939): 379-80.

723 _____. "A Survey of New Testament Studies During Half a Century, 1901–1950." LQHR 6th ser. 21 (1952): 6-16.

724 Hrychok, William D. "A Case Study in the Synoptic Problem." B.D. thesis: Union Theological Seminary, 1968.*

725 Hubbard, B.J. *The Matthean Redaction of a Primitive Apostolic Commissioning: An Exegesis of Matthew 28:16-20.* Missoula MT: Society of Biblical Literature, 1974. 187pp. (SBLDS 19.) Includes bibl.
Diss., University of Iowa, 1973.
OCLC: 1195035 ISB; (Photocopy of typescript. Ann Arbor: University Microfilms, 1983.) 9929067 MNJ.

726 Hübner, Hans. *Das Gesetz in der synoptischen Tradition: Studien zur These einer progressiven Qumranisierung und Judaisierung innerhalb der synoptischen Tradition.* Witten: Luther-Verlag, 1973. 261pp. Includes bibl.
Habilitationsschrift, Ruhr-Universität Bochum, 1971.
OCLC: 785335 BWE.

727 Huby, Joseph. *L'Évangile et les évangiles.* Nouv. éd., rev. Paris: Beauchesne, 1940. 250pp. Nouv. éd. rev. augmenteée par Xavier Léon-Dufour. 1954. 304pp. (Verbum Salutis 11.)
OCLC: 904327 DAY; 820476 ISB.

728 Huck, Albert. *Synopsis of the First Three Gospels.* 9th ed. rev. by Hans. Lietzmann; English ed. by Frank Leslie Cross. New York: American Bible Society, 1936 (several subsequent photo. rpts.). Oxford: Basil Blackwell, 1951 (several subsequent photo. rpts.). xx + 213pp. Trans. of *Synopse der drei ersten Evangelien.* 9. Aufl. Tübingen: J. C. B. Mohr (Paul Siebeck) 1936. 213pp. 3. Aufl. 1906. 208pp. 1. Aufl. 1892.
Greek text; preface and prolegomena in English.
The last revision of Huck's synopsis was the 9th ed. (1936); the 10th, 11th, and 12th eds. (1950, 1970, 1975) are photomechanical rpts. of the 9th ed. Throckmorton's synopsis (1567B) with RSV text is based on the Huck-Lietzmann 9th ed.; Greeven's synopsis (576B) with a ''new recension'' of the Greek text is intended as a ''fundamental revision'' of Huck-Lietzmann.
OCLC: 3098816 ALL; 2149621 MIA; 3356653 BHA; 7373320 IDJ; 3356463 BHA; 3336397 ISB.

729 Hug, J. L. *Introduction to the New Testament.* Trans. from the 3rd German ed. by David Fosdick, Jr. with notes by M. Stuart. Andover: Gould and Newman, 1836. 788pp. Trans. of *Einleitung in die Schriften des Neuen Testaments.* 2 vols. Stuttgart: J. G. Cotta, 1826. 2. Aufl. 1821. 1. Aufl. 1808.
OCLC: 4546202 TEJ; 6714754 MBS; 13747159 ISB.

730 Hultgren, Arland J. ''The Double Commandment of Love in Mt. 22:34-40. Its Sources and Compositions.'' CBQ 36 (1974): 373-78.

731 Hummel, Reinhart. *Die Auseinandersetzung zwischen Kirche und Judentum im Matthäusevangelium.* München: Chr. Kaiser, 1963. 167pp. 2. durchges. und verm. Aufl. 1966. 183pp. (Beiträge zur evangelischen Theologie. Theologische Abhandlungen 33.) Includes bibl.
A revision of the author's thesis, Kiel, 1960.
OCLC: 4720138 ISB; 766381.

732 Hunkin, J. W. ''The Composition of the Third Gospel, with Special Reference to Canon Streeter's Theory of 'Proto-Luke.' '' JThS 28 (1926–1927): 250-62.

733 _____. ''Pleonastic ἄρχομαι in the New Testament.'' JThS 25 (1923–1924): 390-402.

734 Hunt, Bernard Patterson Wathen Stather. *Primitive Gospel Sources.* New York: Philosophical Library, 1951. London: James Clarke, 1951. 344pp. Includes bibl.
OCLC: 5928766 KCC.

735 Hunter, Archibald M. *The Gospel according to Saint Mark.* London: SCM Press, 1948. 1967. Microfiche. Chattanooga TN: Expositor's Microfilm Library, 1978?. 153pp. (Torch Bible Commentaries.) Includes bibl.
OCLC: 392322 ISB; 13542808 JFS; 6971375 TBI.

736 _____. *Interpreting the New Testament, 1900–1950.* Philadelphia: Westminster Press; London: SCM Press, 1951. 144pp.
OCLC: 378199 ISB; 3133197 EBS.

737A Huston, Hollis W. "The 'Q Parties' at Oxford." JBR 25 (1957): 123-28.

737B Idowu, E. Bolaji. "The Relation of the Gospels to African Culture and Religion." In *Jesus and Man's Hope,* Donald G. Miller and Dikran Y. Hadidian, eds., 2:263-72. Pittsburgh: Pittsburgh Theological Seminary, 1971. (Perspective 2.)
OCLC: 142572 ISB.

738 Isenberg, W. W. "A Short Catechism of the Gospel of Mark." CTM 2 (1975): 316-25.

739 Jackson, H. Latimer. "The Present State of the Synoptic Problem." In *Essays on Some Biblical Questions of the Day,* by Members of the University of Cambridge, H. B. Swete, ed., 421-60. London: Macmillan, 1909.
OCLC: 418070 ISB.

740 Jacobson, Arland D. "The Literary Unity of Q." JBL 101 (1982): 365-89.

741 _____. "The Literary Unity of Q: Lc 10, 2-16 and Parallels as a Test Case." In *Logia. Les paroles de Jésus = The Sayings of Jesus: Mémorial Joseph Coppens,* Joël Delobel, ed., 419-23. Leuven: University Press and Peeters, 1982. (BEThL 59.)
OCLC: 9450792 ISB; 11043145 UTS.

742 _____. "Wisdom Christology in Q." Ph.D. diss., Claremont Graduate School, 1978. 259 leaves. Includes bibl. Photocopy. Ann Arbor MI: University Microfilms International, 1978. Microfiche. 1978.
OCLC: 4045205 HDC; 11208428 BHA; 8513772 VYN.

743 Jacoby, Felix. *Die Fragmente der griechischen Historiker (FGrHist).* Berlin: Weidmann, 1923–1958. Photomechanischer Nachdruck. Leiden: Brill, 1961–1969. 3 vols. in 14.
OCLC: 1472724 DRB; 2271735 ISB; 6965587 ALM.

744 Jacquier, Eugène. *History of the Books of the New Testament.* Trans. J. Duggan. London: Kegan Paul, Trench, Trübner & Co., 1907– . New York: Benziger, 1907– . Trans. of *Histoire des livres du Nouveau Testament.* Paris: J. Gabalda, 1903–1908. 4 eme ed. Paris: Victor Lecoffre, 1904– . 1928–1935. 4 vols. Includes bibl.
OCLC: 3408510 RSC; 6950411 ODC; 10083179 TSW; 6909667 ISB.

745 James, Montague Rhodes, trans. *The Apocryphal New Testament. Being the Apocryphal Gospels, Acts, Epistles, and Apocalypses with Other Narratives and Fragments.* London: Oxford University Press (Clarendon), 1924. xxxi+584pp. Corrected rpt 1953 (and several subsequent rpts). New York: Oxford University Press, 1983. xxxi+594pp. Includes bibl.
OCLC: 386365 WSU; 2937654 DMM; 10332916 IBV.

---- ———. *See* Robinson, Joseph A. (1278).

746 Jameson, H. G. *The Origin of the Synoptic Gospels: A Revision of the Synoptic Problem.* Oxford: Blackwell, 1922. 132pp.
OCLC: 8988470 SDN.
Reviews: Burkitt, Francis C. JThS 24 (1922–1923): 441-43; Streeter, B. H. Th 7 (1923): 60.

747 Jepsen, A. "Anmerkungen eines Aussenseiters zum Synoptikerproblem." NovT 14 (1972): 106-14.

748 Jeremias, Joachim. *The Eucharistic Words of Jesus.* Trans. from the 2d German ed. by Arnold Ehrhardt. New York: Macmillan, 1955. Oxford: Blackwell, 1955. 195pp. Trans. from the German 3rd ed. by Norman Perrin, with the author's revisions to July 1964. London: SCM Press, 1966. New York: Scribner's, 1966. London: SCM Press, 1973. Philadelphia: Fortress Press, 1977. 278pp. (New Testament Library.) Trans. of *Die Abendmahlsworte Jesu.* First pub. in 1935. 2., völlig neu bearbeitete Aufl. Göttingen: Vandenhoeck & Ruprecht, 1949. 128pp. 3., völlig neu bearbeitete Aufl. 1960. 175pp. French. *La dernière cène: Les paroles de Jesus.* Traduit de l'allemand [4. ed., 1967] par M. Benzerath et R. Henning. Paris: Editions du Cerf, 1972. 337pp. (Lectio divina 75.)
OCLC: 1464918 BPS; 1464891 ISB; 582393 DRB; 383784 ISB; 1018531 YNG; 3353413 BWE; 6172311 WTS; 6172366 ISB; 11120541 ITC; 891547 BHA.

749 ———. *Jesus' Promise to the Nations.* Trans. S. H. Hooke. London: SCM Press, 1958. Naperville IL: Alec R. Allenson, 1958. Rev. Eng. ed. London: SCM Press, 1967. 84pp. (Studies in Biblical Theology 24.) Trans. of *Jesu Verheissung für die Völker.* Stuttgart: Kohlhammer, 1956. 69pp. (Franz Delitzsch-Vorlesungen 1953.) Includes bibl.
OCLC: 2567968 ISB; 357876 ATO; 3410602 EBS; 1541860 VWM; 5155393 ISB.

750 _____. "Kennzeichen der ipsissima vox Jesu." In *Synoptische Studien: Alfred Wikenhauser zum siebzigsten Geburtstag am 22. Februar 1953 dargebracht von Freunden, Kollegen und Schülern,* J. Schmidt and A. Vögtle, eds. 86-93. München: Karl Zink Verlag, 1953.
OCLC: 6765909 ISB.

751 _____. "Die Lampe unter dem Scheffel." ZNW 39 (1940): 237-40.

752 _____. "Die Muttersprache des Evangelisten Matthäus." ZNW 50 (1959): 270-74.

753 _____. *New Testament Theology.* Vol. 1. *The Proclamation of Jesus.* Trans. John Bowden. New York: Scribner's, 1971. London: SCM Press, 1971. (New Testament Library.) Trans. of *Neutestamentliche Theologie. 1. Die Verkündigung Jesu.* Gütersloh: Gütersloher Verlagshaus G. Mohn, 1971. Includes bibl.
OCLC: 135064 ISB; 159830; 785254 ISB.

754 _____. *The Parables of Jesus.* Trans. S. H. Hooke. London: SCM Press, 1954. 178pp. 2nd rev. ed. trans. from the 6th German ed. of 1962 with revs. which take account of the 8th German ed. of 1970. New York: Scribner's, 1972. 3rd rev. ed. London: SCM Press, 1972. 248 pp. Trans. of *Die Gleichnisse Jesu.* Zürich: Zwingli-Verlag, 1947. 119pp. (Abhandlungen zur Theologie des Alten und Neuen Testaments 11.) 8., durchges. Aufl. Göttingen: Vandenhoeck & Ruprecht, 1970. 243pp. *Die Gleichnisse Jesu: Kurzausgabe.* 9. Aufl. 1984. 155pp. (Kleine Vandenhoeck-Reihe 1500.) Spanish. *Las parabolas Jesu.* Tradujo. Francisco J. Calvo. 3. ed. Estella (Navarra): Editorial Verbo Divino, 1974. 4. ed. 1976. 302pp. (Buena noticia 4.)
OCLC: 1264877 ISB; 1404816 BNG; 699058 ISB; 1336726 ISB; 5950747 TJC; 10980704 YSM; 3325541 ISB; 5811179 IDK.

755 _____. *Die Sprache des Lukasevangeliums: Redaktion und Tradition im Nicht-Markusstoff des dritten Evangeliums.* Göttingen: Vandenhoeck & Ruprecht, 1980. 323pp. (Kritisch-exegetischer Kommentar über das Neue Testament. Sonderband.) Includes bibl.
Some text in Greek.
OCLC: 6210869 ICU.

756 _____. "Tradition und Redaktion in Lukas 15." ZNW 62 (1971): 172-89.

757 Jervell, J. "The Law in Luke-Acts." HThR 64 (1971): 21-36.

758 _____. "Matteusevangelit?" NTT 79 (1978): 241-48.
Critique of H. Hogestad's exegesis of Matthew.

759 Johns, Eric, and David Major. *Witness in a Pagan World: A Study of Mark's Gospel.* Guildford: Lutterworth Press, 1980. 154pp. Includes bibl.
OCLC: 8953137 DTM.

760 Johnson, Elizabeth A. "Jesus, The Wisdom of God: A Biblical Basis for Non-Androcentric Christology." EThL 61 (1985): 261-94.
"Q and Matthew," 280-84.

761 Johnson, M. D. "Reflections on a Wisdom Approach to Matthew's Christology." CBQ 36 (1974): 44-64.

762A Johnson, Sherman E. *A Commentary on the Gospel According to St. Mark.* London: A. & C. Black, 1960. (Black's New Testament Commentaries.) New York: Harper, 1960. (Harper's New Testament Commentaries.) 279pp. 2nd ed., rpt. with corrections. 1977. 283pp. OCLC: 3298334 VZI; 384268 ISB; 5041038 EXQ.

762B Joiner, Earl. "Synoptic Problem." In *Mercer Dictionary of the Bible,* Watson E. Mills, gen. ed. Macon GA: Mercer University Press, forthcoming.

763 Jones, Maurice. *The New Testament in the Twentieth Century: A Survey of Recent Christological and Historical Criticism of the New Testament.* London: Macmillan, 1914. 467pp. Includes bibls. OCLC: 733944 DAY.

764 Juel, Donald. *Messiah and Temple: The Trial of Jesus in the Gospel of Mark.* Missoula MT: Scholars Press, 1977. 223pp. (SBLDS 31.) Includes bibl. OCLC: 2524881 ISB.

765 Jülicher, Adolf. "Der echte Tatiantext." JBL 43 (1924): 132-71.

766 _____. *An Introduction to the New Testament.* Trans. by Janet Penrose Ward. New York: G. P. Putnam's Sons, 1904. London: Smith, Elder, & Co., 1904. 635pp. Trans. of *Einleitung in das Neue Testament.* 1. und 2. Aufl. Freiburg i.B.; Leipzig: J. C. B. Mohr (Paul Siebeck), 1894. 404pp. 5. und 6. Aufl. 1906. 5. und 6., neu bearb. Aufl.; 3., unveranderter Abdruck. 1919. 581pp. (Grundriss der theologischen Wissenschaften 3. T, 1 Bd.) OCLC: 6695995 ACL; 382556 ISB; 6149367 TSW; 6540450 CFT; 2159982 EXC.

767 _____. *Neue Linien in der Kritik der evangelischen Überlieferung.* Gielsen: A. Töpelmann, 1906. 76pp. (Vorträge des Hessischen und Nassauischen theologischen Ferienkurses 3.) OCLC: 9443904 EXC.

768A Kähler, Martin. *The So-Called Historical Jesus and the Historic, Biblical Christ.* Trans., ed., and with an intro. by Carl E. Braaten; foreword by Paul J. Tillich. Philadelphia: Fortress Press, 1964. (Seminary Editions.) 1977. 153pp. (Fortress Texts in Modern Theology.) 1988 (to be published in November 1988). Translation of the first and second essays in *Der sogenannte historische Jesus und der geschichtliche, biblische Christus.* 2. erw. und erläuterte Aufl. Leipzig: George Böhme, 1896. 206pp. Neu hrsg. von E. Wolf, 2. erweiterte Aufl. (Theologische Bücherei 2.) München: C. Kaiser, 1965. 4. Aufl. 1969. 126pp. Microfiche of 1896 printing. Chicago: American Theological Library Association, 1985. (ATLA Monograph Preservation Program. ATLA Fiche 1985-1824.) OCLC: 17042 ISB; 5169125 WAU; 17983215 (announced for November 1988); 9141308 CFT; 6163029 TJC; 1426482 TOL; 17493464 TJC.

768B Kahnis, Karl Friedrich August. *Die lutherische Dogmatik: historisch-genetisch dargestellt.* Vol. 1. *Die lutherische Dogmatik.* Leipzig: Dörffing und Franke, 1861–1868. 3 vols.
OCLC: 11791304 VUT.

769 Kappstein, Th. "A New Book by Harnack (Sprüche und Reden Jesu. Leipzig: J. C. Hinrichs, 1907)." ET 18 (1906–1907): 355-56.

770 Käsemann, Ernst. "Die Anfänge christlicher Theologie." ZThK 57 (1960): 162-85.

771 _____. *Essays on New Testament Themes.* Trans. W. J. Montague from selections of *Exegetische Versuche und Besinnungen,* erster Band, 2. Aufl., 1960. London: SCM Press, 1964. Naperville IL: Alec R. Allenson, 1964. 200pp. (Studies in Biblical Theology 41.) Philadelphia: Fortress Press, 1982. *Exegetische Versuche und Besinnungen.* 2 vols. Göttingen: Vandenhoeck & Ruprecht, 1960–1964. 2 vols. in 1. 1970.
A collection of essays and lectures previously published in various periodicals in a 2nd unrevised edition.
OCLC: 1158492 ISB; 357881 ATO; 7947298 ISB; 1068452 ISB; 839312 BHA.

772 _____. "Sätze heiligen Rechtes im Neuen Testament." NTS 1 (1955): 248-60.
ET: "Sentences of Holy Law in the New Testament." In his *New Testament Questions of Today,* trans. W. J. Montague, 66-81. Philadelphia: Fortress Press, 1969. London: SCM Press, 1969. (New Testament Library.)
OCLC: 24322; 60891 ISB.

773 _____. "Zum Thema der urchristlichen Apokalyptik." ZThK 59 (1962): 257-84.
ET: "On the Subject of Primitive Christian Apocalyptic." In his *New Testament Questions of Today,* trans. W. J. Montague, 108-37. Philadelphia: Fortress Press, 1969. London: SCM Press, 1969. (New Testament Library.)
OCLC: 24322; 60891 ISB.

774 Katz, Friedrich. "Lk 9, 52-11, 36. Beobachtungen zur Logienquelle und ihrer hellenistisch-judenchristlichen Redaktion." Thesis, Mainz University, 1973.

775 Kealy, Sean P. *Mark's Gospel: A History of Its Interpretation from the Beginning until 1979.* New York: Paulist Press, 1982. 269pp. Includes bibl.
OCLC: 8589830 ISB.

776 Keck, Leander E. "Ethos and Ethics in the New Testament." In *Essays in Morality and Ethics. The Annual Publication of the College Theology Society,* J. Gaffney, ed., 29-49. New York: Paulist Press, 1980.
OCLC: 6447869 ISB.

777A _____. "Mark, 3, 7-12 and Mark's Christology." JBL 84 (1965): 341-58.

777B _____. "Oral Traditional Literature and the Gospels: The Seminar." In *The Relationships among the Gospels: An Interdisciplinary Dialogue,* William O. Walker, Jr., ed., 103-22. San Antonio: Trinity University Press, 1978. (Trinity University Monograph Series in Religion 5.) OCLC: 4365624 ISB.

777C _____. "The Sermon on the Mount." In *Jesus and Man's Hope,* Donald G. Miller and Dikran Y. Hadidian, eds. 2:311-22. Pittsburgh: Pittsburgh Theological Seminary, 1971. (Perspective 2.) OCLC: 142572 ISB.

778 Keck, Leander E., and J. Louis Martyn. *Studies in Luke-Acts: Essays Presented in Honor of Paul Schubert.* Nashville: Abingdon Press, 1966. 316pp. Includes bibls. OCLC: 392394 ISB.

779A Kee, Howard Clark. *Jesus in History: An Approach to the Study of the Gospels.* New York: Harcourt, Brace, & World, 1970. 280pp. 2nd ed. 1977. 312pp. "Jesus as God's Eschatological Messenger: The Q Document," ch. 3, 62-103; 2nd ed., 76-120. OCLC: 66531 ISB; 3205311 ISB.

779B _____. "Mark, Long Ending of." In *Mercer Dictionary of the Bible,* Watson E. Mills, gen. ed. Macon GA: Mercer University Press, forthcoming.

780 _____. "The Q Source: A Formal Analysis." App. 3 in his *Understanding the New Testament,* 4th ed., 391-93. Englewood-Cliffs: Prentice-Hall, 1983. OCLC: 8729342 ISB.

781 _____. "The Q Source." A sec. in ch. 3 in his *Understanding the New Testament,* 4th ed., 86-96. Englewood-Cliffs: Prentice-Hall, 1983. OCLC: 8729342 ISB.

782 _____. "Wisdom Tradition and Christology in Q." In *AAR/SBL Abstracts 1984,* K. H. Richards and J. B. Wiggins, eds., 224-25. Chico CA: Scholars Press, 1984.

783 Keech, Finley M. "The Agreements of Matthew and Luke Against Mark in the Triple Tradition." Ph.D. diss., Drew University, 1962.*

784 Keim, Theodor. *The History of Jesus of Nazara: Considered in Its Connection with the Natural Life of Israel, and Related in Detail.* Trans. from the German. 6 vols. London: Williams and Norgate, 1873–1883. 2nd ed. 1876–1883. (Theological Translation Fund Library 1, 11, 14, 19, 25, 30.) Trans. of *Geschichte Jesu von Nazara in ihrer Verkettung mit dem Gesammtleben seines Volkes, frei untersucht und ausführlich erzählt.* 3 vols. Zürich; Orell: Füssli, 1867–1872. OCLC: 4986981 WYU; 3419341 ISB; 7781487 TJC.

785 Kelber, W. H. "From Aphorism to Sayings Gospel and from Parable to Narrative Gospel." *Forum* 1/1 (1985): 23-30.
A review article of J. D. Crossan, *In Fragments* (319).

786 _____. *The Oral and the Written Gospel: The Hermeneutics of Speaking and Writing in the Synoptic Tradition, Mark, Paul, and Q.* Philadelphia: Fortress Press, 1983. 254pp. Includes bibl.
OCLC: 8431377 ISB.
Reviews: Boomershine, T. E. JBL 104 (1985): 538-40; Brodie, T. L. CBQ 46 (1984): 574-75; Patte, D. JAAR 53 (1985): 136-37.

787 Kelly, John Norman Davidson. *Early Christian Doctrines.* London: A. & C. Black, 1958. 2nd ed. 1960. 501pp. 3rd ed. 1965. 446pp. 5th rev. ed. San Francisco: Harper & Row, 1978. 511pp.
OCLC: 1200293 BWE; 5700158 ISB; 3121923 EXN; 5183498 BHA; 3753468 ISB.

788 Kennedy, G. "Classical and Christian Source Criticism." In *The Relationships among the Gospels: An Interdisciplinary Dialogue*, William O. Walker, Jr., ed., 125-55. San Antonio: Trinity University Press, 1978. (Trinity University Monograph Series in Religion 5.)
OCLC: 4365624 ISB.

789A Kenyon, Frederick George. *Handbook to the Textual Criticism of the New Testament.* London: Macmillan, 1901. 321pp.
OCLC: 3911821 MBS.

789B Kern, Friedrich Heinrich. "Über den Ursprung des Evangeliums Matthaei." TZTh 7/2 (1834): 3-132.

790 Kertelge, K. "Das Doppelgebot der Liebe im Markusevangelium." In *À cause de l'évangile: Études sur les Synoptiques et les Actes: Offertes au P. Jacques Dupont, O. S. B. à l'occasion de son 70e anniversaire,* 303-22. Paris: Cerf, 1985. (Lectio divina 123.)
OCLC: 14377925 DTM.

791 _____. "Die Funktion der 'Zwölf' im Markusevangelium. Eine redaktionsgeschichtliche Auslegung, zugleich ein Beitrag zur Frage nach dem neutestamentlichen Amtsverstandnis." TThZ 78 (1969): 193-206.

792A Kilpatrick, G. D. "The Disappearance of Q." JThS 42 (1941): 182-84.

792B _____. "Griesbach and the Development of Text Criticism." In *J. J. Griesbach, Synoptic and Text-Critical Studies, 1776–1976,* Bernard Orchard and Thomas R. W. Longstaff, eds., 136-53. Cambridge; New York: Cambridge University Press, 1978. (SNTSMS 34.)
OCLC: 3541663 ISB.

793A _____. "Ἰδού and ἴδε in the Gospels." JThS N.S. 18 (1967): 425-26.

793B _____. "Matthew on Matthew." In *Synoptic Studies: The Ampleforth Conferences of 1982 and 1983,* C. M. Tuckett, ed., 177-85. Sheffield: JSOT Press, 1984. (JSNT Supplement Series 7.)
OCLC: 12451599 ISB.

794 _____. "The Order of Some Noun and Adjectival Phrases in the New Testament." NovT 5 (1962): 111-14.

795 _____. *The Origins of the Gospel According to St. Matthew.* Oxford: Clarendon Press, 1946. 151pp.
OCLC: 383203 ISB.

796 _____. "Scribes, Lawyers, and Lucan Origins." JThS 1 (1950): 56-60.

797 _____. "Some Notes on Marcan Usage." BTr 7 (1956): 2-9, 51-56, 146.

798 Kingsbury, Jack Dean. *Jesus Christ in Matthew, Mark and Luke.* Philadelphia: Fortress Press, 1981. 134pp. (Proclamation Commentaries, the New Testament Witnesses for Preaching.)
"The Document Q," 1-27.
OCLC: 7175998 ISB.

799 _____. *Matthew: Structure, Christology, Kingdom.* Philadelphia: Fortress Press, 1975. London: SPCK, 1976. 178pp.
OCLC: 1952998 ISB; 2821162.

800 _____. "Observations on the 'Miracle Chapters' of Matthew 8-9." CBQ 40 (1978): 559-73.

801A _____. *The Parables of Jesus in Matthew 13: A Study in Redaction-Criticism.* Richmond: John Knox, 1969. St. Louis: Clayton, 1977. London: SPCK, 1977. 180pp. Includes bibl.
Revised version of a doctoral diss. submitted to the University of Basel, 1966.
OCLC: 3929804 IGR.

801B _____. "The Theology of St. Matthew's Gospel according to the Griesbach Hypothesis." In *New Synoptic Studies: The Cambridge Gospel Conference and Beyond,* William R. Farmer, ed., 331-61. Macon GA: Mercer University Press, 1983.
OCLC: 9783753 ISB.

802 Kister, Menahem. "The Sayings of Jesus and the Midrash." *Immanuel* 15 (1982–1983): 39-50.

803 Klein, H. "Zur Frage nach dem Abfassungsort der Lukasschriften." EvTh 32 (1972): 467-77.

804 Klein, Peter. "Die lukanischen Weherufe Lk 6, 24-26." ZNW 71 (1980): 150-59.

805 Klijn, A. F. J. "A Survey of the Researches into the Western Text of the Gospels and Acts (1949–1959)." NovT 3 (1959): 1-27, 161-73.

---- _____. *See* Baarda, T. (46).

806 Kloppenborg, J. S. "Bibliography of Q." In *Society of Biblical Literature 1985 Seminar Papers,* K. H. Richards, ed., 103-26. Atlanta: Scholars Press, 1985. (SBLSPS 24.)

807 _____. *The Formation of Q: Trajectories in Ancient Wisdom Collections.* Philadelphia: Fortress Press, 1987. 377pp. (Studies in Antiquity and Christianity.) Includes bibl. OCLC: 13861210 ISB.

808 _____. "The Literary Genre of the Synoptic Sayings Source." Ph.D. diss., University of St. Michael's College, Toronto School of Theology, 1984. 461 leaves. Photocopy. 1984. Includes bibl. OCLC: 12333934 OKG.

809 _____. "Q 11:14-20: Work Sheets for Reconstruction." In *Society of Biblical Literature 1985 Seminar Papers,* K. H. Richards, ed., 133-51. Atlanta: Scholars Press, 1985. (SBLSPS 24.)

810 _____. "Q and Ancient Sayings Collections." In *AAR/SBL Abstracts 1984,* K. H. Richards and J. B. Wiggins, eds., 224. Chico CA: Scholars Press, 1984.

811 _____. "A Synopsis for Q [11:14-26.]" In *Society of Biblical Literature 1985 Seminar Papers,* K. H. Richards, ed., 127-32. Atlanta: Scholars Press, 1985. (SBLSPS 24.)

812 _____. "Tradition and Redaction in the Synoptic Sayings Source." CBQ 46 (1984): 34-62.

813 _____. "Wisdom Christology in Q." LTP 34 (1978): 129-47.

814 Klostermann, Erich. "Evangelien Synoptische." RGG 2 (1928): 422-33.

815 _____. *Das Lukasevangelium.* Unter Mitwirkung von Hugo Gressman. Tübingen: J. C. B. Mohr (Paul Siebeck), 1919. Pp. 360-612. 2. völlig neubearb. Aufl. 1929. 3. Aufl., unveränd. Nachdruck der 2. Aufl. (Handbuch zum Neuen Testament 5.) 1975. 246pp. (Handbuch zum Neuen Testament 2/1.) OCLC: 5093003 ELW; 5987653 ISB; 1688571 BWE.

816 _____. *Das Markusevangelium.* 2. völlig neubearb. Aufl. Tübingen: J. C. B. Mohr (Paul Siebeck), 1926. 194pp. 3., neubearb. Aufl. 1936. 174pp. 4. Aufl. 1950. 5. Aufl. unveränd. Nachdruck der 4., erg. Aufl. 1971. 180pp. (Handbuch zum Neuen Testament 3.) OCLC: 5281816 AZU; 7674461 WTS; 4734644 ISB; 1327456 BWE; 802427 DRB.

817A _____. *Das Matthäusevangelium.* 2. völlig neubearb. Aufl. Tübingen: J. C. B. Mohr (Paul Siebeck), 1927. 235pp. 3. photomechanisch gedruckte Aufl. 1938. 4. Aufl. unveränd. Nachdruck der 3. photomechanisch gedrückten Aufl. 1971. 233pp. (Handbuch zum Neuen Testament 4.) OCLC: 5113676 ISB; 5366392 ITC; 1572864 VA@ ; 802420 DRB.

817B Knight, Douglas A. "Sources, Literary." In *Mercer Dictionary of the Bible,* Watson E. Mills, gen. ed. Macon GA: Mercer University Press, forthcoming.

818   Knox, John. "Marcion's Gospel and the Synoptic Problem." In *Jesus, the Gospels, and the Church,* E. P. Sanders, ed., 25-31. Macon GA: Mercer University Press, 1987.

819   Knox, W. L. *The Sources of the Synoptic Gospels.* H. Chadwick, ed. 2 vols. Cambridge: Cambridge University Press, 1953. Vol. 2 rpt in 1957. Microfilm. Ann Arbor MI: University Microfilms International, 1980 (MI 48106.)
Contents: 1. St. Mark; 2. St. Luke and St. Matthew.
OCLC: 387630 ISB; 7430844 ODC; 7430886 ODC; 6819014.

820   Koester, Helmut. "Die ausserkanonischen Herrenworte als Produkte der christlichen Gemeinde." ZNW 48 (1957): 220-37.

821   _____. "Dialog und Spruchüberlierferung in den gnostischen Texten von Nag Hammadi." EvTh 39 (1979): 532-56.

822   _____. "ΓΝΩΜΑΙ ΔΙΑΦΟΡΟΙ: The Origin and Nature of Diversification in the History of Early Christianity." HThR 58 (1965): 279-318.
Reissued in *Trajectories Through Early Christianity,* by James M. Robinson and Helmut Koester, 114-57. Philadelphia: Fortress Press, 1971. 1977.
OCLC: 153829 ISB; 7808237 OBE.

823A   _____. "Gnostic Writings as Witnesses for the Development of the Sayings Tradition." In *The Rediscovery of Gnosticism. Proceedings of the International Conference on Gnosticism at Yale, New Haven, Connecticut, March 28-31, 1978,* Bentley Layton, ed., 1:238-61. 2 vols. Leiden: Brill, 1980-81. (Studies in the History of Religions. Supplements to Numen 41.)
OCLC: 8284344 ISB.

823B   _____. "History and Development of Mark's Gospel (From Mark to *Secret Mark* and 'Canonical' Mark)." In *Colloquy on New Testament Studies. A Time for Reappraisal and Fresh Approaches,* Bruce C. Corley, ed., 35-57. Macon GA: Mercer University Press, 1983.
First presented at the Colloquy on N.T. Studies, Southwestern Baptist Theological Seminary, Fort Worth, Texas, 5 November 1980. (Transcript of a seminar dialogue with Koester follows on 35-57. Omission from dialogue supplied by Robert Lee Williams [1709B].)

824   _____. *Introduction to the New Testament.* 2 vols. Berlin and New York: Walter de Gruyter, 1982. Philadelphia: Fortress Press, 1982. xxxii + 429pp. and xxxii + 365pp. (Hermeneia—Foundations and Facets.) Trans. of *Einführung in das Neue Testament: Im Rahmen der Religionsgeschichte und Kulturgeschichte der hellenistischen und römischen Zeit.* Berlin; New York: Walter de Gruyter, 1980. 801pp. (De Gruyter Lehrbuch.)
OCLC: 8669669 ISB; 6616008 TSM.

825 _____. "One Jesus and Four Primitive Gospels." HThR 61 (1968): 203-47.
Reissued in *Trajectories Through Early Christianity*, by James M. Robinson and Helmut Koester, 158-204. Philadelphia: Fortress Press, 1971. 1977.
OCLC: 153829 ISB; 7808273 OBE.

826 _____. *Synoptische Überlieferung bei den apostolischen Vätern*. Berlin: Akademie-Verlag, 1957. 274pp. (Texte und Untersuchungen zur Geschichte der altchristlichen Literatur 65. Bd., 5. Reihe, Bd. 10.) Includes bibl.
Die vorliegende Untersuchung war im Januar 1954 von der Theologischen Fakultät der Universität Marburg als Dissertation angenommen worden.
OCLC: 889583 ISB.

827 _____. "The Synoptic Sayings Source and Wisdom Sayings of Jesus." In *AAR/SBL Abstracts 1984*, K. H. Richards and J. B. Wiggins, eds., 225. Chico CA: Scholars Press, 1984.

828 Koppe, Johann Benjamin. *Marcus non epitomator Matthaei*. Programme Univ. Göttingen. Helmstadii, 1782.
Rpt in *Sylloge commentationum theologicarum*, D. J. Pott and G. A. Ruperti, eds., 1:35-69. Helmstadii: C. G. Fleckeisen, 1800.
OCLC: 7412567 BTI; 8732773 WTS.

829 Körtner, Ulrich H. J. *Papias von Hierapolis: Ein Beitrag zur Geschichte des frühen Christentums*. Göttingen: Vandenhoeck & Ruprecht, 1983. 371pp. (Forschungen zur Religion und Literatur des Alten und Neuen Testaments 133.)
OCLC: 10816591 ISB.

830 Kosch, Daniel. "Mt. 11,12f ‖ Lk 16,16 in der Logienquelle Q." In his *Die Gottesherrschaft im Zeichen des Widerspruchs: Traditions- und redaktionsgeschichtliche Untersuchung von Lk 16,16 ‖ Mt 11,12f. bei Jesus, Q und Lukas*, 50-64. Bern; Frankfurt; New York: Peter Lang, 1985. (Europäische Hochschulschriften 23/257.)
OCLC: 13060813 ISB.

831 Köstlin, Karl Reinhold. *Der Ursprung und die Komposition der synoptischen Evangelien*. Stuttgart: Mächen, 1853. 400pp.
OCLC: 8078184 TJC.

832 Kraeling, Carl H., ed. *A Greek Fragment of Tatian's Diatessaron, from Dura*. Ed. with facsimile, transcription and intro. by C. H. Kraeling. London: Christophers, 1935. 37pp. (Studies and Documents 3.)
The Fragment with which the text deals is now preserved in the parchment and papyrus collection of Yale University where it is listed as Dura parchment 24 (D Pg. 24.)
OCLC: 1194068 ISB.

833 Kraeling, Emil G. H. *The Clarified New Testament*. Vol. 1. *Four Gospels*. New York: McGraw-Hill, 1962. Includes bibl.
OCLC: 1689237 ISB.

834 Kremer, Jacob, ed. *Les Actes des Apôtres: Traditions, rédaction, théologie*. Gembloux: J. Duculot; Leuven: University Press, 1979. 590pp. (BEThL 48.)
English, French, or German.
OCLC: 5090463 ISB.

835 Küchler, Max. *Frühjüdische Weisheitstraditionen: Zum Fortgang weisheitlichen Denkens im Bereich des frühjüdischen Jahweglaubens*. Freiburg, Schweiz: Universitätsverlag, 1979. 703pp. (Orbis biblicus et orientalis 26.) Includes bibl.
Revision of thesis (doctoral), Universität Freiburg, 1979.
OCLC: 6685444 ISB.

836A Kuhn, Heinz-Wolfgang. *Ältere Sammlungen in Markusevangelium*. Göttingen: Vandenhoeck & Ruprecht, 1971. 270pp. (Studien zur Umwelt des Neuen Testaments 8.) Includes bibl.
Habilitationsschrift—Heidelberg.
OCLC: 751671 DRB.

836B Kuhn, Johannes von. *Das Leben Jesu, wissenschaftlich bearbeitet*. Vol. 1 (no more published). Mainz: Florian Kupferberg, 1838. 488pp. French. *La vie de Jésus-Christ, au point de vue de la science*. Traduit de l'allemand, par Fr. Nettement. Pour faire suite a la raison du christianisme. Paris: Dufour, 1842. [Cover has Paris: A. Royer, 1843.] xxvii + 294pp. (Bibliothèque chrétienne du dix-neuvième siécle.)
OCLC: 6254267 CUF; 5743566 CUF.

837 Kümmel, Werner G. "Äussere und innere Reinheit des Menschen bei Jesus." In *Das Wort und die Wörter: Festschrift Gerhard Friedrich zum 65. Geburtstag,* Horst Balz and Siegfried Schulz, eds., 34-46. Stuttgart: W. Kohlhammer, 1973.
OCLC: 811804 DRB.

838 _____. "Das Gesetz und die Propheten gehen bis Johannes—Lukas 16, 16 im Zusammenhang der heilsgeschichtlichen Theologie der Lukasschriften." In *Verborum veritas: Festschrift für Gustav Stählin zum 70. Geburtstag,* Otto Böcher and Klaus Haacker, eds., 89-102. Wuppertal: Theologischer Verlag Brockhaus, 1970.
OCLC: 3136383 KAT.

839 _____. "In Support of Q." In *The Two-Source Hypothesis: A Critical Appraisal,* A. J. Bellinzoni, Jr., ed., 227-43. Macon GA: Mercer University Press, 1985.
OCLC: 11599674 ISB.

840 _____. *Introduction to the New Testament*. Founded by Paul Feine
(¹1913); reedited by Johannes Behm (⁸1936); completely reedited by
Werner Georg Kümmel (¹²1963). Revised and enlarged English ed. trans.
from the 17th rev. German ed. (1973) by Howard Clark Kee. Nashville:
Abingdon; London: SCM, 1975. 629pp. Trans. from the 14th rev. German ed. (1965) by A. J. Mattill, Jr. Nashville: Abingdon; London: SCM,
1966. 444pp. (New Testament Library.) Trans. of *Einleitung in das Neue
Testament*. 14., durchges. Aufl. Heidelberg: Quelle & Meyer, 1965.
467pp. 17., wiederum völlig neu bearb. Aufl. 1973. 548pp. 18.,
durches. u. durche. Literaturnachtur. erg. Aufl. d. völligen Neubearb.
1976. 574pp. 19., durches. u. erw. Aufl. 1978. 580pp. 20., erneuterg.
Aufl. 1980. 582pp.
"§5. The Synoptic Problem," 33-60 (Mattill, 1966); 38-80 (Kee, 1975).
Pages 56-76 (Kee, 1975) are reissued in *The Two-Source Hypothesis: A
Critical Appraisal,* Arthur J. Bellinzoni, Jr., ed., 53-62, 227-43. Macon GA: Mercer University Press, 1985.
OCLC: 387279 ISB; 1200532 CSU; 1525942; 2931918; 889781 BWE;
7101605 KSU; 976985 BWE; 3273912; 5775421; 8164429 ISB.

841 _____. "Jesus und der jüdische Traditionsgedanke." ZNW 33 (1934):
105-30.

842 _____. "Jesusforschung seit 1965." ThR 45 (1980): 40-84; 46 (1981):
317-63; 47 (1982): 136-65.

843 _____. *The New Testament: The History of the Investigation of Its
Problems*. Trans. S. McLean Gilmour and Howard C. Kee. 2nd ed.
Nashville: Abingdon, 1972. 510pp. 1st British ed. (2nd ed.). London:
SCM Press, 1973. 510pp. (New Testament Library.) Trans. of *Das Neue
Testament: Geschichte der Erforschung seiner Probleme*. Freiburg: K.
Alber, 1958. 596pp. 1970. 612pp. (Orbis academicus; Problemgeschi-
chten der Wissenschaft in Dokumenten und Darstellungen 3/3.) In-
cludes bibl.
While the main text of the 2nd English ed. is essentially the same as the
1st ed., the notes, bibliography, and biographical summaries have been
completely revised and brought up to date.
OCLC: 446851 ISB; 765559 BHA; 3072947; 2550367 ISB; 5285482 MNJ.

844 _____. *Promise and Fulfilment: The Eschatological Message of Jesus*.
Trans. from the 3rd, completely rev. German ed. London: SCM, 1957.
Naperville IL: Alec R. Allenson, 1957. 1961. 1966. Rpt: 1974. 168pp.
(Studies in Biblical Theology 23.) Trans. of *Verheissung und Erfül-
lung: Untersuchungen zur eschatologischen Verkündigung Jesu*. Basel:
H. Majer, 1945. 2., völlig neu bearb. Aufl. Zürich: Zwingli-Verlag,
1953. 3. Aufl. 1956. 156pp. (Abhandlungen zur Theologie des Alten
und Neuen Testaments 6.) Includes bibl.
OCLC: 4307225 ISB; 1018239; 6439244 MOG; 6696563 TNM; 4302334
ISB; 2069796 BWE; 5663308 EZC.

845 _____. "Das Verhalten Jesu gegenüber und das Verhalten des Menschensohns, Markus 8,38 par und Lukus 12,3f. par Matthäus 10,32f." In *Jesus und der Menschensohn: für Anton Vögtle*, Rudolf Pesch, Rudolf Schnackenburg, and Odilo Kaiser, eds., 210-24. Freiburg im Breisgau: Herder, 1975. OCLC: 2318718 ICU.

---- Kundsin, Karl. *See* Bultmann, Rudolf. (193).

846 Kürzinger, J. "Irenäus und sein Zeugnis zur Sprache des Matthäusevangeliums." NTS 10 (1963): 108-15.

847 _____. "Papias." LThK 8 (1963): 34-35.

848 _____. "Papias von Hierapolis: Zu Titel und Art seines Werkes." BZ 23 (1979): 172-86.

849 _____. *Papias von Hierapolis und die Evangelien des Neuen Testaments: Gesammelte Aufsätze, Neuausgabe, und Übersetzung der Fragmente, kommentierte Bibliographie.* Regensburg: F. Pustet, 1983. 250pp. (Eichstätter Materialien. Abt. Philosophie und Theologie 4.) OCLC: 10207067 ICU.

850 _____. "Das Papiaszeugnis und die Erstegestalt des Matthäusevangeliums." BZ 4 (1960): 19-38.

851 _____. "Das Wort, das ergeht durch Gottes Mund (Mt 4, 4.) Zum Verständnis der ersten Versuchung Jesu." In *Der Dienst für den Menschen in Theologie und Verkündigung: Festschrift für Alois Brems, Bischof von Eichstätt, zum 75. Geburtstag*, R. M. Hübner, et al., eds., 157-64. Regensburg: F. Pustet, 1981. (Eichstätter Studien 13.) OCLC: 7742003 PTS.

852 Lachmann, Karl. "De ordine narrationum in Evangeliis synopticis." ThStKr 8 (1835): 570-90.

853 Laconi, Karl. "Vangeli sinottici: Gli eredi della tradizione ecclesiale." SacDot 29 (1984): 8-28.

854 Lafontaine, R., and P. Mourlon Bearnaert. "Essai sur la structure de Marc 8, 27-9, 13." RSR 57 (1969): 543-61.

855 Lagrange, Marie Joseph. *Évangile selon saint Luc*. 8. éd. Paris: J. Gabalda, 1948. clxvii + 634pp. (Études bibliques.) Includes bibl. Greek and French on facing pages. OCLC: 883255 BWE.

856 _____. *Évangile selon saint Marc*. Paris: J. Gabalda, 1911. cl + 455pp. Ed. corr. et augm., 8. mille. 1947. Paris: Librairie Lecoffre, 1966. cxci + 480pp. (Études bibliques.) Includes bibl. Greek text, with trans., intro., and commentary in French. The 1966 ed. has Greek text with Latin trans. on facing quarter pages. OCLC: 5366910 DAY; 883260 BWE; 2707558 IEG.

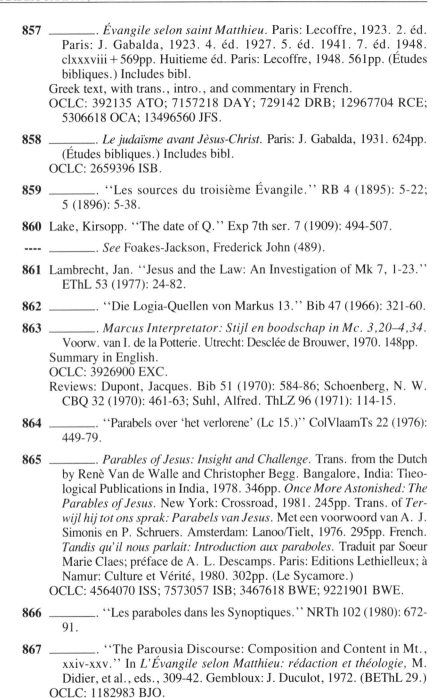

857 _____. *Évangile selon saint Matthieu*. Paris: Lecoffre, 1923. 2. éd. Paris: J. Gabalda, 1923. 4. éd. 1927. 5. éd. 1941. 7. éd. 1948. clxxxviii + 569pp. Huitieme éd. Paris: Lecoffre, 1948. 561pp. (Études bibliques.) Includes bibl.
Greek text, with trans., intro., and commentary in French.
OCLC: 392135 ATO; 7157218 DAY; 729142 DRB; 12967704 RCE; 5306618 OCA; 13496560 JFS.

858 _____. *Le judaïsme avant Jèsus-Christ*. Paris: J. Gabalda, 1931. 624pp. (Études bibliques.) Includes bibl.
OCLC: 2659396 ISB.

859 _____. "Les sources du troisième Évangile." RB 4 (1895): 5-22; 5 (1896): 5-38.

860 Lake, Kirsopp. "The date of Q." Exp 7th ser. 7 (1909): 494-507.

---- _____. *See* Foakes-Jackson, Frederick John (489).

861 Lambrecht, Jan. "Jesus and the Law: An Investigation of Mk 7, 1-23." EThL 53 (1977): 24-82.

862 _____. "Die Logia-Quellen von Markus 13." Bib 47 (1966): 321-60.

863 _____. *Marcus Interpretator: Stijl en boodschap in Mc. 3,20–4,34*. Voorw. van I. de la Potterie. Utrecht: Desclée de Brouwer, 1970. 148pp. Summary in English.
OCLC: 3926900 EXC.
Reviews: Dupont, Jacques. Bib 51 (1970): 584-86; Schoenberg, N. W. CBQ 32 (1970): 461-63; Suhl, Alfred. ThLZ 96 (1971): 114-15.

864 _____. "Parabels over 'het verlorene' (Lc 15.)" ColVlaamTs 22 (1976): 449-79.

865 _____. *Parables of Jesus: Insight and Challenge*. Trans. from the Dutch by Renè Van de Walle and Christopher Begg. Bangalore, India: Theological Publications in India, 1978. 346pp. *Once More Astonished: The Parables of Jesus*. New York: Crossroad, 1981. 245pp. Trans. of *Terwijl hij tot ons sprak: Parabels van Jesus*. Met een voorwoord van A. J. Simonis en P. Schruers. Amsterdam: Lanoo/Tielt, 1976. 295pp. French. *Tandis qu'il nous parlait: Introduction aux paraboles*. Traduit par Soeur Marie Claes; préface de A. L. Descamps. Paris: Editions Lethielleux; à Namur: Culture et Vérité, 1980. 302pp. (Le Sycamore.)
OCLC: 4564070 ISS; 7573057 ISB; 3467618 BWE; 9221901 BWE.

866 _____. "Les paraboles dans les Synoptiques." NRTh 102 (1980): 672-91.

867 _____. "The Parousia Discourse: Composition and Content in Mt., xxiv-xxv." In *L'Évangile selon Matthieu: rédaction et théologie*, M. Didier, et al., eds., 309-42. Gembloux: J. Duculot, 1972. (BEThL 29.)
OCLC: 1182983 BJO.

868 ———. "Q-Influence on Mark 8, 34-9, 1." In *Logia. Les paroles de Jésus* = *The Sayings of Jesus: Mémorial Joseph Coppens,* Joël Delobel, ed., 277-304. Leuven: University Press and Peeters, 1982. (BEThL 59.)
OCLC: 9450792 ISB; 11043145.

869 ———. "Redaction and Theology in Mk. IV." In *L'Évangile selon Marc: Tradition et rédaction,* M. Sabbe, et al., eds., 269-307. Leuven: University Press, 1974. (BEThL 34.)
OCLC: 2345456 ISB.

870 ———. *Die Redaktion der Markus-Apokalypse. Literarische Analyse und Strukturuntersuchung.* Hrsg. mit Unterstützung der Universitaire Stichting von Belgien. Rome: Päpstliches Bibelinstitut, 1967. 321pp. (Analecta Biblica 28.) Includes bibl.
OCLC: 688390 ISB.

871 ———. "The Relatives of Jesus in Mark." NovT 17 (1975): 241-58.

872 ———. *The Sermon on the Mount: Proclamation and Exhortation.* Wilmington DE: M. Glazier, 1985. 255pp. (Good News Studies 14.) Trans. of *Maar ik zeg u: De programmatische rede van Jezus (Mt. 5–7; Lc. 6,20-49.)* Leuven: Vlaamse bijbelstichting & Acco, 1983. 296pp. German. *Ich aber sage euch: Die Bergpredigt als programmatische Rede Jesu (Mt. 5–7; Lk. 6,20-49.* Stuttgart: Katholisches Bibelwerk, 1984. 252pp. French. *'Eh bien, moi je vous dis': Le discours-programme de Jésus (Mt. 5–7, Lc. 6,20-49).* Paris: Cerf, 1986. 265pp. (Lectio divina 125.)
OCLC: 12530747 ESJ; 12263665 BHA; 12865466 VFW; 15244197 CUF.

873 ———. "De vijf Parabels van Mc. 4, Structuur en gie van de Parabelrede." *Bijdragen* 29 (1968): 25-53.

874 ———. "Ware Verwantschap en eeuwige Zonde. Ontstaan en Structuur van Mc. 3, 20-35." *Bijdragen* 29 (1968): 114-50.

875 ———. "Ware Verwantschap en eeuwige Zonde. Ontstaan en Structuur van Mc. 3, 20-35 (II.)" *Bijdragen* 29 (1968): 234-58.

876 ———. "Ware Verwantschap en eeuwige Zonde. Ontstaan en Structuur van Mc. 3, 20-35 (III.)" *Bijdragen* 29 (1968): 369-93.

877A Lange, Joachim. *Das Erscheinen des Auferstandenen im Evangelium nach Matthäus: Eine traditions- u. redaktionsgeschichtl. Untersuchung zu Mt. 28, 16-20.* Würzburg: Echter-Verlag, 1973. 573pp. (Forschung zur Bibel 11.) Includes bibl.
Slightly revised edition of the author's thesis, Würzburg, 1972/73.
OCLC: 1153998 ISB.
Review: Murphy-O'Connor, J. RB 83 (1976): 97-102.

877B Langen, Josef. *Grundriss der Einleitung in das Neue Testament.* Freiburg: Herder, 1868. 2nd ed. Bonn: E. Weber, 1873. 208pp.
OCLC: 2nd ed. (ATLA Fiche 1986-0911) 18332039.

878 LaPotterie, Ignace de, ed. *De Jésus aux évangiles: Tradition et rédaction dans les évangiles synoptiques.* Gembloux: J. Duculot, 1967. 271pp. (BEThL 25.)
OCLC: 1020231 ISB.

879 Larfeld, Wilhelm. *Die neutestamentlichen Evangelien nach ihrer Eigenart und Abhängigkeit.* Gütersloh: C. Bertelsmann, 1925. 388pp.
OCLC: 13757640 ISB.

880 Latourelle, René. "Authenticité historique des miracles de Jésus. Essai de critériologie." Gr 54 (1973): 225-62.

881 Laufen, Rudolf. *Die Doppelüberlieferungen der Logienquelle und des Markusevangeliums.* Königstein/Ts.; Bonn: Peter Hanstein, 1980. 614pp. (Bonner biblische Beiträge 54.) Includes bibl.
Doctoral thesis, Bonn, 1978.
OCLC: 6657276 ISB; 13599914 PAU.

882 _____. "ΒΑΣΙΛΕΙΑ und ΕΚΚΛΗΣΙΑ. Eine traditions- und redaktionsgeschichtliche Untersuchung des Gleichnisses vom Senfkorn." In *Begegnung mit dem Wort: Festschrift für Heinrich Zimmermann*, Joseph Zmijewski and Ernst Nellessen, eds., 105-140. Bonn: Hanstein Verlag, 1980. (Bonner biblische Beiträge 53.)
OCLC: 6033286 ISB.

883 Launderville, Dale. "Jacob's Well: The Synoptic Problem and 'Q.' "
BiTod 21 (1983): 74-76.

884 Leaney, Alfred R. C. *A Commentary on the Gospel According to St. Luke.* London: A. & C. Black, 1958. 2nd ed. 1971. Rpt: 1976. 300pp. (Black's New Testament Commentaries.)
OCLC: 1004799 ISB; 1022311 DAY; 3807979 ISS; 5698656 CLE.

885 _____. "The Resurrection Narratives in Luke (xxiv.12-53.)" NTS 2 (1955): 110-14.

886A LeClerc, Jean. *Historia ecclesiastica duorum primorum a christo nato saeculorum.* Amsterdam: David Mortier, 1716. 813pp.
OCLC: 5141979 TFW.

886B Lee, Jong-Yun. "Rediscussion of the Problem of the Synoptic Gospels." In *The 60th Birthday Celebration of Dr. Han Chul-Ha, President of ACTS, Seoul, Asia United Theological College, 1984.* Seoul: Asia United Theological College, 1984.*

886C _____. "Reexamination of the Synoptic Gospel Problem (II)." In *Bible and Theology.* Vol. 2. Seoul: Emmaus Publishing House, 1984.*

887 Legasse, Simon. "Le logion sur le fils révélateur (Mt. xi,27 par. Lc. x,22. Essai d'analyse prérédactionnelle." In *La notion biblique de Dieu: Le Dieu de la Bible et le Dieu des philosophes,* Joseph Coppens, ed., 245-74. Gembloux: J. Duculot, 1976.
OCLC: 2705773 ISB.

888 ———. "L'oracle contre 'cette génération' (Mt. 23,34-36 par. Lc. 11,49-51) et la polémique judéo-chrétienne dans la source des Logia." In *Logia. Les paroles de Jésus* = *The Sayings of Jesus: Mémorial Joseph Coppens,* Joël Delobel, ed., 237-56. Leuven: University Press and Peeters, 1982. (BEThL 59.) OCLC: 9450792 ISB; 11043145.

889 Lehmann, Martin. *Synoptische Quellenanalyse und die Frage nach dem historischen Jesus: Kriterien der Jesusforschung untersucht in Auseinandersetzung mit Emanuel Hirschs Frühgeschichte des Evangeliums.* Berlin: Walter de Gruyter, 1970. 218pp. (Beiheft zur Zeitschrift für die neutestamentliche Wissenschaft und die Kunde der älteren Kirche 38.) Includes bibl. Revision of the author's thesis, Kirchliche Hochschule, Berlin 1967. OCLC: 775227 ISB.

890 Lemke, Werner Erich. "Synoptic Studies in the Chronicler's History." Th.D. diss., Harvard Divinity School, 1963. 256 leaves. Microfilm. Cambridge MA: Harvard University Library Microreproduction Dept., 1982. OCLC: 8784025 IGR.

891 Lentzen-Deis, F. "Entwicklungen in der synoptischen Frage?" ThPh 55 (1980): 559-70.

892 Léon-Dufour, Xavier. "Autour de la question synoptique." RSR 42 (1954): 549-84.

893 ———. "Autour de la question synoptique." RSR 60 (1972): 494-518.

894 ———. *Concordance of the Synoptic Gospels. In Seven Colors.* Trans. from the French by Robert J. O'Connell. Paris; New York: Desclée, 1956. Trans. of *Concordance des évangiles synoptiques.* Paris; New York: Desclée, 1956. 21pp. + folded diagrams (in color). OCLC: 4597550 ISB; 387731 ATO.

895 ———. *Études d'évangile: Parole de Dieu.* Paris: Editions du Seuil, 1965. 396pp. OCLC: 387497 ATO.

896 ———. "Les évangiles synoptiques." In *Introduction à la Bible,* A. Robert and A. Feuillet, eds. T. 2. *Nouveau Testament,* 143-334. Tournai: Desclée, 1959. 2. éd., rev. et corr. 1959. Ed. nouv. 1976. ET: "The Synoptic Gospels." In *Introduction to the New Testament,* trans. from the French, 139-324. New York: Desclée, 1965. OCLC: 944231 BWE; 3502099 IQU; 5728019.

897 ———. "Le fait synoptique." RSR 60 (1972): 495-96.

898   _____. *The Gospels and the Jesus of History*. Trans. from the French, ed. by John McHugh. New York: Image Books, 1968. 312pp. London: Collins, 1968. 288pp. New York: Image Books, 1970. Trans. of *Les Évangiles et l'histoire de Jésus*. Paris: Editions de Seuil, 1963. 525pp. German. *Die Evangelien und der historische Jesus*. Aschaffenburg: Paul Pattloch, 1966. 599pp. Spanish. *Los evangelios y la historia de Jesus*. Traducción castellana por Pedro Darnell. Barcelona: Editorial Estela, 1966. 457pp. (Colección theologia 3.) Includes bibl.
OCLC: 12998940 TCT; 462477 CSU; 387510 ATO; 7788044 TJC; 13846166 CLU.

899A   _____. "Interprétation des évangiles et problème synoptique." EThL 43 (1967): 5-16.

899B   _____. *Problèm synoptique et Formgeschichte*. Esp. pp. 85-115. Louvain, 1957.*

900   _____. "*Redaktionsgeschichte* of Matthew and Literary Criticism." In *Jesus and Man's Hope*, D. G. Buttrick, ed., 9-35. Pittsburgh: Pittsburgh Theological Seminary, 1970. (Perspective 1.)
OCLC: 142572 ISB.

901   _____. "The Synoptic Gospels." In *In Search of the Historical Jesus*, Harvey K. McArthur, ed. New York: Scribner's, 1969. (Scribner's Source Book in Religion.)
OCLC: 4288 ISB.

902   _____. "Théologie de Matthieu et paroles de Jésus." RSR 50 (1962): 90-111.

903 Leonardi, G. "Il racconto sinottico delle tentazioni di Gesu: fonti, ambiente e dottrina." StPat 16 (1969): 391-429.*

904 Lessing, Gotthold Ephraim. "Neue Hypothese über die Evangelisten als bloss menschliche Geschichtsschreiber betrachtet." In *Theologischer Nachlass*, 45-72. Berlin, 1784. ET: *Lessing's Theological Writings*. Selections in translation with an introductory essay by Henry Chadwick, 45-72. London: A. & C. Black, 1956. Stanford CA: Stanford University Press, 1957. 1967. (Library of Modern Religious Thought.) Written in 1778.
OCLC: 864034 BCT; 669466 DAY; 6714575 BHA; 6060443 CCH.

905 Levesque, E. "La catéchèse primitive et le problème synoptique." RAp 56 (1933): 129-48; "La catéchèse et le question synoptique" 66 (1938): 402-22.

906   _____. *Nos quatre évangiles; leur composition et leur position respective. Étude suive de quelques procédés littéraires de Saint Matthieu*. Paris: Beauchesne, 1917. 2nd ed. 1917. viii + 352pp.
NUC: MiU; NjPT; MH; DCU-H.

907 Levie, Jean. "La complexité du problème synoptique." EThL 31 (1955): 619-36.

908 _____. ''Critique littéraire évangelique et l'évangile araméen de l'apôtre Matthieu.'' In *La formation des évangiles: Problème synoptique et Formgeschichte*, J. Cambier, et al., eds., 34-69. Bruxelles: Desclée de Brouwer, 1957.
OCLC: 2038719 ISB.

909 _____. ''L'évangile Araméen de S. Matthieu est-il la source de l'évangile de S. Marc?'' NRTh 76 (1954): 689-715, 812-43.

910 Lewis, P. B. ''Indications of a Liturgical Source in [boat-narrative] the Gospel of Mark.'' *Encounter* 39 (1978): 385-94.

---- Lietzmann, Hans. *See* Huck, Albert (728).

911 Lightfoot, Joseph Barber. *Essays on the Work Entitled Supernational Religion*. London; New York: Macmillan, 1889. 234pp. 2nd ed. 1893. 324pp.
Contents: Silence of Eusebius; The Ignatian Epistles; Polycarp of Smyrna; Papias of Hierapolis; The Later School of St. John; The Churches of Gaul; Tatian's Diatessaron; Discoveries Illustrating the Acts of the Apostles.
OCLC: 3112850 YNG; 654211 ATO; 3510887 MBS; 13381109 CFT.

912 Lindars, Barnabas. ''From Jesus to the Gospels.'' NBl 50 (1968): 61-65.

913 _____. ''Jesus as Advocate: A Contribution to the Christology Debate.'' BJRL 62 (1980): 476-97.

914 _____. *Jesus Son of Man. A Fresh Examination of the Son of Man Sayings in the Gospels in the Light of Recent Research*. London: SPCK, 1983. 244pp. Includes bibl.
OCLC: 9613665 ISB.

915 _____. ''The New Look on the Son of Man.'' BJRL 63 (1981): 437-62.

916 _____. *New Testament Apologetic. The Doctrinal Significance of the Old Testament Quotations*. Philadelphia: Westminster Press, 1961. London: SCM, 1961. 303pp.
Originally presented as the author's thesis (B.A.), Cambridge.
OCLC: 383115 ISB; 3029147 KKU.

---- Lindemann, Andreas. *See* Conzelmann, Hans (297).

917 _____. ''Literaturbericht zu den synoptischen Evangelien 1978–1983.'' ThR 49 (1984): 223-76, 311-71.

918 Lindemans, Jean, and H. Demeester, eds. *Liber amicorum Monseigneur Onclin: actuele thema's van kerkelijk en burgerlijk recht = thèmes actuels de droit canonique et civil*. Gembloux: J. Duculot, 1976. 398pp. (BEThL 42.)
Preface in Latin; text in Dutch, English, French, German, Italian, or Spanish.
OCLC: 3273434 ISB.

919 Lindeskog, Gösta. "Logia-studien." StTh 4 (1951): 129-89.

920 Lindsey, R. L. *A Hebrew Translation of the Gospel of Mark. Greek-Hebrew Diglot.* With Eng. intro. by Robert L. Lindsey; foreword by David Flusser. Jerusalem: Dugith Publishers, 1969. 2nd ed. 1973. 159pp.
OCLC: 334705 IXA; 3155405 EXN.

921 _____. "A Modified Two-Document Theory of the Synoptic Dependence and Interdependence." NovT 6 (1963): 239-63.

922 Linnemann, Eta. *Parables of Jesus. Introduction and Exposition.* Trans. from the 3rd German ed. by John Sturdy. London: SPCK, 1966. 216pp. 1st U.S. ed. *Jesus of the Parables: Introduction and Exposition.* New York: Harper & Row, 1967. 218pp. Trans. of *Gleichnisse Jesu: Einführung und Auslegung.* Göttingen: Vandenhoeck & Ruprecht, 1961. 195pp. 3., erg. Aufl. 1964. 6., durchges. und ergänzte Aufl. 1975. 207pp. Includes bibl.
OCLC: 4058299 ISB; 816725 ISB; 9452817 EXC; 3256481 EBS; 1516479 BWE.

923 Linton, O. "Coordinated Sayings and Parables in the Synoptic Gospels. Analysis versus Theories." NTS 26 (1980): 139-63.

924 _____. "Das Dilemma der Synoptikerforschung." ThLZ 101 (1976): 881-92.

925 _____. "Evidences of a Second-Century Revised Edition of St. Mark's Gospel." NTS 14 (1968): 321-55.

926 _____. "The Parable of the Children's Game. Baptism and Son of Man (Matt. xi.16-19 = Luke vii.31-5). A Synoptic Text-Critical Structural and Exegetical Investigation." NTS 22 (1976): 159-79.

927 _____. "The Q Problem Reconsidered." In *Studies in New Testament and Early Christian Literature. Essays in Honor of Allen P. Wikgren,* David Edward Aune, ed., 43-59. Leiden: Brill, 1972. (NovTSup 33.)
OCLC: 707874 ISB.

928 _____. "Den synoptiske forsknings dilemma." DTT 35 (1972): 47-62.

929 Lockton, William. *Certain Alleged Gospel Sources: A Study of Q, Proto-Luke and M.* London; New York: Longmans, Green, 1927. 74pp.
OCLC: 5021662 TSW.

930 _____. "The Origin of the Gospels." CQR 94 (1922): 216-39.*

931 _____. *The Resurrection and Other Gospel Narratives and The Narratives of the Virgin Birth. Two Essays.* London: Longmans, Green, 1924. 184pp.
OCLC: 5001500 CFT.

932 _____. *The Three Traditions in the Gospels: An Essay.* London; New York: Longmans, Green, 1926. 306pp.
NUC: IEG; MB.

933 Lohmeyer, Ernst. *Das Evangelium des Markus.* Göttingen: Vandenhoeck & Ruprecht, 1951. 1959. 17. Aufl., nach dem Handexemplar des Verfassers durchgesehene Ausg. mit Ergänzungsheft (3rd ed., 44pp., edited by Gerhard Sass.) 1967. 368pp. (Kritisch-exegetischer Kommentar über das Neue Testament 1 Abt., 2. Bd.) Includes bibl. OCLC: 1179449 BPS; 6126425 IDJ; 3314615 JHE.

934 _____. *Das Evangelium des Matthäus.* Nachgelassene Ausarbeitungen und Entwürfe zur Übersetzung und Erkrlärung von Ernst Lohmeyer. Göttingen: Vandenhoeck & Ruprecht, 1956. 2. durchges. Aufl. 1958. 3. durchges. Aufl. 1962. 1967. 429pp. (Kritisch-exegetischer Kommentar über das Neue Testament; Sonderband.) Includes bibl. OCLC: 5175996 ISB; 8361289 ISB; 1246066 ISB; 381618 ATO.

935 _____. *Galiläa und Jerusalem.* Göttingen: Vandenhoeck & Ruprecht, 1926. 104pp. (Forschungen zur Religion und Literatur des Alten und Neuen Testaments n.F., 34.) OCLC: 504805 ISB.

936 _____. *"Our Father": An Introduction to the Lord's Prayer.* Trans. John Bowden. New York: Harper & Row, 1966. 320pp. Trans. of *Das Vater-unser.* 2. unveränderte Aufl. Göttingen: Vandenhoeck & Ruprecht, 1947. 3. Aufl. 1952. 4., unveränderte Aufl. 1960. 5., unveränderte Aufl. 1962. 216pp. (Abhandlungen zur Theologie des Alten und Neuen Testaments 23.) OCLC: 680997 ISB; 5237135 PKT; 4856013 ISB; 8703199 CFT; 833912 BWE; 4801915 DRU.

937 Lohr, C. H. "Oral Techniques in the Gospel of Matthew." CBQ 23 (1961): 403-35.

938 Lohse, Eduard. "Jesu Worte über den Sabbat." In *Judentum, Urchristentum, Kirche: Festschrift für Joachim Jeremias,* Walter Eltester, ed., 79-89. Berlin: A. Töpelmann, 1960. 2. veilfach berichtigte und ergänzte um eine wissenschaftliche Würdigung und eine Bibliographie des Jubilars erweiterte Aufl. 1964. 259pp. (Beihefte zur Zeitschrift für die neutestamentliche Wissenschaft und die Kunde der älteren Kirche 26.) OCLC: 3716276 NOC; 4796450 AZS.

939 Loisy, Alfred Firmin. *Les évangiles synoptiques.* 2 vols. Ceffonds: Loisy, 1907–1908. Rpt: Frankfurt: Minerva, 1971. OCLC: 4588413 ISB; 942309 BXM.

940 _____. *L'évangile selon Luc.* Paris: Emile Nourry, 1924. Rpt: Frankfurt: Minerva, 1971. 600pp. OCLC: 9775999 WTS; 996302 BXM.

941 _____. *The Origins of the New Testament.* Trans. L. P. Jacks. New York: Macmillan, 1950. London: Allen & Unwin, 1950. 332pp. New York: Collier Books, 1962. 384pp. *The Birth of the Christian Religion and The Origins of the New Testament.* New Hyde Park NY: University Books, 1962. 413, 332pp. (Library of the Mystic Arts, a Library of Ancient and Modern Classics.) Trans. of *La naissance du christianisme.* Paris: E. Nourry, 1933. 452pp. Italian. *Le origini del cristianesimo.* Firenze: Il Saggiatore, 1964. 491pp. (I Gabbiani.)
OCLC: 8369010 IAY; 383107 ISB; 7780101 PLF; 2271218 YAH; 5846273 ISB; 6459572 TJC; 11432974 PIT.

942 Lonergan, Bernard Joseph Francis. *Insight: A Study of Human Understanding.* London: Longmans, Green, 1958. 3rd ed. New York: Philosophical Library, 1970. Rev. student ed. New York. Philosophical Library; London: Darton, Longman, and Todd, 1973. New York: Harper & Row, 1978. London: Darton, Longman, and Todd, 1983. 785pp.
OCLC: 90659; 2180134 TXU; 4041967 AKC; 4233682.

943 _____. *Method in Theology.* New York: Herder and Herder, 1972. London: Darton, Longman and Todd, 1972. 405pp. French. *Pour une methode en théologie.* Traduit de l'anglais sous la direction de Louis Roy. Montréal: Les éditions Fides; Paris: Les éditions du Cerf, 1978. 468pp. (Cogitatio fide.)
OCLC: 376104 ISB; 540559; 4532180 DRU; 8276716 NDD.

---- Longstaff, Thomas Richmond Willis. *See* Orchard, Bernard. (1151).

---- _____. *See* Fuller, Reginald H. (512).

944 _____. 1981. As reviewer see Rist, John M. *On the Independence of Matthew and Mark* (1251).

---- _____. *See* Tyson, Joseph B. (1607).

945 _____. ''At the Colloquium's Conclusion.'' In *J. J. Griesbach, Synoptic and Text Critical Studies, 1776–1976,* Bernard Orchard and Thomas R. W. Longstaff, eds., 170-75. Cambridge; New York: Cambridge University Press, 1978. (SNTSMS 34.)
OCLC: 3541663 ISB.

946 _____. ''Crisis and Christology: The Theology of the Gospel of Mark.'' PSThJ 33/4 (1980): 28-40.
Reissued in 1983 in *New Synoptic Studies: The Cambridge Gospel Conference and Beyond,* William R. Farmer, ed., 373-92. Macon GA: Mercer University Press, 1983.
OCLC: 9783753 ISB.

947 _____. ''A Critical Note in Response to J. C. O'Neill.'' NTS 23 (1976): 116-17.

948 _____. ''Empty Tomb and Absent Lord: Mark's Interpretation of Tradition.'' In *Society of Biblical Literature 1976 Seminar Papers,* George MacRae, ed., 269-77. Cambridge MA: SBL, 1976.

949 _____. *Evidence of Conflation in Mark? A Study in the Synoptic Problem.* Missoula MT: Scholars Press for the SBL, 1977. 245pp. (SBLDS 28.) Includes bibl.
Originally presented as the author's thesis, Columbia University, 1973.
OCLC: 3003358 ISB.

950 _____. "Mark and Roger of Hovedon: A Response." CBQ 41 (1979): 118-20.

951 _____. "The Minor Agreements: An Examination of the Basic Argument." CBQ 37 (1975): 184-92.

952 _____. "The Woman at the Tomb: Matthew 28:1 Reexamined." NTS 27 (1981): 277-82.

---- Loomis, Louise R. *See* Shotwell, James T. (1434).

953A _____, trans. and intro. *The Book of the Popes. I. To the Pontificate of Gregory I.* New York: Columbia University Press, 1916. (Records of Civilization: Sources and Studies.)
OCLC: 1941708 BWE.

953B Lord, Albert B. "The Gospels as Oral Traditional Literature." In *The Relationships among the Gospels: An Interdisciplinary Dialogue,* William O. Walker, Jr., ed., 33-91. San Antonio: Trinity University Press, 1978. (Trinity University Monograph Series in Religion 5.)
OCLC: 4365624 ISB.

954 Lovison, T. "La pericopa della Cananea Mt 15, 21-28." RivBib 19 (1971): 273-305.

955 Lowe, M. "The Demise of Arguments from Order for Markan Priority." NovT 24 (1982): 27-36.

956 _____, and David Flusser. "Evidence Corroborating a Modified Proto-Matthean Synoptic Theory." NTS 29 (1983): 25-47.

957 Ludlum, J. H., Jr. "New Light on the Synoptic Problem." ChrTo 3/3 (1958): 6-9; 3/4 (1958): 10-14.

958 Lührmann, Dieter. 1970. As reviewer see Wrege, Hans T. *Die Überlieferungsgeschichte* (1725).

959 _____. "Jesus und seine Propheten Gesprächsbeitrag." In *Prophetic Vocation in the New Testament and Today,* J. Panagopoulos, ed., 210-17. Leiden: Brill, 1977. (NovTSup 45.)
OCLC: 3659230 ISB; 4035784.

960 _____. "Liebet eure Feinde (Lk 6, 27-37/Mt 5, 39-48.)" ZThK 69 (1972): 412-38.

961 _____. "Noah and Lot (Lk 17, 26-29)—ein Nachtrag." ZNW 63 (1972): 130-32.

962 ⸻. *Die Redaktion der Logienquelle. Ahn.: Zur weiteren Überlieferung der Logienquelle.* Neukirchen-Vluyn: Neukirchener Verlag, 1969. 138pp. (Wissenschaftliche Monographien zum Alten und Neuen Testament 33.) Includes bibl.
A revision of the author's Habilitationsschrift, Heidelberg, 1968, entitled "Studien zur Redaktion und weiteren Überlieferung der Logienquelle".
OCLC: 2174235 ISB.
Review: McArthur, Harvey K. CBQ 33 (1971): 445-47.

963 ⸻. "The Relation between the Gospel of Mark and the Sayings Collection Q." In *AAR/SBL Abstracts 1985,* K. H. Richards and J. B. Wiggins, eds., 160. Atlanta: Scholars Press, 1985.

964 Lummis, E. W. "A Case Against Q." HibJ 24 (1925–1926): 755-65.

965A ⸻. *How Luke was Written. (Considerations Affecting the Two-Document Theory with Special Reference to the Phenomena of Order in the Non-Marcan Matter Common to Matthew and Luke.)* Cambridge: University Press, 1915. 141pp.
OCLC: 8609704 ACL.

965B Lutteroth, Henri. *Essai d'interprétation de quelques parties de l'évangile de selon saint Matthieu.* Paris: Librairie Sandoz et Fischbacher, 1860–1876. 4 vols.
Greek and French in parallel columns.
OCLC: 13757695 ISB.

966 Luz, Ulrich. *Das Evangelium nach Matthäus. 1. Teilband. Mt 1-7.* Zürich: Benziger Verlag; Neukirchen-Vluyn: Neukirchener Verlag, 1985. (Evangelisch-Katholischer Kommentar zum Neuen Testament 1.) Includes bibl.
OCLC: 12410996 ISB.

967 ⸻. "Das Jesusbild der vormarkinischen Tradition." In *Jesus Christus in Historie und Theologie: Neutestamentliche Festschrift für Hans Conzelmann zum 60. Geburtstag,* George Strecker, ed., 347-74. Tübingen: J. C. B. Mohr (Paul Siebeck), 1975.
OCLC: 2129453 ISB.

968 ⸻. "Q 3-4." In *Society of Biblical Literature 1984 Seminar Papers,* K. H. Richards, ed., 375-76. Chico CA: Scholars Press, 1984. (SBLSPS 23.)

969 ⸻. "Q 10:2-16; 11:14-23." In *Society of Biblical Literature 1985 Seminar Papers,* K. H. Richards, ed., 101-102. Atlanta: Scholars Press, 1985. (SBLSPS 24).

970 ⸻. "Sermon on the Mount/Plain: Reconstruction of Q^{MT} and Q^{LK}." In *Society of Biblical Literature 1983 Seminar Papers,* K. H. Richards, ed., 473-79. Chico CA: Scholars Press, 1983. (SBLSPS 22).

971 ⸻. "Die wiederentdeckte Logienquelle." EvTh 33 (1973): 527-33.

---- Macgregor, G. H. C. *See* Morton, A. Q. (1064).

972A Mahnke, Hermann. *Die Versuchungsgeschichte im Rahmen der synoptischen Evangelien: Ein Beitrag zur frühen Christologie.* Frankfurt am Main; Bern; Las Vegas: Lang, 1978. 445pp. (Beiträge zur biblischen Exegese und Theologie 9.) Includes bibl.
An abridgement of the author's thesis, Kiel, 1977.
OCLC: 5801787 DTM.

972B Maier, Adalbert. "Beiträge zur Einleitung in das Neue Testament. Die drei ersten Evangelien im Allgemeinen." ZTh 20 (1848): 3-76.

972C _____. *Einleitung in die Schriften des Neuen Testaments.* Freiburg: Herder, 1852. 601pp.
OCLC: 15244273 DAY.

---- Major, David. *See* Johns, Eric (759).

---- Mann, C. S. *See* Albright, W. F. (18).

973 _____. *Mark: A New Translation with Introduction and Commentary.* Garden City NY: Doubleday, 1986. 714pp. (Anchor Bible 27.)
OCLC: 11813386 ISB.

974 Manson, Thomas Walter. "The Sayings of Jesus." In *The Mission and Message of Jesus: An Exposition of the Gospels in the Light of Modern Research,* by H. D. A. Major, T. W. Manson, and C. J. Wright, bk. 2 (299-639). New York: E. P. Dutton, 1938. 1961. Photocopy. Ann Arbor MI: University Microfilms International, 1981.
OCLC: 2094193 ISB; 186431 PCJ; 7935641.

975 _____. *The Sayings of Jesus, as Recorded in the Gospels according to St. Matthew and St. Luke.* Arranged with introduction and commentary. London: SCM, 1969. Study ed. 1971. 1977. 1st American ed. Grand Rapids MI: Eerdmans, 1979. 347pp. Italian. *I detti di Gesù ne Vangeli di Matteo e Luca.* Brescia: Paideia, 1980. 562pp. (Biblioteca teologica 17.) Includes bibl.
First published as bk. 2 (299-639) of the *Mission and Message of Jesus,* by H. D. A. Major, T. W. Manson, and C. J. Wright.
OCLC: 777903 STC; 4837564 ZBM; 5171481 ISB; 7387352 IDJ.

976 _____. *Studies in the Gospels and Epistles.* Ed. Matthew Black. Philadelphia: Westminster Press; Manchester, Eng.: Manchester University Press, 1962. 293pp.
OCLC: 377500 ISB; 862034 BPS.

977 _____. *The Teaching of Jesus: Studies in its Form and Content.* Cambridge: University Press, 1935. 2nd ed. 1951. Reprint. 1955. 1st pbk. ed. 1963. 1967. 351pp.
OCLC: 2949953 ISB; 9658692 LNE; 1077323 BPS; 346331 WSU; 9908783 MUU; (pbk.) 12900933 GFC.

978 Manson, William. *The Gospel of Luke.* New York: Harper & Row, 1930. 282pp. London: Hodder and Stoughton, 1930. 1937. 1963. 286pp. Microfiche. Chattanooga TN: Expositor's Microfilm Library, 1978. (Moffatt New Testament Commentary.) Includes bibl.
OCLC: 384925 WSU; 8374064 ISB; 1153747 IWU; 1030661 DAY; 7096988 TBI.

979 Marcheselli Casale, Cesare. "Andate e annunciate a Giovanni ciò che udite e vedete (Mt. 11,4; Lc. 7,22)." In *Testimonium Christi: Scritti in onore di Jacques Dupont,* 257-88. Brescia: Paideia, 1985.
OCLC: 13792588 DTM.

980 Marconcini, B. "La predicazione del Battista in Marco e Luca confrontata con la redazione di Matteo." RivBib 20, suppl. 45 (1972): 451-66.

981 Marsh, Herbert. *A Dissertation on the Origin and Composition of Our Three First Canonical Gospels.* Cambridge: Printed by John Burges, and sold by F. & C. Rivington, London, and J. Deighton, Cambridge, 1801. 243pp.
Reissued in *Introduction to the New Testament,* by John David Michaelis; trans. from the 4th German ed. and considerably augmented with notes and *A Dissertation on the Origin & Composition of the First Three Gospels,* by Herbert Marsh. London: Rivington, 1823. Microfiche. Beltsville MD: Reproduced by the NCR Corp. for the ATLA Board of Microtext, 1978.
OCLC: 9174154 IME; 3724018 ISB (Original in the Princeton Theological Seminary Library.)

982 Marshall, A. "A Note on τε . . . καί." BTr 5 (1954): 182-83.

983 Marshall, I. Howard. *The Gospel of Luke: A Commentary on the Greek Text.* Grand Rapids MI: Eerdmans; Exeter, Eng.: Paternoster Press, 1978. 928pp. (New International Greek Testament Commentary.) Includes bibl.
OCLC: 4037038 ICU; 4215510 ISB.

984 ———. "How to Solve the Synoptic Problem: Luke 11:43 and Parallels." In *The New Testament Age: Essays in Honor of Bo Reicke,* William C. Weinrich, ed., 2:313-25. Macon GA: Mercer University Press, 1984.
OCLC: 10458733 ISB.

985 ———. *Luke: Historian and Theologian.* Exeter, Eng.: Paternoster Press, 1970. Grand Rapids MI: Zondervan, 1971. 238pp. (Contemporary Evangelical Perspective: Biblical Theology.)
OCLC: 133333 ISB; 1020317 BCT; 11817755 GCL.

986 ———. "Son of God or Servant of Yahweh?—A Reconsideration of Mark 1:11." NTS 15 (1969): 326-36.

987 Marshall, J. T. "The Aramaic Gospel." Exp 4th ser. 3 (1891): 1-17, 109-24, 205-20, 275-91, 375-90, 452-76.

988 _____. "The Aramaic Gospel: A *résumé* of the Theory in Accordance with its Genesis." ET 4 (1892–1893): 260-67, 515.

989 _____. "Did St. Paul Use a Semitic Gospel?" Exp 4th series 2 (1890): 69-80.

990 Martin R. P. "St. Matthew's Gospel in Recent Study." ET 80 (1968–1969): 132-36.

991 Martin, W. H. Blyth. "The Indispensability of Q." Th 59 (1956): 182-88.

992 Martinez Dalmau, Eduardo. *A Study on the Synoptic Gospel: A New Solution to an Old Problem: The Dependence of the Greek Gospels of St. Matthew and St. Luke upon the Gospel of Mark.* New York: R. Speller, 1964. 122pp.
OCLC: 1865222 DGU.

---- Martyn, J. Louis. *See* Keck, Leander E. (778).

993 _____. "Source Criticism and *Religionsgeschichte* in the Fourth Gospel." In *Jesus and Man's Hope,* D. G. Buttrick, ed., 1:247-73. Pittsburgh: Pittsburgh Theological Seminary, 1970. (Perspective 1.)
OCLC: 142572 ISB.

994 Marxsen, Willi. *Introduction to the New Testament: An Approach to Its Problems.* Trans. G. Buswell. Philadelphia: Fortress Press, 1968. 1970. 284pp. Trans. of *Einleitung in das Neue Testament: Eine Einführung in ihre Probleme.* Gütersloh: G. Mohn, 1963. 2. Aufl. 1964. 3. Aufl. 1964. 239pp. 4. völlig neu bearb. Aufl. 1978. 295pp. Spanish. *Introducción al Nuevo Testamento: una Iniciación a sus Problemas.* Tradujo, Marcelino Legido López. Salamanca: Ediciones Sígueme, 1983. 285pp. (Biblioteca de estudios bíblicos.)
OCLC: 376994 ISB; 12656151 ISB; 8700798 SOI; 5358590 BHA; 1147671 IYU; 5012397 DRU; 5358617 BHA; 5830989.

995 _____. *Mark the Evangelist: Studies on the Redaction History of the Gospel.* Trans. by James Boyce, et al. Nashville: Abingdon Press, 1969. 222pp. Trans. of *Der Evangelist Markus: Studien zur Redaktionsgeschichte des Evangeliums.* Göttingen: Vandenhoeck & Ruprecht, 1956. 2. durchgesehene Aufl. 1959. 149pp. (Forschungen zur Religion und Literatur des Alten und Neuen Testaments n. F. 49.) Spanish. *El Evangelista Markos: Estudio sobre la historia de la redaccion del evangelio.* Salamanca: Ediciones Sigueme, 1981. 211pp. (Biblioteca de estudios bíblicos 33.)
OCLC: 4313 ISB; 3930080 ISB; 7259639 IDI; 10567401 ISB.

996 März, C.-P. "Feuer auf die Erde zu werfen, bin ich gekommen. Zum Verständnis und zur Entstehung von Lk 12,49." In *À cause de l'évangile: Études sur les Synoptiques et les Actes. Offertes au P. Jacques Dupont, O. S. B., à l'occasion de son 70e anniversaire.* Paris: Cerf, 1985. (Lectio divina 123.)
OCLC: 14377925 DTM.

997 _____. "Zur Traditionsgeschichte von Mk 14,3-9 und Parallelen." StNTSU 6-7 (1981–1982): 89-112.

998 Massaux, Édouard. *Influence de L'Evangile de saint Matthieu sur la littérature chrétienne avant saint Iréné.* Louvain: University Press, 1950. 730pp. (Universitas Catholica Lovaniensis. Dissertations ad gradum magistri in Facultate Theologica vel in Facultate Iuris Canonici consequendum conscriptae. Ser. 2, 42.) Includes bibl. OCLC: 16644347 ISB.

999 McArthur, Harvey K. 1969. As reviewer see Wrege, Hans T. *Die Überlieferungsgeschichte* (1725).

1000 _____1971. As reviewer see Luhrmann, Dieter. *Die Redaktion* (962).

1001 _____. "Basic Issues. A Survey of Recent Gospel Research." Interp 18 (1964): 39-55.

1002 _____. "The Burden of Proof in Historical Jesus Research." ET 82 (1970–1971): 116-19.

1003 _____. "Καί Frequency in Greek Letters." NTS 15 (1969): 339-49.

1004 _____. "The Origin of the 'Q' Symbol." ET 88 (1976–1977): 119-20.

1005 _____. "The Parable of the Mustard Seed." CBQ 33 (1971): 198-210.

1006 McCaughey, J. D. "Three 'Persecuted Documents' of the New Testament." ABR 17 (1969): 27-40.

1007 McDermott, John M. "Luc xii,8-9: Pierre angulaire." RB 85 (1978): 381-401.

1008 _____. "Luke xii,8-9: Stone of Scandal." RB 84 (1977): 523-37.

1009 McEleney, N. J. "Authenticating Criteria and Mark 7:1-23." CBQ 34 (1972): 431-60.

1010 McGinley, Laurence J. *Form-Criticism of the Synoptic Healing Narratives: A Study in the Theories of Martin Dibelius and Rudolf Bultmann.* Woodstock MD: Woodstock College Press, 1944. 165pp. Includes bibl. OCLC: 3471506 ISB.

1011 McHugh, J. "The Literary Origins of the Gospels." CleR 58 (1973): 421-28. Review of Benoit, P. *Synopse* 2 (98).

1012 McIndoe, J. H. "The Young Man at the Tomb." ET 80 (1968–1969): 125.

----- McKnight, Edgar V. *See* Talbert, Charles H. (1534).

1013 McLoughlin, S. "Les accords mineurs Mt-Lc contra Mc et le problème synoptique: Vers la théorie des deux sources." In *De Jésus aux évangiles: tradition et rédaction dans les évangiles synoptiques,* I. de La Potterie, ed., 17-40. Gembloux: J. Duculot, 1967. (BEThL 25.) Also issued in *EThL* 43 (1967): 17-40. OCLC: 1020231 ISB.

1014 _____. "The Gospels and the Jesus of History." DRev 87 (1969): 183-200.

1015A _____. "The Synoptic Theory of Xavier Léon-Dufour: An Analysis and Evaluation." Thesis, Leuven, 1965.

1015B McMahon, Edward. "The New Center." PSThJ 40/2 (1987): 17-25.
Critical review of *New Synoptic Studies: The Cambridge Gospel Conference and Beyond,* William R. Farmer, ed. (449B).
First read at a colloquy on "New Critical Approaches in Synoptic Studies" held at Southern Methodist University, fall semester 1986.

1016 McNeile, Alan Hugh, ed. *The Gospel according to St. Matthew.* The Greek Text with introduction, notes, and indexes. London; New York: Macmillan, 1915. 1938. 1961. New York: St. Martin's Press, 1965. Grand Rapids MI: Baker Book House, 1980. 448pp. Microfiche. Huntington Beach CA: Vision Press, 1982.
OCLC: 5154631 ISB; 978793 BHA; 13851706 OKU; 4061753 TXD; 611419 MIA; 6847758 DDC; 10203659 ICU.

1017A _____. *An Introduction to the Study of the New Testament.* 2nd ed., rev., by C. S. C. Williams. London: Oxford University Press, 1953. Rpt from corr. sheets of the 2nd ed. 1957. viii + 486pp. 1st ed. 1927. viii + 478pp. "The Synoptic Problem," 59-91.
OCLC: 376970 ISB; 680378 ISB; 9937468 IAY.

1017B McNicol, Allan J. "The Two-Gospel Hypothesis under Scrutiny: A Response to C. M. Tuckett's Analysis of Recent Neo-Griesbachian Gospel Criticism." PSThJ 40/3 (1987): 5-13.
First read at a colloquy on "New Critical Approaches in Synoptic Studies" held at Southern Methodist University, fall semester 1986.

1017C _____, and William O. Walker, Jr. "A Statement of Closure: Items for Further Research." PSThJ 40/3 (1987): 32.

1017D Meeks, Wayne A. "Hypomnemata from a Untamed Sceptic: A Response to George Kennedy." In *The Relationships among the Gospels: An Interdisciplinary Dialogue,* William O. Walker, Jr., ed., 157-72. San Antonio: Trinity University Press, 1978. (Trinity University Monograph Series in Religion 5.)
OCLC: 4365624 ISB.

1018 Mees, M. "Rassegna di 'logia' e 'sentenze' nella ricerche degli anni 1968–1970." VetChr 8 (1971): 322-31.

1019 _____. "Zur Frage der Logienquelle." ThG 14 (1971): 103-106.

1020 Meier, John P. *The Gospel According to Matthew.* New York: W. H. Sadlier, 1980. 118pp. Discussion leader's edition, ed. by E. F. Gordon. 1983. 174, 32pp. (Access Guide for Scripture Study.) Includes bibl.
OCLC: 8025403 BWE; 9854103.

1021 _____. *Law and History in Matthew's Gospel: A Redactional Study of Mt. 5:17-48.* Rome: Biblical Institute Press, 1976. 206pp. (Analecta Biblica 71.) Includes bibl.
Originally presented as the author's thesis, Biblical Institute, 1975 (S.S.L.)
OCLC: 2895749 ISB.

1022A _____. *Matthew.* Wilmington DE: M. Glazier; Dublin: Veritas Publications in Cooperation with M. Glazier, 1980. Rev. ed. 1981. 377pp. (New Testament Message 3.) Includes bibl.
OCLC: 6268592 ISB; 10122611; 12457817; 8397405 MOG.

---- Meijboom, Hajo Uden. *See* Meyboom, Hajo Uden.

1022B Meredith, A. "The Evidence of Papias for the Priority of Matthew." In *Synoptic Studies: The Ampleforth Conferences of 1982 and 1983,* C. M. Tuckett, ed., 187-96. Sheffield: JSOT Press, 1984. (JSNT Supplement Series 7.)
OCLC: 12451599 ISB.

1023 Merino, Luis Diez. "Testimonios judíos sobre la existencia de un evangelio arameo." EstBib 41 (1983): 157-63.

1024 Merkel, Helmut. "Das Gleichnis von den 'Ungleichen Söhnen' (Matt. xxi.28-32.)" NTS 20 (1974): 254-61.

1025A _____. "Markus 7, 15-Das Jesuswort über die innere Verunreinigung." ZRGG 20 (1968): 340-63.

1025B _____. *Die Pluralität der Evangelien als theologisches und exegetisches Problem in der Alten Kirche.* Berne; Las Vegas: Peter Lang, 1978. (Traditio christiana 3.) French. *La pluralité des Evangiles comme problème théologique et exégétique dans l'Eglise ancienne.* 172pp. Includes bibl.
Selections from various church fathers in Greek or Latin with German translation on facing pages; French translation by Jean-Louis Maier on facing pages.
OCLC: 4834511; 4989165 VYF.

1026 _____. *Die Widersprüche zwischen den Evangelien: Ihre polemische und apologetische Behandlung in der Alten Kirche bis zu Augustin.* Tübingen: J. C. B. Mohr (Paul Siebeck), 1971. 295pp. (Wissenschaftliche Untersuchungen zum Neuen Testament 13.) Includes bibl.
Originally presented as the author's thesis, Univerität Erlangen-Nürnberg, Erlangen.
OCLC: 8993983 CMC.

1027 Merklein, Helmut. *Die Gottesherrschaft als Handlungsprinzip: Untersuchung zur Ethik Jesu.* Würzburg: Echter, 1978. 2nd ed. 1981. 3rd ed. 1984. 339pp. (Forschung zur Bibcl 34.) Includes bibl.
Habilitationsschrift—Würzburg, 1977.
OCLC: 5311543; 7937977 PKT; 13474504 ISB.

1028 _____. *Jesu Botschaft von der Gottesherrschaft: Eine Skizze*. Stuttgart: Katholisches Bibelwerk, 1983. 189pp. (Stuttgarter Bibelstudien 111.) Includes bibl.
OCLC: 10971705 ISB.

1029 Merli, D. "Il segno di Giona." BibOr 14 (1972): 61-77.

1030 Metzger, Bruce M. *Chapters in the History of New Testament Textual Criticism*. Grand Rapids MI: W. B. Eerdmans, 1963. Leiden: Brill, 1963. 164pp. (New Testament Tools and Studies 4.)
OCLC: 2805002 ISB; 270095 CIN.

1031 _____. *Index to Periodical Literature on Christ and the Gospels*. Grand Rapids MI: Eerdmans, 1966. Leiden: Brill, 1966. 602pp. (New Testament Tools and Studies 6.)
OCLC: 582916 WSU; 851296 ISB.

1032 _____. "Tatian's Diatessaron and a Persian Harmony of the Gospels." JBL 69 (1950): 261-80.

1033 _____. *The Text of the New Testament: Its Transmission, Corruption, and Restoration*. London; New York: Oxford University Press, 1964. 268pp. 2nd ed. 1968. 281pp. German. *Der Text des Neuen Testaments: Eine Einfuhrung in die neutestamentliche Textkritik*. Stuttgart: W. Kohlhammer Verlag, 1964. 271pp. Includes bibl.
OCLC: 1550913 ISB; 383123 WSU; 2036316; 13148339 TCT.

1034 _____. *A Textual Commentary on the Greek New Testament. A Companion Volume to the United Bible Societies' Greek New Testament (third edition)*. London; New York: United Bible Societies, 1971. xxxiii + 775pp.
OCLC: 683422 ISB; 502821 UTS.

1035 Meyboom, Hajo Uden. *Geschiedenis en critiek der Marcushypothese*. Amsterdam: Gebroeders Kraay, 1866. 248pp.
Proefschriff, Groningen.
NUC: ICU; MH-AH; NjPT.

1036 _____. "Proeve eener Geschiedenis der Logia-Hypothese." ThT 6 (1872): 303-24, 361-402, 481-506.

1037 Meyer, Arnold O. "Die Entstehung des Markusevangeliums." In *Festgabe für Adolf Jülicher zum 70. Geburtstag, 26. Januar 1927*, Rudolf Bultmann and Hans von Soden, eds., 35-60. Tübingen: J. C. B. Mohr (Paul Siebeck), 1927.
OCLC: 13948892 GTX.

1038 _____. *Jesu Muttersprache; das galiläische Aramaisch in seiner Bedeutung für die Erklärung der Reden Jesu und der Evangelien überhaupt*. Freiburg: J. C. B. Mohr (Paul Siebeck), 1896. 176pp.
OCLC: 1906725 ISB.

1039A Meyer, Ben F. *The Aims of Jesus*. London: SCM Press, 1979. 335pp.
OCLC: 4760225 ISB.

1039B _____. ''The World Mission and the Emergent Realization of Christian Identity.'' In *Jesus, the Gospels, and the Church*, E. P. Sanders, ed., 243-63. Macon GA: Mercer University Press, 1987. OCLC: 16130939 ISB.

1040 Meyer, Eduard. *Ursprung und Anfänge des Christentums*. 1. *Die Evangelien*. Stuttgart; Berlin: J. G. Cotta, 1923. 4. Aufl. 1924. Rpt: 1961. OCLC: 2484832 BUF; 3850388 ISB; 6568959 KSW.

1041A Meyer, Heinrich August Wilhelm. *Kritisch exegetisches Kommentar über die Evangelien des Matthäus, Markus, und Lukas*. Göttingen: Vandenhoeck und Ruprecht, 1832. xvi + 419pp. (His *Kritisch exegetischen Kommentar über das Neue Testament* 1; *Das Neue Testament Griechisch* 2/1.) OCLC: 5113774 STS.

1041B _____. *Kritisch exegetisches Handbuch über die Evangelien des Markus und Lukas*. 2. verb. und verm. Aufl. Göttingen: Vandenhoeck und Ruprecht, 1846. 493pp. 3. verb. und verm. Aufl. 1855. x + 518pp. (His *Kritisch exegetischen Kommentar über das Neue Testament* 1/2.) ET: *Critical and Exegetical Hand-Book to the Gospels of Mark and Luke*. Trans. from the 5th German ed. by R. E. Wallis. Trans., rev., and ed. by W. P. Dickson. Edinburgh: T. & T. Clark, 1880. 2. vols. With a preface, trans. of references, and supplementary notes to the American ed. by M. B. Riddle. New York: Funk & Wagnalls, 1884. Rpts: Winona Lake IN: Alpha Publications, 1979. Peabody MA: Hendrickson, 1983. 598pp. (His *Commentary on the New Testament* 2.) Microfiche. Chattanooga TN: Expositor's Microfilm Library, 1983. OCLC: 5114150 STS; 10381101 CFT; 5810304 OKO; 12435566 NOC; 6995736 TBI.

1042 Meyer, Paul Donald. ''The Community of Q.'' Ph.D. diss., University of Iowa, 1967. Microfilm. Ann Arbor MI: University Microfilms International, 1968. Photocopy. 1973. Includes bibl. OCLC: 5095866 NVS; 616974 DAY.

1043 _____. ''The Gentile Mission in Q.'' JBL 89 (1970): 405-17.

1044 Meynell, Hugo. ''A Note on the Synoptic Problem.'' DRev 90 (1972): 196-200.

1045 _____. ''The Synoptic Problem: Some Unorthodox Solutions.'' LoS 17 (1963): 451-59.

1046 Meynet, Roland. ''Qui donc est 'le plus fort'? Analyse rhétorique de Mc 3, 22-30; Mt 12, 22-37; Luc 11, 14-26.'' RB 90 (1983): 334-50.

1047 Michaelis, Christine. ''Die II-Alliteration der Subjektsworte der ersten 4 Seligpreisungen in Mt. v.3-6 und ihre Bedeutung für den Aufbau der Seligpreisungen bei Mt., Lk. und in Q.'' NovT 10 (1968): 148-61.

1048 Michaelis, Johann David. *Introduction to the New Testament*. Trans. from
the 4th German ed. and considerably augmented with notes, explanatory and supplemental by Herbert Marsh. 2 vols. Cambridge: Printed by
J. Archdeacon, and sold by J. & J. Merrill, 1793. 2nd ed., with a dissertation on the origin and composition of the three first Gospels by Herbert Marsh. London: Printed for F. & C. Rivington, 1802. 4th ed. 4 vols.
in 6. 1823. Trans. of *Einleitung in die göttlichen Schriften des Neuen
Bundes*. 2. und vermehrte Aufl. 3 vols. Göttingen: Witme Bandenhoek,
1765–1766. 4. sehr vermehrte und geänderte Ausgabe. 2 vols. Göttingen: Vandenhoeck und Ruprechtschen Buchhandlung, 1788.
OCLC: 8886876 TCL; 4415662 IND; 5212191 RSC; 2114545 GDC.

1049 Michaelis, Wilhelm. *Einleitung in das Neue Testament: Die Entstehung,
Sammlung und Ueberlieferung der Schriften des Neuen Testaments*.
Bern: Buchhandlung der Evangelischen Gesellschaft, 1946. 410pp. 3.
Aufl., mit einem Anhang versehener Nachdruck der 2. Aufl. 2 vols.
Bern: B. Haller, 1961, c1954.
OCLC: 6349806 ISB; 6651220 ISB.

1050 _____. *Die Erscheinungen des Auferstandenen*. Basel: Heinrich Majer,
1944. 160pp.
OCLC: 9262435 ISB.

1051A Michiels, R. "Het passieverhaal volgens Lucas." CBG 30 (1984): 191-
210.

1051B Mill, John. *Novum testamentum graecum, cum lectionibus variantibus mss.
exemplarium, versionum, editionum, ss. patrum et scriptorum eccle-
siasticorum, et in easdem notis. Accedunt loca scripturae parallela, al-
iaque exegetica. Praemittitur dissertatio de libris N.T. canonis
constitutione, et s. textus n. foederis ad nostra usque tempora historia*.
2nd ed. Lipsiae: Filii J. Friderici Gleditschii, 1723.
First ed. appeared at Amsterdam in 1710. Ludolph Kuster supplements the
readings in Mill's edition, which was published at Oxford in 1707.
OCLC: 3041133 PKT; 4750084 MSM.

1051C Miller, Donald G. "The Gospel of Luke." In *Jesus and Man's Hope*,
Donald G. Miller and Dikran Y. Hadidian, eds., 2:345-48. Pittsburgh:
Pittsburgh Theological Seminary, 1971. (Perspective 2.)
OCLC: 142572 ISB.

1051D _____, and Dikran Y. Hadidian, eds. *Jesus and Man's Hope*. Vol. 2.
Pittsburgh: Pittsburgh Theological Seminary, 1971. (Perspective 2.)
Vol. 2 of 2-vol. collection of written contributions to the Pittsburgh Fes-
tival of the Gospels, hosted by the Pittsburgh Theological Seminary on
its 175th anniversary celebration, 6-10 April 1970. *See* Buttrick, David
G. (222) for vol. 1.
OCLC: 142572 ISB.

---- Milligan, George. *See* Moulton, James H. (1073).

1051E Minear, Paul S. "Gospel History: Celebration or Reconstruction." In *Jesus and Man's Hope*, Donald G. Miller and Dikran Y. Hadidian, eds., 2:13-27. Pittsburgh: Pittsburgh Theological Seminary, 1971. (Perspective 2.) OCLC: 142572 ISB.

1052A Mitton, Charles L. "Notes on Recent Exposition." ET 77 (1965–1966): 1-3.

1052B Moeller, Charles. "How the Gospels Have Affected the Arts and Culture, and How the Arts and Culture Have Affected the Interpretation of the Gospels." In *Jesus and Man's Hope*, Donald G. Miller and Dikran Y. Hadidian, eds., 2:151-92. Pittsburgh: Pittsburgh Theological Seminary, 1971. (Perspective 2.) OCLC: 142572 ISB.

1053 Moffatt, James. *The Historical New Testament. Being the Literature of the New Testament Arranged in the Order of Its Literary Growth and According to the Dates of the Documents.* A new trans., ed., with prolegomena, historical tables, critical notes, and an appendix. Edinburgh: T. & T. Clark, 1901. New York: Scribner's, 1901. 726pp. 2nd and rev. ed. 1901. 724pp. OCLC: 13747231 ISB; 4756237 TEJ; 6483819 CFT.

1054 _____. *An Introduction to the Literature of the New Testament.* New York: Scribner's, 1911. Edinburgh: T. & T. Clark, 1911. 630pp. 3rd and rev. ed. 1949. 1961. 659pp. (International Theological Library.) Includes bibl. OCLC: 383596 ISB; 8700796 SOI; 13300020 RCE; 6807456 IAZ.

1055 Monaghan, F. J. *Reflections on the Synoptic Gospels, and Their Special Design.* Staten Island NY: Alba House, 1970. 204pp. OCLC: 91491 ICU.

1056 Montague, G. T. 1972. As reviewer see Gaboury, Antonio. *La Structure* (516).

1057 Montefiore, Claude G. *The Synoptic Gospels.* Ed., with an intro. and a commentary. London: Macmillan, 1909. 2nd ed. rev. and partly rewritten. London: Macmillan, 1927. Rpt of the 1927 edition with a new prolegomenon by Lou H. Silberman. New York: Ktav Pub. House, 1968. 2 vols. (Library of Biblical Studies.) Microfiche. Louisville: Lost Cause Press, 1976. OCLC: 5786745 CFT; 4268236 ISB; 3926192 EXC; 160245; 4726866 ISB.

----- Montefiore, Hugh. *See* Turner, H. E. W. (1596).

1058 Montgomery, Robert M. *The Two-Source Theory and the Synoptic Gospels.* Nashville: Abingdon Press, 1970. 64pp. (Auxiliary Studies in the Bible.) OCLC: 1015403 ICU.

1059 Mora, Vincent. *Le signe de Jonas.* Paris: Editions du Cerf, 1983. 151pp. (Lire la Bible 63.) Includes bibl. OCLC: 11067148 DTM.

1060 Morgenthaler, Robert. *Statistik des neutestamentlichen Wortschatzes.* Zürich: Gotthelf-Verlag, 1958. 188pp.
OCLC: 861846 ISB.

1061 _____. *Statistische Synopse.* Zürich; Stuttgart: Gotthelf-Verlag, 1971. 328pp. Includes bibl.
OCLC: 291084 UTS; 773202 BAN.

1062 Morghen, R. ''Critica neo-testamentaria e storia del cristianesimo in uno scritto inedito di Ernesto Buonaiuti sulla datazione dei Sinottici.'' CrNSt 4 (1983): 205-28.

1063 Morin, Emile. *L'événement Jésus dans les structures de la société juive.* Paris: Editions du Cerf, 1978. 172pp. (Dossiers libres.) Includes bibl.
OCLC: 4902260 MBB.

1064 Morton, A. Q., and G. H. C. Macgregor. *The Structure of Luke and Acts.* New York: Harper & Row; London: Hodder and Stoughton, 1964. 155pp.
OCLC: 766932 BWE; 6081115 ISB.

1065 Mosley, A. W. ''Jesus' Audiences in the Gospels of St. Mark and St. Luke.'' NTS 10 (1963): 139-49.

1066 Moule, Charles F. D. *The Birth of the New Testament.* New York: Harper & Row, 1962. 2nd ed. London: Black, 1966. New York: Harper & Row, 1976. 252pp. 3rd ed., rev. and rewritten. San Francisco: Harper & Row, 1981. London: A. & C. Black, 1981. San Francisco: Harper & Row, 1982. 382pp. (Harper's New Testament Commentaries. Black's New Testament Commentaries.) French. *La genèse du Nouveau Testament.* Version française par Robert Mazerand. Neuchâtel: Delachaux et Niestlé, 1971. 218pp. (Le monde de la Bible.)
OCLC: 538227 OUN; 1068513; 11993909 DTM; 8039482 VYN; 8324216 NNM; 7672819 ISB; 814375 ISB.

1067 _____. ''The Gravamen Against Jesus.'' In *Jesus, the Gospels, and the Church*, E. P. Sanders, ed., 177-95. Macon GA: Mercer University Press, 1987.
OCLC: 16130939 ISB.

1068 _____. *An Idiom Book of New Testament Greek.* 2nd ed. Cambridge: Cambridge University Press, 1959. 1960. 1963. 1975. 246pp. 1st ed., 1953. Includes bibl.
OCLC: 463722 ITD; 3760189 TLT; 4995770 LSL.

1069A _____. ''The Intention of the Evangelists.'' In *New Testament Essays. Studies in Memory of Thomas Walter Manson, 1893–1958*, A. J. B. Higgins, ed., 165-79. Manchester, Eng.: Manchester University Press, 1959.
OCLC: 2879047 ISB.

1069B ————. "The Techniques of New Testament Research." In *Jesus and Man's Hope*, Donald G. Miller and Dikran Y. Hadidian, eds., 2:29-45. Pittsburgh: Pittsburgh Theological Seminary, 1971. (Perspective 2.) OCLC: 142572 ISB.

1070 ————, and A. M. G. Stephenson. "R. G. Heard on Q and Mark." NTS 2 (1955–1956): 114-18.

1071 Moulton, James H. *A Grammar of New Testament Greek.* 4 vols. Edinburgh: T. & T. Clark, 1908–1976.
Contents. 1. Prolegomena by James Hope Moulton, 1908; 2. Accidence and Word-Formation by J. H. Moulton and W. H. Howard, 1929; 3. Syntax by N. Turner, 1963; 4. Style by N. Turner, 1976.
OCLC: 5140278 CWR; 3645404 ISB; 4069814 CFT.

1072 ————. "Synoptic Studies, III. Some Criticism on Professor Harnack's 'Sayings of Jesus.' " Exp 7th ser. 7 (1909): 411-23.

1073 ————, and George Milligan. *The Vocabulary of the Greek Testament Illustrated from the Papyri and Other Non-Literary Sources.* London: Hodder and Stoughton, 1930. Grand Rapids MI: Eerdmans, 1930. Rpts: 1976. 1985. 705pp. Originally issued as eight fascicles, 1914–1929.
OCLC: 5021084 IAY; 554297 ASC; 8681339 MRT; 13510551 PVU.

1074 Moulton, William F., and Alfred S. Geden, eds. *A Concordance to the Greek Testament According to the Texts of Westcott and Hort, Tischendorf, and the English Revisers.* 3rd ed. Edinburgh: T. & T. Clark, 1950. 4th ed., rev. by Harold K. Moulton, 1963. Rpt: 1967. xiv + 1,033pp. 5th ed. 1978. xvi + 1,110pp. With suppl. according to the text of the United Bible Societies' third edition.
OCLC: 12311137 KUK; 167087 IVD; 4157761 ICU.

1075 Muddiman, John. "John's Use of Matthew: A British Exponent of the Theory." EThL 59 (1983): 333-37.

1076 Mudiso Mbâ Mundla, Jean-Gaspard. *See* Mundla, J.-G. Mudiso Mbâ (1080).

1077 Müller, G. H. *Zur Synopse. Untersuchung über die Arbeitsweise des Lukas und Matthäus und ihre Quellen namentlich die Spruchquelle, im Anschluss an eine Synopse Mk–Lk–Mt.* Göttingen: Vandenhoeck & Ruprecht, 1908. 60pp. (Forschungen zur Religion und Literatur des Alten und Neuen Testaments 11.)
OCLC: 3590451 ISB.

1078 Müller, Ulrich B. "Zur Rezeption gesetzeskritischer Jesusüberlieferung im frühen Christentum." NTS 27 (1981): 158-85.

1079 Munck, Johannes. "Presbyters and Disciples of the Lord in Papias. Exegetical Comments on Eusebius, *Ecclesiastical History,* III.39." HThR 52 (1959): 223-43.

1080 Mundla, J.-G. Mudiso Mbâ. *Jesus und die Führer Israels. Studien zu den sog. Jerusalemer Streitgesprächen.* Münster: Aschendorff, 1984. 377pp. (Neutestamentliche Abhandlungen n. F. 17.) Includes bibl.
Originally presented as the author's doctoral thesis, Universität München, 1982-1983, and entitled "Jesu Wirken in Jerusalem."
OCLC: 11238214 ISB.

1081 Muraoka, T. "The Use of ΩΣ in the Greek Bible." NovT 7 (1964): 51-72.

1082 Murphy-O'Connor, J. 1972. As reviewer see Benoit, Pierre, and M.-É. Boismard, *Synopse* (98).

1083A _____. 1976. As reviewer see Lange, Joachim. *Das Erscheinen* (877).

1083B Murray, Gregory. "Did Luke Use Mark?" DR 106 (1986): 268-71.

1083C _____. *The Origin and Purpose of St. Mark's Gospel.* Bath: Downside Abbey, 1987. 6pp.
OCLC: 17983002.

1083D _____. "The Rich Young Man [Table of Synoptic Parallels]." DR 103 (1985): 144-46.

1083E _____. "Saint Peter's Denials." DR 103 (1985): 296-98.

1084 Mussner, Franz. "Das 'Gleichnis' vom gestrengen Mahlherrn (Lk 13,22-30): Ein Beitrag zum Redaktionsverfahren und zur Theologie des Lukas." In his *Praesentia salutis. Gesammelte Studien zu Fragen und Themen des Neuen Testaments,* 113-24. Düsseldorf: Patmos-Verlag, 1967. (Kommentare und Beiträge zum Alten und Neuen Testament.)
OCLC: 8055027 IVD.

1085 Narborough, Frederick D. V. "The Synoptic Problem." In *A New Commentary on Holy Scripture, Including the Apocrypha,* Charles Gore, Henry L. Goudge, and Alfred Guillaume, eds., 2:33-42. London: SPCK; New York: Macmillan, 1928. Rpts: 1929. 1951. 1958.
OCLC: 4108707 OSU; 381771 ISB; 13324396 GCL.

1086 Neill, Stephen. *The Interpretation of the New Testament, 1861–1961.* London; New York: Oxford University Press, 1964. 1st ed., rpt with corrections. 1964. 1966. 360pp. (Firth Lectures 1962.) New ed. *The Interpretation of the New Testament, 1861–1986,* by Stephen Neill and Tom Wright. 1988.
OCLC: 377510 ATO; 6130392 ISB; 3173171 LRU; 16801441.

1087 Neirynck, Frans. "Les accords mineurs et la rédaction des Evangiles, L'épisode du paralytique (Mt IX,1-8/Lc V, 17-26, par. Mc II, 1-12.)" EThL 50 (1974): 215-30.

1088 _____. "The Argument from Order and St. Luke's Transpositions." EThL 49 (1973): 784-815.

_____. *See* Boismard. M.-É. (141).

1089 _____. "Deuteromarcus et les accords Matthieu-Luc." EThL 56 (1980): 397-408.

1090 _____. "Le discours anti-apocalyptique de Mc. XIII." EThL 45 (1969): 154-64.

1091 _____. *Duality in Mark: Contributions to the Study of the Markan Redaction.* Leuven: University Press, 1972. 214pp. (BEThL 31.)
Originally published as "Mark in Greek." EThL 47 (1971): 144-98; "Duality in Mark." EThL 47 (1971): 394-463; "Duplicate Expressions in the Gospel of Mark." EThL 48 (1972): 150-209.
OCLC: 763125 ISB.

1092 _____. "L'Edition du text de Q." EThL 55 (1979): 373-81.
Reissued in *Evangelica: Gospel Studies = Études d'évangile: Collected Essays,* by F. Neirynck, edited by F. van Segbroeck, 925-33. Leuven: University Press and Peeters, 1982. (BEThL 60.)
OCLC: 10403283 ISB.

1093 _____. *Evangelica: Gospel Studies = Evangelica: études d'évangile. Collected Studies.* Ed. by F. van Segbroeck. Leuven: University Press and Peeters, 1982. 1,036pp. (BEThL 60.)
English, Dutch, or French.
OCLC: 10403283 ISB.

1094 _____, ed. *L'Évangile de Luc: problèmes littéraires et théologiques: mémorial Lucien Cerfaux.* Gembloux: J. Duculot, 1973. 385pp. (BEThL 32.)
OCLC: 763098 ISB.

1095 _____. "Les expressions doubles chez Marc et le problème synoptique." EThL 59 (1983): 303-30.

1096 _____. "Le Femmes au tombeau: étude de la redaction Matthéenne (Matt. xxviii.1-10.)" NTS 15 (1969): 168-90.

1097 _____"The Gospel of Matthew and Literary Criticism: A Critical Analysis of A. Gaboury's Hypothesis." In *Society of Biblical Literature 1972 Seminar Papers,* L. C. McGaughy, ed., 147-79. Missoula MT: Society of Biblical Literature, 1972.

1098 _____. "The Griesbach Hypothesis; The Phenomenon of Order." EThL 58 (1982): 111-22.

1099 _____. "Hawkins's Additional Notes to His 'Horae synopticae.' " EThL 46 (1970): 78-111.

1100 _____. "John and the Synoptics: The Empty Tomb Stories." NTS 30 (1984): 161-87.

1101 _____. "La matière marcienne dans l'évangile de Luc." In *L'Évangile de Luc, problèmes littéraires et théologiques: mémorial Lucien Cerfaux,* Frans Neirynck, ed., 157-201. Gembloux: J. Duculot, 1973. (BEThL 32.)
OCLC: 763098 ISB.

1102 _____. "The Matthew-Luke Agreements in Mt 14,13-14 / Lk 9,10-11 (par. Mk 6,30-34.) The Two-Source Theory Beyond the Impasse." EThL 60 (1984): 25-44.

1103 _____. "Minor Agreements Matthew-Luke in the Transfiguration Story." In *Orientierung an Jesus: Zur Theologie der Synoptiker: für Josef Schmid,* P. Hoffmann, et al., eds., 253-66. Freiburg: Herder, 1973. OCLC: 786219 ISB.

1104 _____, ed. *The Minor Agreements of Matthew and Luke Against Mark with a cumulative list.* Ed. Frans Neirynck, in collaboration with Theo Hansen and Frans van Segbroeck. Leuven: University Press, 1974. 330pp. (BEThL 37.) OCLC: 1722135 ISB.

1105 _____. "Mt 12,25a / Lc 11,17a et la rédaction des évangiles." EThL 62 (1986): 122-33.

1106A _____. "Une nouvelle théorie synoptique (à propops de Mc 1, 1-6 et par.) Notes critiques." EThL 44 (1968): 149-53.

1106B _____. "Once More: The Making of a Synopsis." EThL 62 (1986): 141-54.
(CR) Review of Kurt Aland's (15) and Denaux-Vervenne's (357B) synopses.

1107 _____. "Once More: The Symbol Q." EThL 55 (1979): 382-83. Reissued in his *Evangelica: Gospel Studies = Études d'évangile. Collected Essays,* ed. F. van Segbroeck, 689-90. Leuven: University Press and Peeters, 1982. (BEThL 60.) OCLC: 10403283 ISB.

1108 _____. "Paul and the Sayings of Jesus." In *L'Apôtre Paul: Personnalité, style et conception du ministère,* par A. Vanhoye, J. N. Aletti, et al., 265-321. Leuven: University Press and Peeters, 1986. (BEThL 73.) OCLC: 14981178 IDK.

1109 _____, et al., eds. *Proceedings of the Jerusalem Symposium.* See Boismard, M.-É., David L. Dungan, William R. Farmer, and Frans Neirynck, eds. (141).

1110 _____. "Q." In *The Interpreter's Dictionary of the Bible.* Suppl. vol., Keith Crim, ed., 715-16. Nashville: Abingdon Press, 1976.

1111 _____. "Recent Developments in the Study of Q." In *Logia. Les paroles de Jésus = The Sayings of Jesus: Mémorial Joseph Coppens,* Joël Delobel, ed., 29-75. Leuven: University Press and Peeters, 1982. (BEThL 59.) OCLC: 9450792 ISB; 11043145.

1112 _____. "La rédaction matthéenne et la structure du premier évangile." EThL 43 (1967): 41-73.

1113 _____. "The Redactional Text of Mark." EThL 57 (1981): 144-62.

1114 _____. "The Sermon on the Mount in the Gospel Synopsis." EThL 52 (1976): 350-57.

1115 _____. "Studies on Q Since 1972." EThL 56 (1980): 409-13.

1116 _____. "The Symbol Q (= Quelle)." EThL 54 (1978): 119-25. Reissued in his *Evangelica: Gospel Studies = Études d'évangile. Collected Essays,* ed. F. van Segbroeck, 683-89. Leuven: University Press and Peeters, 1982. (BEThL 60.) OCLC: 10403283 ISB.

1117 _____. "Synoptic Problem." In *The Interpreter's Dictionary of the Bible.* Suppl. vol., Keith Crim, ed., 845a-48b. Nashville: Abingdon Press, 1976. Reissued in *The Two-Source Hypothesis: A Critical Appraisal,* Arthur J. Bellinzoni, Jr., ed., 85-93. Macon GA: Mercer University Press, 1985. OCLC: 11599674 ISB.

1118 _____. *Synoptica. Het argument van de acoloethie in de synoptische kwestie.* (Studiorum Novi Testamenti Auxilia 5.) Leuven, 1967.

1119 _____. "Urmarcus redivivus? Examen critique de l'hypothèse des insertions matthéennes dans Mc." In *L'Évangile selon Marc: Tradition et rédaction,* M. Sabbe, et al., eds., 103-45. Leuven: University Press, 1974. (BEThL 34.) OCLC: 2345456 ISB.

1120 _____, et al. *Jean et les synoptiques: Examen critique de l'exégèse de M.-É. Boismard.* Leuven: University Press, 1979. 427pp. (BEThL 49.) OCLC: 6251058 ISB.

1121A _____, and Frans van Segbroeck. "The Griesbach Hypothesis: A Bibliography." In *J. J. Griesbach, Synoptic and Text-Critical Studies, 1776–1976,* Bernard Orchard and Thomas R. W. Longstaff, eds., 176-81. Cambridge; New York: Cambridge University Press, 1978. (SNTSMS 34.) OCLC: 3541663 ISB.

1121B _____, and Frans van Segbroeck. *New Testament Vocabulary. A Companion Volume to the Concordance.* Leuven: University Press, 1984. (BEThL 65.) OCLC: 10889439 ISB.

1122 _____, and Frans van Segbroeck. "Q Bibliography." In *Logia. Les paroles de Jésus = The Sayings of Jesus: Mémorial Joseph Coppens,* Joël Delobel, ed., 561-86. Leuven: University Press and Peeters, 1982. (BEThL 59.) OCLC: 9450792 ISB; 11043145.

1123 _____, and Frans van Segbroeck. "Q Bibliography: Additional List 1981–1985." EThL 62 (1986): 157-65.

1124A Nepper-Christensen, Poul. *Das Matthäusevangelium, ein judenchrist-liches Evangelium.* Aarhus: Universitetsforlaget, 1958. 227pp. (Acta theologica Danica 1.) Includes bibl.
Thesis—Aarhus universitet.
OCLC: 1647538 ISB.

1124B Neudecker, Johann Christian Gotthold. *Lehrbuch der historischkritischen Einleitung in das Neue Testament.* Leipzig: Breitkopf und Härtel, 1840. 736pp.
NUC: NjPT; ICU; MH.

1125 Neugebauer, Fritz. "Die dargebotene Wange und Jesu Gebot der Feindesliebe. Erwägungen zu Lk 6, 27-36/Mt 5, 38-48." ThLZ 110 (1985): 865-76.

1126 _____. "Geistsprüche und Jesuslogien. Erwägungen zu der von der formgeschichtlichen Betrachtungsweise R. Bultmanns angenommenen grundsätzlichen Möglichkeit einer Identität von prophetischen Geistsprüchen mit Logien des irdischen Jesus." ZNW 53 (1962): 218-28.

1127 Neusner, Jacob. *The Idea of Purity in Ancient Judaism.* With a critique and a commentary by Mary Douglas. Leiden: Brill, 1973. 155pp. (Studies in Judaism in Late Antiquity 1. Haskell Lectures 1972–73.) Includes bibl.
OCLC: 896752 ISB.

1128 Newman, Robert C. "Jesus' Self-Understanding According to the So-called Q Material." In *The New Testament Student and His Field,* J. Skilton and C. Ladley, eds., 70-97. Phillipsburg NJ: Presbyterian and Reformed Publishing Co., 1982. (New Testament Student 5.)
OCLC: 9141944 ISB.

1129 _____. "The Synoptic Problem! A Proposal for Handling Both Internal and External Evidence." WThJ 43 (1980): 132-51.

1130 Nicolardot, Firmin. *Les procédés de rédaction des trois premiers évangélistes.* Paris: Fischbacher, 1908. 315pp. Includes bibl.
OCLC: 4476370 IND.

1131 Nineham, Dennis E. 1977. As reviewer see Farmer, William R. *Synoptic Problem* (458).

1132 _____. "Eye-Witness Testimony and the Gospel Tradition." JThS 9 (1958): 13-25, 243-52; 11 (1960): 253-64.

1133 _____. *The Gospel of St. Mark.* Baltimore: Penguin Books, 1963. New York: Seabury Press, 1968. 477pp. (Pelican Gospel Commentaries.) *St. Mark.* Philadelphia: Westminster Press, 1978. 477pp. (Westminster Pelican Commentaries.)
OCLC: 5664461 ISB; 967855; 3120679.

1134A _____. "The Order of Events in St. Mark's Gospel—An Examination of Dr. Dodd's Hypothesis." In *Studies in the Gospels: Essays in Memory of R. H. Lightfoot*, D. E. Nineham, ed., 223-39. Oxford: Blackwell, 1955.
OCLC: 2394516 ISB.

1134B Nissiotis, Nicos A. "The Gospels in the Faith and Life of the Church: A Theological Perspective." In *Jesus and Man's Hope*, Donald G. Miller and Dikran Y. Hadidian, eds., 2:119-39. Pittsburgh: Pittsburgh Theological Seminary, 1971. (Perspective 2.)
OCLC: 142572 ISB.

1135 North, Robert. "Chenoboskion and Q." CBQ 24 (1962): 154-70.

1136 Nunez, M. de Burgos. "Marcos: Las problemas de su communidad y sus objectivos como evangelista." *Communio* 17 (1984): 127-52.

1137 O'Connell, L. J. "Boismard's Synoptic Theory: Exposition and Response." ThTo 26 (1978): 325-42.

1138 O'Neill, J. C. "The Silence of Jesus." NTS 15 (1969): 153-67.

1139 _____. "The Synoptic Problem." NTS 21 (1975): 273-85.

1140 O'Rourke, J. J. "The Article as a Pronoun in the Synoptic Gospels." CBQ 37 (1975): 492-99.

1141 _____. "The Construction with a Verb of Saying as an Indication of Sources in Luke." NTS 21 (1975): 421-23.

1142 _____. "Some Observations on the Synoptic Problem and the Use of Statistical Procedures." NovT 16 (1974): 272-77.

1143 Oberlinner, Lorenz. *Historische Überlieferung und christologische Aussage: zur Frage der Brüder Jesu in der Synopse.* Stuttgart: Verlag Katholisches Bibelwerk, 1975. 396pp. (Forschung zur Bibel 19.) Includes bibl.
Originally presented as the author's thesis, Freiburg i.B., 1974.
OCLC: 2048630 EMU.

1144 Oliver A. *Évangile et critique moderne.* Vol 1: *Prolegomenes;* vol. 2: *Texte et Traduction.* Saint Maurice: Chez l'auteur, 1969.**

1145 Ong, Walter J. *The Presence of the Word: Some Prolegomena for Cultural and Religious History.* New Haven: Yale University Press, 1967. New York: Simon and Schuster, 1970. Minneapolis: University of Minnesota Press, 1981. 360pp. (Terry Lectures.) Includes bibl.
OCLC: 586274; 237329 DRB; 7463915

1146A Orchard, Bernard. "Are All Gospel Synopses Biassed?" ThZ 34 (1978): 149-62.

1146B _____. "The 'Common Step' Phenomenon in the Synoptic Pericopes." In *New Synoptic Studies: The Cambridge Gospel Conference and Beyond,* William R. Farmer, ed., 393-407. Macon GA: Mercer University Press, 1983.
OCLC: 9783753 ISB.

1146C _____, trans. "A Demonstration That Mark Was Written After Matthew and Luke." In *J. J. Griesbach, Synoptic and Text-Critical Studies, 1776–1976*, Bernard Orchard and Thomas R. W. Longstaff, eds., 103-35. Cambridge; New York: Cambridge University Press, 1978. (SNTSMS 34.)
ET of J. J. Griesbach's *Commentatio* (579).
OCLC: 3541663 ISB.

1147A _____. *Matthew, Luke, and Mark*. Manchester: Koinonia Press, 1976. 168pp. (Griesbach Solution to the Synoptic Question 1.)
OCLC: 2400796 ISB.

1147B _____. "The Solution of the Synoptic Problem." *Scripture Bulletin* 18/ 1 (1987): 2-14.

1148A _____. "Some Reflections on the Relationship of Luke to Matthew." In *Jesus, the Gospels, and the Church*, E. P. Sanders, ed., 33-46. Macon GA: Mercer University Press, 1987.
OCLC: 16130939 ISB.

1148B _____. *A Synopsis of the Four Gospels in a New Translation. Arranged according to the Two-Gospel Hypothesis and edited by John Bernard Orchard*. Macon GA: Mercer University Press, 1982. xxv + 294pp. Greek ed.: *A Synopsis of the Four Gospels in Greek. Arranged according to the Two-Gospel Hypothesis and edited by John Bernard Orchard*. Edinburg: T. & T. Clark; Macon GA: Mercer University Press, 1983. xxxiv + 342pp. (Griesbach Solution to the Synoptic Question 2.)
OCLC: 10415086 MNU; 10501588 ISB.

1149A _____. "Thessalonians and the Synoptic Gospels." Bib 19 (1938): 19-42.

1149B _____. "The Two-Gospel Hypothesis or, Some Thoughts on the Revival of the Griesbach Hypothesis." DRev 98 (1980): 267-79.

1150 _____. "Why THREE Synoptic Gospels? A Statement of the Two-Gospel Hypothesis." IThQ 46 (1979): 240-55.

1151 _____, and Thomas R. W. Longstaff, eds. *J. J. Griesbach, Synoptic and Text-Critical Studies, 1776–1976*. Cambridge; New York: Cambridge University Press, 1978. 224pp. (SNTSMS 34.)
Selected papers from the Johann Jakob Griesbach Bicentenary Colloquium, 1776–1976, held at Münster (Westfalen) 26-31 July 1976 on the theme Johann Jakob Griesbach and the development of the investigation of the synoptic problem, 1776–1976.
OCLC: 3541663 ISB.
Review: Cause, M. ETR 55 (1980): 113-19.

1152 _____, and Harold Riley. *The Order of the Synoptics: Why Three Synoptic Gospels*. Macon GA: Mercer University Press, 1987. xiv + 294pp. (Griesbach Solution to the Synoptic Question 3.) Includes bibl.
OCLC: 15283083 ISB.

1153 _____, and J. A. T. Robinson. "Redating Revelation. Two Reviews of Books Redating New Testament Documents." *Ampleforth Journal* 82 (1977): 41-45.*

1154 Ortensio, da Spinetoli. *Matteo: Commento al vangelo della chiesa.* Assisi: Cittadella editrice, 1971. 711pp. 2. ed. rinnovata. 1973. Includes bibl. OCLC: 998906 BWE; 831785 BHA.

1155 Ortiz de Urbina, I. "Una nueva reconstrucción del Diatessaron de Taciano." EE 44 (1969): 519-26.

1156 Osburn, C. D. "The Historical Present in Mark as a Text-Critical Criterion." Bib 64 (1983): 486-500.

1157A Ott, Wilhelm. *Gebet und Heil: Die Bedeutung der Gebetsparänese in der lukanischen Theologie.* München: Kösel-Verlag, 1965. 160pp. (Studien zum Alten und Neuen Testament 12.) Includes bibl. OCLC: 5048369 ISB.

1157B Outler, Albert C. "The Gospel according to St. Mark." PSThJ 33/4 (1980): 3-9.
Revised from a lecture at the University of Dallas, 7 September 1976. Reissued under new title: "Canon Criticism and the Gospel of Mark" in *New Synoptic Studies: The Cambridge Gospel Conference and Beyond,* William R. Farmer, ed., 233-43. Macon GA: Mercer University Press, 1983.
OCLC: (new title) 9783753 ISB.

1157C _____. " 'Gospel Studies' in Transition." In *The Relationships among the Gospels: An Interdisciplinary Dialogue,* William O. Walker, Jr., ed., 17-29. San Antonio: Trinity University Press, 1978. (Trinity University Monograph Series in Religion 5.)
OCLC: 4365624 ISB.

1157D _____. "The Interpretation of the Gospels Today: Some Questions about Aims and Warrants." In *Jesus and Man's Hope,* Donald G. Miller and Dikran Y. Hadidian, eds., 2:47-57. Pittsburgh: Pittsburgh Theological Seminary, 1971. (Perspective 2.)
OCLC: 142572 ISB.

1158 Owen, Henry. *Observations on the Four Gospels: Tending Chiefly to Ascertain the Times of the Publication, and to Illustrate the Form and Manner of Their Composition.* London: T. Payne, 1764. 114pp.
OCLC: 5745295 NDD.

1159 Page, Allen. "Proto-Luke Reconsidered: A Study of Literary Method and Theology in the Gospel of Luke." Ph.D. diss. in progress, Duke University, 1985.*

1160 Palmer, Humphrey. *The Logic of Gospel Criticism: An Account of the Methods and Arguments used by Textual, Documentary, Source, and Form Critics of the New Testament.* London: Macmillan, 1968. New York: St. Martin's Press, 1968. 260pp. Includes bibl.
OCLC: 387608 ISB.

1161A Palmer, N. H. "Lachmann's Argument." NTS 13 (1967): 368-78. Reissued in *The Two-Source Hypothesis: A Critical Appraisal,* Arthur J. Bellinzoni, Jr., ed., 119-31. Macon GA: Mercer University Press, 1985. OCLC: 11599674 ISB.

1161B Panikkar, Raymond. "The Relation of the Gospels to Hindu Culture." In *Jesus and Man's Hope,* Donald G. Miller and Dikran Y. Hadidian, eds., 247-61. Pittsburgh: Pittsburgh Theological Seminary, 1971. (Perspective 2.) OCLC: 142572 ISB.

1162 Parker, Pierson. *Good News in Matthew: Matthew in Today's English Version.* London: Fontana Books in cooperation with the Bible Reading Fellowship, 1976. Cleveland: Collins & World, 1976. 283pp. OCLC: 13948931 GTX; 3866828 TWS.

1163 _____. *The Gospel Before Mark.* Chicago: University of Chicago Press, 1953. 266pp. OCLC: 3051141 ISB.

1164A _____. "Herod Antipas and the Death of Jesus." In *Jesus, the Gospels, and the Church,* E. P. Sanders, ed., 197-208. Macon GA: Mercer University Press, 1987. OCLC: 16130939 ISB.

1164B _____. "The Posteriority of Mark." In *New Synoptic Studies: The Cambridge Gospel Conference and Beyond,* William R. Farmer, ed., 67-142. Macon GA: Mercer University Press, 1983. OCLC: 9783753 ISB.

1165 _____. "A Second Look at *The Gospel Before Mark.*" JBL 100 (1981): 389-413.
Reissued in *Society of Biblical Literature 1979 Seminar Papers,* 1:151-61. Chico CA: Scholars Press, 1979. *The Two-Source Hypothesis: A Critical Appraisal,* Arthur J. Bellinzoni, Jr., ed., 205-17. Macon GA: Mercer University Press, 1985. OCLC: 11599674 ISB.

1166A Paschen, Wilfrid. *Rein und unrein: Untersuchung zur biblischen Wortgeschichte.* München: Kösel-Verlag, 1970. 219pp. (Studien zum Alten und Neuen Testament 24.) Includes bibl.
Originally presented as the author's thesis, Würzburg. OCLC: 364505 ISB.

1166B Patte, Daniel. *The Gospel according to Matthew: A Structural Commentary on Matthew's Faith.* Philadelphia: Fortress Press, 1987. xvi+432pp. Includes bibl. OCLC: 13861205 ISB.

1167 Patton, C. S. "Did Mark Use Q? Or Did Q Use Mark?" AJT 16 (1912): 634-42.

1168A ———. *Sources of the Synoptic Gospels.* New York; London: Macmillan, 1915. Rpt: New York: Johnson Reprint Corp, 1967. 263pp. (University of Michigan Studies. Humanistic Series 5.)
The author's doctoral dissertation, University of Michigan, but not published as a thesis.
OCLC: 2577398 ISB; 350665 YNG.

1168B Paulus, Heinrich Eberhard Gottlob. *Exegetisches Handbuch über die drei ersten Evangelien.* Heidelberg: C. F. Winter, 1830–1833. 3 vols. 2nd ed. 1842.
OCLC: 14765120 ISB.

1168C ———. *Philologisch-kritischer und historischer Commentar über die drey ersten Evangelien.* Lübeck: J. F. Bohn, 1800–1804. 2. verb. Ausg. 1804–1805. Reissued in Leipzig in 1812. 4 vols. (His *Philologisch-kritischer und historischer Commentar über das neue Testament 1-3.*)
NUC: ICU; 1812 IEG, MH-AH. OCLC: 1804–1805 10094701 WTS.

1168D ———. *Theologisch-exegetisches Conservatorium, oder, Auswahl aufbewahrungswerther Aufsätze und Zerstreuter Bemerkungen über die alt- und neutestamentlichen Religionsurkunden.* 1ste Lieferung: *Eine Reihe von Erörterungen über den Ursprung der drey ersten Evangelien.* Heidelberg: A. Oswald, 1822.
NUC: ICU; NNUT; MH-AH.

1169 Pautrel, R. "Des Abréviations subies par quelques sentences de Jésus dans la rédaction synoptique." RSR 24 (1934): 344-65.

1170 Peabody, David B. "Augustine and the Augustinian Hypothesis: A Reexamination of Augustine's Thought in *De consensu evangelistarum.*" In *New Synoptic Studies: The Cambridge Gospel Conference and Beyond,* W. R. Farmer, ed., 37-64. Macon GA: Mercer University Press, 1983.
First presented at the Southwest Seminar on the Development of Early Catholic Christianity, September 1982.
OCLC: 9783753 ISB.

1171 ———. "Chapters in the History of the Linguistic Argument for Solving the Synoptic Problem: The Nineteenth Century in Context." In *Jesus, the Gospels, and the Church,* E. P. Sanders, ed., 47-68. Macon GA: Mercer University Press, 1987.
First presented at a Colloquy of the Graduate Program in Religious Studies, Southern Methodist University, 23 March 1984, and subsequently at the Symposium de interrelatione evangeliorum, Jerusalem, Israel, 7-23 April 1984.
OCLC: 16130939 ISB.

1172A ———. "In Retrospect and Prospect." PSThJ 40/2 (1987): 9-16.
A contextual review of *The Two-Source Hypothesis: A Critical Appraisal,* ed. by Arthur J. Bellinzoni, Jr. (94). First read at a colloquy on "New Critical Approaches in Synoptic Studies" held at Southern Methodist University, fall semester, 1986.

1172B _____. ''The Late Secondary Redaction of Mark's Gospel and the Griesbach Hypothesis: A Response to Helmut Koester.'' In *Colloquy on New Testament Studies: A Time for Reappraisal and Fresh Approaches*, Bruce C. Corley, ed., 87-132. Macon GA: Mercer University Press, 1983.

First presented at the Colloquy on New Testament Studies, Southwestern Baptist Theological Seminary, Fort Worth, Texas, 5 November 1980. OCLC: 9489011 ISB.

1173 _____. ''The Logical Development of 'Reception' Sayings Within the Synoptic Tradition.'' 1984.

Presented and discussed at a conference on the topic, ''Order in the Synoptic Gospels: Patterns of Agreement Within Pericopes,'' sponsored by the Center for the Study of Religion in the Greco-Roman World, Southern Methodist University, Dallas, Texas, 9-10 November 1984.

1174 _____. *Mark as Composer*. Macon GA: Mercer University Press; Leuven: Peeters, 1987. 216pp. (New Gospel Studies 1.)

A revision of the author's Ph.D. diss., Southern Methodist University, 1983, ''The Redactional Features of the Author of Mark'' (1176). OCLC: 13525188 ISB.

1175 _____. ''A Pre-Markan Prophetic Sayings Tradition and the Synoptic Problem.'' JBL 97 (1978): 391-409.

Previously read at the Southwestern Regional Meeting of the Society of Biblical Literature, Enid, Oklahoma, March 1977. Response by Werner Kelber. Paper developed while participating in the Southwest Regional Seminar on Gospel Studies, Dallas, Texas, 1976-1979.

1176 _____. ''The Redactional Features of the Author of Mark: A Method Focusing on Recurrent Phraseology and Its Application.'' Ph.D. diss., Southern Methodist University, 1983. 455 leaves. Photocopy. Ann Arbor MI: University Microfilms International, 1984. Microfilm, 1984. Microfiche. 1984. Includes bibl.

Revision published in 1987 as *Mark as Composer* (1174). OCLC: 10326177 ISB; 13343220 EXN; 10862200 VYN.

1177 _____. ''A Response to Multi-Stage Theories of Synoptic Relationships.'' Forthcoming in *Proceedings of the Jerusalem Symposium*. See Boismard, M.-É., David L. Dungan, William R. Farmer, and Frans Neirynck, eds. (141).

First presented at the Symposium de interrelatione evangeliorum, Jerusalem, Israel, 7-23 April 1984.

1178 _____. ''St. Augustine on the Interrelationships among the Gospels,'' 1982.

Read in the Section on the Synoptic Gospels, Society of Biblical Literature national meeting, New York, December 1982.

1179 _____. "William Reuben Farmer: A Biographical and Bibliographical Essay." In *Jesus, the Gospels, and the Church*, E. P. Sanders, ed., ix-xxx. Macon GA: Mercer University Press, 1987.
OCLC: 16130939 ISB.

1180 Perler, Othmar. "L'Evangile de Pierre et Méliton de Sardes." RB 71 (1964): 584-90.

1181 Perrin, Norman. "Apocalyptic Christianity: The Synoptic Source 'Q'; The Apocalyptic Discourses; The Book of Revelation." In *Visionaries and Their Apocalypses*, P. D. Hanson, ed., 121-45. Philadelphia: Fortress Press; London: SPCK, 1983. (Issues in Religion and Theology 2.) "The Source Q," 131-34. First published in 1974 (1184, pp. 65-85).
OCLC: 9371261 ISB.

1182 _____. "The Composition of Mark ix 1." NovT 11 (1969): 67-70.

1183 _____. "Historical Criticism, Literary Criticism, and Hermeneutics: The Interpretation of the Parables of Jesus and the Gospel of Mark Today." JR 52 (1972): 361-75.

1184 _____. *The New Testament, An Introduction: Proclamation and Parenesis, Myth and History.* New York: Harcourt Brace Jovanovich, 1974. 385pp. 2nd ed., under the general editorship of Robert Ferm. 1982. 516pp. Includes bibl.
OCLC: 900760 ISB; 8585215.

1185 _____. *Rediscovering the Teaching of Jesus.* London: SCM, 1967. New York: Harper & Row, 1967. 1st paperback ed. 1976. 272pp. Includes bibl.
OCLC: 1987342 CIN; 382610 ISB; 2922350 KKU; 2967318.

1186 _____. "The Son of Man in the Synoptic Tradition." BR 13 (1968): 3-25.

1187 _____. *What is Redaction Criticism?* Philadelphia: Fortress Press, 1969. London: SPCK, 1970. 86pp. (Guides to Biblical Scholarship.) Includes bibl.
OCLC: 27247 ISB; 121657.

1188 Perrot, Charles. "Les prophètes de la violence et la nouveauté des temps. Matthieu 11,12-13." In *L'Ancien et le nouveau.* J. Doré, et al., eds., 93-109. Paris: Cerf, 1982. (Cogitatio fidei 111.)
OCLC: 8995581 DDC.

1189A Perry, Alfred M. "The Growth of the Gospels." In *The Interpreter's Bible*, George A. Buttrick, et al., eds., 7:60-74. New York; Nashville: Abingdon Press, 1951.
Esp. "The Synoptic Problem," 61-62.

1189B _____. *The Sources of Luke's Passion-Narrative.* Chicago: University of Chicago Press, 1920. 128pp. (Historical and Linguistic Studies in Literature Related to the New Testament 2nd ser., IV/2.)
OCLC: 4555884 ISB.

1190 Pesce, Mauro. "Ricostruzione dell'archetipo letterario comune a Mt 22, 1-10 e Lc 14, 15-24." In *La Parabola degli invitati al banchetto: dagli évangelisti a Gesù,* Jacques Dupont, et al., eds., 167-236. Brescia: Paideia, 1978. (Testi e ricerche di Scienze Religiose 14.) OCLC: 4779789.

1191 Pesch, Rudolf. "Berufung und Sendung, Nachfolge und Mission. Eine Studie zu Mk I, 16-20." ZKTh 91 (1969): 1-31.

1192 _____. *Das Markusevangelium.* Freiburg im Breisgau; Basel; Wien: Herder, 1976–1977. 2., durchges. Aufl. 1977–1980. 3., erneut durchges. Aufl., mit einem Nachtrag. 1980– . 2 vols. (Herder's theologischer Kommentar zum Neuen Testament 2. *Das Markus-Evangelium.*) Darmstadt: Wissenschaftliche Buchgesellschaft, 1979. 413pp. (Wege der Forschung 411.) Italian. *Il vangelo di Marco, parte prima: testo greco e traduzione, introduzione e commento ai capp. 1, 1-8, 26.* Traduzione italiana di Marcello Soffritti. Ed. italiana, a cura di Omero Soffritti. Brescia: Paideia, 1980. 658pp. (Commentario teologico del Nuovo Testamento 2/1.)
Contents: 1. Teil. *Einleitung und Kommentar zu Kap. 1.1-8.26,* 2. Teil. *Kommentar zu Kap. 8.27-16.20.*
OCLC: 2600878; 4189839; 10966998 CLU; 7402623 ISB; 5398173; 7387462 IDJ.

1193 _____. *Naherwartungen: Tradition und Redaktion in Mark 13.* Düsseldorf: Patmos-Verlag, 1968. 275pp. (Kommentare und Beiträge zum Alten und Neuen Testament.)
Issued also as thesis, Freiburg i. B.
OCLC: 392224 ATO.

1194 _____. "Ein Tag vollmächtigen Wirkens Jesu in Kapharnaum (Mk 1, 21-34; 35-39). (Dritter Teil)." BiLe 9 (1968): 114-28.

1195 _____. "Über die Autorität Jesu: eine Rückfrage anhand des Bekenner- und Verleugnerspruchs Lk 12, 8f. par." In *Kirche des Anfangs: Festschr. für Heinz Schürmann zum 65. Geburtstag,* Rudolf Schnackenburg, Josef Ernst, and Joachim Wanke, eds., 25-55. Leipzig: St.-Benno-Verlag, 1977. Freiburg; Basel; Wien: Herder, 1978. (Erfurter theologische Studien 38.)
OCLC: 4079038; 6381479 DRU; 4476698 NOC.

1196 Petrie, C. Sewart. "The Proto-Luke Hypothesis." ET 54 (1942–1943): 172-77.

1197 _____. " 'Q' Is Only What You Make It." NovT 3 (1959): 28-33.

1198 Philips, Gérard. *L'union personnelle avec le Dieu vivant: essai sur l'origine et le sens de la grâce créée.* Gembloux: J. Duculot, 1974. 299pp. (BEThL 36.) Spanish. *Inhabitación Trinitaria y Gracia: La Union personal con el Dios vivo. Ensayo sobre el origen y el sentido de la gracia creada.* Presentación y traducción de Julián Lopez Martín. Salamanca: Secretariado Trinitario, 1980. 379pp. (Koinonia 12.)
OCLC: 1159065 EMU; 15534903 EBS.

1199 Piper, Otto A. "The Origin of the Gospel Pattern." JBL 78 (1959): 115-24.

1200 Piper, Ronald A. "Matthew 7, 7-11 par. Luke 11, 9-13. Evidence of Design and Argument in the Collection of Jesus' Sayings." In *Logia. Les paroles de Jésus = The Sayings of Jesus: Mémorial Joseph Coppens,* Joël Delobel, ed., 411-18. Leuven: University Press and Peeters, 1982. (BEThL 59.)
OCLC: 9450792 ISB; 11043145 UTS.

1201 Plooij, Daniel. *A Further Study of the Liège Diatessaron.* Leiden: Brill, 1925. 92pp.
OCLC: 2692716 ISB.

1202 Plummer, Alfred. *A Critical and Exegetical Commentary on the Gospel According to St. Luke.* Edinburgh: T. & T. Clark; New York: Scribner's, 1896. 2nd ed. 1898. 10th ed. 1914. lxxxviii + 590pp. (International Critical Commentary.)
OCLC: 1283072 BHA; 4585259 CIN; 4830630 COI.

1203 _____. *An Exegetical Commentary on the Gospel According to S. Matthew.* London: James Clarke, 1909. 2nd ed. 1910. xlvi + 451pp. 3rd ed. 1915. Rpts of 2nd ed.: Minneapolis: James Family Christian Pub. Co., 1979; Grand Rapids MI: Eerdmans, 1960. Microfiche. Pastors Resource Services, 1971. Chattanooga TN: Expositor's Microfilm Library, 1978? Rpt: Grand Rapids: Baker Book House, 1982. 451pp. (Thornapple Commentaries.) Includes bibl.
OCLC: 7356670 ISB; 6495371 IHT; 6368172 CDC; 7002398 TBI; 9240677 BWE.

1204 _____. *The Gospel According to St. Mark.* Cambridge: Cambridge University Press, 1915. xlviii + 211pp. 1920. 1926. 1938. Grand Rapids MI: Baker Book House, 1982. lvi + 392pp. (Cambridge Bible for Schools and Colleges.) Microfiche. Chicago: American Theological Library Association, 1985. (ATLA monograph preservation program; ATLA Fiche 1985–3448.)
OCLC: 3406516 ISB; 8951558 MRT; 17493234.

1205 Plummer, Charles. "A Medieval Illustration of the Documentary Theory of the Origin of the Synoptic Gospels." Exp 3rd ser. 10 (1889): 23-35.

1206 Pokorny, Petr. "The Temptation Stories and Their Intention." NTS 20 (1974): 115-27.

1207 _____. "Die Worte Jesu nach der Logienquelle im Lichte des zeitgenössischen Judentums." *Kairos* 11 (1969): 172-80.

1208 Polag, Athanasius. *Die Christologie der Logienquelle.* Neukirchen-Vluyn: Neukirchener-Verlag, 1977. 213pp. (Wissenschaftlichen Monographien zum Alten und Neuen Testament 45.) Includes bibl.
A revision of the author's thesis, Trier, 1969.
OCLC: 3277808 ISB.
Reviews: Hoffmann, P. ThRv 79 (1983): 205-208; Moloney, F. J. Salm 44 (1982): 848-49.

1209 _____. *Fragmenta Q: Textheft zur Logienquelle.* Neukirchen-Vluyn: Neukirchener Verlag, 1979. 102pp. Includes bibl.
Text in Greek; prefatory matter in English and German.
OCLC: 7178302; 6758639 EMT.
Review: Kingsbury, J. D. RelStR 5 (1979): 224.

1210 _____. "Die theologische Mitte der Logienquelle." In *Das Evangelium und die Evangelien: Vorträge vom Tübinger Symposium 1982,* P. Stuhlmacher, ed., 103-11. Tübingen: J. C. B. Mohr (Paul Siebeck), 1983. (Wissenschaftliche Untersuchungen zum Neuen Testament 28.)
OCLC: 10371104 ISB.

1211 _____. "Der Umfang der Logienquelle." Diss. Lic. Theol. Trier, 1966 (see 1208).

1212 _____. "Zu den Stufen der Christologie in Q." In *Studia Evangelica,* IV:72-74. Berlin: Akademie-Verlag, 1968. (Texte und Untersuchungen 102.)
OCLC: 1637245 ISB; 13641309 BZM.

1213 Porúbcan, Štefan. "Form Criticism and the Synoptic Problem." NovT 7 (1964): 81-118.

1214A Powers, B. W. "The Shaking of the Synoptics. A Report on the Cambridge Conference on the Synoptic Gospels, August, 1979." RTR 39 (1980): 33-39.

1214B _____. "The Writing of the Synoptic Gospels: A Study in the History and the Solution of the Synoptic Problem." Petersham, Australia: Powers, 1985.
A limited photocopy edition circulated by the author. Available from the author: 259A Trafalgar Street, Petersham, N.S.W. 2049, Australia.

1215 Preuschen, Erwin. *Untersuchungen zum Diatessaron Tatians.* Heidelberg: C. Winter, 1918. 63pp. (Sitzungsberichte der Heidelberger Akademie der Wissenschaften. Philosophisch-historische Klasse, 1918, 15. Abhandlung.)
OCLC: 7719956 COO.

1216 Pryke, E. J. "ἴδε and ἰδού ." NTS 14 (1968): 418-24.

1217 _____. *Redactional Style in the Marcan Gospel. A Study of Syntax and Vocabulary as Guides to Redaction in Mark.* Cambridge; New York: Cambridge University Press, 1978. 196pp. (SNTSMS 33.) Includes bibl.
OCLC: 3073587 ISB.

1218 Puig i Tàrrech, Armand. "La parabole des talents (Mt 25, 14-30) ou des mines (Lc 19, 11-28.)" In *À cause de l'évangile: Études sur les Synoptiques et les Actes: Offertes au P. Jacques Dupont, O. S. B. à l'occasion de son 70e anniversaire,* 165-94. Paris: Cerf, 1985. (Lectio divina 123.)
OCLC: 14377925 DTM.

1219 Ramsay, William Mitchell. "The Oldest Written Gospel." In his *Luke, the Physician and Other Studies in the History of Religion*, 69-101. London; New York: Hodder and Stoughton, 1908. Rpts: Minneapolis: James Family Christian Pub. Co., 1978; Grand Rapids MI: Baker Book House, 1979.
Ramsay thinks that Q was written when Jesus was still alive.
OCLC: 3222576 ISB; 9084931 PLF; 4757725 IGR; 7501878 TBI.

1220 Randellini, L. "Recenti tentativi per risolvere la questione sinottica." RivBib 7 (1959): 159-72, 242-57.

1221 Rawlinson, A. E. J. *St. Mark*. With introduction, commentary, and additional notes. London: Methuen, 1925. 2nd ed. 1927. 3rd ed. 1931. 4th ed. 1936. 5th ed. 1942. 7th ed. 1949. 278pp. (Westminster Commentaries.)
OCLC: 6395369 ISB; 3067214 CSM; 6044636 ISB; 1970111 TYC; 3954133 AFU; 4184451 CFT.

1222 Redlich, Edwin B. *The Student's Introduction to the Synoptic Gospels*. London: Longmans, Green, and Co., 1936. 275pp.
OCLC: 1025012 ISB.

1223 Rehkopf, Friedrich. *Die lukanische Sonderquelle: Ihr Umfang und Sprachgebrauch*. Tübingen: J. C. B. Mohr (Paul Siebeck), 1959. 106pp. (Wissenschaftliche Untersuchungen zum Neuen Testament 5.) Includes bibl.
OCLC: 1276147 ISB.

1224A Reicke, Bo. "Griesbach und die synoptische Frage. Beiträge zu einem Griesbach Symposium an der Universität Münster im Juli 1976." ThZ 32 (1976): 341-59.

1224B _____. "From Strauss to Holtzmann and Meijboom. Synoptic Theories Advanced During the Consolidation of Germany, 1830–1870." NovT 29/1 (1987): 1-21.

1225 _____. "Griesbach's Answer to the Synoptic Question." In *J. J. Griesbach, Synoptic and Text-Critical Studies, 1776–1976*, Bernard Orchard and Thomas R. W. Longstaff, eds., 50-67. Cambridge; New York: Cambridge University Press, 1978. (SNTSMS 34.)
OCLC: 3541663 ISB.

1226A _____. "The Historical Setting of John's Baptism." In *Jesus, the Gospels, and the Church*, E. P. Sanders, ed., 209-24. Macon GA: Mercer University Press, 1987.
OCLC: 16130939 ISB.

1226B _____. "Den primära israelsmissionen och hednamissionen engligt Synoptikerna." SvTK 26 (1950): 77-100.

1226C _____. *The Roots of the Synoptic Gospels*. Philadelphia: Fortress Press, 1986. x + 191pp.
OCLC: 13124951.

1226D ———. "A Test of Synoptic Relationships: Matthew 10:17-23 and 24:9-14 with Parallels." In *New Synoptic Studies: The Cambridge Gospel Conference and Beyond,* William R. Farmer, ed., 209-29. Macon GA: Mercer University Press, 1983.
OCLC: 9783753 ISB.

1227 Reiling, J. "The Use and Translation of *kai egeneto,* 'and It Happened' in the New Testament." BTr 16 (1965): 153-63.

1228 Rengstorf, Karl Heinrich. *Das Evangelium nach Lukas.* Göttingen: Vandenhoeck & Ruprecht, 1936. 8. überarbeitete und vielfach ergänzte Aufl. 1958. 9., durchges. und ergänzte Aufl. 1962. 10., durchges. Aufl. 1965. 16. Aufl. 1975. 294pp. (Das Neue Testament Deutsch 3.)
OCLC: 1198314 BPS; 6808948 SDN; 6076305 VYN; 3253939 YU#.

1229 Resch, Alfred. *Agrapha: aussercanonische Evangelienfragmente.* Gesammelt und untersucht von Alfred Resch. Anhang: *Das Evangelienfragment von Fajjum,* von Adolf Harnack. Leipzig: J. C. Hinrichs, 1889. 520pp. (Texte und Untersuchungen 5/4.)
OCLC: 1105478 BHA.

1230 ———. *Agrapha: aussercanonische Schriftfragmente.* Gesammelte und untersucht und in zweiter völlig neu bearbeiteter durch alttestamentliche Agrapha vermehrter Auflage hrsg. von Alfred Resch, mit fünf Registern. Leipzig: J. C. Hinrichs, 1906. Rpt: Darmstadt: Wissenschaftliche Buchgesellschaft, 1967. 426pp. (Texte und Untersuchungen, 30/3-4.)
OCLC: 1101841 BHA; 4046947 TXR.

1231 ———. *Aussercanonische Paralleltexte zu den Evangelien.* Leipzig: J. C. Hinrichs, 1893–1897. 5 vols. in 3. (Texte und Untersuchungen 10/1-5.)
OCLC: 1105459 BHA.

1232 ———. "Τὰ λόγια ᾽Ιησοῦ—יֵשׁוּעַ דִּבְרֵי. Ein Beitrag zur synoptischen Evangelienforschung." In *Theologische Studien.* Herrn Wirkl. Oberkonsistorialrath Professor D. Bernhard Weiss zu seiner 70. Geburtstage dargebracht, C. R. Gregory, et al., 95-128. Göttingen: Vandenhoeck & Ruprecht, 1897.
OCLC: 6712206 NDD.

1233 ———. "Die Kriterien einer objektiven Quellenforschung." ZKWL 9 (1888): 495-504.

1234 ———. *Die Logia Jesu nach dem griechischen und hebräischen Text wiederhergestellt.* Leipzig: J. C. Hinrichs, 1898. 301pp.
OCLC: 10093219 MBB.

1235 ———. "Miscellen zur neutestamentlichen Schriftforschung." ZKWL 8 (1888): 84-91, 144-48, 177-86, 232-45, 279-95.

1236 _____. *Der Paulinismus und die Logia Jesu in ihrem gegenseitigen Verhältnis.* Leipzig: J. C. Hinrichs, 1904. 656pp. (Texte und Untersuchungen 27.) Includes bibl.
OCLC: 1097381 BHA.

1237 _____. "Pragmatische Analyse der grossen Einschaltung des Lukas. Lukas 9, 51-18, 14." JDTh 21 (1876): 654-96; JDTh 22 (1877): 65-92.

1238 Rese, Martin. "Das Lukas-Evangelium. Ein Forschungsbericht." ANRW 25/3 (1985): 2258-2328.

1239 Reuss, Eduard W. E. "Étude comparative sur les trois premiers évangiles au point de vue de leurs rapports d'origine et de dependance mutuelle." RThPh 10 (1855): 65-83; RThPh 11 (1856): 163-88; RThPh 15 (1860): 1-32.
Also published in RTh(P) 2 (1859): 15-72.

1240 _____. *History of the Sacred Scriptures of the New Testament.* Trans. from the 5th rev. and enl. German ed., with numerous bibl. add's. by Edward L. Houghton. 2 vols. Edinburgh: T. & T. Clark; Boston: Houghton, Mifflin and Co., 1884. 638pp. Trans. of *Die Geschichte der Heiligen Schriften Neuen Testaments.* Halle: C. A. Schwetschke und Sohn, 1842. 278pp. 2., durchaus umgearbeitete und stark vermehrte Ausgabe. Braunschweig: C. A. Schwetschke und Sohn, 1853. 586pp. 4. verm. und verb. Aufl. 1864. 626pp.
OCLC: 3463295 ISB; 3411739 RSC; 13757392 ISB; 6888085 ISB; 8980212 IWT.

1241 Reville, Albert. *Étude critiques sur l'Évangile selon Saint Matthieu.* Leiden: D. Noothoven van Goor, 1862. 346pp.
OCLC: 16713937 IXT.

1242 Richardson, Alan. *The Gospels in the Making: An Introduction to the Recent Criticism of the Synoptic Gospels.* London: Student Christian Movement Press, 1938. 190pp. Includes bibl.
OCLC: 4227712 ISB.

1243 Richardson, Peter. "The Thunderbolt in Q and the Wise Man in Corinth." In *From Jesus to Paul: Studies in Honour of Francis Wright Beare,* P. Richardson and J. C. Hurd, eds., 91-111. Waterloo: Wilfrid Laurier University Press, 1984.
OCLC: 11357157 ISB.

1244 _____, and P. Gooch. "Logia of Jesus in 1 Corinthians." In *The Jesus Tradition Outside the Gospels,* D. Wenham, ed., 39-62. Sheffield: JSOT Press, 1985. 419pp. (Gospel Perspectives 5.)
OCLC: 12509903 DTM.

1245 Riesenfeld, Harald. *The Gospel Tradition and Its Beginnings: A Study in the Limits of "Formgeschichte." An Address Delivered at the Opening Session of the Congress on the Four Gospels in 1957, in the Examination Schools, Oxford, on 16 September, 1957.* London: A. R. Mowbray, 1957. 1961. 30pp.
OCLC: 3926943 EXC; 4070222 TXD.

1246 _____. *The Gospel Tradition: Essays.* Foreword by W. D. Davies. Oxford: Blackwell, 1970. Philadelphia: Fortress Press, 1970. 214pp. Eight chs. trans. from the Swedish and French by E. Margaret Rowley; one ch. trans. from the German by Robert A. Kraft. OCLC: 162312 TWH; 98164 ISB.

1247 Riesner, Rainer. *Jesus als Lehrer: Eine Untersuchung zum Ursprung der Evangelien-Überlieferung.* 2., verbesserte Auflage. Tübingen: J. C. B. Mohr (Paul Siebeck), 1984. xii + 615pp. (Wissenschaftliche Untersuchungen zum Neuen Testament. 2. Reihe.) Includes bibl. OCLC: 10584559

1248 _____. "Wie sicher ist die Zwei-Quellen-Theorie?" ThBe 8 (1977): 49-73.

1249 _____. "Wie steht es um die synoptische Frage? Gedanken zur Cambridge Griesbach Conference 1979." ThBe 11 (1980): 80-83.

1250 Rigaux, Beda. "Le petite apocalypse de Luc (XVII, 22-37.)" In *Ecclesia a Spiritu Sancto Edocta: Mélanges théologiques hommages à Mgr Gérard Philips,* J. Coppens, et al., eds., 407-38. Gembloux: J. Duculot, 1970. (BEThL 27.) OCLC: 626935 ISB.

---- Riley, Harold. *See* Orchard, Bernard (1152).

1251 Rist, John M. *On the Independence of Matthew and Mark.* Cambridge; New York: Cambridge University Press, 1978. 132pp. (SNTSMS 32.) OCLC: 2542593. Review. Longstaff, T. R. W. JBL 100 (1981): 127-30.

1252A Ritschl, Albrecht B. *Das Evangelium Marcions und das Kanonische Evangelium des Lukas.* Tübingen: Osiander, 1846. 301pp. NUC: ICU; MH; NjPT; CtY-D.

1252B _____. "Über den Gegenwartigen Stand der Kritik der synoptischen Evangelien." ThJb(T) 10 (1851): 480-538.

1253 Robbins, V. K. "Picking Up the Fragments: From Crossan's Analysis to Rhetorical Analysis." *Forum* 1/2 (1985): 31-64. Review article of John D. Crossan, *In Fragments* (319).

1254 Roberts, James Hall. *The Q Document.* New York: Morrow, 1964. Greenwich: Fawcett, 1965. 289pp. Fiction (a spy-style novel). OCLC: 770316 BRL; 13072554 XCA.

1255A Robertson, Archibald Thomas. *A Harmony of the Gospels for Students of the Life of Christ. Based on the Broadus Harmony in the Revised Version.* New York; London: Harper & Bros., 1922. xxxvii + 305pp. Based on Broadus's *Harmony* which Robertson edited and revised (175B). Esp. "About Harmonies of the Gospels," 253-54; "Synoptic Criticism," 25-56.

1255B _____. "The Christ of the Logia." Ch. 1 in his *The Christ of the Logia,*
15-41. New York: George H. Doran; London: Hodder & Stoughton;
Nashville: Southern Baptist Convention, 1924. 247pp.
This ch. is the only one of the 13 chs. to deal with Q.
OCLC: 2678562 ISB; 11258334 MCM; 8860398 CBS.

1256 _____. *A Grammar of the Greek New Testament in the Light of Histor-*
ical Research. London: Hodder & Stoughton; New York: George H.
Doran Co., 1914. 1,360pp. 2nd ed. with addenda. 1915. 1,367pp. 3rd
ed. with addenda and indexes to addenda of 2nd and 3rd eds. 1920. 4th
ed. 1923. 5th ed. 1931. Rpt: Nashville: Broadman Press, c1934.
lxxxvi + 1,454pp. Includes bibl.
OCLC: 2482851 ISB; 3087543 ISB; 878300 BPS; 1878774 BWE; 6634245
MOG; 3511617 NBC; 1619582 BCT.

1257 _____. *An Introduction to the Textual Criticism of the New Testament.*
New York: Doran; London: Hodder & Stoughton; Nashville: Broadman
Press, 1925. 2nd ed. Garden City: Doubleday, Doran & Co., 1928.
300pp. Includes bibl.
OCLC: 5807846 NNM; 3603208 CSM; 9368232 EXN; 4634760 IDA;
3652691 IWW.

1258 Robinson, James M. "Basic Shifts in German Theology." Interp 16 (1962):
76-97.

1259 _____. "Early Collections of Jesus' Sayings." In *Logia. Les paroles*
de Jésus = The Sayings of Jesus: Mémorial Joseph Coppens, Joël Delobel, ed., 389-94. Leuven: University Press and Peeters, 1982. (BEThL
59.)
OCLC: 9450792 ISB; 11043145.

1260 _____. "Jesus—From Easter to Valentinus (or to the Apostles' Creed)."
JBL 101 (1982): 5-37.

1261 _____. "Jesus as Sophos and Sophia: Wisdom Tradition and the Gos-
pels." In *Aspects of Wisdom in Judaism and Early Christianity,* Robert
Louis Wilken, ed., 1-16. Notre Dame IN: University of Notre Dame
Press, 1975. (Studies in Judaism and Christianity in Antiquity 1.)
OCLC: 1418485 ISB.

1262 _____. "Judaism, Hellenism, Christianity: Jesus' Followers in Galilee
until 70 C.E." AF 53 (1985): 241-50.

1263 _____. "Kerygma and History in the New Testament." In *The Bible in*
Modern Scholarship. Papers Read at the 100th Meeting of the Society
of Biblical Literature, December 28-30, 1964, J. Philip Hyatt, ed., 114-
50. Nashville: Abingdon Press, 1965.
OCLC: 339444 ISB.

1264 _____. "The Mission and Beelzebul: Pap. Q 10:2-16; 11:14-23." In
Society of Biblical Literature 1985 Seminar Papers, K. H. Richards, ed.,
97-99. Atlanta: Scholars Press, 1985. (SBLSPS 24.)

1265 _____. *A New Quest of the Historical Jesus.* London: SCM, 1959. Naperville IL: Alec R. Allenson, 1959. 1966. Missoula MT: Scholars Press, 1979. 128pp. (Studies in Biblical Theology 25.)
OCLC: 385797 ISB; 2521109 GSU; 11706910 CLO; 6330676.

1266 _____. "On the *Gattung* of Mark (and John.)" In *Jesus and Man's Hope,* D. G. Buttrick, ed., 99-129. Pittsburgh: Pittsburgh Theological Seminary, 1970. (Perspective 1.)
OCLC: 142572 ISB.

1267 _____. *Pap. Q.* Claremont: Institute for Antiquity and Christianity, 1985.*

1268 _____. "The Preaching of John. Work Sheets for the Reconstruction of Q." In *Society of Biblical Literature 1984 Seminar Papers,* K. H. Richards, ed., 305-46. Chico CA: Scholars Press, 1984. (SBLSPS 23.)

1269 _____. *The Problem of History in Mark.* London: SCM; Naperville IL: Alec R. Allenson, 1957. London: SCM, 1962. *The Problem of History in Mark and Other Marcan Studies.* Philadelphia: Fortress Press, 1982. 95pp. (Studies in Biblical Theology 21.)
OCLC: 6029012 ISB; 383475; 335131 YNG; 8281434 ISB.

1270 _____. "Q and Wisdom Traditions." In *AAR/SBL Abstracts 1984,* K. H. Richards and J. B. Wiggins, eds., 264. Chico CA: Scholars Press, 1984.

1271 _____. "Reconstruction of the Q Text: Q 3-4 (The Preaching of John and the Temptation of Jesus)." In *AAR/SBL Abstracts 1984,* K. H. Richards and J. B. Wiggins, eds., 265. Chico CA: Scholars Press, 1984.

1272 _____. "The Sayings of Jesus: Q." DrewG 54/1 (1983): 26-38.

1273 _____. "The Sermon on the Mount/Plain. Work Sheets for the Reconstruction of Q." In *Society of Biblical Literature 1983 Seminar Papers,* K. H. Richards, ed., 451-54. Chico CA: Scholars Press, 1983. (SBLSPS 22.)

1274 _____. "Zur Gattung der Spruchquelle Q." In *Zeit und Geschichte: Dankesgabe an Rudolf Bultmann zum 80. Geburtstag.* Im Auftrage der Alten Marburger und in Zusammenarbeit mit Hartwig Thyen, E. Dinkler, ed., 77-96. Tübingen: J. C. B. Mohr (Paul Siebeck), 1964.
OCLC: 1411809 ISB.

---- Robinson, John A. T. *See* Orchard, Bernard (1153).

1275 _____. "The Parable of the Wicked Husbandmen: A Test of Synoptic Relationships." NTS 21 (1975): 443-61.

1276 _____. *Redating the New Testament.* London: SCM, 1976. Philadelphia: Westminster, 1976. 369pp.
OCLC: 2912693; 2414777 BCT; 2225158 ISB.

1277 Robinson, Joseph A. *The Study of the Gospels.* London; New York: Longmans, Green, 1902. 1911. 161pp. (Handbooks for the Clergy.) Includes bibl.
OCLC: 4101590 ISB.

1278 _____, and Montague R. James. *The Gospel According to Peter, and The Revelation of Peter. Two Lectures on the Newly Recovered Fragments, Together with the Greek Texts.* London: C. J. Clay, 1892. 96pp. OCLC: 3478401 ISB.

1279 Robinson, Theodore H. *The Gospel of Matthew.* London: Hodder and Stoughton; New York: Harper & Bros.; Garden City NY: Doubleday, Doran & Co., 1928. London: Hodder and Stoughton, 1937. 237pp. 1947. 240pp. (Moffatt New Testament Commentary.)
Includes the text of the gospel in Moffatt's version.
OCLC: 13949659 GTX; 3758048 ISB; 1068591 IWU; 384929 WSU; 1028740 IWU; 10859945 TBC.

1280 Rohde, Joachim. *Rediscovering the Teaching of the Evangelists.* New ed., trans. Dorothea M. Barton, with revisions and additional material by the author. London: SCM; Philadelphia: Westminster, 1968. 278pp. (New Testament Library.) Trans. of *Die redaktionsgeschichtliche Methode: Einführung und Sichtung des Forschungsstandes.* Hamburg: Furche, 1966. 247pp. Includes bibl.
A revision of the author's thesis, Berlin, 1962 entitled "Formgeschichte und Redaktionsgeschichte in der neutestamentlichen Forschung der Gegenwart."
OCLC: 20161; 60576 ISB; 6507661 ISB.

1281 Rolland, Philippe. "L'évangile des craignant-Dieu, source commune à Matthieu et à Luc." In his *Les premiers évangiles: Un nouveau regard sur le probléme synoptique,* 158-80. Paris: Cerf, 1984. (Lectio divina 116.)
OCLC: 11725693 DTM.

1282 _____. "Les Évangiles des premières communautés crétiennes." RB 90 (1983): 161-201.

1283 _____. "Marc, première harmonie évangélique." RB 90 (1983): 23-79.

1284 Roloff, Jürgen. *Das Kerygma und der irdische Jesus: Histor. Motive in d. Jesus-Erzählungen d. Evangelien.* Göttingen: Vandenhoeck & Ruprecht, 1970. 2. Aufl. 1973. 289pp. Includes bibl.
Revision of the author's Habilitationsschrift, Hamburg, 1968.
OCLC: 6153971 TJC; 2603969 ISB.

1285 Romaniuk, K. *Co to jest źródło Q?* Warsaw: Akademia Teologii Katolickiej, 1983. 164pp. Includes bibl.

1286 _____. "Refleksje na temat pewnej krytyki źródla Q." CoTh 52/4 (1982): 31-46.

1287 Ropes, James Hardy. *Die Sprüche Jesu, die in den kanonischen Evangelien nicht überliefert sind. Eine kritische Bearbeitung des von D. Alfred Resch gesammelten Materials,* von James Hardy Ropes. Leipzig: J. C. Hinrichs, 1896. 176pp. (Texte und Untersuchungen 14/2.)
OCLC: 1001076 BHA.

1288 _____. *The Synoptic Gospels*. Cambridge MA: Harvard University Press, 1934. 2nd impression with new preface. London: Oxford University Press, 1960. 117pp.
OCLC: 2928375 ISB; 3165098 ISB.

1289 Rosché, Theodore R. "The Words of Jesus and the Future of the 'Q' Hypothesis." JBL 79 (1960): 210-20.
Reissued in *The Two-Source Hypothesis: A Critical Appraisal*, A. J. Bellinzoni, Jr., ed., 357-69. Macon GA: Mercer University Press, 1985.
OCLC: 11599674 ISB.

1290 Roth, Cecil. "The Cleansing of the Temple and Zechariah xiv. 21." NovT 4 (1960): 174-81.

1291 Rowlingson, D. T. "Q." In *The Interpreter's Dictionary of the Bible*, George A. Buttrick, ed., 3:973. New York; Nashville: Abingdon, 1962.

1292 _____. "Synoptic Problem." In *The Interpreter's Dictionary of the Bible*, George A. Buttrick, ed., 4:491-95. New York; Nashville: Abingdon Press, 1962.

1293 Ruddick, C. T., Jr. "Behold, I Send my Messenger." JBL 88 (1969): 381-417.

1294 Rushbrooke, W. G. *Synopticon. An Exposition of the Common Matter of the Synoptic Gospels*. London: Macmillan and Co., 1880. 239 leaves.
OCLC: 4547119 ISB.

---- _____. *See* Abbott, E. A. (6).

1295 Sabbe, M. "Can Mt 11,25-27 and Lc 10,22 Be Called a Johannine Logion?" In *Logia. Les paroles de Jésus = The Sayings of Jesus: Mémorial Joseph Coppens*, Joël Delobel, ed., 363-71. Leuven: University Press and Peeters, 1982. (BEThL 59.)
OCLC: 9450792 ISB; 11043145.

1296 _____, ed. *L'Évangile selon Marc: Tradition et rédaction*. Leuven: University Press, 1974. Gembloux: J. Duculot, 1974. 594pp. (BEThL 34.)
English, French, or German.
OCLC: 2345456 ISB.

1297 Sabourin, L. "Christological Texts from 'Q.' " In his *Christology: Basic Texts in Focus*, 15-28. New York: Alba House, 1984.
OCLC: 10913754 DTM.

1298 _____. *The Gospel According to St. Matthew*. 2 vols. in 1: 1. *General Introduction, Commentary 1:10–7:27*; 2. *Commentary 7:28–28:20*. *Bombay: St. Paul Publications, 1982*. 945pp.
OCLC: 13952426 GTX; 10671488 ITC.

1299 _____. "Is Mark the Earliest Gospel?" RelStB 4 (1984): 61-72.

1300 _____. *L'Évangile de Luc: Introduction et commentaire*. Rome: Editrice Pontificia Università Gregoriana, 1985. 412pp. Includes bibl.
Text in French includes trans. into French of the Greek Gospel of Luke.
OCLC: 15130039 EMT.

1301 ———. "Recent Gospel Studies." BibThB 3 (1974): 283-315.

1302 Sabugal, S. "La embajada mesiánica del Bautista (Mt 11, 2-6 = Lc 7, 18-23.)" Aug 14 (1974): 5-39.

1303 ———. "La embajada mesiánica del Bautista, IV: La fuente (Q) et Mt y Lc." Aug 17 (1977): 395-424.

1304 ———. "La embajada mesiánica del Bautista (Mt 11, 2-6 par), V: Hacia el evento historico." Aug 17 (1977): 511-39.

1305 ———. "La tradición pre-redaccional del Padre-nuestro." NatGrac 32 (1985): 233-66.

1306 Salmon, George. *A Historical Introduction to the Study of the Books of the New Testament. Being an Expansion of Lectures Delivered in the Divinity School of the University of Dublin.* London: John Murray, 1885. 692pp. 3rd ed. 1888. 643pp. 4th ed. 1889. 654pp. 9th ed. 1899. 643pp. Microfiche. Louisville KY: Lost Cause Press, 1977.
OCLC: 8208845 EXN; 3374782 CBC; 11410968 WBS; 5846174 ISB; 3317440 ISB.

1307 Sanday, William. "The Apocalyptic Element in the Gospels." HibJ 10 (1911–1912): 83-109.

1308 ———. *The Authorship and Historical Character of the Fourth Gospel, Considered in Reference to the Contents of the Gospel Itself. A Critical Essay.* London: Macmillan, 1872. 307pp.
OCLC: 4162992 ACL.

1309 ———. "The Conditions Under Which the Gospels Were Written, in Their Bearing Upon Some Difficulties of the Synoptic Problem." In *Studies in the Synoptic Gospels,* by Members of the University of Oxford, W. Sanday, ed., 1-26. Oxford: Clarendon Press, 1911. Microfiche. Louisville KY: Lost Cause Press, 1977.
OCLC: 753275 ISB; 4045911 ISB.

1310 ———. "The Criticism of the New Testament." In *Criticism of the New Testament,* by W. Sanday, et al., 1-30. London: J. Murray; New York: Scribner's, 1902. 2nd ed. 1903. Microfiche. Chicago: American Theological Library Association, 1985. (ATLA monograph preservation program; ATLA Fiche 1985–0777.) (St. Margaret's Lectures 1902.)
OCLC: 2822666 MBS; 4107994 ISB; 15624846 CBC.

1311 ———. *The Gospels in the Second Century: An Examination of the Critical Part of a Work Entitled "Supernatural Religion".* London: Macmillan, 1876. 384pp.
OCLC: 3456311 ISB.

1312 ———. "Gospels." In *A Dictionary of the Bible, Comprising its Antiquities, Biography, Geography, and Natural History,* William Smith, ed., 1,217-43. London: J. Murray, 1893.
OCLC: 3783132 IQU.

1313 _____. "History of the Criticism of the Synoptic Gospels." First section in his article on the "Gospels" (1312).

1314 _____. *Inspiration. Eight Lectures on the Early History and Origin of the Doctrine of Biblical Inspiration.* London; New York: Longmans, Green and Co., 1893. 2nd ed. 1894. Microfiche. Louisville KY: Lost Cause Press, 1981. 464pp. (Bampton Lectures 1893.)
OCLC: 6411742 ISB; 382957 KEN; 7367646 ISB.

1315 _____. *The Life of Christ in Recent Research.* New York: Oxford University Press, 1907. Oxford: Clarendon Press, 1911. Microfiche. Louisville KY: Lost Cause Press, 1977. 1978. 328pp. (New Cambridge Bibliography of English Literature.)
OCLC: 4348278 ISB; 13928397 UBY.

1316 _____. "A Plea for the Logia." ET 11 (1899–1900): 471-73.

1317 _____. "A Survey of the Synoptic Question." Exp 4th ser. 3 (1891): 81-91; 179-94; 302-16; 345-61; 411-26.

1318 _____, ed. *Studies in the Synoptic Problem.* By Members of the University of Oxford. Oxford: Clarendon Press, 1911. Microfiche. Louisville KY: Lost Cause Press, 1977. 456pp.
Essays by W. Sanday, John C. Hawkins, B. H. Streeter, W. C. Allen, J. Vernon Bartlet, W. E. Addis, and N. P. Williams.
OCLC: 753275 ISB; 4045911 ISB.

---- Sanders, Ed Parish. *See* Fuller, Reginald H. (512).

1319 _____. 1975. As reviewer see Benoit, P., and M.-É. Boismard. *Synopse* (98).

1320A _____. "The Argument from Order and the Relationship between Matthew and Luke." NTS 15 (1969): 249-61.
Reissued in *The Two-Source Hypothesis: A Critical Appraisal,* A. J. Bellinzoni, Jr., ed., 409-25. Macon GA: Mercer University Press, 1985.
OCLC: 11599674 ISB.

1320B _____. *Jesus and Judaism.* London: SMC Press, 1985. 1st Fortress Press ed. Philadelphia: Fortress Press, 1985. xiv + 444pp. Includes bibl.
OCLC: 12222737 CUY; 11345326 ISB.

1321 _____. "Jesus and the Kingdom: The Restoration of Israel and the New People of God." In *Jesus, the Gospels, and the Church,* E. P. Sanders, ed., 225-39. Macon GA: Mercer University Press, 1987.
OCLC: 16130939 ISB.

1322 _____, ed. *Jesus, the Gospels, and the Church. Essays in Honor of William R. Farmer.* Macon GA: Mercer University Press, 1987. xxxviii + 286pp.
OCLC: 16130939 ISB.

1323A _____. "Literary Dependence in Colossians." JBL 85 (1966): 28-45.

1323B _____. "New Testament Studies Today." In *Colloquy on New Testament Studies: A Time for Reappraisal and Fresh Approaches,* Bruce Corley, ed., 11-28. Macon GA: Mercer University Press, 1983. OCLC: 9489011 ISB.

1324 _____. "The Overlaps of Mark and Q and the Synoptic Problem." NTS 19 (1973): 453-65.

1325 _____. "Priorités et dépendances dans la tradition synoptique." RSR 60 (1972): 519-40.

1326 _____. *The Tendencies of the Synoptic Tradition.* London: Cambridge University Press, 1969. 328pp. (SNTSMS 9.) Includes bibl.
Revision of thesis, Union Theological Seminary.
Pages 290-93, "Appendix 2. Suggested Exceptions to the Priority of Mark," are reissued in *The Two-Source Hypothesis: A Critical Appraisal,* Arthur J. Bellinzoni, Jr., ed., 199-203. Macon GA: Mercer University Press, 1985.
OCLC: 32360 ISB; 11599674 ISB.
Review: Sparks, H. F. D. JThS 21 (1970): 469-73.

1327A Sanders, Jack T. "Tradition and Redaction in Luke xv.11-32." NTS 15 (1969): 433-38.

1327B Sanders, James A. "The Gospels and the Canonical Process: A Response to Lou H. Silberman." In *The Relationships among the Gospels: An Interdisciplinary Dialogue,* William O. Walker, Jr., ed., 219-36. San Antonio: Trinity University Press, 1978. (Trinity University Monograph Series in Religion 5.)
OCLC: 4365624 ISB.

1328 Sato, Migaku. *Q und Prophetie: Studien zur Gattungs- und Traditionsgeschichte der Quelle Q.* Tübingen: J. C. B. Mohr (Paul Siebeck), 1988. xii + 437pp. (Wissenschaftliche Untersuchungen zum Neuen Testament. 2. Reihe 29.) Includes bibl.
Revision of the author's diss. with same title, University of Bern, 1977.
OCLC: 17885158 ISB.

1329 Sauer, Jürgen. "Traditionsgeschichtliche Erwägungen zu den synoptischen und paulinischen Aussagen über Feindesliebe und Wiedervergeltungsverzicht." ZNW 76 (1985): 1-28. "Rekonstruktion der ältesten Überlieferungselemente der Q-Überlieferung," 5-17.

1330 Saunier, Heinrich. *Über die Quellen des Evangeliums des Marcus. Ein Beitrag zu den Untersuchungen über die Entstehung unsrer kanonischen Evangelien.* Berlin: Ferdinand Dümmler, 1825. 187pp.
NUC: MH-AH; ICU.

1331 Sawyer, H. "The Marcan Framework." SJTh 14 (1961): 279-94.

1332 Schelkle, Karl Hermann. "Israel und Kirche im Anfang." ThQ 163 (1983): 86-95.

1333 Schenk, W. "Der Einfluss der Logienquelle auf das Markusevangelium." ZNW 70 (1979): 141-65.

1334 _____. *Synopse zur Redenquelle der Evangelien. Q-Synopse und Rekonstruktion in deutscher Übersetzung mit kurzen Erläuterungen.* Düsseldorf: Patmos, 1981. 138pp.
OCLC: 9232108 BHA.

1335 Schenke, Hans-Martin, and Karl Martin Fischer. *Einleitung in die Schriften des Neuen Testaments. 2. Die Evangelien und die anderen neutestamentlichen Schriften.* Berlin: Evangelische Verlagsanstalt; Gütersloh: Gütersloher Verlagshaus, 1978.
OCLC: 5240643; 5716287 ISB.

1336 Schillebeeckx, E. *Jezus, het verhaal, van een levende.* 3rd ed. Bloemendaal: Nelissen, 1975. 641pp. Negende druk. 1982. ET: *Jesus. An Experiment in Christology.* New York: Seabury Press, 1979. 767pp. Italian: *Gesù. La Storia di un Vivente.* Brescia: Queriniana, 1976. 774pp. (Biblioteca di Teologia Contemporanea 26.)
OCLC: 5008741; 4496535 ISB; 3626718 BWE; 15268400.

1337 _____. "Schoonenberg en de Exegese." TTh 16 (1976): 44-55.

1338 Schille, Gottfried. "Literarische Quellenhypothesen im Licht der Wahrscheinlichkeitsfrage." ThLZ 97 (1972): 331-40.

1339 Schlatter, Adolf von. *Das Evangelium des Lukas: aus seinen Quellen erklärt.* Stuttgart: Calwer, 1931. 722pp. 2. Aufl. 1960. 3. Aufl. 1975. 720pp.
OCLC: 6049861 ELW; 5319098 ISB; 5035845 BCT.

1340 _____. *Das Evangelium des Matthäus, ausgelegt für Bibelleser.* Stuttgart: Verlag der Vereinsbuchhandlung, 1895. 447pp. 2., durchges. Aufl. 1900. 418pp. *Der Evangelist Matthäus: Seine Ziel, seine Selbständigkeit; ein Kommentar zum ersten Evangelium.* 3. Aufl. Stuttgart: Calwer, 1948. 4. Aufl. 1957. 5. Aufl. 1959. 6. Aufl. 1963. 815pp.
OCLC: 8066553 TJC; 6689410 WTS; 2055297 BCT; 5122886 AZU; 6809018 SDN.

1341 _____. *Markus: der Evangelist für die Griechen.* Stuttgart: Calwer, 1935. 2. Aufl., mit einem Geleitwerk von Karl Heinrich Rengstorf. 1984. 279pp.
OCLC: 1007213 BCT; 12598833 NVS.

1342 Schleiermacher, Friedrich. *A Critical Essay on the Gospel of St. Luke. With an introduction by the translator, containing an account of the controversy respecting the origin of the three first Gospels since Bishop Marsh's dissertation.* ET by Connop Thirlwall. London: J. Taylor, 1825. 320pp. Microfiche. ATL. 1977. Louisville KY: Lost Cause Press, 1979. 1980. Trans. of *Über die Schriften des Lucas, ein kritischer Versuch.* Berlin: G. Reimer, 1817.
OCLC: 1543962 ICU; 6831834 ISB; 13975259 UBY; 3436668 ATL.

1343 _____. *Einleitung ins Neue Testament. Aus Schleiermacher's hand-schriftlichen Nachlasse und nachgeschriebenen Vorlesungen.* Mit einer Vorrede von Dr. Friedrich Lücke. Vol. 1 of *Friedrich Schleiermacher's Sämmtliche Werke.* Berlin: G. Reimer, 1845. Rpt: Ann Arbor MI: University Microfilms, 1969.
OCLC: 6096770 ISB; 4979369 TXA.

1344 _____. "Über die Zeugnisse des Papias von Unsern Ersten Beiden Evangelien." In *Friedrich Schleiermacher's Sämmtliche Werke,* 1:361ff. Berlin: G. Reimer, 1835. Rpt: Ann Arbor MI: University Microfilms, 1969.
OCLC: 6096770 ISB; 4979369 TXA.

1345 Schlosser, Jacques. "Lk 17, 2 und die Logienquelle." StNTSU 8 (1983): 70-78.

1346 _____. *Le Règne de Dieu dans les dits de Jésus.* 2 vols. Paris: J. Ga-balda, 1980. 747pp. (Études bibliques.) Includes bibl.
OCLC: 7194668 ICU.

1347 Schmid, Josef. *Das Evangelium nach Lukas. Übersetzt und erklärt.* Re-gensburg: Friedrich Pustet, 1951. 2., umgearb. Aufl. 1951. 296pp. 3., von neuem umgearb. Aufl. 1955. 4., durchges. Aufl. 1960. 366pp. (Regensburger Neues Testament 3.)
OCLC: 9004216 CFT; 949435 WIT.

1348 _____. *Das Evangelium nach Matthäus. Übersetzt und erklärt.* Re-gensburg: F. Pustet, 1948. 277pp. (Veröffentlichung des Katholischen Bildungswerks.) 2., umgearb. Aufl. 1952. 309pp. 3., von neuem um-gearb. Aufl. 1956. 4. durchges. Aufl. 1959. 5., durchges. Aufl. 1965. 401pp. (Regensburger Neues Testament 1.)
OCLC: 1233908 BWE; 9004183 CFT; 3390316 IAL; 5362116 ISB; 1375622 BCT.

1349 _____. "Markus und der aramäische Matthäus." In *Synoptische Stu-dien: Alfred Wikenhauser zum siebzigsten Geburtstag am 22. Februar 1953 dargebracht von Freunden, Kollegen und Schülern,* J. Schmidt and A. Vögtle, eds., 148-83. München: K. Zink, 1953.
OCLC: 6765909 ISB; 13953567 GTX.

1350 _____. *Matthäus und Lukas: Eine Untersuchung des Verhältnisses ihrer Evangelien.* Freiburg: Herder and Co., 1930. (Biblische Studien 28.)
OCLC: 16753219 IXA.

1351 _____. "Neue Synoptiker-Literatur." ThRv 52 (1956): 49-62.

1352 _____. "Synoptiker." LThK 9 (1964): 1,240-45.

1353 _____, and A. Vögtle, eds. *Synoptische Studien: Alfred Wikenhauser zum siebzigsten Geburtstag am 22. Februar 1953 dargebracht von Freunden, Kollegen und Schülern.* München: K. Zink, 1953. 293pp.
OCLC: 6765909 ISB; 13953567 GTX.

1354A Schmidt, Daryl. "The LXX Gattung 'Prophetic Correlative.' " JBL 96 (1977): 517-22.

1354B _____. "Tyson's Approach to the Literary Death of Luke's Jesus." PSThJ 40/2 (1987): 33-38.
First read at a colloquy on "New Critical Approaches in Synoptic Studies" held at Southern Methodist University, fall semester 1986.

1355 Schmidt, Karl Ludwig. *Der Rahmen der Geschichte Jesu: literarkritische Untersuchungen zur ältesten Jesusüberlieferung.* Berlin: Trowitzsch, 1919. Rpt: Darmstadt: Wissenschaftliche Buchgesellschaft, 1964. 1969. 322pp.
OCLC: 3857703 ISB; 7211126 LYC; 232116.

1356 Schmiedel, P. W. "Gospels." In *Encyclopaedia Biblica,* T. K. Cheyne and J. S. Black, eds., 2:1,839-98. New York: Macmillan, 1901.
OCLC: 1084084 ISB.

1357 Schmithals, Walter. 1967. As reviewer see Farmer, William R. *The Synoptic Problem* (458).

1358 _____. *Einleitung in die drei ersten Evangelien.* Berlin; New York: Walter de Gruyter, 1985. 494pp. (De Gruyter Lehrbuch.) Includes bibl.
OCLC: 12601876 ISB.

1359 _____. *Das Evangelium nach Lukas.* Zürich: Theologischer Verlag, 1980. 240pp. (Züricher Bibelkommentare. Neues Testament 3/1.)
OCLC: 7364580 VXM.

1360 _____. *Das Evangelium nach Markus.* Gütersloh: Gütersloher Verlagshaus Mohn, 1979. (Ökumenischer Taschenbuchkommentar zum Neuen Testament 2.) Includes bibl.
OCLC: 5677624 DTM.

1361 _____. "Evangelien, Synoptische." In TRE 10:570-626. 1982. "Die Spruchsammlung-Q," 597-99; "Die Spruchsammlung (Q)," 620-23.

1362 _____. "Kritik der Formkritik." ZThK 77 (1980): 149-85.

1363 _____. *Neues Testament und Gnosis.* Darmstadt: Wissenschaftliche Buchgesellschaft, 1984. 194pp. (Erträge der Forschung 208.) Includes bibl.
"Die Spruchquelle (Q)," 125-26.
OCLC: 11327357 ISB.

1364 _____. "Paulus und der historische Jesus." ZNW 53 (1962): 145-60.

1365 _____. "Die Worte vom leidenden Menschensohn: Ein Schlüssel zur Lösung des Menschensohn-Problems." In *Theologia crucis, signum crucis: Festschrift für Erich Dinkler zum 70. Geburtstag,* Carl Andresen and Günter Klein, eds., 417-45. Tübingen: J. C. B. Mohr (Paul Siebeck), 1979.
OCLC: 5682595 ISB.

1366 Schmitt, John J. "In Search of the Origin of the *Siglum* Q." JBL 100 (1981): 609-11.

1367A Schnackenburg, Rudolf. "Der eschatologische Abschnitt Lk 17, 20-37." In *Mélanges bibliques: en hommage au R. P. Béda Rigaux*, Albert Descamps and R. P. André de Halleux, eds., 213-34. Gembloux: J. Duculot, 1970.
OCLC: 506223 ISB.

1367B ————. "On the Origin of the Fourth Gospel." In *Jesus and Man's Hope*, D. G. Buttrick, ed., 1:223-46. Pittsburgh: Pittsburgh Theological Seminary, 1970. (Perspective 1.)
OCLC: 142572 ISB.

1368 ————, J. Ernst, and J. Wanke, eds. *Die Kirche des Anfangs: Festschrift für Heinz Schürmann zum 65. Geburtstag*. Leipzig: St.-Benno-Verlag, 1977. Freiburg im Breisgau; Basel; Wien: Herder, 1978. 667p. (Erfurter theologische Studien 38.)
Includes 3 contributions in French.
OCLC: 4079038 TJC; 6381479 DRU; 4476698 NOC.

1369 Schneider, Gerhard. *Das Evangelium nach Lukas*. Gütersloh: Gütersloher Verlagshaus Mohn, 1977. 2 vols. (Ökumenischer Taschenbuchkommentar zum Neuen Testament 3.) Includes bibl.
OCLC: 3840158 EMU.

1370 ————. "Gab es eine vorsynoptische Szene 'Jesus vor dem Synedrium'?" NovT 12 (1970): 22-39.

1371 ————. "Der Menschensohn in der lukanischen Christologie." In *Jesus und der Menschensohn: Für Anton Vögtle*, Rudolf Pesch and Rudolf Schnackenburg, eds., 267-82. Freiburg im Breisgau: Herder, 1975.
OCLC: 2318718 ICU.

1372 ————. *Parusiegleichnisse im Lukas-Evangelium*. Stuttgart: KBW Verlag, 1975. 106pp. (Stuttgarter Bibelstudien 74.) Includes bibl.
OCLC: 1429879 ISB.

1373 ————. "Das Vaterunser des Matthäus." In *À cause de l'évangile: Études sur les Synoptiques et les Actes. Offertes au P. Jacques Dupont, O. S. B. à l'occasion de son 70e anniversaire*, 57-90. Paris: Cerf, 1985. (Lectio divina 123.)
OCLC: 14377925 DTM.

1374 ————. *Verleugnung, Verspottung und Verhör Jesu nach Lukas 22, 54-71: Studien zur lukanischen Darstellung der Passion*. Munich: Kosel Verlag, 1969. (Studien zum Alten und Neuen Testament 22.) Includes bibl.
Habilitationsschrift—Würzburg.
OCLC: 2948463 ISB.

1375 Schniewind, Julius. *Das Evangelium nach Markus. Übersetzt und erklärt von Julius Schniewind, mit einer Einleitung zum Gesamtwerk: Die Entstehung und der Wortlaut des Neuen Testaments von Hermann Strathmann.* Göttingen: Vandenhoeck & Ruprecht, 1949. 5. Aufl. 1949. 6. durchges. Aufl. 1952. 7. Aufl. 1956. 210pp. (Das Neue Testament Deutsch 1.)
OCLC: 5152048 ECO; 1201728 ISB; 4733955 CFT; 1194619 BPS.

1376 _____. *Das Evangelium nach Matthäus. Übersetzt und erklärt.* Göttingen: Vandenhoeck & Ruprecht, 1936. 4., durchges. Aufl. 1937. 274pp. 1950. 282pp. 12. Aufl. 1968. 285pp. (Das Neue Testament Deutsch; Neues Göttinger Bibelwerk 2.) Includes bibl.
OCLC: 7583273 OKO; 1245416 ISB; 10359228 OKO.

1377 _____. "Zur Synoptiker-Exegese." ThR n.F. 2 (1930): 129-89.

1378 Schoenberg, M. W. 1970. As reviewer see Lambrecht, Jan. *Marcus* (863).

1379 Scholer, David M. "Q Bibliography: 1981–1986." In *Society of Biblical Literature 1986 Seminar Papers,* 27-36. Atlanta: Scholars Press, 1986. (SBLSPS 25.)

1380 Scholten, J. H. *Das älteste Evangelium: kritische Untersuchung der Zusammensetzung, des wechselseitigen Verhältnisses, des geschichtlichen Werths und des Ursprungs der Evangelien nach Matthäus und Marcus.* Aus dem Holländischen mit Genehmigung des Verfassers übersetzt von Ernst Rud. Redempenning. Elberfeld: R. L. Friderichs, 1869. Microfiche. Chicago: American Theological Library Association, 1985. xxiv + 256pp. (ATLA Monograph Preservation Program; ATLA Fiche 1985-3134.)
OCLC: (ATLA Fiche) 17492645 IND.

1381 Schönle, Volker. *Johannes, Jesus und die Juden: Die theologische Position des Matthäus und des Verfassers der Redenquelle im Lichte von Mt. 11.* Frankfurt am Main: P. Lang, 1982. 288pp. (Beiträge zur biblischen Exegese und Theologie 17.)
OCLC: 9101815 DRU.
Review: Viviano, B. T. CBQ 46 (1984): 589-90.

1382A Schoonenberg, P. "Schillebeeckx en de exegese. Enige gedachten bij 'Jezus, het verhaal, van een levende'." TTh 15 (1975): 255-68.

1382B Schott, Heinrich August. *Isagoge historico-critica in libros Nove Foederis sacros.* Jenae: C. H. Walzii, 1830. viii + 642pp.
OCLC: 10166029 WTS.

1383 Schottroff, Luise. "Gewaltverzicht und Feindesliebe in der urchristlichen Jesustradition [Mk 12:13-17]." In *Jesus Christus in Historie und Theologie: Neutestamentliche Festschrift für Hans Conzelmann zum 60. Geburtstag,* Georg Strecker, ed., 197-221. Tübingen: J. C. B. Mohr (Paul Siebeck), 1975.
ET: "Non-Violence and the Love of One's Enemies." In *Essays on the Love Commandment,* trans. Reginald H. Fuller and Ilse Fuller, 9-39. Philadelphia: Fortress Press, 1978.
OCLC: 2120453 ISB; 4076205 ISB.

1384 _____, and Wolfgang Stegemann. *Jesus von Nazareth, Hoffnung der Armen.* Stuttgart; Berlin; Köln; Mainz: Kohlhammer, 1978. 2. Aufl. 1981. 164pp. (Urban-Taschenbücher 639.) OCLC: 5521302 TSW; 10566330 IME.

1385 Schramm, Tim. *Der Markus-Stoff bei Lukas: eine literarkritische und redaktionsgeschichtliche Untersuchung.* Cambridge: Cambridge University Press, 1971. 207pp. (SNTSMS 14.) Includes bibl. Diss. Hamburg. OCLC: 224026 ISB. Review: Gaboury, Antonio. CBQ 34 (1972): 540-41.

1386 Schreiber, J. *Die Markuspassion. Wege zur Erforschung der Leidensgeschichte Jesu.* Hamburg: Furche, 1969. 70pp. Includes bibl. OCLC: 230704 WIT.

1387 Schreiner, Josef, ed. *Forma y propósito del Nuevo Testamento: introducción a su problemática.* Barcelona: Editorial Herder, 1973. 474pp. (Biblioteca Herder: sección de Sagrada Escritura 129.) Includes bibl. OCLC: 1937910 BWE.

1388 Schubert, Hans von. *The Gospel of Peter. Synoptical Tables with Translations and Critical Apparatus.* Trans. John MacPherson. Edinburgh: T. & T. Clark, 1893. 31pp. Trans. of *Die Composition des Pseudopetrinischen Evangelien-fragments: Mit einer synoptischen Tabelle als Ergänzungsheft.* Berlin: Reuther und Reichard, 1893. Synoptic table 31pp. at end. NUC: TxFTC; MH; ICU; MH-AH.

1389 Schulz, Siegfried. "Die Bedeutung des Markus für die Theologiegeschichte des Urchristentums." In *Studia Evangelica,* F. L. Cross, ed., 2:135-45. Berlin: Akademische-Verlag, 1964. (Texte und Untersuchungen 87.) OCLC: 1637245 ISB; 13641309 BZM.

1390 _____. "Die Gottesherrschaft ist nahe herbeigekommen (Mt 10, 7/Lk 10, 9): Der kerygmatische Entwurf der Q-Gemeinde Syriens." In *Das Wort und die Wörter. Festschrift Gerhard Friedrich zum 65. Geburtstag,* Horst Balz and Siegfried Schulz, eds., 57-67. Stuttgart: W. Kohlhammer, 1973. OCLC: 811804 DRB.

1391 _____. *Griechisch-deutsche Synopse der Q-Überlieferungen.* Zürich: Theologischer Verlag, 1972. 106pp. Selections from the Gospels of Matthew and Luke in German and Greek on opposite pages. Supplement to his *Q—Die Spruchquelle der Evangelisten* (1395). OCLC: 1560384 TSM.

1392 _____. "Der historische Jesus. Bilanz der Fragen und Lösungen." In *Jesus Christus in Historie und Theologie: Neutestamentliche Festschrift für Hans Conzelmann zum 60. Geburtstag*, Georg Strecker, ed., 3-25. Tübingen: J. C. B. Mohr (Paul Siebeck), 1975. OCLC: 2120435 ISB.

1393 _____. "Markus und das Alte Testament." ZThK 58 (1961): 184-97.

1394 _____. "Die neue Frage nach dem historischen Jesus." In *Neues Testament und Geschichte: historisches Geschehen und Deutung im Neuen Testament. Oscar Cullmann zum 70. Geburtstag,* Heinrich Baltensweiler and Bo Reicke, eds., 33-42. Zürich: Theologischer Verlag, 1972. Tübingen: J. C. B. Mohr (Paul Siebeck), 1972. OCLC: 594856 ISB.

1395 _____. *Q—Die Spruchquelle der Evangelisten.* Zürich: Theologischer Verlag, 1972. 508pp. Includes bibl. Supplement (1391). OCLC: 838592 BAN. Review: Hoffmann, P. BZ 19 (1975): 104-15.

1396 _____. *Die Stunde der Botschaft: Einführung in die Theologie der vier Evangelisten.* Hamburg: Furche, 1967. 2. durchges. Aufl. Zürich: Zwingli Verlag, 1970. 392pp. OCLC: 6507005 ELW; 652847 UTS; 4238846 CSU.

1397 Schulze, Johann Daniel. "Über den schriftstellerischen Charakter und Werth des Evangelisten Marcus: Ein Beitrag zur Special-Hermeneutik des N. T." In *Analekten für das Studium der exegetischen und systematischen Theologie.* "Erster Abschnitt," 2:2 (1814): 104-51; "Zweiter Abschnitt: Erster Hälfte," 2:3 (1815): 69-132; "Zweiter Abschnitt: Zweiter Hälfte," 3:1 (1816): 88-127. The periodical was complete in 4 vols., published in Leipzig by J. A. Barth from 1812 to 1822. Vols. 1-3 were edited by Karl August Gottlieb Keil; vol. 4, by Heinrich Gottlieb Tzschirner.

1398 Schuppan, C. "Gottes Herrschaft und Gottes Wille: Eine Untersuchung zur Struktur der Rede von Gott in der Spruchquelle Q in Vergleich mit dem Frühjudentum und den Matthäus- und Lukasevangelium." Diss. Griefswald, 1978.*

1399 Schürmann, Heinz. "Beobachtungen zum Menschensohn-Titel in der Redenquelle: Sein Vorkommen in Abschluss- und Einleitungswendungen." In *Jesus und der Menschensohn: für Anton Vögtle,* Rudolf Pesch and Rudolf Schnackenburg, eds., 124-47. Freiburg im Breisgau: Herder, 1975. Reissued in his *Gottes Reich, Jesu Geschick: Jesu ureigener Tod im Licht seiner Basileia-Verkündigung,* 153-82. Freiburg: Herder, 1983. OCLC: 2318718 ICU; 10920891 EXN.

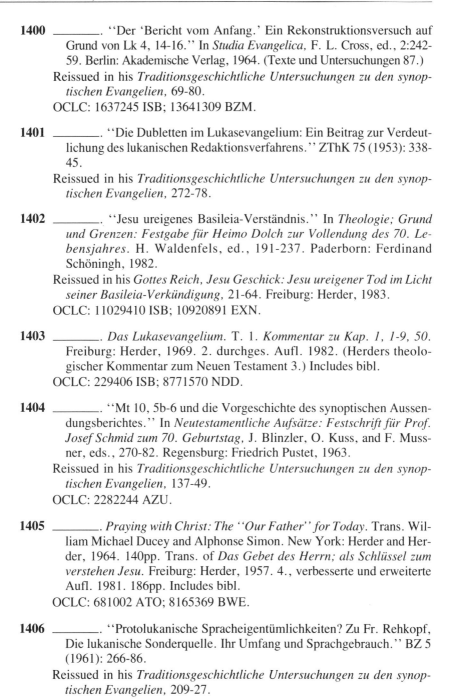

1400 _____. "Der 'Bericht vom Anfang.' Ein Rekonstruktionsversuch auf Grund von Lk 4, 14-16." In *Studia Evangelica*, F. L. Cross, ed., 2:242-59. Berlin: Akademische Verlag, 1964. (Texte und Untersuchungen 87.) Reissued in his *Traditionsgeschichtliche Untersuchungen zu den synoptischen Evangelien*, 69-80.
OCLC: 1637245 ISB; 13641309 BZM.

1401 _____. "Die Dubletten im Lukasevangelium: Ein Beitrag zur Verdeutlichung des lukanischen Redaktionsverfahrens." ZThK 75 (1953): 338-45.
Reissued in his *Traditionsgeschichtliche Untersuchungen zu den synoptischen Evangelien*, 272-78.

1402 _____. "Jesu ureigenes Basileia-Verständnis." In *Theologie; Grund und Grenzen: Festgabe für Heimo Dolch zur Vollendung des 70. Lebensjahres*. H. Waldenfels, ed., 191-237. Paderborn: Ferdinand Schöningh, 1982.
Reissued in his *Gottes Reich, Jesu Geschick: Jesu ureigener Tod im Licht seiner Basileia-Verkündigung*, 21-64. Freiburg: Herder, 1983.
OCLC: 11029410 ISB; 10920891 EXN.

1403 _____. *Das Lukasevangelium*. T. 1. *Kommentar zu Kap. 1, 1-9, 50*. Freiburg: Herder, 1969. 2. durchges. Aufl. 1982. (Herders theologischer Kommentar zum Neuen Testament 3.) Includes bibl.
OCLC: 229406 ISB; 8771570 NDD.

1404 _____. "Mt 10, 5b-6 und die Vorgeschichte des synoptischen Aussendungsberichtes." In *Neutestamentliche Aufsätze: Festschrift für Prof. Josef Schmid zum 70. Geburtstag*, J. Blinzler, O. Kuss, and F. Mussner, eds., 270-82. Regensburg: Friedrich Pustet, 1963.
Reissued in his *Traditionsgeschichtliche Untersuchungen zu den synoptischen Evangelien*, 137-49.
OCLC: 2282244 AZU.

1405 _____. *Praying with Christ: The "Our Father" for Today*. Trans. William Michael Ducey and Alphonse Simon. New York: Herder and Herder, 1964. 140pp. Trans. of *Das Gebet des Herrn; als Schlüssel zum verstehen Jesu*. Freiburg: Herder, 1957. 4., verbesserte und erweiterte Aufl. 1981. 186pp. Includes bibl.
OCLC: 681002 ATO; 8165369 BWE.

1406 _____. "Protolukanische Spracheigentümlichkeiten? Zu Fr. Rehkopf, Die lukanische Sonderquelle. Ihr Umfang und Sprachgebrauch." BZ 5 (1961): 266-86.
Reissued in his *Traditionsgeschichtliche Untersuchungen zu den synoptischen Evangelien*, 209-27.

1407 _____. *Einer quellenkritischen Untersuchung des lukanischen Abend-mahlsberichtes Lk. 22, 7-38.* Münster Westf.: Aschendorffsche Verlagsbuchhandlung, 1953–1956. 3 vols. (Neutestamentliche Abhandlungen 19/5, 20/4, 20/5.) Contents. 1. Teil. *Der Paschamahlbericht, Lk 22,(7-14),15-18; 2.* Teil. *Der Einsetzungsbericht, Lk 22,19-20; 3.* Teil. *Jesu Abschiedsrede, Lk 22,21-38.* OCLC: 1178706 RSC.

1408 _____. "Die Sprache des Christus: Sprachliche Beobachtungen an den synoptischen Herrenworten." BZ 2 (1958): 54-84. Reissued in his *Traditionsgeschichtliche Untersuchungen zu den synoptischen Evangelien,* 83-108.

1409 _____. "Sprachliche Reminiszenzen an Abgeänderte oder ausgelassene Bestandteile der Spruchsammlung im Lukas- und Matthäusevangelium (Max Meinertz zum 80. Geburtstag)." NTS 6 (1960): 193-210. Reissued under slightly different title in his *Traditionsgeschichtliche Untersuchungen zu den synoptischen Evangelien,* 111-25.

1410 _____. "Das Thomasevangelium und das lukanische Sondergut." *BZ* 7 (1963): 236-60. Reissued in his *Traditionsgeschichtliche Untersuchungen zu den synoptischen Evangelien,* 228-47.

1411 _____. *Traditionsgeschichtliche Untersuchungen zu den synoptischen Evangelien: Beiträge.* Düsseldorf: Patmos-Verlag, 1968. 367pp. (Kommentare und Beiträge zum Alten und Neuen Testament.) OCLC: 3926922 ISB.

1412 _____. "Die vorösterlichen Anfänge der Logientradition: Versuch eines formgeschichtlichen Zugangs zum Leben Jesu." In *Der historische Jesus und der kerygmatische Christus: Beiträge zum Christusverständnis in Forschung und Verkündigung,* Helmut Ristow and Karl Matthiae, eds., 342-70. Berlin: Evangelische Verlagsanstalt, 1960. 2. Aufl. 1961. 3. Aufl. 1964. Reissued in his *Traditionsgeschichtliche Untersuchungen zu den synoptischen Evangelien,* 39-65. OCLC: 864284 ISB; 1077359 BPS.

1413 _____. "Die Warnung des Lukas von der Falschlehre in der 'Predigt am Berge' Lk 6, 20-49." BZ 10 (1966): 57-81.

1414 _____. "Wer daher eines dieser geringsten Gebote auflöst. . . . Wo fand Matthäus das Logion Mt 5, 19?" BZ 4 (1960): 238-50. Reissued in his *Traditionsgeschichtliche Untersuchungen zu den synoptischen Evangelien,* 126-36.

1415 ————. "Das Zeugnis der Redenquelle für die Basileia-Verkündigung Jesu: Eine traditionsgeschichtliche Untersuchung." In *Logia. Les paroles de Jésus = The Sayings of Jesus. Mémorial Joseph Coppens,* Joël Delobel, ed., 121-200. Leuven: University Press and Peeters, 1982. Reissued in Schürmann's *Gottes Reich, Jesu Geschick: Jesu ureigener Tod im Licht seiner Basileia-Verkündigung,* 65-152. Freiburg: Herder, 1983. OCLC: 9450792 ISB; 11043145; 10920891 EXN.

1416 ————. "Zur Traditions- und Redaktionsgeschichte von Mt 10, 23." BZ 3 (1959): 82-88. Reissued in his *Traditionsgeschichtliche Untersuchungen zu den synoptischen Evangelien,* 150-56.

1417 ————. "Zur Traditionsgeschichte der Nazareth-Perikope Lk 4, 16-30." In *Mélanges bibliques en hommage au R. P. Béda Rigaux,* Albert Descamps and R. P. André de Halleux, eds., 187-205. Gembloux: J. Duculot, 1970. OCLC: 506223 ISB.

1418 Schüssler-Fiorenza, Elisabeth. *See* Fiorenza, Elisabeth Schüssler (477B).

1419A Schwarz, Franz J. "Evangelien (und Apostelgeschichte)." In *Kirchen-Lexikon,* H. J. J. Wetzer and B. Welte, eds., 3:779-801; French trans.: 8:183-207. Freiburg: Herder, 1849. French. *Dictionnaire encyclopédique de la théologie catholique.* Paris, 1860. 3rd ed. Paris: Gaume Fréres et J. Duprey, 1868. OCLC: 2842224 MBS; (3rd ed.) 2422694 LLM.

1419B ————. *Neue Untersuchungen über das Verwandtschafts-Verhältniss der synoptischen Evangelien; mit besonderen Berücksichtigung der Hypothese vom schöpferischen Urevangelisten.* Tübingen: H. Laupp, 1844. 339pp. Eine von der katholisch-theologischen Fakultät zu Tübingen gekrönte Preisschrift. OCLC: 12325956 CUF.

1420 Schwarz, Günther. *Und Jesus sprach: Untersuchungen zur aramäischen Urgestalt der Worte Jesu.* Stuttgart: Kohlhammer, 1985. 362pp. (Beiträge zur Wissenschaft vom Alten und Neuen Testament 6.) Includes bibl. OCLC: 12394366 ISB.

1421A Schwegler, Albert. *Das nachapostolische Zeitalter in den Hauptmomenten seiner Entwicklung.* Tübingen: L. F. Fues, 1846. Rpt: Graz: Akademische Druck- and Verlagsanstalt, 1977. 2 vols. OCLC: 4839807 IND; 7985402 DWT.

1421B ————. "Die Hypothese vom schöpferischen Urevangelisten in ihrem Verhältnis zur Traditionshypothese." ThJb(T) 2 (1843): 203-78.

1422 Schweitzer, Albert. *The Quest of the Historical Jesus. A Critical Study of Its Progress from Reimarus to Wrede*. With a pref. by F. C. Burkitt. New York: Macmillan, 1961. ix + 413pp. Trans. by W. Montgomery from the 1st German ed. entitled *Von Reimarus zu Wrede. Eine Geschichte der Leben-Jesu-Forschung*. Tübingen: J. C. B. Mohr (Paul Siebeck), 1906.
OCLC: 7004112 IDI; 6104323 ISB.

1423A Schweizer, Eduard. "Die Christologie von Phil 2, 6-11 und Q." ThZ 41 (1985): 258-63.

1423B _____. "The Gospel of Matthew." In *Jesus and Man's Hope*, Donald G. Miller and Dikran Y. Hadidian, eds., 2:339-41. Pittsburgh: Pittsburgh Theological Seminary, 1971. (Perspective 2.)
OCLC: 142572 ISB.

1424 _____. "Eine hebräisierende Sonderquelle des Lukas?" ThZ 6 (1950): 160-85.

1425 _____. "Matth. 5, 17-20-Anmerkungen zum Gesetzesverständnis des Matthäus." ThLZ 77 (1952): 479-84.

1426 Scott, B. B. "Picking up the Pieces." *Forum* 1/1 (1985): 15-21.
Review of D. Crossan, *In Fragments* (319).

1427 Scott-Moncrieff, C. E. *St. Mark and the Triple Tradition*. London: James Nisbet & Co., 1907. 142pp.
OCLC: 8676584 ISB.

1428 Segalla, G. "La cristologia escatologica della Quelle." TeItSett 4 (1979): 119-68.

  ---- Segbroeck, Frans Van. *See* Neirynck, Frans (1121).

  ---- _____. *See* Neirynck, Frans (1122).

  ---- _____. *See* Neirynck, Frans (1123).

1429A Seitz, O. J. F. "The Rejection of the Son of Man: Mark Compared with Q." In *Studia Evangelica*, E. A. Livingstone, ed., 7:451-65. Berlin: Akademie Verlag, 1982. (Texte und Untersuchungen 126.)
OCLC: 9237313 ISB.

1429B Selby, Donald J. "To Compile a Narrative: The Study of the Gospels." In his *Introduction to the New Testament: "The Word Became Flesh,"* 27-81. New York: Macmillan; London: Collier-Macmillan, 1971. (Also published simultaneously and bound with James King West's *Introduction to the Old Testament: "Hear O Israel"* as *Introduction to the Bible*. Identical pagination.)
Esp. "1. Why Four Gospels?" 35-45; and "2. The Quest for Sources," 45-55.
OCLC: 142201; 210062 ISB.

1430 Sellin, G. "Komposition, Quellen und Funktion des lukanischen Reiseberichtes (Lk. ix.51–xix.28.)" NovT 20 (1978): 100-35.

1431 _____. "Das Leben des Gottessohnes. Taufe und Verklärung Jesu als Bestandteile eines vormarkinischen 'Evangeliums'." *Kairos* 25 (1983): 237-53.

1432 _____. "Lukas als Gleichniserzähler: Die Erzählung vom barmherzigen Samariter (Lk 10, 25-37)." ZNW 65 (1974): 166-89.

1433 Senior, D. P. *The Passion Narrative according to Matthew. A Redactional Study.* Leuven: University Press, 1975. 433pp. (BEThL 39). Adaptation of a doctoral dissertation presented to the Theology Faculty of Leuven University in 1972.
OCLC: 1722400 ISB; 3073844.

1434 Shotwell, James T., and Louise R. Loomis. *The See of Peter.* New York: Columbia University Press, 1927. New York: Octagon Books, 1965. 737pp. (Records of Civilization: Sources and Studies 7.)
A documentary study containing extracts of essential texts relating to the history of the rise of the papacy.
OCLC: 1419968 BPS; 1441203 TOL.

1435A Shuler, Philip L. "Genre Criticism and the Synoptic Problem." In *New Synoptic Studies: The Cambridge Gospel Conference and Beyond,* William R. Farmer, ed., 467-80. Macon GA: Mercer University Press, 1983.
OCLC: 9783753 ISB.

1435B _____. *A Genre for the Gospels: The Biographical Character of Matthew.* Philadelphia: Fortress Press, 1982. x + 133pp. Includes bibl.
Originally presented as his Ph.D. diss., McMaster University, 1975. Microfiche of diss. 1976.
OCLC: 8345521 ISB; 15817052.

1435C _____. "The Genre of the Gospels and the Two Gospel Hypothesis." In *Jesus, the Gospels, and the Church,* E. P. Sanders, ed., 69-88. Macon GA: Mercer University Press, 1987.
OCLC: 16130939 ISB.

1436A _____. "The Griesbach Hypothesis and Gospel Genre." PSThJ 33/4 (1980): 41-49.

1436B _____. "Questions of a Holistic Approach to Luke-Acts." PSThJ 40/2 (1987): 43-47.
Critical review of Joseph Tyson's *The Death of Jesus in Luke-Acts* (1603). First read at a colloquy on "New Critical Approaches in Synoptic Studies" held at Southern Methodist University, Fall semester 1986.

1437 Sieber, John Howard. "A Redactional Analysis of the Synoptic Gospels with Regard to the Question of the Sources of the Gospel according to Thomas." Ph.D. diss., Claremont, 1966. 274 leaves. Includes bibl. Photocopy. Ann Arbor MI: University Microfilms International, 1976. Microfilm, 1986.
OCLC: 2830111 BHA; 14161580 UTS.

1438A Sieffert, Friedrich L. *Über den Ursprung des ersten kanonischen Evangeliums: Eine kritische Abhandlung.* Königsberg: J. H. Bon, 1832. 179pp.
OCLC: 4266703 YU#.

1438B Sigal, Phillip. "Aspects of Mark Pointing to Matthean Priority." In *New Synoptic Studies: The Cambridge Gospel Conference and Beyond,* William R. Farmer, ed., 185-208. Macon GA: Mercer University Press, 1983.
OCLC: 9783753 ISB.

1439A Silberman, Lou H. " 'Habent Sua Fata Libelli': The Role of Wandering Themes in Some Hellenistic Jewish and Rabbinic Literature." In *The Relationships among the Gospels: An Interdisciplinary Dialogue,* William O. Walker, Jr., ed., 195-218. San Antonio: Trinity University Press, 1978. (Trinity University Monograph Series in Religion 5.)
OCLC: 4365624 ISB.

1439B _____. "Whence *Siglum* Q? A Conjecture." JBL 98 (1979): 287-88.

1440 Simons, Eduard. *Hat der dritte Evangelist den kanonischen Matthäus benutzt?* Bonn: Carl Georgi, 1880. Microfiche. Chicago: ATLA, 1985. (ATLA monograph preservation program; ATLA Fiche 1984–3263.) 112pp.
OCLC: 17492161.
Review: Holtzmann, Heinrich J. ThLZ 6 (1881): 180-83.

1441A Simpson, R. T. "The Major Agreements of Matthew and Luke Against Mark." NTS 12 (1966): 273-84.
Reissued in *The Two-Source Hypothesis: A Critical Appraisal,* A. J. Bellinzoni, Jr., ed., 381-95. Macon GA: Mercer University Press, 1985.
OCLC: 11599674 ISB.

1441B Smith, B. T. D. "Sources and Plan of the Gospel," "Non-Marcan Parallels in Matthew and Luke," and "Matter Peculiar to Matthew." In *The Gospel according to St. Matthew,* B. T. D. Smith, ed., xviii-xxxiii. London: Cambridge University Press, 1933. (Cambridge Bible for Schools and Colleges.)
OCLC: 5530036 CPT.

1442 Smith, Charles W. F. "Dr. Parker's Synoptic Theory." AThR 36 (1954): 210-13.

---- Smith, D. Moody, Jr. *See* Spivey, Robert A. (1472).

1443 Smith, Morton. *Clement of Alexandria and a Secret Gospel of Mark.* Cambridge: Harvard University Press, 1973. 452pp. Includes bibl. English, Greek, or Latin.
OCLC: 695310 ISB.

---- _____. *See* Hadas, Moses (602).

1444 _____. "The Jewish Element in the Gospels." JBR 24 (1956): 90-96.

1445 _____. "Palestinian Judaism in the First Century." In *Israel: Its Role in Civilization,* Moshe Davis, ed., 67-81. New York: Seminary Israel Institute of the Jewish Theological Seminary of America; dist. by Harper, 1956. New York: Arno Press, 1977. (America and the Holy Land.) Spanish. *Israel en la civilización moderna.* Buenos Aires: Edit. Candelabro. 1961.
OCLC: 910492 ISB; 2911991; 10564636 MBB.

1446 Smith, Robinson. "Fresh Light in the Synoptic Problem: Matthew a Lucan Source." HibJ 10 (1911–1912): 615-25.

1447 Snape, H. C. 1966. As reviewer see Farmer, W. R. *The Synoptic Problem* (458).

1448 _____. "Christian Origins in Rome with Special Reference to Mark's Gospel." MCM n.s. 13 (1970): 230-44.

1449 _____. "The Composition of the Lukan Writings: A Re-Assessment." HThR 53 (1960): 27-46.

1450 Snoy, T. "La Rédaction marcienne de la marche sur les éaux (Mc VI,45-52.)" EThL 44 (1968): 205-41.

1451 Soden, Hermann von. *The History of Early Christian Literature: The Writings of the New Testament.* Trans. J. R. Wilkinson, ed. W. D. Morrison. New York: G. P. Putnam; London: Williams and Norgate, 1906. 476pp. Trans. of *Urchristliche Literaturgeschichte: Die Schriften des Neuen Testaments.* Berlin: Alexander Duncker, 1905. 237pp. Esp. part 2. "The Gospel Literature."
OCLC: 4153462 ISB; 3425930 IAL.

1452 Soiron, Thaddaus. *Die Bergpredigt Jesu: Formgeschichtliche, exegetische und theologische Erklärung.* Freiburg im Breisgau: Herder, 1941. 480pp.
OCLC: 7356676 ISB.

1453 _____. *Die Logia Jesu: Eine literarkritische und literaturgeschichtliche Untersuchung zum synoptischen Problem.* Münster: Aschendorffsche Verlagsbuchhandlung, 1916. 173pp. (Neutestamentliche Abhandlungen 6/4.)
OCLC: 1258881 ISB.

1454 Solages, Bruno de. "Analyse ordinale des Évangiles Synoptiques." BLE 75 (1974): 205-209.

1455 _____. *Comment sont nés les évangiles: Marc, Luc, Matthieu.* Toulouse: Privat, 1973. 206pp.
OCLC: 691612 IXA.

1456 _____. *La composition des évangiles: De Luc et de Matthieu et leurs sources.* Leiden: Brill, 1973. 319pp.
French or Greek.
OCLC: 754804.

1457 _____. *A Greek Synopsis of the Gospels: A New Way of Solving the Synoptic Problem.* English ed. trans. from the French by J. Baissus, with a preface by Cardinal Tisserant. Leiden: E. J. Brill, 1959. Trans. of *Synopse grecque des évangiles: méthode nouvelle pour résoudre le problème synoptique.* Toulouse: Institut Catholique, 1959. 1,128pp.
OCLC: 387621 ISB; 2660492 ISB.
Reviews of French ed.: Benoit, Pierre. RB 67 (1960): 93-102; Boismard, M.-É. RB 80 (1973): 588-93.

1458 _____. "L'évangile de Thomas et les évangiles canoniques: l'ordre des péricopes." BLE 80 (1979): 102-108.

1459 _____. "Mathématiques et Évangiles: Réponse au R. P. Benoit." BLE 61 (1960): 287-311.

1460 _____. "À propos de la 'Théorie' des deux sources. Réponse au R. P. [M.-É.] Boismard." BLE 76 (1975): 61-64.

1461 _____. "Une question de méthode: à propos de la théorie synoptique du P. M.-É. Boismard." BLE 74 (1973): 139-41.

1462 _____. "Le témoignage de Papias." BLE 71 (1970): 3-14.

1463 Soltau, Wilhelm. *Unsere Evangelien, ihre Quellen und ihr Quellenwert vom Standpunkt des Historikers aus betrachtet.* Leipzig: Dieterich, 1901. 149pp.
OCLC: 6765991 TJC.

1464 Soulen, R. N. "Q." In his *Handbook of Biblical Criticism,* 137-38; 2nd ed., 157-59. Atlanta: John Knox Press, 1976. 2nd ed. 1981.
OCLC: 2401586 ISB; 7328973 ICU.

1465 Sparks, H. F. D. 1970. As reviewer see Sanders, Ed Parish. *Tendencies* (1326).

1466 _____. 1975. As reviewer see Gaston, L. *Horae* (521).

1467 _____. "The Semitisms of St. Luke's Gospel." JTS 44 (1943): 129-38.

1468 _____. "Some Observations on the Semitic Background of the New Testament." BSNTS 2 (1951): 33-43.

1469 _____. "St. Luke's Transpositions." NTS 3 (1956–1957): 219-23.

1470 Spitta, Friedrich. "Beiträge zur Erklärung der Synoptiker." ZNW 5 (1904): 303-26.

1471 _____. *Die synoptische Grundschrift in ihrer Überlieferung durch das Lukasevangelium.* Leipzig: J. C. Hinrichs, 1912. 512pp. (Untersuchungen zum Neuen Testament 1.)
OCLC: 1344369 BCT.

1472   Spivey, Robert A., and D. Moody Smith, Jr. *Anatomy of the New Testament. A Guide to Its Structure and Meaning.* New York: Macmillan, 1969. xviii + 510pp. 2nd ed. 1974. 3rd ed. 1982. xviii + 539pp. Includes bibl.
Esp. "Note on the Gospel of Mark and the Synoptic Problem," 61-65 (1st ed.). "Notes on the Nature of a Gospel, Gospel Criticism, and the Gospel of Mark," 61-67 (3rd ed.).
OCLC: 745857 ISB.

1473   Springer, J. F. "The Synoptic Problem I-IV." BS 81 (1924): 59-88; 201-39; 323-62; 493-514.

1474   Stacpoole, A. J. "A Note on the Dating of St. Mark's Gospel." Scrip 16 (1964): 106-10.

1475   Stanley, D. "Didache as a Constructive Element of the Gospel-Form." CBQ 17 (1955): 216-28.

1476   Stanton, Graham. "The Origin and Purpose of Matthew's Gospel: Matthean Scholarship from 1945–1980." In ANRW 25/3: 1,889-1,951. Berlin; New York: Walter de Gruyter, 1985.
Esp. "Source Criticism," 1,899-1,903.

1477   Stanton, Vincent Henry. "Gospels." In *A Dictionary of the Bible, Dealing with Its Language, Literature, and Contents, Including the Biblical Theology,* James Hastings, ed., 2:234-49. New York: Scribner's, 1899.
OCLC: 382363 ISB.

1478   _____. *The Gospels as Historical Documents.* 3 vols. Cambridge: Cambridge University Press, 1903–1920. Microfilm. Chicago: Dept. of Photoduplication, University of Chicago Library, for the ATLA Board of Microtext, 1971.
Contents. 1. The Early Use of the Gospels; 2. The Synoptic Gospels; 3. The Fourth Gospel.
OCLC: 11490250 ICW.

1479   _____. "Some Points in the Synoptic Problem. 1. The Part Played by Oral Tradition in Determining the Form and Contents of the Synoptic Gospels." Exp 4th ser. 37 (1893): 81-97.

1480   _____. "Some Points in the Synoptic Problem. 2. The Supposed Relation of St. Matthew and St. Luke to the 'Logia' as a Common Source." Exp 4th ser. 37 (1893): 179-96.

1481   _____. "Some Points in the Synoptic Problem. 3. Some Secondary Features." Exp 4th ser. 37 (1893): 256-66.

1482   _____. "Some Points in the Synoptic Problem. 4. The Authorship and Composition of the Third Gospel." Exp 4th ser. 37 (1893): 336-53.

1483   Stead, F. H. "Does the Original Collection of Logia ('Q') Contain Prediction of Our Lord's Resurrection?" Exp 8 (1921): 397-400.

1484 Stegeman, Wolfgang. "Vagabond Radicalism in Early Christianity: A Historical and Theological Discussion of a Thesis Proposed by Gerd Theissen." In *God of the Lowly. Socio-Historical Interpretation of the Bible.* Trans. from the German by M. J. O'Connell, 148-68. Maryknoll NY: Orbis Books, 1984. Trans. of "Wanderradikalismus im Urchristentum? Historische und theologische Auseinandersetzung mit einer interessanten These." In *Der Gott der kleinen Leute: Sozialgeschichtliche Bibelauslegungen,* Willy Schottroff and Wolfgang Stegeman, eds., 2:94-120. München: Kaiser; Gelnhauses: Burckhardthaus, 1979. OCLC: 10558943 ISB; 5772480.

1485 _____. "Wanderradikalismus im Urchristentum? Historische und theologische Auseinandersetzung mit einer interessanten These." In *Der Gott der kleinen Leute: Sozialgeschichtliche Bibelauslegungen,* Willy Schottroff and Wolfgang Stegemann, eds., 2:94-120. München: Kaiser; Gelnhauses: Burckhardthaus, 1979. OCLC: 5772480 STS; (ET) 10558943 ISB.

---- _____. *See* Schottroff, Luise (1384).

1486 Stegner, W. R. "Lucan Priority in the Feeding of the Five Thousand." BR 21 (1976): 19-28.

1487 _____. "The Priority of Luke: An Exposition of Robert Lindsey's Solution to the Synoptic Problem." BR 27 (1982): 26-38.

1488 Stein, Robert H. "Luke 1:1-4 and *Traditionsgeschichte.*" JETS 26 (1983): 421-30.

1489 _____. "The Proper Methodology for Ascertaining a Markan Redaction History." NovT 13 (1971): 181-98.

1490 _____. "The *Redaktionsgeschichtlich* Investigation of a Markan Seam (Mc 1,21f.)." ZNW 61 (1970): 70-94.

1491 _____. *The Synoptic Problem. An Introduction.* Grand Rapids MI: Baker Book House, 1987. 292pp. OCLC: 16633461 MCB.

1492 _____. "What is *Redaktionsgeschichte?*" JBL 88 (1969): 45-56.

1493 Steinhauser, Michael G. *Doppelbildworte in den synoptischen Evangelien: Eine form- and traditionskritische Studie.* Würzburg: Echter Verlag; Stuttgart: Katholisches Bibelwerk, 1981. Toronto: Echter, 1981. 467pp. (Forschung zur Bibel 44.) A revision of the author's doctoral thesis, Universität Würzburg, 1977–1978. OCLC: 8599000 ELW; 9281568 ISB.

1494 Stendahl, Krister. *The School of St. Matthew, and Its Use of the Old Testament.* Lund: Gleerup, 1954. 2nd ed. 1968. (Acta Seminarii neotestamentici Upsaliensis 20.) 1st American ed. Philadelphia: Fortress Press, 1968. 249pp. OCLC: 15814 CUF; 441208 ISB.

---- Stephenson, A. M. G. *See* Moule, Charles F. D. (1069).

1495 Stephenson, T. "The Classification of Doublets in the Synoptic Gospels." JThS 20 (1918–1919): 1-8.

1496 _____. "The Overlapping of Sources in Matthew and Luke." JThS 21 (1919–1920): 127-45.

1497 Stoldt, Hans-Herbert. *History and Criticism of the Marcan Hypothesis.* Trans. and ed. by Donald L. Niewyk; intro. by William R. Farmer. Macon GA: Mercer University Press; Edinburgh: T. & T. Clark, 1980. Trans. of *Geschichte und Kritik der Markushypothese.* Göttingen: Vandenhoeck & Rupecht, 1977. 241pp. Includes bibl. OCLC: 6847895 ISB; 3330200 ISB.

1498 _____. "Reflections on Legitimacy and Limits of Theological Criticism." PSThJ 33/4 (1980): 49-54. Trans. and ed. by Virgil Howard from the German original published in *Bibel und Gemeinde* 79 (1979): 283ff.

1499 Stonehouse, N. B. *Origins of the Synoptic Gospels: Some Basic Questions.* Grand Rapids MI: Eerdmans, 1963. 201pp. (Peyton Lectures 1962.) OCLC: 804053 ISB.

1500 Storr, Gottlob C. *Ueber den Zweck der evangelischen Geschichte und der Briefe Johannis.* Tübingen: J. F. Heerbrandt, 1786. 526pp. OCLC: 7674620 NDD.

1501 Strack, Hermann Leberecht, and Paul Billerbeck. *Kommentar zum Neuen Testament aus Talmud und Midrasch.* 6 vols. München: Beck, 1922–1961. 5., unveränderte Aufl. 1969. 6., unveränderte Aufl. 1974–1975. 7., unveränderte Aufl. 1978. OCLC: 848243 ISB; 5626752 VYN; 419029 DAY; 1867461 BNG; 4022155 CPC.

1502A Strauss, David Friedrich. *The Life of Jesus, Critically Examined.* (1) Trans. from the 4th German ed. by George Eliot [i.e., Mary Ann Evans]. 3 vols. London: Chapman Brothers, 1846. (2) Trans. from the 4th German ed. by Marvin Evans. 2 vols. New York: C. Blanchard, 1855–1860. Microfiche. Louisville KY: Lost Cause Press, 1979. ET: 2nd ed. 2 vols in 1. London: Swan Sonnenschein; New York: Macmillan, 1892. ET: 3rd ed. (Eliot trans.) with notes and intro. by Peter C. Hodgson. (Lives of Jesus Series.) Philadelphia: Fortress Press, 1972. London: SCM, 1975. 812pp. Trans. of *Das Leben Jesu, kritisch bearbeitet.* 2 vols. 4th ed. Tübingen: Osiander, 1840. 3rd ed. rev. 1838, 1839. 2nd ed. 1837. 1st ed. 1835, 1836. Rpt: Darmstadt: Wissenschaftliche Buchgesellschaft, 1969. OCLC: 8167917 ISB; 1052308 OUN; 683046; 2666113; 5937738 ISB.

1502B _____. *Das Leben Jesu für das deutsche Volk bearbeitet.* 2 vols. Leipzig: F. A. Brockhaus, 1864. 663pp. 5. Aufl. 2 vols. in 1. Bonn: Emil Strauss, 1889. 18. Aufl. 2 vols. Stuttgart: Alfred Kröner, 1964. ET: *A New Life of Jesus.* "Authorized trans." London; Edinburgh: Williams and Norgate, 1865. *The Life of Jesus for the People.* 2nd ed. London: Williams and Norgate, 1879.
OCLC: 5204628 DUQ; 16278676 CLU; 6840184 CLE; 4818775 IND; 3804259 TLM.

1503 Strecker, Georg. "Die Antithesen der Bergpredigt (Mt 5, 21-48 par.)" ZNW 69 (1978): 36-72.

1504 _____. *Die Bergpredigt: Ein exegetischer Kommentar.* Göttingen: Vandenhoeck & Rupecht, 1984. 194pp. Includes bibl.
OCLC: 11197083 ISB.

1505 _____. "Die Makarismen der Bergpredigt." NTS 17 (1971): 255-75.

1506 _____. *Der Weg der Gerechtigkeit: Untersuchung zur Theologie des Matthäus.* Göttingen: Vandenhoeck & Ruprecht, 1962. 267pp. 2., durchges, um einen Nachtrag erw. Aufl. 1966. 283pp. 3., durchges. und erw. Aufl. 1971. 310pp. (Forschungen zur Religion und Literatur des Alten und Neuen Testaments 82.) Includes bibl.
Based on the author's Habilitationsschrift, Bonn, 1958/1959.
OCLC: 5258783 COO; 6818495 ISB; 702707 CSU.

1507 _____, and Schnelle Udo. "Die Logienquelle." In *Einführung in die neutestamentliche Exegese.* By G. Strecker and S. Udo, 52-57. Göttingen: Vandenhoeck & Ruprecht, 1983. (Uni-Taschenbücher 1253.)
OCLC: 9938778 DWT.

1508 Streeter, Burnett Hillman. 1923. As reviewer see Jameson, H. G. *Origin* (746).

1509 _____. "The Document Q." In *The Two-Source Hypothesis. A Critical Appraisal,* A. J. Bellinzoni, Jr., ed., 221-25. Macon GA: Mercer University Press, 1985.
OCLC: 11599674 ISB.

1510 _____. *The Four Gospels. A Study of Origins, Treating of the Manuscript Tradition, Sources, Authorship, and Dates.* London: Macmillan, 1924. 4th impression, rev. 1930. New York: St. Martin's Press, 1956. 10th impression. 1961. 1964. 624pp.
Pages 157-69, 182-86, 195-97 are reissued in *The Two-Source Hypothesis: A Critical Appraisal,* Arthur J. Bellinzoni, Jr., ed., 23-36, 221-25. Macon GA: Mercer University Press, 1985.
OCLC: 7083711 GZE; 2848086 ISB; 3695137 UUM; 1068490 BPS; 383217 WSU; 11599674 ISB.
Review: Burkett, Francis. JTS 26 (1924–1925): 278-94.

1511 _____. "Fresh Light on the Synoptic Problem." HibJ 20 (1921–1922): 103-12.

1512 _____. "The Literary Evolution of the Gospels." In *Studies in the Synoptic Problem*, by Members of the University of Oxford, W. Sanday, ed., 209-27. Oxford: Clarendon Press, 1911. Microfiche. Louisville KY: Lost Cause Press, 1977.
OCLC: 753275 ISB; 4045911 ISB.

1513 _____. "On the Original Order of Q." In *Studies in the Synoptic Problem*, by Members of the University of Oxford, W. Sanday, ed., 141-64. Oxford: Clarendon Press, 1911. Microfiche. Louisville KY: Lost Cause Press, 1977.
OCLC: 753275 ISB; 4045911 ISB.

1514 _____. "On the Trial of Our Lord before Herod: A Suggestion." In *Studies in the Synoptic Problem*, by Members of the University of Oxford, W. Sanday, ed., 229-31. Oxford: Clarendon Press, 1911. Microfiche. Louisville KY: Lost Cause Press, 1977.
OCLC: 753275 ISB; 4045911 ISB.

1515 _____. "The Original Extent of Q." In *Studies in the Synoptic Problem*, by Members of the University of Oxford, W. Sanday, ed., 185-208. Oxford: Clarendon Press, 1911. Microfiche. Louisville KY: Lost Cause Press, 1977.
OCLC: 753275 ISB; 4045911 ISB.

1516 _____. "St. Mark's Knowledge and Use of Q." In *Studies in the Synoptic Problem*, by Members of the University of Oxford, W. Sanday, ed., 165-83. Oxford: Clarendon Press, 1911. Microfiche: Louisville KY: Lost Cause Press, 1977.
OCLC: 753275 ISB; 4045911 ISB.

1517 _____. "Synoptic Criticism and the Eschatological Problem." Apppendix in *Studies in the Synoptic Problem*, by Members of the University of Oxford, W. Sanday, ed., 425-38. Oxford: Clarendon Press, 1911. Microfiche. Louisville KY: Lost Cause Press, 1977.
OCLC: 753275 ISB; 4045911 ISB.

1518 _____. "The Synoptic Gospels." In *A Commentary on the Bible*, Arthur S. Peake, ed., 672-80. London: T. C. and E. C. Jack, Ltd., 1929.
OCLC: 6617374 TJC.

1519A Strobel, August. "In dieser Nacht (Luk 17, 34). Zu einer älteren Form der Erwartung in Luk 17, 20-37." ZThK 58 (1961): 16-29.

1519B Stroth, Friedrich Andreas. "Von Interpolationen im Evangelium Matthaei." *Repertorium für biblische und morgenländische Litteratur* 9 (1781): 99-156.
Published anonymously. Stroth was later identified as the author by J. G. Eichhorn, editor of the series. *See* J. G. Eichhorn, *Einleitung in das Neue Testament* (421), 2nd ed. vol. 1, 1820, 465n1.

1520 Sturch, R. L. "The Markan Miracles and the Other Synoptists." ET 89 (1978): 375-76.

1521 Styler, G. M. "The Priority of Mark." Excursus 4 in *The Birth of the New Testament*, by C. F. D. Moule, 223-32. New York: Harper & Row, London: A. & C. Black, 1962. 3rd ed., revised and rewritten, 285-316. San Francisco: Harper & Row, 1982. (Harper's New Testament Commentaries. Black's New Testament Commentaries.)
Reissued in *The Two-Source Hypothesis: A Critical Appraisal*, Arthur J. Bellinzoni, Jr., ed., 63-75. Macon GA: Mercer University Press, 1985.
OCLC: 538227 OUN; 1005383 ISB; 11599674 ISB.

1522A Suggs, M. Jack. "The Passion and Resurrection Narratives." In *Jesus and Man's Hope*, Donald G. Miller and Dikran Y. Hadidian, eds., 2:323-37. Pittsburgh: Pittsburgh Theological Seminary, 1971. (Perspective 2.)
OCLC: 142572 ISB.

1522B _____. *Wisdom, Christology, and Law in Matthew's Gospel*. Cambridge: Harvard University Press, 1970. 132pp.
OCLC: 81999 ISB.
Reviews: Hamerton-Kelly, Robert. JAAR 39 (1971): 528-30; Brogan, W. J. ThSt 32 (1971): 304-306; Sweetman, L. CTJ 6 (1971): 228-34.

1523 Suhl, Alfred. 1971. As reviewer see Lambrecht, Jan. *Marcus Interpretator* (863).

1524 _____. *Die Funktion der alttestamentlichen Zitate und Anspielungen im Markusevangelium*. Gütersloh: G. Mohn, 1965. 198pp.
Revision of the author's thesis, Münster.
OCLC: 925191 ISB.

1525 Sullivan, Clayton. *Rethinking Realized Eschatology*. Macon GA: Mercer University Press, 1988. Forthcoming.
A critique of Dodd's "realized eschatalogy" as based on the questionable two-source hypothesis of gospel origins.

1526 Summers, Ray. *The Secret Sayings of the Living Jesus: Studies in the Coptic Gospel according to Thomas*. Waco TX: Word Books, 1968. 159pp.
Includes bibl.
OCLC: 231474 DTM.

1527 Sundwall, J. "Die Zusammensetzung des Markusevangeliums." AAAboH 9 (1934):*

1528A Swanson, Donald C. "Diminutives in the Greek New Testament." JBL 77 (1958): 134-51.

1528B Swanson, Reuben J. *The Horizontal Line Synopsis of the Gospels*. Rev. ed. Pasadena CA: William Carey Library, 1984. 1st ed. 1975. xlviii + 557pp. Greek ed.: *The Horizontal Line Synopsis of the Gospels. Greek Edition*. Vol. 1. *The Gospel of Matthew*. Dillsboro NC: Western North Carolina Press, 1982. xxii + 448pp.
English ed. employs the RSV text; Greek ed. employs the text of the United Bible Societies' 3rd ed. of *The Greek New Testament* (1966, 1968, 1975).

1529 Sweetland, D. M. "Discipleship and Persecution: A Study of Luke 12:1-12." Bib 65 (1984): 61-80.

1530 Sweetman, L. 1971. As reviewer see Suggs, M. Jack. *Wisdom* (1522).

1531 Swete, Henry Barclay, ed. *Essays on Some Biblical Questions of the Day.* By Members of the University of Cambridge. London: Macmillan, 1909. 556pp.
OCLC: 418070 ISB; 13954256 GTX.

1532 _____. *The Gospel according to St. Mark. The Greek text with introduction, notes, and indices.* London; New York: Macmillan, 1898. cix + 412pp. 2nd ed. 1902. 3rd ed. 1920. Rpt: Grand Rapids MI: Eerdmans, 1951. Microfiche. Pastors Resource Services, 1971. Chattanooga TN: Expositor's Microform Library, 1978?. cxviii + 434pp.
OCLC: 2319201 CPL; 6184027 BUF; 8594297 BCT; 13840024 BNG; 3647465 CSM; 6841169 CDC; 7118852 TBI.

1533A Talbert, Charles H. "Oral and Independent or Literary and Interdependent? A Response to Albert B. Lord." In *The Relationships among the Gospels: An Interdisciplinary Dialogue,* William O. Walker, Jr., ed., 93-102. San Antonio: Trinity University Press, 1978. (Trinity University Monograph Series in Religion 5.)
OCLC: 4365624 ISB.

1533B _____. "The Redaction Critical Quest for Luke the Theologian." In *Jesus and Man's Hope,* D. G. Buttrick, ed., 1:171-222. Pittsburgh: Pittsburgh Theological Seminary, 1970. (Perspective 1.)
OCLC: 142572 ISB.

1534 _____, and Edgar V. McKnight. "Can the Griesbach Hypothesis Be Falsified?" JBL 91 (1972): 338-68.

1535 Taylor, Robert Oswald Patrick. *The Groundwork of the Gospels. With some collected papers.* Oxford: Blackwell, 1946. xiii + 151pp.
OCLC: 3595097 ISB.

1536 Taylor, Vincent. *Behind the Third Gospel: A Study of the Proto-Luke Hypothesis.* Oxford: Clarendon Press, 1926. Microfilm. Ann Arbor MI: University Microfilms International, 1981. 279pp. Includes bibl.
OCLC: 5154300 ISB; 11197771 VYN.

1537 _____. "The Elusive Q." ET 46 (1934–1935): 68-74.

1538 _____. *The First Draft of St. Luke's Gospel.* With a preface by E. G. Selwyn. London: SPCK, 1927. 40pp. (Theology Reprints 1.)
Includes the text of Proto-Luke (pp. 9-39.)
OCLC: 988410 ISB.

1539 _____. *The Formation of the Gospel Tradition. Eight Lectures.* 2nd ed. London: Macmillan; New York: St. Martin's, 1935. 1st ed. 1933. Rpts: 1945. 1949. 1953. 1957. 1960. 1964. 1968. xii + 217pp.
Lectures originally presented at the University of Leeds during the spring term of 1932.
OCLC: 11529226 CDS; 3426528 UUM; 3048866 MST; 6255564 KSW.

1540 _____. *The Gospel According to St. Mark. The Greek Text with intro-duction, notes, and indexes.* 2nd ed. London: Macmillan; New York: St. Martin's Press, 1966. 1st ed. 1952. 8th ed. 1969. 1974. Grand Rapids MI: Baker Book House, 1981. 696pp. (Thornapple Commentaries.) Spanish. *Evangelio según San Marcos.* Presentación de D. Mínguez Fernández. Madrid: Ediciones Cristiandad, 1979. 835pp. (Biblioteca Biblica cristiandad.)
OCLC: 2993768 BCT; 175907 CSU; 10088837 MBB; 8229936 VYF; 9337316 IDK.

1541 _____. *The Gospels. A Short Introduction.* London: Epworth Press, 1930. 128pp. 11th ed. 1967. 111pp.
OCLC: 1814234 BPS; 349908 WSU.

1542 _____. "Is the Proto-Luke Hypothesis Sound?" JThS 29 (1927–1928): 147-55.

1543 _____. *The Life and Ministry of Jesus.* Nashville: Abingdon Press, 1955. Photocopy. Ann Arbor MI: University Microfilms International, 1977. 240pp.
Reissued as pt. 2 ("Historical and Theological") of his *The Person of Christ in New Testament Teaching,* 153-304. London: Macmillan; New York: St. Martin's, 1958.
A revision and enlargement of his "The Life and Ministry of Jesus." In *The Interpreter's Bible,* George A. Buttrick, et al., eds., 7:114-44. New York: Abingdon Press, 1951.
OCLC: 560317 ISB; 12018927 PZI.

1544 _____. "Modern Issues in Biblical Studies. Methods of Gospel Criticism." ET 71 (1959–1960): 68-72.

1545 _____. *New Testament Essays.* London: Epworth Press, 1970. Grand Rapids MI: Eerdmans, 1972. 146pp.
OCLC: 97231 ISB; 344130 CCL.

1546 _____. "The Order of Q." JThS 4 (1953): 27-31. Reissued in his *New Testament Essays,* 90-94 (1545).

1547 _____. "The Original Order of Q." In *New Testament Essays. Studies in Memory of Thomas Walter Manson, 1893–1958,* A. J. B. Higgins, ed., 246-69. Manchester: Manchester University Press, 1959.
Reissued in Taylor's *New Testament Studies.* 95-118; and in *The Two-Source Hypothesis: A Critical Appraisal,* A. J. Bellinzoni, Jr., ed., 295-317. Macon GA: Mercer University Press, 1985.
OCLC: 2879047 ISB; 1159967 ISB.

1548 _____. *The Passion Narrative of St. Luke.* A critical and historical investigation. Ed. Owen E. Evans. Cambridge: Cambridge University Press, 1972. 141pp. (SNTSMS 19.)
OCLC: 195556 ISB.

1549 _____. "The Proto-Luke Hypothesis." ET 67 (1955–1956): 12-16.

1550 Taylor, W. S. "Memory and the Gospel Tradition." ThTo 21 (1973): 302-17.

1551 Teeple, Howard M. "The Greek Article with Personal Names in the Synoptic Gospels." NTS 19 (1973): 302-17.

1552 _____. "The Oral Tradition That Never Existed." JBL 89 (1970): 56-68.

1553 Testa, G. "Studio di Mc 6, 6b-13 secondo il metodo della storia della tradizione." DT(P) 93 (1972): 177-91.

1554A Tevis, Dennis Gordon. "An Analysis of Words and Phrases Characteristic of the Gospel of Matthew." Ph.D. diss., Southern Methodist University, 1982. 317 leaves. Includes bibl. Photocopy. Ann Arbor MI: University Microfilms International, 1984. Microfilm. 1985.
OCLC: 11493802 IYU; 13379798 HGS, ISB.

1554B Theile, Carl Gottfried Wilhelm. *De trium Evangeliorum necessitudine.* Dissertatio prima, quam . . . defendent auctor Carol. Godofr. Guilielm. Theile . . . et socius Christianus Guilielmus Niedner. Lipsiae: Fridr. Gluick, 1823. 70pp.
NUC: NjPT.

1554C _____. "Kritik der verschiedenen Berichten über das Wechselverhältniss der synoptischen Evangelien." *Neues kritisches Journal der theologischen Literatur* 5/4 (1828?): 385ff.*

1554D _____. *Zur Biographia Jesu.* Leipzig: Eisenach, 1837. iv + 170pp.
NUC: MB; OO; MH-AH; PPLT.

1555 Theissen, Gerd. *The Social Setting of Pauline Christianity. Essays on Corinth.* Ed. and trans. and with an intro. by John H. Schütz. Philadelphia: Fortress Press; Edinburgh: T. & T. Clark, 1982. 210pp. (Studies in the New Testament and Its World.) Trans. of *Studien zur Soziologie des Urchristentums.* Tübingen: J. C. B. Mohr (Paul Siebeck), 1979. 317pp. 2., erw. Aufl. 1983. 364pp. (Wissenschaftliche Untersuchungen zum Neuen Testament 19.) Includes bibl.
OCLC: 7737429 ISB: 9107708 VFY; 6230492 ISB; 10527797.

1556 _____. "Wanderradikalismus. Literatursoziologische Aspekte der Überlierferung von Wörten Jesu im Urchristentum." ZThK 70 (1973): 245-71.

1557 Theron, Daniel J. *Evidence of Tradition. Selected Source Material for the Study of the History of the Early Church, the New Testament Books, the New Testament Canon.* Grand Rapids MI: Baker Book House, 1958. 1980. 135pp.
Greek and Latin texts, with parallel English translations.
OCLC: 894801 BWE; 6263260 IFB.

1558 Thils, Gustave. *Histoire doctrinale du mouvement oecuménique.* Louvain: Warny, 1955. 260pp. Nouv. éd. Paris: Desclée de Brouwer, 1962. 338pp. (BEThL 8).
OCLC: 1250287 FAU; 5159049 COO.

1559 ————. *L'infaillibilité du peuple chrétien "In credendo": Notes de théologie posttridentine.* Paris: Desclée de Brouwer; Louvain: Warny, 1963. 66pp. (BEThL 21.)
OCLC: 1813524 BWE.

1560 ————. *Orientation de la théologie.* Louvain: Ceuterick, 1958. Photorpt. ed. 1964. 188pp. (BEThL 11.)
OCLC: 13955931 GTX; 920009 BXM; 13949973 GTX.

1561 ————. *Primauté Pontificale et prérogatives Episcopales: (potestas ordinaria) au Concile du Vatican.* Louvain: Warny, 1961. 102pp.
OCLC: 656666 ATO.

1562 ————, and R. E. Brown, eds. *Exégèse et théologie. Les saintes écritures et leur interprétation théologique.* Gembloux: J. Duculot, 1968. 327pp. (BEThL 26.) Includes bibl.
French, German, or English.
OCLC: 1074393 ISB; 4984978 COO.

1563 Thomas, Page A. "William R. Farmer: Bibliography." In *Jesus, the Gospels, and the Church,* E. P. Sanders, ed., xxxi-xxxviii. Macon GA: Mercer University Press, 1987.
OCLC: 16130939 ISB.

1564 Thomas, R. L. "An Investigation of the Agreements between Matthew and Luke Against Mark." JETS 19 (1976): 103-12.

1565 Thompson, P. J. "The Infancy Gospels of St. Matthew and St. Luke Compared." In *Studia Evangelica. Papers presented to the International Congress on "The Four Gospels in 1957," held at Christ Church, Oxford, 1957,* Kurt Aland, F. L. Cross, et al., eds., 217-22. Berlin: Akademie-Verlag, 1959. (Texte und Untersuchungen 73.)
OCLC: 1637245 ISB; 13641309 BZM.

1566 Thompson, William G. "Reflections on the Composition of Mt. 8:1-9:34." CBQ 33 (1971): 365-88.

1567A Throckmorton, Burton Hamilton, Jr. "Did Mark Know Q?" JBL 67 (1948): 319-29.

1567B ————. *Gospel Parallels. A Synopsis of the First Three Gospels. With Alternate Readings from the Manuscripts and Noncanonical Parallels.* 3rd ed. rev. Nashville; New York: Thomas Nelson, 1967. 2nd ed. 1957. 1st ed. 1949. xxvi + 191pp.
Employs the RSV, 1952, and follows the Huck-Lietzmann *Synopsis* 9th ed. (728).

1568 ————. "Mark and Roger of Hoveden." CBQ 39 (1977): 103-106.

1569 Timmer, John. *Julius Wellhausen and the Synoptic Gospels. A Study in Tradition Growth.* Rotterdam: Drukkerij Bronder-Offset N.V., 1970. 127pp.
Proefschrift—Vrije Universiteit te Amsterdam.
OCLC: 1720697 HUC.

1570 Tischendorf, Constantin von, ed. *Evangelia apocrypha: adhibitis plurimis codicibus graecis et latinis maximam partem nunc primum consultis atque ineditorum copia insignibus.* Lipsiae: Avenarius et Mendelssohn, 1853. lxxxviii + 463pp. Ed. altera, ab ipso Tischendorfio recognita et locupletata. 1876. xcv + 486pp. Hildesheim: G. Olms, 1966.
OCLC: 3487925 RSC; 7868816 CLU; 910837 TOL.

1571 ———. *Origin of the Four Gospels.* Trans. under the author's sanction by W. L. Gage from the 4th German ed., revised and greatly enlarged. New York: American Tract Society, 1867. London: Jackson, 1868. 287pp.
OCLC: 1949490 BSC; 3834581 TLM.

1572 ———, ed. *Synopsis evangelica: ex quattuor evangeliis ordine chronologico concinnavit praetexto brevi commentario illustravit apposito apparatu critico.* Edito in commodum academicum repetita. Lipsiae: Avenarius & Mendelssohn, 1854. 204pp. 2. ed., emendata. Lipsiae: Hermann Mendelssohn, 1864. Ed. 7a., novis curis auctior et emendatior. 1898. 184pp.
OCLC: 3964087 MBS; 11401120 RCE; 9561324 EXN.

1573 ———. *When Were Our Gospels Written? An Argument. With a narrative of the discovery of the Sinaitic manuscript.* Boston: Massachusetts Sabbath School Society, 1867. 167pp. 4th ed. London: Religious Tract Society, 1869. New ed. 1890? (Religious Tract Society: Library books 97.) 119pp. Trans. of *Wann wurden unsere Evangelien verfasst?* Leipzig: J. C. Hinrichs, 1865. 70pp. New York: Amerikansichen Traktat-Gesellschaft, 1865? 112pp. 4. wesentlich erweiterte Aufl. 1880. 132pp. French. *À quelle époque nos évangiles ont-ils été composés?* Traduit de l'allemand, sur la seconde édition, par L. Durand. Paris: C. Meyrueis, 1866. 48pp.
OCLC: 12377766 CBY; 11528933 WBS; 8985040 ISB; 7068743 IGR; 519052 STS; 967231 BCT; 12536637 ITC; 10445266 IUL.

1574 Titius, A. "Das Verhältnis der Herrnworte im Markusevangelium zu den Logia des Matthäus." In *Theologische Studien.* Herrn Wirkl. Oberkonsistorialrath Professor D. Bernard Weiss zu seiner 70. Geburtstage dargebracht, C. R. Gregory, et al., 284-331. Göttingen: Vandenhoeck & Ruprecht, 1897.
OCLC: 6712206 NDD.

1575 Tödt, Heinz E. *The Son of Man in the Synoptic Tradition.* Trans. Dorothea M. Barton. Philadelphia: Westminster Press, 1965. 366pp. (New Testament Library.) London: SCM, 1965. Trans. of *Der Menschensohn in der synoptischen Überlieferung.* 1963. Includes bibl.
OCLC: 387227 WSU; 6025888 ISB.

1576 Toews, J. E. "The Synoptic Problem and the Genre Question." *Direction* 10 (1981): 11-18.

1577 Torrey, C. C. *Our Translated Gospels. Some of the Evidence.* New York; London: Harper & Bros.; London: Hodder & Stoughton, 1936. 1937. Rpt: Ann Arbor MI: University Microfilms, 1976. 172pp. OCLC: 530639 ISB; 3728562 MBS; 3081718 SNN; 4521960 COI.

1578 Torris, J. "L'énigme du quatrième évangile, à propos des livres de Siegfried Schulz." CCER 28 (1980): 20-27.

1579 Trilling, Wolfgang. "Der Einzug in Jerusalem Mt. 21, 1-17." In *Neutestamentliche Aufsätze: Festschrift für Prof. Josef Schmid zum 70. Geburtstag,* J. Blinzler, O. Kuss, and F. Mussner, eds., 303-309. Regensburg: F. Pustet, 1963. OCLC: 2282244 AZU.

1580 _____. "Die Täufertradition bei Matthäus." BZ 3 (1959): 271-89.

1581 _____. *Das wahre Israel: Studien zur Theologie des Matthäusevangeliums.* Leipzig: St. Benno-Verlag, 1959. 209pp. 3. umgearbeitete Aufl. München: Kösel, 1964. 3. Aufl. Leipzig: St. Benno-Verlag, 1975. 247pp. (Erfurter theologische Studien 7.) Spanish. *El verdadero Israel: estudio de la theologia de Mateo.* Madrid: Fax, 1974, 370pp. (Actualidad biblica 36.) Includes bibl.
Revision of the author's thesis "Die Theologie des Matthäusevangelium," Münich, 1958.
OCLC: 5252492 COO; 766364 ISB; 5366293 BHA; 3296819 BHA.

1582 Trocmé, Étienne. *The Formation of the Gospel according to Mark.* Trans. Mela Gaughan. Philadelphia: Westminster Press; London: SPCK, 1975. 293pp. Trans. of *La Formation de l'Évangile selon Marc.* Paris: Presses Universitaires de France, 1963. 231pp. (Études d'histoire et de philosophie religieuses 57.) Includes bibl.
OCLC: 1366159 ISB; 2155849; 760077 ISB.

1583 Tuckett, C. M. "1 Corinthians and Q." JBL 102 (1983): 607-19.

1584A _____. "The Argument from Order and the Synoptic Problem." ThZ 36 (1980): 338-54.

1584B _____. "Arguments from Order: Definition and Evaluation." In *Synoptic Studies: The Ampleforth Conferences of 1982 and 1983,* C. M. Tuckett, ed., 197-219. Sheffield: JSOT Press, 1984. (JSNT Supplement Series 7.)
OCLC: 12451599 ISB.

1585 _____. "The Beatitudes: A Source-Critical Study." NovT 25 (1983): 193-216.

1586 _____. "The Griesbach Hypothesis in the 19th Century." JSNT 3 (1979): 29-60.

1587 _____. "Luke 4, 16-30, Isaiah and Q." In *Logia. Les paroles de Jésus = The Sayings of Jesus. Mémorial Joseph Coppens,* Joël Delobel, ed., 343-54. Leuven: University Press and Peeters, 1982. (BEThL 59.)
OCLC: 9450792 ISB; 11043145 UTS.

1588 ———. "On the Relationship between Matthew and Luke." NTS 30 (1984): 130-42.

1589 ———. "Paul and the Synoptic Mission Discourse?" EThL 60 (1984): 376-81.

1590 ———. "The Present Son of Man." JSNT 14 (1982): 58-81.

1591A ———. *The Revival of the Griesbach Hypothesis: An Analysis and Appraisal.* Cambridge; New York: Cambridge University Press, 1983. 255pp. (SNTSMS 44.) OCLC: 7464607 ISB.

1591B ———, ed. *Synoptic Studies: The Ampleforth Conferences of 1982 and 1983.* Sheffield: JSOT Press, 1984. xii + 231pp. (JSNT Supplement Series 7.) Conference papers. OCLC:12451599 ISB.

1591C ———. "The Two-Gospel Hypothesis under Scrutiny: A Response." PSThJ 40/3 (1987): 25-31.

1592 Turner, C. H. "Historical Introduction of the Textual Criticism of the New Testament. Part 2." JThS 10 (1908–1909): 161-82.

1593 ———. "Marcan Usage. Notes, Critical and Exegetical, on the Second Gospel." JThS 25 (1924): 377-86; 26 (1925): 12-20, 145-56, 225-40, 337-46; 27 (1926): 58-62; 28 (1927): 9-30, 349-62; 29 (1928): 275-89, 346-61.

1594 ———. *The Study of the New Testament, 1883–1920. An Inaugural Lecture Delivered before the University of Oxford on October 22 and 29, 1920.* Oxford: Clarendon Press, 1920. 66pp. 2nd ed., with additional notes. 1924. 3rd ed. 1926. Photocopy. 1985. 72pp. OCLC: 4643709 IND; 4707903 TSW; 12682231 ISB; 12112808 EXN.

1595 Turner, H. E. W. *Historicity and the Gospels. A Sketch of Historical Method and Its Application to the Gospels.* London: A. R. Mowbray, 1963. 108pp. OCLC: 565390 ISB.

1596 ———, and Hugh Montefiore. *Thomas and the Evangelists.* London: SCM, 1962. Naperville IL: Alec R. Allenson, 1962. 128pp. (Studies in Biblical Theology 35.) Includes bibl. OCLC: 2079353 ISB; 383456 WSU.

1597 Turner, N. "The Literary Character of New Testament Greek." NTS 20 (1974): 107-14.

1598 ———. "The Minor Verbal Agreements of Mt. and Lk. Against Mk." In *Studia Evangelica. Papers Presented to the International Congress on "The Four Gospels in 1957," held at Christ Church, Oxford, 1957,* Kurt Aland, et al., eds., 223-34. Berlin: Akademie-Verlag, 1959. (Texte und Untersuchungen 73.) OCLC: 1637245 ISB; 13641309 BZM.

1599 ———. "Papyrus Finds." ET 76 (1964–1965): 44-48.

1600 ———. "Q in Recent Thought." ET 80 (1968–1969): 324-28.

1601 ———. "The Quality of the Greek in Luke-Acts." In *Studies in New Testament Language and Text. Essays in Honour of George D. Kilpatrick on the Occasion of His Sixty-Fifth Birthday,* J. K. Elliott, ed., 387-400. Leiden: E. J. Brill, 1976. 400pp. (NovTSup 44.)
OCLC: 2370190 IVD.

1602 ———. "The Relation of Luke I and II to Hebraic Sources and to the Rest of Luke-Acts." NTS 2 (1956): 100-109.

1603A Tyson, Joseph B. "The Blindness in the Disciples in Mark." JBL 80 (1961): 261-68.

1603B ———. "Conflict as a Literary Theme in the Gospel of Luke." In *New Synoptic Studies: The Cambridge Gospel Conference and Beyond,* William R. Farmer, ed., 303-27. Macon GA: Mercer University Press, 1983.
OCLC: 9783753 ISB.

1603C ———. *The Death of Jesus in Luke-Acts.* Columbia SC: University of South Carolina Press, 1986. xi + 198pp. Includes bibl.
OCLC: 13010821 ISB.

1603D ———. "Further Thoughts on *The Death of Jesus in Luke-Acts.*" PSThJ 40/2 (1987): 48-50.
Response to three critical responses by Daryl Schmidt, David Balch, and Philip L. Shuler in PSThJ 40/2 (1987): 33-47.

1603E ———. "Jesus and Herod Antipas." JBL 79 (1960): 239-46.

1603F ———. "The Jewish Public in Luke-Acts." NTS 30 (1980): 574-83.

1603G ———. "Literary Criticism and the Gospels: The Seminar." In *The Relationships among the Gospels: An Interdisciplinary Dialogue,* William O. Walker, Jr., ed., 323-41. San Antonio: Trinity University Press, 1978. (Trinity University Monograph Series in Religion 5.)
OCLC: 4365624 ISB.

1603H ———. "The Lucan Version of the Trial of Jesus." NovT 3 (1959): 249-58.

1603I ———. "The Opposition to Jesus in the Gospel of Luke." PerspRS 5 (1978): 144-50.

1603J ———. "Scripture, Torah, and Sabbath in Luke-Acts." In *Jesus, the Gospels, and the Church,* E. P. Sanders, ed., 89-104. Macon GA: Mercer University Press, 1987.
OCLC: 16130939 ISB.

1604A ———. "Sequential Parallelism in the Synoptic Gospels." NTS 22 (1976): 276-308.

1604B ———. "Source Criticism and the Gospel of Luke." In *Perspectives on Luke-Acts,* Charles H. Talbert, ed., 24-39. Macon GA: Mercer University Press, 1978.
OCLC: 4410368 ISB.

1604C ————. "The Sources of Luke: A Proposal for the Consultation on the Relationships of the Gospels." In *Society of Biblical Literature 1976 Seminar Papers*, George MacRae, ed., 279-86. Missoula MT: Scholars Press, 1976.

1604D ————. "The Synoptic Problem." In his *The New Testament and Early Christianity*, 148-58. New York; London: Macmillan; Collier Macmillan, 1984.
OCLC: 9464471 ISB.

1605 ————. "The Synoptic Problem." In *Harper's Bible Dictionary*, Paul J. Achtemeier, gen. ed., 1,009. San Francisco: Harper & Row, 1985.
OCLC: 12262764 ISB.

1606 ————. "The Two-Source Hypothesis: A Critical Appraisal." In *The Two-Source Hypothesis: A Critical Appraisal*, A. J. Bellinzoni, Jr., ed., 437-52. Macon GA: Mercer University Press, 1985.
OCLC: 11599674 ISB.

1607 ————, and Thomas R. W. Longstaff. *Synoptic Abstract*. Assisted by E. A. Tipper and L. Marvin Guier. Wooster OH: Biblical Research Associates, 1978. 193pp. (Computer Bible 15.)
OCLC: 4291144 ICU.

---- Udo, Schnelle. *See* Strecker, Georg. (1507).

1608 Urbina, I. Ortiz de. 1969. *See* Oertiz de Urbina, I.

1609 Vaage, Leif Eric. "Q: The Ethos and Ethics of an Itinerant Intelligence." Ph.D. diss., Claremont Graduate School, 1987. 2 vols. 596 leaves. Photocopy. 1987. Includes bibl.
OCLC: 14974287 HDC.

1610 ————. "Q 4. [Lk. 4:1-13]." In *Society of Biblical Literature 1984 Seminar Papers*, K. H. Richards, ed., 347-73. Chico CA: Scholars Press, 1984. (SBLSPS 23.)

1611 Vaganay, Léon. "L'absence du Sermon sur la montagne chez Marc." RB 58 (1951): 5-46.

1612 ————. "Autour de la question synoptique." EThL 31 (1955): 343-56.

1613 ————. *L'Évangile de Pierre*. Préface par M.-J. Lagrange. Paris: Gabalda et fils, 1930. 2. éd. 1930. 357 pp. (Études bibliques.) Includes bibl.
Greek text, translation, and commentary of the Gospel of Peter on pp. 197-340.
OCLC: 5722840 ISB; 13948617 GTX; 743003 BZM.

1614 ————. "Existe-t-il chez Marc quelques traces du sermon sur la montagne?" NTS 1 (1954): 192-200.

1615 ————. "Matthieu (évangile selon saint.)" In DBS 5. 1957.*

1616 _____. *Le problème synoptique: Une hypothèse de travail.* Préf. de L. Cerfaux. Tournai: Desclée, 1954. 474 pp. (Bibliothèque de théologie. Série 3. Théologie biblique 1.) Includes bibl.
OCLC: 2039531 PCJ; 1853322 ISB.

1617 _____. "La question synoptique." EThL 28 (1952): 238-56.

1618 _____. "Le schématisme du discours communautaire à la lumière de la critique des sources." RB 60 (1953): 203-44.

1619 VanCangh, Jean-Marie. " 'Par l'esprit de Dieu'-par le doigt de Dieu. Mt 12, 28 par. Lc 11, 20." In *Logia. Les paroles de Jésus = The Sayings of Jesus: Mémorial Joseph Coppens,* Joël Delobel, ed., 337-42. Leuven: University Press and Peeters, 1982. (BEThL 59.)
OCLC: 9450792 ISB; 11043145.

---- Van Unnik, W. C. *See* Baarda, T. (46).

1620 Vargas-Machuca, A. "(καί) ἰδού en el estilo narrativo de Mateo." Bib 50 (1969): 233-44.

1621 _____. "El paralítico perdonado, en la redacción de Mateo (Mt. 9, 1-8.)" EE 44 (1969): 15-43.

1622 Vassiliadis, Petros. "Behind Mark: Towards A Written Source." NTS 20 (1973): 155-60.

1623 _____. "The Function of John the Baptist in Q and Mark." Theol(A) 46 (1975): 405-13.

1624 _____. "The Nature and Extent of the Q-Document." NovT 20 (1978): 49-73.

1625 _____. "The Original Order of Q: Some Residual Cases." In *Logia. Les paroles de Jésus = The Sayings of Jesus: Mémorial Joseph Coppens,* Joël Delobel, ed., 379-87. Leuven: University Press and Peeters, 1982. (BEThL 59.)
OCLC: 9450792 ISB; 11043145 UTS.

1626 _____. "Prolegomena to a Discussion on the Relationship Between Mark and the Q Document." DeBiM 3 (1975): 31-46.

1627 _____. *The Q-Document Hypothesis: A Critical Examination of Today's Literary and Theological Problems Concerning the Q-Document.* Athens: privately printed [Grigoris' Bookshops], 1977. 167pp. Includes bibl.
Thesis, University of America. Text in Greek; table of contents in Greek and English (pp. 166-67.)
OCLC: 5392205 TSW.

1628 Veit, Karl. *Die synoptischen Parallelen: Und ein alter Versuch ihrer Enträtselung mit neuer Begründung.* Gütersloh: C. Bertelsmann, 1897. 162pp.
Includes the Greek text of synoptic parallels.
OCLC: 4865124 BCT.

1629 Vielhauer, Philipp. *Geschichte der urchristlichen Literatur: Einleitung in das Neue Testament, die Apokryphen und die apostolischen Väter.* Berlin; New York: Walter de Gruyter, 1975. Durchgesehener Nachdruck. 1978. 3. Druck. 1981. 813pp. (De Gruyter Lehrbuch.) Includes bibl. OCLC: 2079375 ISB; 2893583; 6308866 VYN; 7919246 GCL.

1630 _____. "Gottesreich und Meschensohn in der Verkündigung Jesu." In *Aufsätze zum Neuen Testament,* 55-91. München: Kaiser Verlag, 1965. (Theologische Bücherei 31.) OCLC: 774934 ISB.

1631A _____. "Zum synoptischen Problem: Ein Bericht über die Theorien Léon Vaganays." ThLZ 80 (1955): 647-52.

1631B Vinson, Richard Bolling. "The Significance of the Minor Agreements as an Argument against the Two-Document Hypothesis." Ph.D. diss., Duke University, 1984. 438 leaves. Photocopy. Ann Arbor MI: University Microfilms International, 1985. Microfiche. 1985. Includes bibl. OCLC: 11920719 NDD; 13308534 COI; 11989149 EMT.

1631C Voeglin, Eric. "The Gospel and Culture." In *Jesus and Man's Hope,* Donald G. Miller and Dikran Y. Hadidian, eds., 2:59-101. Pittsburgh: Pittsburgh Theological Seminary, 1971. (Perspective 2.) OCLC: 142572 ISB.

1632 Vogels, H. J. *Die Harmonistik im Evangelientext des Codex Cantabrigiensis: Ein Beitrag zur neutestamentlichen Textkritik.* Leipzig: J. C. Hinrichs, 1910. 119pp. (Texte und Untersuchungen 36/1A.) OCLC: 987319 BHA.

1633 Vögtle, Anton. "Bezeugt die Logienquelle die authentische Redeweise Jesu vom 'Menschensohn'." In *Logia. Les paroles de Jésus = The Sayings of Jesus: Mémorial Joseph Coppens,* Joël Delobel, ed., 77-99. Leuven: University Press and Peeters, 1982. Reissued in Vögtle's *Offenbarungsgeschehen und Wirkungsgeschichte: Neutestamentliche Beiträge,* 50-69. Freiburg: Herder, 1985. (BEThL 59.) OCLC: 9450792 ISB; 11043145; 13957315 GTX.

1634 _____. "Die Einladung zum grossen Gastmahl und zum königlichen Hochzeitsmahl: Ein Paradigma für den Wandel des geschichtlichen Verständnishorizonts." In his *Das Evangelium und die Evangelien: Beiträge zur Evangelienforschung,* 171-218. Düsseldorf: Patmos-Verlag, 1971. (Kommentare und Beiträge zum Alten und Neuen Testament.) OCLC: 783321 ICU.

1635 _____. "Herkunft und ursprünglicher Sinn der Taufperikope Mk 1, 9-11." In his *Offenbarungsgeschehen und Wirkungsgeschichte: Neutestamentliche Beiträge,* 70-108. Freiburg: Herder, 1985. Orig. pub. in 1972. OCLC: 13957315 GTX.

1636 ————. "Der Spruch vom Jonaszeichen." In *Synoptische Studien: Alfred Wikenhauser zum siebzigsten Geburtstag am 22. Februar 1953 dargebracht von Freunden, Kollegen und Schülern,* J. Schmidt and A. Vögtle, eds., 230-77. München: K. Zink, 1953. Reissued in Vögtle's *Das Evangelium und die Evangelien,* 103-36. OCLC: 6765909 ISB; 13953567 GTX; 783321 ICU.

---- ————. *See* Schmid, Josef (1353).

1637 Volkmar, Gustav. *Die Evangelien, oder, Marcus und die Synopsis der kanonischen und ausserkanonischen Evangelien nach dem ältesten Text, mit historisch-exegetischen Commentar.* Leipzig: Fues, 1870. 660pp. OCLC: 16463172 IXT.

1638 ————. *Jesus Nazarenus und die erste christliche Zeit.* Mit den beiden ersten Erzählern. Zürich: Caesar Schmidt, 1882. 403pp. OCLC: 9229361 ISB.

1639A ————. *Die Religion Jesu und ihre erste Entwicklung nach dem gegenwärtigen Stande der Wissenschaft.* Leipzig: Brockhaus, 1857. 564pp. NUC: MB; NcD.

1639B ————. "Über das Lukasevangelium nach seinem Verhaltniss zu Marcion und seinem dogmatischen Character, mit besonderer Beziehung auf die kritischen Untersuchungen F. C. Baurs und A. Ritschls." ThJb(T) 9 (1850): 110-38, 185-235.

1640 Vööbus, Arthur. "A New Approach to the Problem of the Shorter and Longer Text in Luke." NTS 15 (1969): 457-63.

1641 ————. *The Prelude to the Lukan Passion Narrative. Tradition-, redaction-, cult-, motif-historical and source-critical studies.* Stockholm: Estonian Theological Society in Exile, 1968. 151pp. (Papers of the Estonian Theological Society in Exile 17.) Includes bibl. OCLC: 93900 STS.

1642 Vorster, Willem S. "Redaction, Contextualisation and the Sayings of Jesus." In *Logia. Des paroles de Jésus = The Sayings of Jesus: Mémorial Joseph Coppens,* Joël Delobel, ed., 491-500. Leuven: University Press and Peeters, 1982. (BEThL 59.) OCLC: 9450792 ISB; 11043145.

1643 Vosté, Jacobus-M. *De synopticorum mutua relatione et dependentia.* Rome: Collegio Angelico, 1928. 68pp. OCLC: 1295485 DAY.

1644 Votaw, C. W. "The Gospels and Contemporary Biographies." AJT 19 (1915): 45-73, 217-49.

1645 Walker, N. "Patristic Evidence and the Priority of Matthew." In *Studia Patristica,* 7:571-75. Berlin: Akademie-Verlag, 1966. (Texte und Untersuchungen 92.) OCLC: 712857 ISB.

1646A Walker, William O., Jr. "Introduction: The Colloquy on the Relationships among the Gospels." In *The Relationships among the Gospels: An Interdisciplinary Dialogue,* William O. Walker, Jr., ed., 1-15. San Antonio: Trinity University Press, 1978. (Trinity University Monograph Series in Religion 5.)
OCLC: 4365624 ISB.

1646B _____. "A Method for Identifying Redactional Passages in Matthew on Functional and Linguistic Grounds." CBQ 39 (1977): 76-93.

1647 _____. "Nazareth: A Clue to Synoptic Relationships." In *Jesus, the Gospels, and the Church,* E. P. Sanders, ed., 105-18. Macon GA: Mercer University Press, 1987.
OCLC: 16130939 ISB.

1648 _____. "The Quest for the Historical Jesus. A Discussion of Methodology." AThR 51 (1969): 38-56.

1649 _____, ed. *The Relationships among the Gospels: An Interdisciplinary Dialogue.* San Antonio: Trinity University Press, 1978. 359pp. (Trinity University Monograph Series in Religion 5.)
Based on proceedings of the Colloquy on the Relationships among the Gospels, sponsored by Trinity University and the Southwest Commission on Religious Studies, and held at Trinity University, San Antonio, Texas, 26-29 May 1977.
OCLC: 4365624 ISB.

1650A _____. "The Son of Man Question and the Synoptic Problem." NTS 28 (1982): 374-88. Rpt in slightly revised version as the second part of "The Son of Man Question and the Synoptic Problem," in *New Synoptic Studies: The Cambridge Gospel Conference and Beyond,* William R. Farmer, ed., 261-301. Macon GA: Mercer University Press, 1983.
OCLC: 9783753 ISB.

1650B _____. "The State of the Synoptic Question: Some Reflections on the Work of Tuckett and McNicol." PSThJ 40/3 (1987): 14-21.
First read at the colloquy on "New Critical Approaches in Synoptic Studies" held at Southern Methodist University, fall semester 1986.

1650C _____, with Allan J. McNicol. "A Statement of Closure: Items for Further Research." PSThJ 40/3 (1987): 32.

1651 Wanke, Joachim. *"Bezugs- und Kommentarworte" in den synoptischen Evangelien: Beobachtungen zur Interpretationsgeschichte der Herrenworte in der vorevangelischen Überlieferung.* Leipzig: St. Benno-Verlag, 1981. 120pp. (Erfurter theologische Studien 44.) Includes bibl.
OCLC: 13953614 GTX; 11263927 RBN.
Review: Turro, J. C. CBQ 45 (1983): 714-15.

1652 Watson, James D. *The Double Helix: A Personal Account of the Discovery of the Structure of DNA.* New York: Atheneum, 1968. 226pp. New York: New American Library, 1969. 140pp. New York: Norton, 1980. (Norton Critical Edition.) A new critical edition including text, commentary, reviews, original papers, ed. by Gunther S. Stent. London: Weidenfeld and Nicolson, 1981. 298pp.
Autobiographical.
OCLC: 439345 MCL; 14018707 UBY; 6016503; 7512108 GZM.

1653 Weder, Hans. *Die Gleichnisse Jesu als Metaphern: Traditions- und redaktionsgeschichtliche Analysen und Interpretationen.* Göttingen: Vandenhoeck & Ruprecht, 1978. 312pp. (Forschungen zur Religion und Literatur des Alten und Neuen Testaments 120.) Includes bibl.
Originally presented as the author's thesis, Zürich.
OCLC: 4435101; 4258951 ISB.

1654 Weeden, Theodore J. ''The Heresy that Necessitated Mark's Gospel.'' ZNW 59 (1968): 145-58.

1655 Wegner, Uwe. *Der Hauptmann von Kafarnaum (Mt. 7, 28a, 8, 5-10.13 par Lk. 7, 1-10): Ein Beitrag zur Q-Forschung.* Tübingen: J. C. B. Mohr (Paul Siebeck), 1985. (Wissenschaftliche Untersuchungen zum Neuen Testament 2/14.)
Revision of the author's thesis (doctoral), Tübingen, 1982–1983.
OCLC: 12146373 ISB; 12281904 UIU.
Review: Fuchs, A. StNTSU 10 (1985): 214-18.

1656 Weiffenbach, Wilhelm. *Die Papias-fragmente über Marcus und Matthäus, eingehend exegetisch Untersucht und kritisch Gewürdigt, Zugleich ein Beitrag zur synoptischen Frage.* Berlin: L. Schleiermacher, 1878. 135pp.
OCLC: 8078232 TJC.

1657 Weinreich, Otto. *Gebet und Wunder: Zwei Abhandlungen zur Religions- und Literaturgeschichte.* Stuttgart: W. Kohlhammer, 1929. 33pp.
OCLC: 13981529 JFS.

1658 Weiser, Alfons. *Die Knechtsgleichnisse der synoptischen Evangelien.* München: Kösel-Verlag, 1971. 312pp. (Studien zum Alten und Neuen Testament 29.) Includes bibl.
Originally presented as the author's thesis, Würzburg.
OCLC: 390283 CMC.

1659 Weiss, Bernhard. *A Commentary on the New Testament.* 4 vols. Trans. George H. Schodde and E. Wilson, with intro. by J. S. Riggs. New York: Funk & Wagnalls, 1906. Microfiche. Chattanooga TN: Expositor's Microfilm Library, 1978.
Contents. 1. Matthew-Mark; 2. Luke–The Acts; 3. Romans-Colossians; 4. Thessalonians–Revelation.
OCLC: 2028159 ISB; 7000975 TBI.

1660 _____. *Entstehungsgeschichte des Neuen Testaments.* Leipzig: J. C. Hinrichs, 1904. 19pp.
Erweiterter Sonderdruck aus Weiss, *Das Neue Testament, deutsch.*
OCLC: 654295 HUC.

1661 _____. "Die Erzählungsstücke des apostolischen Matthäus." JDTh 10 (1865): 319-76.

1662 _____. *A Manual of Introduction to the New Testament.* 2 vols. Trans. A. J. K. Davidson. New York: Funk & Wagnalls, 1889. (Foreign Biblical Library.) Trans. of *Lehrbuch der Einleitung in das Neue Testament.* Berlin: W. Hertz, 1886. 2., verb. Aufl. 1889. 1897. 644pp.
OCLC: 512180 KSU; 8116593 ISB; 7490503 TJC; 10067099 MBB.

1663 _____. *Das Marcusevangelium und seine synoptischen parallelen.* Berlin: W. Hertz, 1872. 515pp.
OCLC: 8059307 ISB.

1664 _____. *Das Matthäus-Evangelium und seine Lucas-Parallelen.* Halle: Waisenhaus, 1876. 584pp.
Greek text of Matt. and passages from Mark and Luke, after Tischendorf's edition of the N.T., followed by the author's notes in German.
OCLC: 7522148 ISB.

1665 _____. *Die Quellen des Lukasevangeliums.* Stuttgart; Berlin: Cotta, 1907. 296pp.
OCLC: 2878392 IEC.

1666 _____. *Die Quellen der synoptischen Überlieferung.* Leipzig: J. C. Hinrichs, 1908. 256pp. (Texte und Untersuchungen 32/3.)
OCLC: 1133725 BHA.

1667 _____. "Die Redestücke des apostolischen Matthäus." JDTh 9 (1864): 49-140.

1668 _____. "Zur Entstehungsgeschichte der drei synoptischen Evangelien." ThStKr 34 (1861): 29-100, 646-713.

1669 Weiss, Johannes. *Das älteste Evangelium: Ein Beitrag zum Verständnis des Markus-Evangeliums und der ältesten evangelischen Überlieferung.* Göttingen: Vandenhoeck & Ruprecht, 1903. 414pp.
OCLC: 7537821 IND.

1670 _____. *Jesus' Proclamation of the Kingdom of God.* Trans., ed., and with an intro. by R. H. Hiers and D. L. Holland. Philadelphia: Fortress Press, 1971. London: SCM, 1971. (Lives of Jesus Series.) Chico CA: Scholars Press, 1985. 148pp. (Scholars Press Reprints and Translations Series.) Trans. of *Die predigt Jesu vom Reiches Gottes.* Göttingen: Vandenhoeck & Ruprecht, 1892. 2. völlig neubearbeiter Aufl. 1900. 214pp. 3. Aufl., hrsg. von Ferdinand Hahn. 1964. 251pp. Includes bibl.
OCLC: 146788 ISB; 11037859 SUC; 11917642 ISB; 8732179 CFT; 7993154 ISB; 4292483 AZU.

1671 _____. *Synoptische Tafeln zu den drei älteren Evangelien mit Unterscheidung der Quellen in vierfachen Farbendruck.* Göttingen: Vandenhoeck & Ruprecht, 1913. 2. Aufl. neu bearb. von Roland Schütz. 1920. 14pp. Rpt from the 3rd ed. of *Die Schriften des Neuen Testaments, neu übersetzt und für die Gegenwart erklärt.* OCLC: 16799500 WEL.

1672 _____. "Die Verteidigung Jesu gegen den Vorwurf des Bündnisses mit Beelzebul." ThStKr 63 (1890): 555-69.

1673 Weisse, Christian H. *Die Evangelienfrage in ihrem gegenwärtigen Stadium.* Leipzig: Breitkopf und Hartel, 1856. 292pp. NUC: NcD.

1674 _____. *Die evangelische Geschichte: Kritisch und philosophisch bearbeitet.* Leipzig: Breitkopf und Hartel, 1838. 2 vols. OCLC: 6765779 ISB.

1675 Weizsäcker, Carl. *The Apostolic Age of the Christian Church.* 2 vols. Trans. from the 2nd and rev. ed., by James Millar. London: Williams and Norgate; New York: Putnam, 1907–1912. (Theological Translation Library 1, 5.) Trans. of *Das apostolische Zeitalter der christlichen Kirche.* Freiburg, i. b.: J. C. B. Mohr (Paul Siebeck), 1886. 2., neu bearbeitete Aufl. 1892. 3. Aufl. 1902. 700pp. OCLC: 2923769 SUS; (Microfilm) 4388336 ATL; 1132424 ISB; 14006316 UBY.

1676 _____. *Untersuchungen über die evangelische Geschichte, ihre Quellen und den Gang ihrer Entwicklung.* Gotha: R. Besser, 1864. 580pp. 2. Ausg. Tübingen: J. C. B. Mohr (Paul Siebeck), 1901. 379pp. OCLC: 11116382 NDD; 4533518 IND.

1677 Wellhausen, Julius. *Einleitung in die drei ersten Evangelien.* Berlin: G. Reimer, 1905. 115pp. 2. Ausg. 1911. 176pp. OCLC: 10431065 HLS; 2962566 ISB.

1678 _____. *Das Evangelium Lucae.* Berlin: G. Reimer, 1904. 142pp. OCLC: 2661070 IEC.

1679 _____. *Das Evangelium Marci.* Berlin: G. Reimer, 1903. 146pp. 2. Aufl. 1909. 137pp. OCLC: 4866727 ITC; 3349981 ISB.

1680 _____. *Das Evangelium Matthaei.* Berlin: G. Reimer, 1904. 2. Ausg. 1914. 144pp. OCLC: 961073 BHA.

1681 Wendling, Emil. *Die Entstehung des Marcus-Evangeliums: philologische Untersuchungen.* Tübingen: J. C. B. Mohr (Paul Siebeck), 1908. 246pp. OCLC: 8059350 ISB.

1682 _____. "Neuere Schriften zu den synoptischen Evangelien und zur Apostelgeschichte." ZWTh 51 (1909): 135-68.

1683 ———. *Ur-Marcus: Versuch seiner Wiederherstellung der ältesten Mitteilungen über das Leben Jesu.* Tübingen: J. C. B. Mohr (Paul Siebeck), 1905. 73pp.
OCLC: 6545733 ISB.

1684 Wendt, Hans H. *The Teaching of Jesus.* 2 vols. Trans. John Wilson. Edinburgh: T. & T. Clark, 1892–1901. New York: Scribner, 1892? 1896. Microfilm. New Haven CT: Micrographic Systems of Connecticut, 1985. Trans. of *Die Lehre Jesu.* Göttingen: Vandenhoeck & Ruprecht, 1886–1890. 2., verbesserte Aufl. 1901. 640pp.
OCLC: 12433036 ITC; 3106580 ISB; 12888156 TSW; 14573496 YUS; 7029826 PLT; 1674745 ISB.

1685 Wenham, D. "The Interpretation of the Parable of the Sower." NTS 20 (1974): 299-319.

1686 ———. "A Note on Mark 9:33-42/Matt. 18:1-6/Luke 9:46-50." JSNT 14 (1982): 113-18.

1687 ———. *The Rediscovery of Jesus' Eschatological Discourse.* Sheffield: JSOT Press, 1984. 406pp. (Gospel Perspectives 4.) Includes bibl.
OCLC: 11617047 ICU.

1688 ———. "The Synoptic Problem Revisited. Some New Suggestions about the Composition of Mark 4:1-34." TynB 23 (1972): 3-38.

1689 Wenham, J. W. "Synoptic Independence and the Origin of Luke's Travel Narrative." NTS 27 (1981): 507-15.

1690 Werner, Martin. *Der Einfluss paulinischer Theologie im Markusevangelium: eine Studie zur neutestamentlichen Theologie.* Giessen: A. Töpelmann, 1923. 216pp. (Beihefte zur Zeitschrift für die neutestamentliche Wissenschaft und die Kunde der älteren Kirche 1.)
Also published as the author's "theologische Dissertation," Bern. (Jena: Frommans'sche Buchdr, 1922. 210pp.)
OCLC: 1305345 ISB.

1691 Wernle, Paul. *The Sources of Our Knowledge of the Life of Jesus.* Trans. Edward Lummis. Boston: American Unitarian Association; London: Green, 1907. 163pp.
Contents: 1. Source material outside the four Gospels; 2. Our four evangelists; 3. The Synoptics; 4. The sources of the synoptics.
OCLC: 4948403 VIC; 3886930 ISB.

1692 ———. *Die synoptische Frage.* Freiburg i.B.: J. C. B. Mohr (Paul Siebeck), 1899. 256pp.
OCLC: 1965094 ISB.

1693 West, H. P., Jr. "A Primitive Version of Luke in the Composition of Matthew." NTS 14 (1967): 75-95.

1694 Westcott, Brooke F. *An Introduction to the Study of the Gospels. With historical and explanatory notes.* Cambridge: Macmillan, 1860. 458pp. New ed. with an intro. by Horation B. Hackett. Boston: Gould and Lincoln; New York: Sheldon and Company, 1872. 476pp. Microfiche. Beltsville MD: reproduced by the NCR Corp. for the ATLA Board of Microtext, 1978 (ATLA F57).

The present work is an attempt to define and fill up the outline which the author sketched in "The Elements of the Gospel Harmony," published in 1851.

OCLC: 9990458 VWM; 15165432 ISB; 3811072 ISB.

1695 _____, and Fenton J. A. Hort. *The New Testament in the Original Greek.* 2 vols. Cambridge: Macmillan, 1881. New York: Harper, 1881–1882.

Contents. 1. Text; 2. Introduction and Appendix.

OCLC: 9519565 ISB; 12734511 SUC.

1696 Wettstein, Johann Jacobus, ed. *Novum Testamentum Graecum.* 2 vols. Amsterdam: Ex Officina Dommeriana, 1751–1752. Rpt: Graz, Austria: Akademische Druck- und Verlagsanstalt, 1962.

Contents. 1. *Quattuor evangelia.*

OCLC: 1286241 ISB.

1697 Wetzel, G. *Die synoptischen Evangelien: Eine Darstellung und Prüfung der wichtigsten über die Entstehung derselben aufgetretenen Hypothesen, mit selbständigem Versuch zur Lösung der synoptischen Evangelienfrage.* Heilbronn: G. Henninger, 1883. 229pp.

OCLC: 15270403 OBE.

1698 White, H. J. "The 'Dogmatic' Variations in St. Matthew." CQR 80 (1915): 302-21.**

1699 Wichelhaus, M. "Am ersten Tage der Woche: Mk. i.35-39 und die didaktischen Absichten des Markus-Evangelisten." NovT 11 (1969): 45-66.

1700 Wiefel, Wolfgang. "Erwägungen zum Thema Jesuanismus im Urchristentum." TVers 12 (1981): 11-24.

1701 _____. "Vatersprüche und Herrenworte: Ein Beitrag zur Frage der Bewahrung mündlicher Traditionssätze." NovT 11 (1969): 105-20.

1702A Wikenhauser, Alfred. *New Testament Introduction.* Trans. Joseph Cunningham, based on the 2nd rev., and enl. German ed. New York: Herder and Herder, 1958. 579pp. Trans. of *Einleitung in das Neue Testament.* Freiburg i. B.: Herder 1953. 419pp. 1956. 440pp. 5. Aufl. 1963. 6. völlig neu bearbeitete Aufl. von Josef Schmid. 1973. Italian. *Introduzione al Nuovo Testamento.* Edizione italiana a cura di Felice Montagnini. Nuovo edizione completamente rifata. Brescia: Paideia Editrice, 1981. 734pp. (Biblioteca teologica 9.)

OCLC: 192179 ISB; 1069724 PCJ; 3798439 IQU; 12441292 ITC; 771264 BHA; 753687 CWR; 7589004 BWE.

1702B _____. "Zur synoptischen Frage." *Römische Quartalschrift* 39 (1931): 43-61.

1703 Wilke, Christian Gottlob. *Die neutestamentliche Rhetorik: Ein Seitenstück zur Grammatik des neutestamentlichen Sprachidioms.* Dresden; Leipzig: Arnoldische Buchhandlung, 1843. Photocopy. 1979. 522pp. OCLC: 13949446 GTX.

1704 _____. "Über die Parabel von den Arbeitern im Weinberge." ZWTh 1 (1826): 71-109.**

1705 _____. *Der Urevangelist, oder, exegetisch kritische Untersuchung über das Verwandtschaftsverhältniss der drei ersten Evangelien.* Leipzig: Gerhard Fleischer, 1838. 694pp. OCLC: NUC: MH; NcD; NjPT.

1706 Wilkens, W. "Zur Frage der literarischen Beziehung zwischen Matthäus und Lukas." NovT 8 (1966): 48-57.

1707 Willes, Bartus van (praes. Jodocus Heringa.) *Specimen hermeneuticum de iis, quae ab uno Marco sunt narrata, aut copiosus et explicatius ab eo, quam a caeteris evangelistis exposita.* Traiecti ad Rhenum, 1811.

1708A Williams, C. S. C. *Alterations to the Text of the Synoptic Gospels and Acts.* Oxford: Blackwell, 1951. 93pp. OCLC: 2880056 ISB.

1708B Williams, John. *A Free Enquiry into the Authenticity of the First and Second Chapters of St. Matthew's Gospel.* London, 1771.* With a new preface . . . and a dissertation on the original language of that Gospel. London: B. White and Son, and J. Johnson, 1789. OCLC: 8244868 PKT.

1709A Williams, N. P. "A Recent Theory of the Origin of St. Mark's Gospel." In *Studies in the Synoptic Problem,* by Members of the University of Oxford, W. Sanday, ed., 387-421. Oxford: Clarendon Press, 1911. Microfiche. Louisville KY: Lost Cause Press, 1977. OCLC: 753275 ISB; 4045911 ISB.

1709B Williams, Robert Lee. "Helmut Koester on Mark." PSThJ 40/2 (1987): 26-30.
A focused reveiw on *Colloquy on New Testament Studies: A Time for Reappraisal and Fresh Approaches,* Bruce C. Corley, ed. (307B). First read at a colloquy on "New Critical Approaches in Synoptic Studies" held at Southern Methodist University, fall semester 1986. Supplies omissions from seminar dialogue with Helmut Koester (823B).

1710 Willis, Wendell. "An Irenic View of Christian Origins: Theological Continuity from Jesus to Paul in W. R. Farmer's Writings." In *Jesus, the Gospels, and the Church,* E. P. Sanders, ed., 265-86. Macon GA: Mercer University Press, 1987. OCLC: 16130939 ISB.

1711 Wilson, R. McL. "Farrer and Streeter on the Minor Agreements of Matthew and Luke Against Mark." In *Studia Evangelica. Papers presented to the International Congress on "The Four Gospels in 1957," held at Christ Church, Oxford, 1957,* Kurt Aland, F. L. Cross, et al., eds., 254-57. Berlin: Akademie-Verlag, 1959. (Texte und Untersuchungen 73.) OCLC: 1637245 ISB; 13641309 BZM.

1712 _____. *Studies in the Gospel of Thomas.* London: A. P. Mowbray, 1960. 160pp.
OCLC: 827597 ISB; 721349 VTU.

1713 Windisch, Hans L. *Johannes und die Synoptiker: Wollte der vierte Evangelist die älteren Evangelien ergänzen oder ersetzen?* Leipzig: J. C. Hinrichs, 1926. 189pp. (Untersuchungen zum Neuen Testament 12.) OCLC: 4417384 KAT.

1714 Wink, Walter. *John the Baptist in the Gospel Tradition.* London: Cambridge University Press, 1968. 132pp. (SNTSMS 7.) Includes bibl. OCLC: 387997 ISB.

1715 Winter, Paul. "On Luke and Lucan Sources." ZNW 47 (1956): 217-42.

1716 _____. "The Treatment of His Sources by the Third Evangelist in Luke xxi-xxiv." StTh 8 (1954): 138-72.

1717 Wood, Herbert G. "The Priority of Mark." ET 65 (1953–1954): 17-19. Reissued in *The Two-Source Hypothesis: A Critical Appraisal,* Arthur J. Bellinzoni, Jr., ed., 77-84. Macon GA: Mercer University Press, 1985. OCLC: 11599674 ISB.

1718 Woods, F. H. "The Origin and Mutual Relation of the Synoptic Gospels." In *Studia Biblica et Ecclesiastica: Essays Chiefly in Biblical and Patristic Criticism,* S. R. Driver, T. K. Cheyne, and W. Sanday, eds., 2:59-104. Oxford: Clarendon Press, 1890. OCLC: 3698065 BCT.

1719 Wootton, R. W. F. "The Implied Agent in Greek Passive Verbs in Mark, Luke and John." BTr 19 (1968): 159-64.

1720 Worden, Ronald D. "A Philosophical Analysis of Luke 6:20b-49 and Parallels." Ph.D. diss., Princeton Theological Seminary, 1973. 599 leaves. Photocopy. Ann Arbor MI: Xerox University Microfilms, 1984. Includes bibl.
OCLC: 10642100 LOS.

1721 Worden, Ronald D. "The Q Sermon on the Mount/Plain: Variants and Reconstruction." In *Society of Biblical Literature 1983 Seminar Papers,* K. H. Richards, ed., 455-71. Chico CA: Scholars Press, 1983. (SBLSPS 22.)

1722 _____. "Redaction Criticism of Q: A Survey." JBL 94 (1975): 532-46.

1723 Woschitz, Karl. "Reflexionen zum Zeitverständnis in der Spruchquelle 'Q'." ZKTh 97 (1975): 72-79.

1724 Wrede, William. *The Messianic Secret*. Trans. J. C. B. Grieg. Cambridge: J. Clarke, 1971. Greenwood SC: Attic Press, 1971. 292pp. (Library of Theological Translations.) Trans. of *Das Messiasgeheimnis in den Evangelien: Zugleich ein Beitrag zum Verständnis des Markusevangeliums*. Göttingen: Vandenhoeck & Ruprecht, 1901. 3., unveränderte Aufl. 1963. 5., unveränderte Aufl. 1969. 291pp.
OCLC: 663165 ISB; 6313317 KSW; 6173199 WTS; 3941486 ISB; 5072626 DRU.

1725 Wrege, Hans T. *Die Überlieferungsgeschichte der Bergpredigt*. Tübingen: J. C. B. Mohr (Paul Siebeck), 1968. (Wissenschaftliche Untersuchungen zum Neuen Testament 9.)
OCLC: 4073016 ISB
Reviews: McArthur, Harvey K. JBL 88 (1969): 91-92; Goulder, M. D. JThS 20 (1969): 599-602; Hoffmann, Paul. ThRv 68 (1972): 115-17; Lührmann, Dieter. ThLZ 95 (1970): 199-200.

1726 _____. "Zur Rolle des Geisteswortes in frühchristlichen Traditionen (Lc 12. 10 parr.)" In *Logia. Les paroles de Jésus = The Sayings of Jesus: Mémorial Joseph Coppens,* Joël Delobel, ed., 373-77. Leuven: University Press and Peeters, 1982. (BEThL 59.)
OCLC: 9450792 ISB; 11043145.

1727 Wright, Arthur. *The Composition of the Four Gospels: A Critical Inquiry*. London; New York: Macmillan and Co., 1890. 176pp.
OCLC: 5055644 ISB; 4862593 UUW.

1728 _____. *Some New Testament Problems*. London: Methuen, 1898. 349pp. (Churchman's Library.)
OCLC: 4160061 ACL.

1729 _____. *A Synopsis of the Gospels in Greek. With various readings and critical notes*. 2nd ed. rev. and enl. London: Macmillan and Company, 1903. 3rd ed. rev. 1906. 319pp.
OCLC: 520259 OTC; 3252898 ISB.

---- Wright, Tom. *See* Neill, Stephen (1086).

1730 Yamauchi, Edwin M. "Logia." In *The International Standard Bible Encyclopaedia,* fully revised (3rd ed.) by G. W. Bromiley, et al., eds., 3:152-54. Grand Rapids MI: William B. Eerdmans, 1986.

1731 Yoder, James D. "Semitisms in Codex Bezae." JBL 78 (1959): 317-21.

1732 Zahn, Theodor. *Das Evangelium des Lucas*. 1. und 2. Aufl. Leipzig: Deichert, 1913. 773pp. 3. und 4., durchges. Aufl. 1920. 744pp. (Kommentar zum Neuen Testament 3.)
OCLC: 2848250 DAY; 875900 BHA.

1733 _____. *Das Evangelium des Matthäus*. Leipzig: Deichert, 1903. 2. Aufl. 1905. 716pp. 3. Aufl. 1910. 724pp. 4. Aufl. 1922. (Kommentar zum Neuen Testament 1.) Rpt: Wuppertal: R. Brockhaus, 1984. (Theologische Verlagsgemeinschaft.) 730pp.
OCLC: 7189110 NOC; 4734742 CFT; 12144293 EMT; 12310212 EWF.

1734 _____. *Introduction to the New Testament.* 3 vols. Trans. from the 3rd German ed. by J. M. Trout, W. A. Mather, et al. Edinburgh: T. & T. Clark; New York: Scribner's, 1909. Trans. of *Einleitung in das Neue Testament.* Leipzig: A. Deichert, 1897–1899. 3., vielfach berichtigte und vervollständigte Aufl. 1906–1907. 2 vols. Includes bibl.
OCLC: 3652164 ISB; 11205961 GCL; 3149339 MBS; 3149353 MBS.

1735 Zeller, Dieter. "Entrückung zur Ankunft als Menschensohn (Lk 13, 34f.; 11, 29f.)" In *À cause de l'évangile: Études sur les Synoptiques et les Actes: Offertes au P. Jacques Dupont, O. S. B. à l'occasion de son 70e anniversaire,* 513-30. Paris: Cerf, 1985. (Lectio divina 123.)
OCLC: 14377925 DTM.

1736 _____. *Kommentar zur Logienquelle.* Stuttgart: Katholisches Bibelwerk, 1984. 109pp. (Stuttgarter kleiner Kommentar. Neues Testament 21.) Includes bibl.
OCLC: 12705325 PKT.
Review: Kloppenborg, J. S. CBQ 48 (1986): 353-54.

1737 _____. "Das Logion Mt 8, 11f/Lk 13, 28f und das Motiv der 'Völkerwallfahrt'." BZ 15 (1971): 222-37.

1738 _____. "Das Logion Mt 8, 11f/Lk 13, 28f und des Motiv der 'Völkerwallfahrt' (Schluss.)" BZ 16 (1972): 84-93.

1739 _____. "Redaktionsprozesse und wechselnder 'Sitz im Leben' beim Q-Material." In *Logia. Les paroles de Jésus = The Sayings of Jesus: Mémorial Joseph Coppens,* Joël Delobel, ed., 395-409. Leuven: University Press and Peeters, 1982. (BEThL 59.)
OCLC: 9450792 ISB; 11043145 UTS.

1740 _____. "Die Versuchungen Jesu in der Logienquelle." TThZ 89 (1980): 61-73.

1741 _____. *Die weisheitlichen Mahnsprüche bei den Synoptikern.* Würzburg: Echter, 1977. 2nd ed. 1983. 244pp. (Forschung zur Bibel 217.) Includes bibl.
A revision of the author's Habilitationsschrift, Freiburg i. B., 1976.
OCLC: 3282896 ISB.

1742 _____. "Der Zusammenhang der Eschatologie in der Logienquelle." In *Gegenwart und kommendes Reich: Schülergabe Anton Vögtle zum 65. Geburtstag,* Peter Fiedler and Dieter Zeller, eds., 67-78. Stuttgart: Verlag Katholisches Bibelwerk, 1975. (Stuttgarter biblische Beiträge.)
OCLC: 2297186 IYU.

1743A Zeller, Eduard. "Strauss und Renan." *Historische Zeitschrift* 12 (1864): 70-133.

1743B _____. "Studien zur neutestamentlichen Theologie. 4. Vergleichende Uebersicht über den Wörtervorrath der sämmtlichen neutestamentlichen Schriftsteller." ThJb(T) 2 (1843): 443-543.

1743C _____. "Über den dogmatischen Charakter des dritten Evangeliums. Mit besonderer Rücksicht auf sein Verhältniss zur Apostelgeschichte und zum Johannesevangelium." ThJb(T) 2 (1843): 59-90.

1743D _____. "Zum Marcus-Evangelium." ZWTh 8 (1865): 308-28, 385-408.

1744 Zerwick, Maximilian. *Untersuchungen zum Markus-Stil: Ein Beitrag zur stilistischen Durcharbeitung des Neuen Testaments.* Rome: E. Pontifico Instituto Biblico, 1937. 144pp. (Scripta Pontificii Instituti Biblici.) OCLC: 9552530 ISB.

1745 Ziesler, J. A. "Luke and the Pharisees." NTS 25 (1979): 146-57.

1746 Zmijewski, Josef. *Die Eschatologiereden des Lukas-Evangeliums: Eine traditions- und redaktionsgeschichtliche Untersuchung zu Lk 21,5-36 und Lk 17,20-37.* Bonn: P. Hanstein Verlag, 1972. 591pp. (Bonner biblischer Beiträge 40.) Includes bibl. Originally presented as the author's thesis, Bonn, 1970. OCLC: 556594 HUC.

1747 _____. "Der Glaube und sein Macht: Eine traditionsgeschichtliche Untersuchung zu Mt. 17, 20; 21, 21; Mk. 11,25; Lk 17,6." In *Begegnung mit dem Wort: Festschrift für Heinrich Zimmermann*, Josef Zmijewski and Ernst Nellessen, eds., 81-103. Bonn: P. Hanstein Verlag, 1980. (Bonner biblischer Beiträge 53.) OCLC: 6033286 ISB.

Date of Publication/Writing Index

The bibliography itself is an "index" of works on the synoptic problem arranged alphabetically by author, editor, or compiler. In this date-of-publication index the names of the proprietors are arranged *chronologically* so that at a glance one may observe the concurrence of studies on the synoptic problem throughout the period 1716 to 1988. While the occurrence of works by the same author may readily be observed in the main bibliography, the chronological confluence of works by the same author as well as that of works by different authors is readily apparent in the date-of-publication/writing index. The number occurring before the name in this index is the number of the entry in the bibliography, to which one may readily refer for specific information regarding the work in question.

1796
660. Herder, Johann Gottfried

1797
582. Griesbach, Johann J., ed.

1798–1811
580A. Griesbach, Johann J.

1800–1804
1168C. Paulus, Heinrich Eberhard Gottlob

1801
981. Marsh, Herbert

1804–1827
421. Eichhorn, Johann Gottfried

1805
27. Ammon, Christoph Friedrich von

1808
729. Hug, J. L.

1811
580B. Griesbach, Johann J.
1707. Willes, Bartus van

1812
571. Gratz, Petrus Alois

1814–1816
1397. Schulze, Johann Daniel

1816
528A. Gersdorf, Christoph Gotthelf

1817
1342. Schleiermacher, Friedrich

1818
529. Gieseler, Johann Carl Ludwig

1822
1168D. Paulus, Heinrich Eberhard Gottlob

1825
581. Griesbach, Johann J.
1330. Saunier, Heinrich
1554B. Theile, Karl Gottfried Wilhelm

1826
135C. Bloomfield, Samuel Thomas
366. De Wette, Wilhelm Martin Leberecht
497. Fritzsche, Karl Friedrich August
1704. Wilke, Christian Gottlob

1828
1554C. Theile, Karl Gottfried Wilhelm

1829
283B. Clausen, Henrik Nicolai

1830–1833
1168B. Paulus, Heinrich Eberhard Gottlob

1830
498. Fritzsche, Karl Friedrich August
658. Herder, Johann Gottfried
1382B. Schott, Heinrich August

1832
1041A. Meyer, Heinrich August Wilhelm
1438A. Sieffert. Friedrich L.

1834
789B. Kern, Friedrich Heinrich

1835
852. Lachmann, Karl
1343. Schleiermacher, Friedrich
1344. Schleiermacher, Friedrich

1836
314. Credner, K. A.
365. De Wette, Wilhelm Martin Leberecht

1837
578B. Greswell, Edward
1554D. Theile, Karl Gottfried Wilhelm

1838
528B. Gfrörer, August Friedrich
836B. Kuhn, Johannes von
1674. Weisse, Christian H.
1705. Wilke, Christian Gottlob

1839
79. Baur, Ferdinand C.

1840
1124B. Neudecker, Christian Gotthold

1842
1240. Reusse, Eduard W. E.

1843
1421B. Schwegler, Albert
1703. Wilke, Christian Gottlob
1743B. Zeller, Eduard
1743D. Zeller, Eduard

1844
1419B. Schwarz, Franz J.

1845
634. Hasert, Christian Adolf
    [Philosphotos Alethias]
1343. Schleiermacher, Friedrich

1846
81C. Baur, Ferdinand C.
124. Bleek, Friedrich
1041B. Meyer, Heinrich August Wilhelm
1252A. Ritschl, Albrecht B.
1421A. Schwegler, Albert
1502. Strauss, David Friedrich

1847
80. Baur, Ferdinand C.

1848
439. Ewald, Heinrich
972B. Maier, Adalbert

1848–1951
342A. Davidson, Samuel

1849
661. Hertwig, Otto Robert
1419A. Schwarz, Frans J.

1850
438. Ewald, Heinrich
672. Hilgenfeld, Adolf
1639B. Volkmar, Gustav

1851–1852
78. Bauer, Bruno

1851
81A. Baur, Ferdinand C.
1252B. Ritschl, Albrecht B.

1852
673. Hilgenfeld, Adolf
972C. Maier, Adalbert

1853
81B. Baur, Ferdinand C.
142. Bolton, W. J.
350B. Delitzsch, Franz
831. Köstlin, Karl Reinhold
1570. Tischendorf. Constantin von, ed.

1854
667. Hilgenfeld, Adolf
1572. Tischendorf, Constantin von, ed.

1855
1239. Reuss, Eduard W. E.

1856
1239. Reuss, Eduard W. E.
1673. Weisse, Christian H.

1857
1639A. Volkmar, Gustav

1858
365. DeWette, Wilhelm Martin Leberecht

1860–1876
965B. Lutteroth, Henri

1860
366. DeWette, Wilhelm Martin Leberecht
381B. Dollinger, Johann Joseph Ignaz von
668B. Hilgenfeld, Adolf
1239. Reuss, Eduard W. E.
1694. Westcott, Brooke F.

1861–1868
768B. Kahnis, Karl Friedrich August

1861–1862
28B. Anger, Rudolf

1861
668A. Hilgenfeld, Adolf
1668. Weiss, Bernhard

1862
125. Bleek, Friedrich
127. Bleek, Friedrich
1241. Reville, Albert

1863
669. Hilgenfeld, Adolf
671. Hilgenfeld, Adolf
712. Holtzmann, Heinrich J.

1864
1667. Weiss, Bernhard
1676. Weizsäcker, Carl
1743A. Zeller, Eduard

1865
1573. Tischendorf, Constantin von
1661. Weiss, Bernhard
1743D. Zeller, Eduard

1866
1035. Meyboom, Hajo Uden

1867–1872
784. Keim, Theodore

1867
311. Cowper, B. Harris, trans.
1571. Tischendorf, Constantin von

1868
342B. Davidson, Samuel
877B. Langen, Josef

1869–1870
126. Bleek, Friedrich

1869

1380. Scholten, J. H.

1870

1637. Volkmar, Gustav

1871

196. Burgon, John W.

1872

616. Hammond, C. E.
1036. Meyboom, Hajo Uden
1308. Sanday, William
1663. Weiss, Bernard

1874

66. Baring-Gould, S.

1875

670. Hilgenfeld, Adolf

1876

1237. Resch, Alfred
1311. Sanday, William
1664. Weiss, Bernhard

1877

674. Hilgenfeld, Adolf
1237. Resch, Alfred

1878

1656. Weiffenbach, Wilhelm

1879

5. Abbott, E. A.
675. Hilgenfeld, Adolf

1880

1041. Meyer, Heinrich August Wilhelm
1294. Rushbrooke, W. G.
1440. Simons, Eduard

1881

113. Beyschlag, Willibald
707. Holtzmann, Heinrich J.
1695. Westcott, Brooke F.,
    and Fenton J. A. Hort

1882

1638. Volkmar, Gustav

1883

114. Beyschlag, Willibald
411. Edersheim, Alfred
705. Holsten, Karl C. J.
1697. Wetzel, G.

1884

6. Abbot. E. A.,
    and W. G. Rushbrook

1885

412. Edersheim, Alfred
706. Holsten, Karl C. J.
708. Holtzmann, Heinrich J.
1306. Salmon, George

1886–1890

1684. Wendt, Hans H.

1886

676. Hilgenfeld, Adolf
1662. Weiss, Berhnard
1675. Weizsäcker, Carl

1887

541. Godet, Frédérick Louis

1888

1233. Resch, Alfred
1235. Resch, Alfred

1889

711. Holtzmann, Heinrich J.
911. Lightfoot, Joseph Barber
1205. Plummer, Charles
1229. Resch, Alfred

1890

249. Carpenter, J. E.
440. Ewald, Paul
627. Harris, J. Rendel
989. Marshall, J. T.
1672. Weiss, Johannes
1718. Woods, F. H.
1727. Wright, Arthur

1891

163. Bousset, Wilhelm
472. Feine, Paul
987. Marshall, J. T.
1317. Sanday, William

1892–1893

988. Marshall, J. T.

1892

728. Huck, Albert
1278. Robinson, Joseph A.,
    and Montague R. James
1670. Weiss, Johannes

1893–1897

1231. Resch, Alfred

1893

175B. Broadus, John Albert
618. Harnack, Adolf von
620. Harnack, Adolf von
629. Harris, J. Rendel
677. Hilgenfeld, Adolf
1312. Sanday, William
1314. Sanday, William
1388. Schubert, Hans von
1479. Stanton, Vincent Henry
1480. Stanton, Vincent Henry
1481. Stanton, Vincent Henry
1482. Stanton, Vincent Henry

1894–1899

542. Godet, Frédérick Louis

1894

253. Cassels, Walter Richard
551. Goodwin, W. W.
561. Graffin, R., ed.
577. Gregory, J. B.
628. Harris, J. Rendel
680. Hill, J. Hamlyn, ed. and trans.
766. Jülicher, Adolf

1895–1898

101. Bergsma, J., ed.

1895

180. Brown, David
859. Lagrange, Marie Joseph
1340. Schlatter, Adolf von

1896

184B. Bruce, Alexander B.
552. Gould, Ezra Palmer
768A. Kähler, Martin
1038. Meyer, Arnold O.
1202. Plummer, Alfred
1287. Ropes, James Hardy

1897

55A. Badham, F. P.
184A. Bruce, Alexander Balmain
709. Holtzmann, Heinrich J.
1232. Resch, Alfred
1574. Titius, A.
1628. Veit, Karl

1898

331. Dalman, Gustaf H.
603. Hadorn, Wilhelm
1234. Resch, Alfred
1532. Swete, Henry Barclay
1728. Wright, Arthur

1899–1900

25. Allen, Willoughby C.
1316. Sanday, William

1899

639. Hawkins, John C.
650. Heinrici, C. F. Georg
701. Holcombe, John J.
1477. Stanton, Vincent Henry
1692. Wernle, Paul

1900–1901

641. Hawkins, John C.

1900

1. Abbott, E. A.
26. Allen, Willoughby C.

1901–1902

21. Allen, Willoughby C.

1901–1917

3. Abbott, E. A.

1901

2. Abbott, E. A.
95. Belser, Johannes
205. Burkitt, Francis C.
789A. Kenyon, Frederick George
1053. Moffatt, James
1356. Schmiedel, P. W.
1463. Soltau, Wilhelm
1724. Wrede, William

1902

331. Dalman, Gustaf H.
644. Headlam, Arthur C.
1277. Robinson, Joseph A.
1310. Sanday, William

1903–1920

1478. Stanton, Vincent Henry

1903–1908

744. Jacquier, Eugène

1903

248. Carpenter, J. E.
1669. Weiss, Johannes
1679. Wellhausen, Julius
1729. Wright, Arthur
1733. Zahn, Theodor

1904–1905

276. Chapman, John

1904

172. Briggs, Charles A.
201. Burkitt, Francis C., ed.
208. Burton, Ernest Dewitt
656. Hennecke, Edgar
685. Hobson, A. A.
699. Hoffmann, R. A.
1236. Resch, Alfred
1470. Spitta, Friedrich
1660. Weiss, Bernhard
1678. Wellhausen, Julius
1680. Wellhausen, Julius

1905

275. Chapman, John
1677. Wellhausen, Julius
1683. Wendling, Emil

1906–1907

769. Kappstein, Th.

1906

164. Bousset, Wilhelm
202. Burkitt, Francis C.
710. Holtzmann, Heinrich J.
767. Jülicher, Adolf
1230. Resch, Alfred
1422. Schweitzer, Albert
1451. Soden, Hermann
1659. Weiss, Bernhard

1907–1908

428. Emmet, Cyril W.
939. Loisy, Alfred Firmin

1907

23. Allen, Willoughby C.
621. Harnack, Adolf von
624. Harnack, Adolf von
1315. Sanday, William
1427. Scott-Moncrieff, C. E.
1665. Weiss, Bernhard
1691. Wernle, Paul

1908–1909

1592. Turner, C. H.

1908–1976

1071. Moulton, James H.

1908

53. Bacon, Benjamin W.
74. Barth, Fritz
625. Harnack, Adolf von
651. Heinrici, C. F. Georg
1077. Müller, G. H.
1130. Nicolardot, Firmin

1219. Ramsay, W. M.
1666. Weiss, Bernhard
1681. Wendling, Emil

1909–1910

186. Buchler, A.

1909

47. Bacon, Benjamin W.
284. Cohu, John Rougier
739. Jackson, H. Latimer
860. Lake, Kirsopp
1057. Montefiore, Claude G.
1072. Moulton, James H.
1203. Plummer, Alfred
1531. Swete, Henry Barclay, ed.
1682. Wendling, Emil
1734. Zahn, Theodor

1910–1911

288. Connolly, R. H.

1910

27A. Amann, E.
99. Berg, P.
200. Burkitt, Francis C.
410. Easton, Burton S.
1632. Vogels, H. J.

1911–1912

530. Gilbert, George H.
1307. Sanday, William
1446. Smith, Robinson

1911

13A. Addis, W. E.
20. Allen, Willoughby C.
22. Allen, Willoughby C.
76. Bartlet, J. Vernon
373. Dibelius, Martin
619. Harnack, Adolf von
640. Hawkins, John C.
642. Hawkins, John C.
856. Lagrange, Marie Joseph
1054. Moffatt, James
1309. Sanday, William
1313. Sanday, William
1318. Sanday, William, ed.
1512. Streeter, Burnett Hillman
1513. Streeter, Burnett Hillman
1514. Streeter, Burnett Hillman
1515. Streeter, Burnett Hillman
1516. Streeter, Burnett Hillman
1517. Streeter, Burnett Hillman
1709A. Williams, N. P.

1912

50. Bacon, Benjamin W.
187. Buckley, Eric R.
207. Burton, Ernest Dewitt
256. Castor, George Dewitt
277. Chapman, John
1167. Patton, C. S.
1471. Spitta, Friedrich

1913–1917

4. Abbott, E. A.

1913

192. Bultmann, Rudolf
203. Burkitt, Francis C.
636. Haupt, Walther
702. Holdsworth, William W.
1671. Weiss, Johannes
1732. Zahn, Theodor

1914

24. Allen, Willoughby C.
283A. Clark, A. C.
340. Dausch, Petrus
623. Harnack, Adolf von
763. Jones, Maurice
1256. Robertson, Archibald Thomas

1915

646. Headlam, Arthur C.
965A. Lummis, E. W.
1016. McNeile, Alan Hugh, ed.
1168A. Patton, C. S.
1204. Plummer, Alfred
1644. Votaw, C. W.
1698. White, H. J.

1916

44. Ayles, H. H. B.
953A. Loomis, Louise Ropes, trans.
1453. Soiron, Thaddaus

1917

8. Abrahams, Israel
117. Bindley, T. H.
906. Levesque, E.

1918–1919

1495. Stephenson, T.

1918

282. Clark, A. C.
1215. Preuschen, Erwin

1919–1920

1496. Stephenson, T.

1919

49. Bacon, Benjamin W.
281. Cladder, Herman J.
370. Dibelius, Martin
815. Klostermann, Erich
1355. Schmidt, Karl Ludwig

1920

227. Cadbury, Henry J.
489. Foakes-Jackson, John Frederick John,
    and Kirsopp Lake
1189B. Perry, A. M.
1594. Turner, C. H.

1921–1922

1511. Streeter, Burnett Hillman

1921

17. Albertz, Martin
189. Bultmann, Rudolf
622. Harnack, Adolf von
1483. Stead, F. H.

1922–1926

543. Goguel, Maurice

1922–1961

1501. Strack, Hermann Leberecht
    and Paul Billerbeck

1922

746. Jameson, H. G.
930. Lockton, William
1255A. Robertson, Archibald Thomas

1923–1924

51. Bacon, Benjamin W.
204. Burkitt, Francis C.
290. Conybeare, F. C.
733. Hunkin, J. W.

1923–1958

743. Jacoby, Felix

1923

198. Burkitt, Francis C.
223. Cadbury, Henry J.
477A. Findlay, Adam F.
645. Headlam, Arthur C.
857. Lagrange, Marie Joseph
1040. Meyer, Eduard
1508. Streeter, Burnett Hillman
1690. Werner, Martin

1924–1928

1593. Turner, C. H.

1924

745. James, Montague R., trans.
765. Jülicher, Adolf
931. Lockton, William
940. Loisy, Alfred Firmin
1255B. Robertson, Archibald T.
1473. Springer, J. F.
1510. Streeter, Burnett Hillman

1925–1926

325. Crum, John Macleod Campbell
964. Lummis, E. W.

1925–1931

213. Bussmann, W.

1925

48. Bacon, Benjamin W.
199. Burkitt, Francis C.
206. Burney, Charles F.
328. Cullmann, Oscar
879. Larfeld, Wilhelm
1201. Plooij, Daniel
1221. Rawlinson, Alfred E. J.
1257. Robertson, Archibald T.

1926–1927

732. Hunkin, J. W.

1926

190. Bultmann, Rudolf
309. Couchoud, P. L.
326. Crum, John Macleod Campbell
408. Easton, Burton S.
545. Goguel, Maurice
547. Goodspeed, Edgar J.
816. Klostermann, Erich
932. Lockton, William
935. Lohmeyer, Ernst
1536. Taylor, Vincent
1713. Windisch, Hans L.

1927–1928

1542. Taylor, Vincent

1927

226. Cadbury, Henry J.
327. Crum, John Macleod Campbell
372. Dibelius, Martin
817A. Klostermann, Erich
929. Lockton, William
1017A. McNeile, Alan Hugh
1037. Meyer, Arnold O.
1434. Shotwell, James T.,
         and Louise R. Loomis
1538. Taylor, Vincent

1928

102. Bertram, Georg
409. Easton, Burton S.
814. Klostermann, Erich
1085. Narborough, Frederick D. V.
1279. Robinson, Theodore H.
1643. Vosté, Jacobus-M.

1929

225. Cadbury, Henry J.
1518. Streeter, Burnett Hillman
1657. Weinreich, Otto

1930

52. Bacon, Benjamin W.
315. Creed, John M.
371. Dibelius, Martin
978. Manson, William
1073. Moulton, James Hope,
          and George Milligan
1350. Schmid, Josef
1377. Schniewind, Julius
1541. Taylor, Vincent
1613. Vaganay, Léon

1931–1932

377. Dodd, Charles Harold
379. Dodd, Charles Harold

1931

407. Easton, Burton S.
720. Hoskyns, Edwin C.
858. Lagrange, Marie Joseph
1339. Schlatter, Adolf von
1702B. Wikenhauser, Alfred

1933

544. Goguel, Maurice
566. Grant, Frederick C.
905. Levesque, E.
941. Loisy, Alfred Firmin
1441B. Smith, B. T. D.
1539. Taylor, Vincent

1934–1935

316. Creed, John M.
317. Creed, John M.
1537. Taylor, Vincent

1934

193. Bultmann, Rudolf,
         and Karl Kundsin
370. Dibelius, Martin
841. Kümmel, Werner G.
1169. Pautrel, R.
1288. Ropes, James Hardy
1527. Sundwall, J.

1935

228. Cadoux, Arthur T.
368. Dibelius, Martin
378. Dodd, Charles Harold
748. Jeremias, Joachim
832. Kraeling, Carl H., ed.
977. Manson, Thomas W.
1341. Schlatter, Adolf von

1936

289. Connolly, R. H.
1222. Redlich, Edwin B.
1228. Rengstorf, Karl Heinrich
1376. Schniewind, Julius
1577. Torrey, C. C.

1937

170. Branscomb, B. Harvie
274. Chapman, John
369. Dibelius, Martin
549. Goodspeed, Edgar J.
585. Grobel, Kendrick
1744. Zerwick, Maximilian

1938

68. Barr, Allan
209A. Busch, Friedrich
430. Enslin, Morton Scott
519. Gardner-Smith, Percival
974. Manson, Thomas W.
1149B. Orchard, Bernard
1242. Richardson, Alan

1939

218. Butler, B. C.
722. Howard, W. F.

1940

727. Huby, Joseph
751. Jeremias, Joachim

1941–1942

567. Grant, Frederick C.

1941

54. Badcock, F. J.
188. Bultmann, Rudolf
792A. Kilpatrick, G. D.
1452. Soiron, Thaddaus

1942–1943

73. Barrett, C. K.
1196. Petrie, C. Sewart

1942

548. Goodspeed, Edgar J.
681. Hirsch, Emmanuel

1943–1944

69A. Barr, Allan
533. Glasson, T. F.

1943

564. Grant, Frederick C.
715. Honey, T. E. Floyd
1467. Sparks, H. F. D.

1944

273. Chapman, John
1010. McGinley, Laurence J.
1050. Michaelis, Wilhelm

1945

546. Goodenough, Erwin R.
844. Kümmel, Werner G.

1946

120. Black, Matthew
145. Bonsirven, Joseph
795. Kilpatrick, G. D.
1049. Michaelis, Wilhelm
1535. Taylor, Robert Oswald Patrick

1947–1948

122. Black, Matthew

1947

16. Albertz, Martin
754. Jeremias, Joachim

1948–1949

38. Argyle, A. W.

1948

214. Butler, B. C.
219. Butler, B. C.
287. Connolly, Hugh
531. Gilmour, S. MacLean
735. Hunter, Archibald M.
855. Lagrange, Marie Joseph
1348. Schmid, Josef
1567A. Throckmorton, Burton H., Jr.

1949

1375. Schniewind, Julius
1567B. Throckmorton, Burton H., Jr.

1950–1951

39. Argyle, A. W.

1950

97. Benoit, Pierre
796. Kilpatrick, G. D.
941. Loisy, Alfred Firmin
998. Massaux, Edouard
1032. Metzger, Bruce M.

1074. Moulton, W. F.,
    and A. S. Geden, eds.
1226B. Reicke, Bo
1424. Schweizer, Eduard

1951–1955

191. Bultmann, Rudolf

1951

217. Butler, B. C.
605. Haenchen, Ernst
682. Hirsch, Emmanuel
736. Hunter, Archibald M.
919. Lindeskog, Gösta
933. Lohmeyer, Ernst
1189A. Perry, Alfred M.
1347. Schmid, Josef
1468. Sparks, H. F. D.
1611. Vaganay, Léon
1708A. Williams, C. S. C.

1952

465. Farrer, Austin M.
469. Farrer, Austin M.
490. Fonseca, Aloisius Gonzaga da
532. Gilmour, S. MacLean
723. Howard, W. F.
1425. Schweizer, Eduard
1540. Taylor, Vincent
1617. Vaganay, Léon

1953–1956

1407. Schürmann, Heinz

1953–1954

211. Bussby, Frederick
1717. Wood, Herbert G.

1953

134. Blinzler, Joseph von
216. Butler, B. C.
381A. Doeve, Jan Willem
653. Helmbold, Heinrich
750. Jeremias, Joachim
819. Knox, W. L.
1068. Moule, Charles F. D.
1163. Parker, Pierson
1349. Schmid, Josef
1353. Schmid, Josef,
    and A. Vögtle, eds.
1401. Schürmann, Heinz
1546. Taylor, Vincent
1618. Vaganay, Léon
1636. Vögtle, Anton
1702A. Wikenhauser, Alfred

1954

118. Birkeland, Harris
158. Bornkamm, Günther
221. Butler, B. C.
272. Cerfaux, Lucien
295. Conzelmann, Hans
468. Farrer, Austin M.
647. Heard, Richard G.
648. Heard, Richard G.
892. Léon-Dufour, Xavier
909. Levie, Jean
982. Marshall, A.
1442. Smith, Charles W. F.
1494. Stendahl, Krister
1614. Vaganay, Léon
1616. Vaganay, Léon
1716. Winter, Paul

1955–1956

31. Argyle, A. W.
1070. Moule, Charles F. D.,
    and A. M. G. Stephenson
1549. Taylor, Vincent

1955

70. Barrett, C. K.
194. Bundy, Walter E.
215. Butler, B. C.
435. Evans, C. F.
466. Farrer, Austin M.
563. Grant, Frederick C.
574. Greenlee, J. H.
598. Guy, Harold A.
772. Käsemann, Ernst
885. Leaney, Alfred R. C.
907. Levie, Jean
1134A. Nineham, Dennis E.
1475. Stanley, D.
1543. Taylor, Vincent
1558. Thils, Gustave
1612. Vaganay, Léon
1631A. Vielhauer, Philipp

1956–1957

168. Bradby, E. L.
437A. Evans, Owen E.
1469. Sparks, H. F. D.

1956

336. Daube, David
467. Farrer, Austin M.
749. Jeremias, Joachim
797. Kilpatrick, G. D.
894. Léon-Dufour, Xavier
934. Lohmeyer, Ernst
991. Martin, W. H. Blyth

995. Marxen, Willi
1351. Schmid, Josef
1444. Smith, Morton
1445. Smith, Morton
1602. Turner, N.
1715. Winter, Paul

1957

232. Cambier, J. L. Cerfaux, et al
380. Doeve, Jan Willem
565. Grant, Frederick C.
570. Grässer, Erich
737A. Huston, Hollis W.
820. Koester, Helmut
826. Koester, Helmut
844. Kümmel, Werner G.
899B. Léon-Durour, Xavier
908. Levie, Jean
1245. Riesenfeld, Harald
1269. Robinson, James M.
1405. Schürmann, Heinz
1615. Vaganay, Léon

1958–1959

147. Borgen, Peder

1958–1973

397. Dupont, Jacques

1958

67. Barnett, Albert E.
159. Bornkamm, Günther
383. Doresse, Jean
537. Glombitza, Otto
787. Kelly, John Norman Davidson
843. Kümmel, Werner G.
884. Leaney, Alfred R. C.
942. Lonergan, Bernard Joseph Francis
957. Ludlum, J. H., Jr.
1060. Morgenthaler, Robert
1124A. Nepper-Christensen, Poul
1132. Nineham, Dennis E.
1408. Schürmann, Heinz
1528A. Swanson, Donald C.
1557. Theron, Daniel J.
1560. Thils, Gustave

1959–1960

576B. Greeven, H.
593. Gundry, Robert H.
1544. Taylor, Vincent

1959

77. Bartsch, H. W.
181. Brown, J. P.
210. Buse, Ivor
254. Cassian, Evéque
255. Cassian, Evéque

296. Conzelmann, Hans
312. Cranfield, C. E. B.
550. Goodspeed, Edgar J.
587. Grundmann, Walter
592. Guillaumont, A., ed. and trans.
604. Haenchen, Ernst
752. Jeremias, Joachim
805. Klijn, A. F. J.
896. Léon-Dufour, Xavier
1069A. Moule, Charles F. D.
1079. Munck, Johannes
1197. Petrie, C. Sewart
1199. Piper, Otto A.
1220. Randellini, L.
1223. Rehkopf, Friedrich
1265. Robinson, James M.
1416. Schürmann, Heinz
1457. Solages, Bruno de
1547. Taylor, Vincent
1565. Thompson, P. J.
1580. Trilling, Wolfgang
1581. Trilling, Wolfgang
1598. Turner, N.
1603H. Tyson, Joseph B.
1711. Wilson, R. McL.
1731. Yoder, James D.

1960–1961

436. Evans, Owen E.

1960

96. Benoit, Pierre
144. Bonnard, Pierre
160. Bornkamm, Günther
250. Carrington, Philip
269. Cerfaux, Lucien
383. Doresse, Jean
405. Duthoit, R.
476A. Filson, Floyd Vivian
522. Gaston, Lloyd
569. Grant, Robert M.
584. Grintz, Jehoshua M.
600. Guy, Harold A.
762A. Johnson, Sherman E.
770. Käsemann, Ernst
771. Käsemann, Ernst
850. Kurzinger, J.
938. Lohse, Eduard
1289. Rosché, Theodore R.
1290. Roth, Cecil
1409. Schürmann, Heinz
1412. Schürmann, Heinz
1414. Schürmann, Heinz
1449. Snape, H. C.
1459. Solages, Bruno de
1603E. Tyson, Joseph B.

1712. Wilson, R. McL.

1961–1962

30. Argyle, A. W.
40. Argyle, A. W.
182. Brown, J. P.
450A. Farmer, William R.

1961

62. Bammel, Ernst
183A. Brown, J. P.
295. Conzelmann, Hans
307A. Coppens, Joseph,
       and Luc Dequeker
384. Doudna, John C.
456. Farmer, William R.
568A. Grant, Robert M.
586. Grundmann, Walter
916. Lindars, Barnabas
922. Linnemann, Eta
937. Lohr, C. H.
1331. Sawyerr, H.
1393. Schulz, Siegfried
1406. Schürmann, Heinz
1519A. Strobel, August
1561. Thils, Gustave
1603A. Tyson, Joseph B.

1962–1963

278. Cherry, R. Stephen

1962

86. Beare, Francis Wright
112. Beyer, Klaus
240. Carlston, Charles E.
344. Davies, William D.
345. Davies, William D.
482. Fitzmyer, Joseph A.
511. Fuller, Reginald H.
773. Käsemann, Ernst
783. Keech, Finley M.
794. Kilpatrick, G. D.
833. Kraeling, Emil G. H.
902. Léon-Dufour, Xavier
976. Manson, Thomas W.
1066. Moule, Charles F. D.
1126. Neugebauer, Fritz
1135. North, Robert
1258. Robinson, James M.
1291. Rowlingson, D. T.
1292. Rowlingson, D. T.
1364. Schmithals, Walter
1506. Strecker, Georg
1596. Turner, H. E. W.,
       and Hugh Montefiore

1963

15. Aland, Kurt, ed.
34. Argyle, A. W.
75. Barth, Gerhard
161. Bornkamm, Günther
189. Bultmann, Rudolf
473. Fenton, John C.
568B. Grant, Robert M.
609. Hahn, Ferdinand
610. Hahn, Ferdinand
652. Held, H. J.
731. Hummel, Reinhart
840. Kümmel, Werner G.
846. Kürzinger, J.
847. Kürzinger, J.
890. Lemke, Werner Erich
899. Léon-Dufour, Xavier
921. Lindsey, R. L.
994. Marxen, Willi
1030. Metzger, Bruce M.
1045. Meynell, Hugo
1065. Mosley, A. W.
1133. Nineham, Dennis E.
1404. Schürmann, Heinz
1410. Schürmann, Heinz
1499. Stonehouse, N. B.
1559. Thils, Gustave
1575. Todt, Heinz E.
1579. Trilling, Wolfgang
1582. Trocmé, Étienne
1595. Turner, H. E. W.

1964–1965

386. Downing, F. G.
1599. Turner, N.

1964

33. Argyle, A. W.
37. Argyle, A. W.
111. Betz, Otto
197. Burkill, T. Alec
332. Dalmau, E. M.
346. Davies, William D.
350A. Deiss, L., ed. and trans.
432. Eppstein, Victor
457A. Farmer, William R.
458. Farmer, William R.
491. Foster, L. A.
525. Gerhardsson, Birger
527. Gerhardsson, Birger
540. Gnilka, Joachim
594. Gundry, Robert H.
992. Martinez Dalmau, Eduardo
1001. McArthur, Harvey K.
1033. Metzger, Bruce M.
1064. Morton, A. Q.,

and G. H. C. Macgregor
1081. Muraoka, T.
1086. Neill, Stephen
1180. Perler, Othmar
1213. Porúbcan, Štefan
1254. Roberts, James Hall
1274. Robinson, James M.
1352. Schmid, Josef
1389. Schulz, Siegfried
1400. Schürmann, Heinz
1474. Stacpoole, A. J.

1965–1966

534. Glasson, T. F.
1052A. Mitton, Charles L.

1965–1977

98. Benoit, Pierre,
    and M.-É. Boismard

1965

14. Akagi, Tai
82. Bea, A.
106. Best, Ernest
167. Bowman, John
174. Briscoe, Hollie L.
489. Foakes-Jackson, Frederick John,
    and Kirsopp Lake
596A. Guthrie, Donald
602. Hadas, Moses,
    and Morton Smith
612. Haik, Paul S.
777A. Keck, Leander E.
822. Koester, Helmut
895. Léon-Dufour, Xavier
1015A. McLoughlin, S.
1157A. Ott, Wilhelm
1227. Reiling, J.
1263. Robinson, James M.
1524. Suhl, Alfred
1630. Vielhauer, Philipp

1966

65. Barclay, Robert
71. Barrett, C. K.
138. Boismard, M. E.
224. Cadbury, Henry J.
236. Campbell, D. B. J.
334. Dambricourt, Georges
348. Davis, Joseph L.
461. Farmer, William R.
464. Farmer, William R.
518. Gander, Georges
535. Glasson, T. F.
606. Haenchen, Ernst
631. Hartman, L.
778. Keck, Leander E.,

and J. Louis Martyn
840. Kümmel, Werner G.
862. Lambrecht, Jan
922. Linnemann, Eta
936. Lohmeyer, Ernst
1031. Metzger, Bruce M.
1211. Polag, Athanasius
1280. Rohde, Joachim
1323A. Sanders, Ed Parish
1413. Schürmann, Heinz
1437. Sieber, John Howard
1441A. Simpson, R. T.
1447. Snape, H. C.
1645. Walker, N.
1706. Wilkens, W.

1967–1968

103. Best, Ernest
447. Farmer, William R.
526. Gerhardsson, Birger

1967

9. Abrahams, Israel
59. Balz, Horst R.
85. Beardslee, William A.
93. Bellinzoni, A. J.
143. Boman, Thorlief
146A. Borchert, Gerald Leo
229. Cain, Marvin F.
443. Farmer, William R.
452. Farmer, William R.
617. Hare, Douglas R. A.
626. Harrington, Wilfrid
694. Hoffmann, Paul
793. Kilpatrick, G. D.
870. Lambrecht, Jan
878. LaPotterie, Ignace de, ed.
899A. Léon-Dufour, Xavier
1013. McLoughlin, S.
1042. Meyer, Paul Donald
1084. Mussner, Franz
1109. Neirynck, Frans
1115. Neirynck, Frans
1145. Ong, Walter J.
1161A. Palmer, N. H.
1185. Perrin, Norman
1357. Schmithals, Walter
1396. Schulz, Siegfried
1693. West, H. P., Jr.

1968–1969

32. Argyle, A. W.
241. Carlston, Charles E.
246. Carmignac, Jean
268. Cave, C. H.
495. Freudenberger, R.
990. Martin, R. P.

1012. McIndoe, J. H.
1600. Turner, N.

1968

84. Beardlsee, William A.
91. Beauvery, R.
119. Bjerkelund, C. J.
129. Bligh, J.
175A. Broadribb, D.
237. Campenhausen, Hans von
270. Cerfaux, Lucien
294. Conzelmann, Hans
353. Delorme, J.
402. Dupont, Jacques
459. Farmer, William R.
520. Gast, Frederick
588. Grundmann, Walter
599. Guy, Harold A.
654. Hengel, Martin
716. Honore, A. M.
724. Hrychok, William D.
825. Koester, Helmut
873. Lambrecht, Jan
874. Lambrecht, Jan
875. Lambrecht, Jan
876. Lambrecht, Jan
898. Léon-Dufour, Xavier
912. Lindars, Barnabas
925. Linton, O.
994. Marxsen, Willi
1025A. Merkel, Helmut
1047. Michaelis, Christine
1106A. Neirynck, Frans
1160. Palmer, Humphrey
1186. Perrin, Norman
1193. Pesch, Rudolf
1194. Pesch, Rudolf
1212. Polag, Athanasius
1216. Pryke, E. J.
1411. Schürmann, Heinz
1450. Snoy, T.
1526. Summers, Ray
1562. Thils, Gustave,
 and R. E. Brown, eds.
1641. Vööbus, Arthur
1652. Watson, James D.
1654. Weeden, Theodore J.
1714. Wink, Walter
1719. Wootton, R. W. F.
1725. Wrege, Hans T.

1969–1970

36. Argyle, A. W.
230. Caird, George B.

1969

56. Bajard, J.
123. Black, Matthew
128. Bligh, J.
130. Bligh, J.
131. Bligh, J.
132. Bligh, J.
133. Bligh, J.
173. Briggs, R. C.
220. Butler, B. C.
245. Carmignac, Jean
416. Edwards, Richard A.
426. Elliott, J. Keith
462. Farmer, William R.
553. Goulder, M. D.
632. Hasel, Gerhard F.
635. Hasler, Victor
655. Hengel, Martin
689. Hoffmann, Paul
690. Hoffmann, Paul
698. Hoffmann, Paul
791. Kertelge, K.
801A. Kingsbury, Jack Dean
854. Lafontaine, R.,
 and P. Mourlon Bearnaert
901. Léon-Dufour, Xavier
903. Leonardi, G.
920. Lindsey, R. L.
962. Lührmann, Dieter
975. Manson, Thomas W.
986. Marshall, I. Howard
995. Marxsen, Willi
999. McArthur, Harvey K.
1003. McArthur, Harvey K.
1006. McCaughey, J. D.
1014. McLoughlin, S.
1090. Neirynck, Frans
1095. Neirynck, Frans
1138. O'Neill, J. C.
1144. Oliver, A.
1155. Ortiz de Urbina, I.
1182. Perrin, Norman
1187. Perrin, Norman
1191. Pesch, Rudolf
1207. Pokorny, Petr
1293. Ruddick, C. T., Jr.
1320A. Sanders, Ed Parish
1326. Sanders, Ed Parish
1327A. Sanders, Jack T.
1374. Schneider, Gerhard
1386. Schreiber, J.
1403. Schürmann, Heinz
1472. Spivey, Robert A.,
 and D. Moody Smith, Jr.
1492. Stein, Robert H.

1608. Urbina, I. Ortiz de
1620. Vargas-Machuca, A.
1621. Vargas-Machuca, A.
1640. Vööbus, Arthur
1648. Walker, William O., Jr.
1699. Wichelhaus, M.
1701. Wiefel, Wolfgang

1970–1971

425. Elliott, J. Keith
704. Holst, R.
1002. McArthur, Harvey K.

1970

12. Achtemeier, Paul J.
57. Baker, Alfred
61. Bammel, Ernst
83. Beardslee, William A.
88. Beare, Francis Wright
156. Bornkamm, Günther
166. Bovon, François
195. Burchard, Christoph
222. Buttrick, David G., ed.
280. Christ, Felix
330. Curtis, Philip
355. Denaux, A.
360. Descamps, A.
375A. Didier, M., ed.
391A. Dungan, David L.
396. Dupont, Jacques
401. Dupont, Jacques
418. Edwards, Richard A.
424. Elliott, J. Keith
483. Fitzmyer, Joseph A.
516. Gaboury, Antonio
607. Hahn, Ferdinand
614. Hamann, H. P.
691. Hoffmann, Paul
693. Hoffmann, Paul
779A. Kee, Howard Clark
838. Kümmel, Werner G.
863. Lambrecht, Jan
889. Lehmann, Martin
900. Léon-Dufour, Xavier
958. Lührmann, Dieter
985. Marshall, I.
993. Martyn, J. Louis
1043. Meyer, Paul Donald
1055. Monaghan, F. J.
1058. Montgomery, Robert M.
1098. Neirynck, Frans
1166A. Paschen, Wilfrid
1246. Riesenfeld, Harald
1250. Rigaux, Beda
1266. Robinson, James M.
1284. Roloff, Jürgen

1367A. Schnackenburg, Rudolf
1367B. Schnackenburg, Rudolf
1370. Schneider, Gerhard
1378. Schoenberg, M. W.
1417. Schürmann, Heinz
1448. Snape, H. C.
1462. Solages, Bruno de
1465. Sparks, H. F. D.
1490. Stein, Robert H.
1522B. Suggs, M. Jack
1533B. Talbert, Charles H.
1545. Taylor, Vincent
1552. Teeple, Howard M.
1569. Timmer, John

1971

7. Abel, Ernest L.
18. Albright, W. F.,
    and C. S. Mann
60. Bammel, Ernst
69B. Barr, James
115B. Bijlefeld, William A.
157. Bornkamm, Günther
179. Brogan, W. J.
183B. Brown, Raymond E.
243. Carlston, Charles E.,
    and D. Norlin
258. Catchpole, D. R.
318. Cribbs, F. L.
347B. Davis, Charles T.
375B. Dillistone, F. W.
393A. Dungan, David L.
413. Edwards, Richard A.
419. Edwards, Richard A.
442C. Farmer, William R.
453C. Farmer, William R.
474. Fernandez, Enrique López
476A. Filson, Floyd Vivian
476B. Filson, Floyd Vivian
500B. Frye, Roland Mushat
504. Fuchs, Albert
513C. Funk, Robert W.
595B. Gustafson, James M.
601. Haacker, K.
615. Hamerton-Kelly, Robert
692. Hoffmann, Paul
717. Hooker, Morna Dorothy
737B. Idowu, E. Bolaji
753. Jeremias, Joachim
756. Jeremias, Joachim
757. Jervell, J.
777C. Keck, Leander E.
836A. Kuhn, Heinz-Wolfgang
954. Lovison, T.
1000. McArthur, Harvey K.
1005. McArthur, Harvey K.

1018. Mees, M.
1019. Mees, M.
1026. Merkel, Helmut
1034. Metzger, Bruce M.
1051C. Miller, Donald G.
1051D. Miller, Donald G. and
    Dikran Y. Hadidian, eds.
1051E. Minear, Paul S.
1052B. Moeller, Charles
1061. Morgenthaler, Robert
1069B. Moule, Charles F. D.
1134B. Nissiotis, Nicos A.
1154. Ortensio, da Spinetoli
1157D. Outler, Albert C.
1161B. Panikkar, Raymond
1385. Schramm, Tim
1423B. Schweizer, Eduard
1429B. Selby, Donald J.
1489. Stein, Robert H.
1505. Strecker, Georg
1522A. Suggs, M. Jack
1523. Suhl, Alfred
1530. Sweetman, L.
1566. Thompson, William G.
1631C. Voeglin, Eric
1634. Vögtle, Anton
1658. Weiser, Alfons
1724. Wrede, William
1737. Zeller, Dieter

1972–1973

329. Curtis, K. P. G.
630. Hartman, L.

1972

11. Achtemeier, Paul J.
19A. Aletti, Jean Noël
43. Aune, David E., ed.
58A. Balch, D. L.
64. Barbour, R. S.
100. Berger, K.
152. Boring, M. Eugene
237. Campenhausen, Hans, von
286E. Connick, C. Milo
291. Conzelmann, Hans
321. Crossan, John D.
322. Crossan, John D.
356. Denaux, A.
361. Devisch, M.
433. Ernst, Josef
485. Fitzmyer, Joseph A.
492. Frankemölle, H.
494. Freudenberg J.
496. Frey, Louis
515. Gaboury, Antonio
554. Goulder, M. D.

688. Hoffmann, Paul
695. Hoffmann, Paul
697. Hoffmann, Paul
703. Holst, R.
747. Jepsen, A.
803. Klein, H.
843. Kümmel, Werner G.
867. Lambrecht, Jan
893. Léon-Dufour, Xavier
897. Léon-Dufour, Xavier
927. Linton, O.
928. Linton, O.
943. Lonergan, Bernard Joseph Francis
960. Lührmann, Dieter
961. Lührmann, Dieter
980. Marconcini, B.
1009. McEleney, N. J.
1029. Merli, D.
1044. Meynell, Hugo
1056. Montague, G. T.
1082. Murphy-O'Connor, J.
1091. Neirynck, Frans
1096. Neirynck, Frans
1183. Perrin, Norman
1325. Sanders, Ed Parish
1338. Schille, Gottfried
1391. Schulz, Siegfried
1394. Schulz, Siegfried
1395. Schulz, Siegfried
1534. Talbert, Charles H.,
    and Edgar V. McKnight
1548. Taylor, Vincent
1553. Testa, G.
1635. Vögtle, Anton
1688. Wenham, D.
1738. Zeller, Dieter
1746. Zmijewski, Josef

1973–1974

679. Hill, David

1973

45. Baarda, T.
137. Boismard, M.-É.
155. Boring, M. Eugene
165. Bouttier, Michel
271. Cerfaux, Lucien
320. Crossan, John D
323. Crossan, John D.
382. Donahue, J. R.
455. Farmer, William R.
493. Frankemölle, H.
499. Frizzi, Guiseppe
513A. Funk, Robert W.
521. Gaston, Lloyd
523. Geiger, Ruthild

597. Güttgemanns, E.
611. Hahn, Ferdinand
726. Hubner, Hans
774. Katz, Friedrich
837. Kümmel, Werner G.
865. Lambrecht, Jan
877A. Lange, Joachim
880. Latourelle, René
971. Luz, Ulrich
1011. McHugh, J.
1088. Neirynck, Frans
1100. Neirynck, Frans
1102. Neirynck, Frans
1117. Neirynck, Frans, ed.
1127. Neusner, Jacob
1324. Sanders, Ed Parish
1387. Schreiner, Josef, ed.
1390. Schulz, Siegfried
1443. Smith, Morton
1455. Solages, Bruno de
1456. Solages, Bruno de
1461. Solages, Bruno de
1550. Taylor, W. S.
1551. Teeple, Howard M.
1556. Theissen, Gerd
1622. Vassiliadis, Petros
1720. Worden, Ronald D.

1974–1982

562. Gransden, Antonia

1974

35. Argyle, A. W.
89. Beare, Francis Wright
105. Best, Ernest
171. Brekelmans, C., et al.
185A. Buchanan, George W.
265. Catchpole, D. R.
305. Coppens, Joseph
310. Courcier, J.
324. Crossan, John D.
363. Devisch, M.
392. Dungan, David L.
434. Etcheverria, R. Trevijano
448A. Farmer, William R.
478. Fitzmyer, Joseph A.
500A. Frizzi, Guiseppe
559. Goulder, M. D.
596B. Guthrie, Donald
725. Hubbard, B. J.
730. Hultgren, Arland J.
761. Johnson, M. D.
869. Lambrecht, Jan
871. Lambrecht, Jan
1024. Merkel, Helmut
1087. Neirynck, Frans

1116. Neirynck, Frans
1118. Neirynck, Frans, ed.
1142. O'Rourke, J. J.
1184. Perrin, Norman
1198. Philips, Gérard
1206. Pokorny, Petr
1296. Sabbe, M., ed.
1301. Sabourin, L.
1302. Sabugal, S.
1432. Sellin, G.
1454. Solages, Bruno de
1597. Turner, N.
1685. Wehnam, D.

1975–1976

231. Caird, George B.

1975

10. Achtemeier, Paul J.
41. Aune, David E.
63. Banks, Robert
72. Barrett, C. K.
297. Conzelmann, Hans,
    and Andreas Lindemann
362. Devisch, M.
364. Devisch, M.
404. Dupont, Jacques, et al.
415. Edwards, Richard A.
442A. Farmer, William R.
509. Fuller, Reginald H.
512. Fuller, Reginald H.,
    E. P. Sanders,
    and Thomas R. W. Longstaff
633. Hasenfratz, H.-P.
643. Hawthorne, Gerald F.
665. Higgins, Angus J. B.
687. Hoffmann, Paul
713. Holtzmann, Heinrich J.
738. Isenberg, W. W.
799. Kingsbury, Jack Dean
845. Kümmel, Werner G.
951. Longstaff, Thomas Richmond Willis
967. Luz, Ulrich.
1139. O'Neill, J. C.
1140. O'Rourke, J. J.
1141. O'Rourke, J. J.
1143. Oberlinner, Lorenz
1261. Robinson, James M.
1275. Robinson, John A. T.
1319. Sanders, Ed Parish
1336. Schillebeeckx, E.
1371. Schneider, Gerhard
1372. Schneider, Gerhard
1382A. Schoonenberg, P.
1383. Schottroff, Luise
1392. Schulz, Siegfried

1399. Schürmann, Heinz
1433. Senior, D. P.
1460. Solages, Bruno de
1466. Sparks, H. F. D.
1528B. Swanson, Reuben J.
1582. Trocmé, Étienne
1623. Vassiliadis, Petros
1626. Vassiliadis, Petros
1629. Vielhauer, Philipp
1722. Worden, Ronald D.
1723. Woschitz, Karl
1742. Zeller, Dieter

1976–1977

1004. McArthur, Harvey K.
1192. Pesch, Rudolf

1976

29. Arai, S.
104. Best, Ernest
148. Boring, M. Eugene
154. Boring, M. Eugene
301B. Cope, O. Lamar
303. Cope, O. Lamar
333. Dalpadado, J. K.
341. Dautzenberg, G.
343. Davies, David
374. Dideberg, Dany,
      and P. Mourlon Bearnaert
388A. Dungan, David L.
414. Edwards, Richard A.
420. Edwards, Richard A.
450D. Farmer, William R.
458. Farmer, William R.
475. Feuillet, A.
481. Fitzmyer, Joseph A.
513D. Furnish, Victor P.
591. Guelich, Robert A.
864. Lambrecht, Jan
888. Legasse, Simon
918. Lindemans, Jean,
      and H. Demeester, eds.
924. Linton, O.
926. Linton, O.
947. Longstaff, Thomas Richmond Willis
948. Longstaff, Thomas Richmond Willis
1021. Meier, John P.
1083A. Murphy-O'Connor, J.
1107. Neirynck, Frans
1111. Neirynck, Frans
1114. Neirynck, Frans
1147A. Orchard, Bernard
1162. Parker, Pierson
1224A. Reicke, Bo
1276. Robinson, John A. T.
1337. Schillebeeckx, E.

1464. Soulen, R. N.
1486. Stegner, W. R.
1564. Thomas, R. L.
1601. Turner, N.
1604A. Tyson, Joseph B.
1604C. Tyson, Joseph B.

1977

149. Boring, M. Eugene
153. Boring, M. Eugene
212. Busse, Ulrich
264. Catchpole, D. R.
266. Catchpole, D. R.
286B. Collison, J. G. F.
351. Delling, Gerhard
387A. Drury, John
395. Dunn, James D. G.
423. Eijl, Edmond J. M. van, ed.
449. Farmer, William R.
590. Grundmann, Walter
764. Juel, Donald
861. Lambrecht, Jan
949. Longstaff, Thomas Richmond Willis
959. Lührmann, Dieter
1008. McDermott, John M.
1131. Nineham, Dennis E.
1153. Orchard, Bernard,
        and J. A. T. Robinson
1195. Pesch, Rudolf
1208. Polag, Athanasius
1248. Riesner, R.
1303. Sabugal, S.
1304. Sabugal, S.
1354A. Schmidt, Daryl
1368. Schnackenburg, Rudolf,
        J. Ernst, and J. Wanke, eds.
1369. Schneider, Gerhard
1497. Stoldt, Hans-Herbert
1568. Throckmorton, Burton Hamilton, Jr.
1627. Vassiliadis, Petros
1646B. Walker, William O., Jr.
1741. Zeller, Dieter

1978–1979

539. Gnilka, Joachim

1978

28A. Amore, R. C.
46. Baarda, T., A. F. J. Klijn,
      and W. C. van Unnik, eds.
162. Bosold, Iris
239. Carlston, Charles E.
259. Catchpole, D. R.
292. Conzelmann, Hans
293. Conzelmann, Hans
441B. Farmer, William R.
442B. Farmer, William R.

446. Farmer, William R.
451. Farmer, William R.
470. Fee, Gordon F.
479B. Fitzmyer, Joseph A.
500C. Frye, Roland Mushat
501. Fuchs, Albert
508A. Fuller, Reginald H.
508B. Fuller, Reginald H.
510. Fuller, Reginald H.
555. Goulder, M. D.
558. Goulder, M. D.
560A. Goulder, M. D.
576C. Greeven, Heinrich
714. Holtzmann, Heinrich J.
721B. Howard, George
742. Jacobson, Arland D.
758. Jervell, J.
777B. Keck, Leander E.
788. Kennedy, G.
792B. Kilpatrick, G. D.
800. Kingsbury, Jack Dean
813. Kloppenborg, J. S.
865. Lambrecht, Jan
910. Lewis, P. B.
945. Longstaff, Thomas Richmond Willis
953B. Lord, Albert B.
972A. Mahnke, Hermann
983. Marshall, I. Howard
1007. McDermott, John M.
1017D. Meeks, Wayne A.
1025B. Merkel, Helmut
1027. Merklein, Helmut
1063. Morin, Emile
1113. Neirynck, Frans
1121A. Neirynck, Frans,
        and Frans van Segbroeck
1137. O'Connell, L. J.
1146A. Orchard, Bernard
1146C. Orchard, Bernard, trans.
1151. Orchard, Bernard,
        and T. R. W. Longstaff, eds.
1157C. Outler, Albert C.
1175. Peabody, David B.
1190. Pesce, Mauro
1217. Pryke, E. J.
1225. Reicke, Bo
1251. Rist, John M.
1327B. Sanders, James A.
1335. Schenke, Hans-Martin,
        and Karl Martin Fischer
1384. Schottroff, Luise,
        and Wolfgang Stegemann
1398. Schuppan, C.
1430. Sellin, G.
1439A. Silberman, Lou H.

1503. Strecker, Georg
1520. Sturch, R. L.
1533A. Talbert, Charles H.
1603G. Tyson, Joseph B.
1603I. Tyson, Joseph B.
1604B. Tyson, Joseph B.
1607. Tyson, Joseph B.,
        and T. R. W. Longstaff
1624. Vassiliadis, Petros
1646A. Walker, William O., Jr.
1649. Walker, William O., Jr.
1653. Weder, Hans

1979–1983

306. Coppens, Joseph

1979–1981

657. Herbst, Karl

1979

116. Binder, H.
136. Bocher, O.
140. Boismard, M.-E.
367. Dewey, Joanna
489. Foakes-Jackson, Frederick John,
        and Kirsopp Lake
525B. Gerhardsson, Birger
613. Hamann, H. P.
678. Hill, David
821. Koester, Helmut
834. Kremer, Jacob, ed.
835. Kuchler, Max
848. Kurzinger, J.
950. Longstaff, Thomas Richmond Willis
1039A. Meyer, Ben F.
1092. Neirynck, Frans
1105. Neirynck, Frans
1120. Neirynck, Frans, et al.
1150. Orchard, Bernard
1209. Polag, Athanasius
1333. Schenk, W.
1360. Schmithals, Walter
1365. Schmithals, Walter
1428. Segalla, G.
1439B. Silberman, Lou H.
1458. Solages, Bruno de
1484. Stegeman, Wolfgang
1485. Stegeman, Wolfgang
1555. Thiessen, Gerd
1586. Tuckett, C. M.
1745. Ziesler, J. A.

1980–1981

823A. Koester, Helmut

1980

176. Broer, Ingo
252. Cartlidge, David R.,
     and David L. Dungan, eds.
267. Causse, M.
286D. Combrink, H. J. B., et al.
308. Correns, Dietrich
385D. Downing, F. G.
389A. Dungan, David L., ed.
393D. Dungan, David L.
441. Farmer, William R.
444B. Farmer, William R.
450B. Farmer, William R.
450E. Farmer, William R.
457C. Farmer, William R.
460. Farmer, William R.
471. Fee, Gordon F.
502. Fuchs, Albert
505. Fuchs, Albert
507. Fuchs, Albert
556. Goulder, M. D.
666. Higgins, Angus J. B.
683. Hobbs, Edward C.
721C. Howard, Virgil, trans.
755. Jeremias, Joachim
759. Johns, Eric, and David Major
776. Keck, Leander E.
804. Klein, Peter
842. Kümmel, Werner G.
866. Lambrecht, Jan
881. Laufen, Rudolf
882. Laufen, Rudolf
891. Lentzen-Deis, F.
913. Lindars, Barnabas
923. Linton, O.
946. Longstaff, Thomas Richmond Willis
1020. Meier, John P.
1022A. Meier, John P.
1089. Neirynck, Frans
1112. Neirynck, Frans
1129. Newman, Robert C.
1149A. Orchard, Bernard
1157B. Outler, Albert C.
1214A. Powers, B. W.
1249. Riesner, R.
1346. Schlosser, Jacques
1359. Schmithals, Walter
1362. Schmithals, Walter
1418. Fiorenza, Elisabeth Schüssler
1436. Shuler, Philip L.
1498. Stoldt, Hans-Herbert
1578. Torris, J.
1584A. Tuckett, C. M.
1603F. Tyson, Joseph B.
1740. Zeller, Dieter

1747. Zmijewski, Josef

1981–1985

479A. Fitzmyer, Joseph A.

1981–1982

262. Catchpole, D. R.
503. Fuchs, Albert
997. März, C.-P.

1981

87. Beare, Francis Wright
107. Betz, Hans Dieter
115A. Biggs, H.
139. Boismard, M.-É.
260. Catchpole, D. R.
304. Coppens, Joseph
406. Dyer, Charles H.
484. Fitzmyer, Joseph A.
487. Fleddermann, Harry
576A. Greeven, Heinrich, ed.
798. Kingsbury, Jack Dean
851. Kurzinger, J.
915. Lindars, Barnabas
944. Longstaff, Thomas Richmond Willis
952. Longstaff, Thomas Richmond Willis
1078. Muller, Ulrich B.
1110. Neirynck, Frans
1165. Parker, Pierson
1334. Schenk, W.
1366. Schmitt, John J.
1493. Steinhauser, Michael G.
1576. Toews, J. E.
1651. Wanke, Joachim
1689. Wenham, J. W.
1700. Wiefel, Wolfgang

1982–1983

802. Kister, Menahem
1148B. Orchard, Bernard

1982

109. Betz, Hans Dieter
151. Boring, M. Eugene
242. Carlston, Charles E.
257. Catchpole, D. R.
313. Crawford, Barry S.
349. Dehandschutter, Boudewijn
352. Delobel, Joël, ed.
357A. Denaux, A.
359. Dermience, Alice
403. Dupont, Jacques
417. Edwards, Richard A.
445B. Farmer, William R.
514A. Fusco, Vittorio
595A. Gundry, Robert H.
662. Heylen, V., ed.

740. Jacobson, Arland D.
741. Jacobson, Arland D.
775. Kealy, Sean P.
824. Koester, Helmut
868. Lambrecht, Jan
887. Legasse, Simon
955. Lowe, M.
1093. Neirynck, Frans
1097. Neirynck, Frans
1108. Neirynck, Frans
1122. Neirynck, Frans,
    and Frans Van Segbroeck
1128. Newman, Robert C.
1178. Peabody, David B.
1188. Perrot, Charles
1200. Piper, Ronald A.
1259. Robinson, James M.
1260. Robinson, James M.
1286. Romaniuk, K.
1295. Sabbe, M.
1298. Sabourin, L.
1361. Schmithals, Walter
1381. Schönle, Volker
1402. Schürmann, Heinz
1415. Schürmann, Heinz
1429A. Seitz, O. J. F.
1435B. Shuler, Philip L.
1487. Stegner, W. R.
1554A. Tevis, Dennis Gordon
1587. Tuckett, C. M.
1590. Tuckett, C. M.
1619. VanCangh, Jean-Marie
1625. Vassiliadis, Petros
1633. Vögtle, Anton
1642. Vorster, Willem S.
1650A. Walker, William O., Jr.
1686. Wenham D.
1726. Wrege, Hans T.
1739. Zeller, Dieter

1983

13B. Agnew, Peter W.
42. Aune, David E.
150. Boring, M. Eugene
185C. Buchanan, George Wesley
238. Cantwell, L.
251. Carruth, Shawn
261. Catchpole, D. R.
263. Catchpole, D. R.
285. Collins, Raymond F.
286A. Collison, J. G. F.
286C. Collison, J. G. F.
298. Cook, M. J.
301A. Cope, O. Lamar
307B. Corley, Bruce C., ed.
319. Crossan, John D.

335. Danner, Dan G.
347A. Davis, Charles T.
376. Dillon, R. J.
391B. Dungan, David L.
427. Ellis, E. Earle
441A. Farmer, William R.
444C. Farmer, William R.
444D. Farmer, William R.
449. Farmer, William R.
450C. Farmer, William R., ed.
454. Farmer, William R.
514B. Gamba, Giuseppe Giovanni
517. Gamber, Klaus
536. Glickman, Steven Craig
589. Grundmann, Walter
637. Havener, Ivan
649. Hedrick, Charles W.
718. Hooker, Morna Dorothy
719A. Horn, Friedrich Wilhelm
780. Kee, Howard Clark
786. Kelber, W. H.
801B. Kingsbury, Jack Dean
823B. Koester, Helmut
829. Körtner, Ulrich H. J.
849. Kürzinger, J.
883. Launderville, Dale
914. Lindars, Barnabas
956. Lowe, M., and David Flusser
970. Luz, Ulrich
1023. Merino, Luis Diez
1028. Merklein, Helmut
1046. Meynet, Roland
1059. Mora, Vincent
1062. Morghen, R.
1075. Muddiman, John
1094. Neirynck, Frans
1146B. Orchard, Bernard
1156. Osburn, C. D.
1164B. Parker, Pierson
1170. Peabody, David B.
1172. Peabody, David B.
1176. Peabody, David B.
1181. Perrin, Norman
1210. Polag, Athanasius
1226D. Reicke, Bo
1272. Robinson, James M.
1273. Robinson, James M.
1282. Rolland, Philippe
1283. Rolland, Philippe
1285. Romaniuk, K.
1323B. Sanders, Ed Parish
1332. Schelkle, Karl Hermann
1345. Schlosser, Jacques.
1431. Sellin, G.
1435A. Shuler, Philip L.

1438B. Sigal, Phillip
1488. Stein, Robert H.
1507. Strecker, Georg, and Schnell Udo
1583. Tuckett, C. M.
1585. Tuckett, C. M.
1591A. Tuckett, C. M.
1603B. Tyson, Joseph B.
1721. Worden, Ronald D.

1984

19B. Alexander, Philip S.
19C. Alexander, Philip S.
110. Betz, Hans Dieter
121. Black, Matthew
135A. Blomberg, Craig L.
146B. Borg, Marcus J.
169. Brandenburger, Egon
177. Broer, Ingo
185B. Buchanan, George Wesley
233. Cameron, Peter Scott
234. Cameron, Ronald
235. Cameron, Ronald
247. Carmignac, Jean
339. Dauer, Anton
354. DelVerme, Marcello
385B. Downing, F. G.
387B. Dschulnigg, Peter
389B. Dungan, David L.
394. Dunn, James D. G.
398. Dupont, Jacques
400. Dupont, Jacques
441C. Farmer, William R.
444A. Farmer, William R.
445A. Farmer, William R.
453D. Farmer, William R.
463. Farmer, William R.
488. Fleddermann, Harry
506. Fuchs, Albert
560B. Goulder, M. D.
560C. Goulder, M. D.
572. Green, H. Benedict
573. Green, H. Benedict
578A. Grelot, P.
583. Grigsby, Bruce
664. Higgins, Angus J. B.
684. Hobbs, Edward C.
696. Hoffmann, Paul
700. Hoffmann, R.
782. Kee, Howard Clark
793B. Kilpatrick, G. D.
808. Kloppenborg, J. S.
810. Kloppenborg, J. S.
812. Kloppenborg, J. S.
827. Köester, Helmut
853. Laconi, Karl
886B. Lee, Jong-Yun

886C. Lee, Jong-Yun
917. Lindemann, Andreas
968. Luz, Ulrich
984. Marshall, I. Howard
1022B. Meredith, A.
1051A. Michiels, R.
1080. Mundla, J.-G. Mudiso Mbâ
1099. Neirynck, Frans
1101. Neirynck, Frans
1121B. Neirynck, Frans,
       and Frans van Segbroeck
1136. Nunez, M. de Burgos
1173. Peabody, David B.
1243. Richardson, Peter
1268. Robinson, James M.
1270. Robinson, James M.
1271. Robinson, James M.
1281. Rolland, Philippe
1297. Sabourin, L.
1299. Sabourin, L.
1328. Sato, Migaku
1363. Schmithals, Walter
1504. Strecker, Georg
1529. Sweetland, D. M.
1584B. Tuckett, C. M.
1588. Tuckett, C. M.
1589. Tuckett, C. M.
1591B. Tuckett, C. M., ed.
1604D. Tyson, Joseph B.
1610. Vaage, Leif Eric
1631B. Vinson, Richard Bolling
1687. Wenham, D.
1736. Zeller, Dieter

1985

94. Bellinzoni, A. J., ed.
108. Betz, Hans Dieter
279A. Chilton, Bruce
338. Daube, David
358. Denker, J.
388B. Dungan, David L.
393C. Dungan, David L.
399. Dupont, Jacques
431. Enslin, Morton Scott
480. Fitzmyer, Joseph A.
486. Fleddermann, Harry
513B. Funk, Robert W.
538. Glover, Richard
557. Goulder, M. D.
608. Hohn, Ferdinand
686. Hodgson, Robert
760. Johnson, Elizabeth A.
785. Kelber, W. H.
790. Kertelge, K.
806. Kloppenborg, J. S.
809. Kloppenborg, J. S.

811. Kloppenborg, J. S.
830. Kosch, Daniel
839. Kümmel, Werner G.
872. Lambrecht, Jan
963. Lührmann, Dieter
966. Luz, Ulrich
969. Luz, Ulrich
979. Marcheselli Casale, Cesare
996. März, C.-P.
1083D. Murray, Gregory
1083E. Murray, Gregory
1125. Neugebauer, Fritz
1159. Page, Allen
1214B. Powers, B. W.
1218. Puig i Tàrrech, Armand
1238. Rese, Martin
1244. Richardson, Peter,
    and P. Gooch
1247. Riesner, R.
1253. Robbins, V. K.
1262. Robinson, James M.
1264. Robinson, James M.
1267. Robinson, James M.
1300. Sabourin, L.
1305. Sabugal, S.
1320B. Sanders, Ed Parish
1329. Sauer, Jürgen
1358. Schmithals, Walter
1373. Schneider, Gerhard
1420. Schwarz, Günther
1423A. Schweizer, Eduard
1426. Scott, B. B.
1476. Stanton, Graham
1509. Streeter, Burnett Hillman
1605. Tyson, Joseph B.
1606. Tyson, Joseph B.
1655. Wegner, Uwe
1735. Zeller, Dieter

1986

90. Beasley-Murray, George Raymond
178. Broer, Ingo
244. Carmignac, Jean
299. Cooper, John Charles
300A. Cooper, John Charles
300B. Cooper, John Chalres
357B. Denaux, Adelbert,
    and Marc Vervenne
441D. Farmer, William R.
453B. Farmer, William R.
973. Mann, C. S.
1083B. Murray, Gregory
1103. Neirynck, Frans
1106B. Neirynck, Frans
1123. Neirynck, Frans,
    and Frans van Segbroeck

1226C. Reicke, Bo
1379. Scholer, David M.
1603C. Tyson, Joseph B.
1730. Yamauchi, E. M.

1987

55B. Baird, William
58B. Balch, D. L.
92. Bellinzoni, A. J.
279B. Chilton, Bruce
302. Cope, O. Lamar
337. Daube, David
390. Dungan, David L.
445C. Farmer, William R., ed.
448B. Farmer, William R.
524. Gerhardsson, Birger
638. Havener, Ivan
719B. Horsley, Richard A.
721A. Howard, George, trans. and ed.
807. Kloppenborg, J. S.
818. Knox, John
1015B. McMahon, Edward
1017B. McNicol, Allan J.
1017C. McNicol, Allan J., and
    William O. Walker, Jr.
1039B. Meyer, Ben F.
1067. Moule, Charles F. D.
1083C. Murray, Gregory
1147B. Orchard, Bernard
1148A. Orchard, Bernard
1152. Orchard, Bernard,
    and Harold Riley
1164A. Parker, Pierson
1166B. Patte, Daniel
1171. Peabody, David B.
1172. Peabody, David B.
1174. Peabody, David B.
1179. Peabody, David B.
1224B. Reike, Bo
1226A. Reicke, Bo
1321. Sanders, Ed Parish
1322. Sanders, Ed Parish, ed.
1354B. Schmidt, Daryl
1435C. Shuler, Philip L.
1436B. Shuler, Philip L.
1491. Stein, Robert H.
1563. Thomas, Page A.
1591C. Tuckett, C. M.
1603D. Tyson, Joseph B.
1603J. Tyson, Joseph B.
1609. Vaage, Leif Eric
1647. Walker, William O. Jr.
1650B. Walker, William O., Jr.
1650C. Walker, William O., Jr.,
    with Allan J. McNicol
1709B. Williams, Robert Lee

1710. Willis, Wendell

1988

385A. Downing, F. G.
385C. Downing, F. G.
453A. Farmer, William R., ed.
457B. Farmer, William R.
762B. Joiner, Earl
779B. Kee, Howard Clark
817B. Knight, Douglas A.
1525. Sullivan, Clayton

1989 (forthcoming)

141. Boismard, M.-É.,
        William R. Farmer,
        and Frans Neirynck, eds.
388C. Dungan, David L.
393B. Dungan, David L., ed.
1177. Peabody, David B.

Keyword Index

"paraboles du maitre dans les tradition synoptique, Les," 165
Parabolic material in Mark 4, 348
Parallel passages, 135A
Parker, Pierson, *The Gospel before Mark* (R), 1442
  reconsidered, 1165
Parousia parables in Luke, 1372
Passion
  and resurrection narratives, 1522A
  in Mark, 106
  narratives
    in John and the Synoptics, 147
    in Luke, 69A, 1051A, 1223, 1548
      sources of, 1189B
    in Mark, 1386
    in Matthew, 130, 1433
  sayings in the gospel tradition, 123
Patristic
  evidence and the Synoptic Problem, 514B
    reexamined, 450C
  quotations and gospel sources, 538
  testimonies regarding the gospels, 1025B
Paucity of sayings of Mark, 153
Paul
  and Jesus, 394
  and Q, 38, 39
  and sayings of Jesus, 1108
  and the historical Jesus, 1364
  and the synoptic mission discourse, 1589
  knowledge of, of Matthew, 219
Pauline
  epistles, 36
  gospels, 66
  theology, influence of, in Mark, 1690
Paulinism and the sayings of Jesus, 1236
Pericope
  first synoptic, 210
  of Nazareth, 56
  of the Canaanite woman, 359
Permutations, 19A
Persecuted documents of the New Testament, 1006
Persecution in Luke 12:1-12, 1529
Personal names in the Synoptic Gospels, Greek article with, 1551
Peter
  apostle, 1434
  denials, 1083E
Petrine Gospel, 66
  and the Griesbach Hypothesis, 347A
Pharisaism, 8, 9
Pharisees in Luke, 1745
Pherein, 485
Philippians 2:6-11 and Q, 1423A

Philo of Alexandria, 784
Philosophers, Cynic, 385C
Pittsburgh Festival of the Gospels, 222, 1051D
Plurality of Q, 663
Polag, Athanasius
  Die Christologie der Logienquelle (R), 1208
  Fragmenta Q. (R), 1209
Pontifical primacy and episcopal perogatives, 1561
Poor and Jesus of Nazareth, 1384
Positive criterion of Jesus' ministry, 240
Post-Apostolic Age in the chief moments of its development, 1421A
Posteriority of Mark, 1164B
Prayer
  and miracle, 1657
  house of, 72
  in Luke, 1157A
Preaching
  of Jesus, kingdom of God and Son of Man in the, 1630
  of John and temptation of Jesus, reconstruction of in Q 3-4, 1271
  of John, worksheets for the reconstruction of Q, 1268
Precanonical tradition used by author of Luke-Acts, 472
Pre-Marcan Gospel, 1431
  miracle catenae, 11, 12
  prophetic sayings tradition that argues for Mark's use of Matthew and Luke, 1175, 1176
  tradition, picture of Jesus in, 967
Pre-Synoptic scene, Jesus before the Sanhedrin, 1370
Presbyters and disciples of the Lord in Papias, 1079
Present Son of Man, 1590
Primitive and early Church, 518, 886A, 935
  apostolic period, 1675
Primitive Christianity, 193
  sociology of, 1555
Primitive text of Gospels and Acts, 283A
Priority
  of Luke, 920, 921, 1486, 1487
  of Mark, 1717
    advocated, 1500, 1510, 1521
    criticized, 1163
  of Matthew
    criticized, 1165
    documented, 1340
    supported, 672

Problem of the Gospels, its present state (1856), 1673
Problem of order and the Griesbach Hypothesis, 389B
Pro-Jewish passages in Matthew, 298
Promise and fulfillment, 844
Prophecies, 305
Prophecy
    and Q, 420
    Christian, 148, 149, 150
    early Christian, in Book of Revelation, 477B
    in New Testament, 678
Prophet(s), 1188
    Christian, 152, 155
    early Christian, 41, 42
Prophetic
    'I', 395
    utterances, 395
    vocation of Jesus, 959
Protévangile de Jacques, 27A
Proto-Luke, 175A
    alleged gospel source, 929
    hypothesis, 1196, 1536, 1549
        is it sound? 1542
        study of, 316
    reconsidered, 1159
    reexamination, 531
    Streeter's theory of, 732
    text of, 1538
    trial narrative of, 317
Proto-Matthew with Mark the earliest canonical Gospel, 1659
Provenance of Matthew, 457A
Purification, law of, 186
Purity, ritual, 1166A
    Judaism, 1127

'Q', 37, 38, 39, 40, 51, 73, 94, 172, 300, 325, 326, 335, 364, 428, 491, 568B, 700, 798, 971, 1181, 1211, 1254, 1301, 1358, 1361, 1363, 1509, 1609, 1739
    3-4 968
        reconstruction of 1271
    4 (Lk 4:1-13) 1610
    10:2-16 969
    11:14-20,
        worksheets for reconstruction of 809
    11:14-23 969
    according to, 1234
    alleged gospel source, 929
    alternative to, 442A
    and ancient sayings collections, 810
    and Christian prophecy, 151, 414
    and 1 Corinthians, 1583
    and Luke

Lk 4:16-30 and Isaiah, 1587
    Lk 10:4-11, 692
    see also use of Q by
    and Mark, 363
        Mk 4:21-25, 403
        function of John the Baptist, 1623
        overlap, 505
    and Matthew, 361, 760
        ch. 11, 417
        see also use of Q by
    and Nag Hammadi manuscripts, 1135
    and Philippians 2:6-11, 1423A
    and prophets, 1328
    and the cross, 239
    and the friend at midnight, 261
    and the Gospel of Thomas, 251
    and the Sermon on the Mount, worksheets for reconstruction of, 1273
    and the Synoptic Problem, 1453
    and Wisdom tradition, 1270
    Aramaic document, 211
    arguments
        against a written sayings source, 756
        for an oral sayings source, 756
    as sayings of Jesus, 1272
    ascetical words of Jesus in, 58A
    authorship and date, 54
    beginning of, 486
        theology in, 689
    bibliography of, 806, 1122
        1981–1985, additional list, 1123
        1981–1986, 1379
    Christ of, 1255
    Christological material in, 1212
    Christological texts from, 1297
    Christology of, 1208
    church's stake in, 441D
    community, 1042
        reproof and reconciliation, 263
    concordance to, 415
    conjecture on the origin of the symbol (Q) of, 1439B
    content of, 563
    critical reflections on, 1286
    criticism of, 556, 560A
    critique of, 388B
    date of, 860
        and authorship of, 54
    debate on, 115
    defense of, 168, 262, 329
    dictionary article on, 1110, 1291, 1464
    elusive character of, 1537
    end of, 61
    eschatology of, 420
    essays on, 327

(SOURCE HYPOTHESIS)

Source Hypothesis in light of the probability
   question, 1338
Sources, literary, 817B
   of Luke, 76
   quest for, 1429B
Spirit of God, 1619
Spruchquelle, 589
Stance of Jesus over against the stance of the
   Son of Man, 845
Statistical synopsis, 1061
Stoldt, Hans-Herbert, 721C
   and Conzelmann, 457C
   defended, 444B
   History and Criticism of the Marcan Hy-
     pothesis (R), 446
Stone of Scandal, 1007, 1008
Strauss, David Frederick
   and Ernest Renan, 1743A
   from, to Holtzmann and Meijboom (1830–
     1870), 1224B
Streeter, B. H., 445A, 505, 544, 1711
   criticized, 217
   The Four Gospels (R), 1510
   fundamental solution of Synoptic Problem
     criticized, 929
   theory of Proto-Luke, 732
Structural commentary on Matthew's faith,
   1166B
Style and method of Luke, 227
Suffering Son of Man, Words of, 1365
Suggs, M. Jack, *Wisdom, Christology, and
   Law in Matthew's Gospel* (R), 1522B
Support of Q, 839
Synopsis
   first modern example, 582
   for Q [11:14-26], 811
   of Q, 1391
   of the Gospels, 405
     Greek, 1729
     horizontal line, 1528B
     statistical, 1061
   Synopsis Quattuor Evangeliorum, 15
   theory of construction of, 393D
Synoptic abstract, computer Bible, 1607
Synoptic criticism, 53, 807
   and eschatological problem, 1517
   since Streeter, 436
Synoptic divorce material, 265
Synoptic eschatology, understanding of, 209A
Synoptic Evangelists, 1741
   their redaction procedure, 1130
Synoptic Gospel research, 1232
Synoptic Gospels, 6, 13A, 15, 82, 84, 85,
   127, 147, 159, 184, 236, 300B, 310, 385D,
   399, 422, 438, 475, 485, 496, 543, 600,

(SYNOPTIC GOSPELS)

   653, 711, 814, 896, 901, 939, 1057, 1252B,
   1361, 1455, 1456, 1554C, 1569, 1682, 1697
   and Acts, 286D
     alterations to the text of, 1708
     dates, 619
   and early Christianity, 972A
   and John, 519, 1713
   and memory, 1550
   and oral tradition, 1479
   and the Gospel of Thomas, 1437
   and the Two-Document Hypothesis, 1058
   and the tradition of the Pentateuch, 334
   and Thessalonians, 1149A
   analysis of their order, 1454
   argues against Q, 1288
   argues for the priority of an Ur-Mark, 852
   article as pronoun in, 1140
   as historical documents, 1478
   bibliography of, 353
   birth of, 244
   concordance in seven colors, 894
   criticize Two-Gospel (Griesbach) Hypoth-
     esis, 712
   defend Two-Source Hypothesis, 712
   dependency of, 406
   developmental history of, 1668
   dictionary articles on, 596B, 1352, 1518
   divorce material in, 265
   doublets in, 1495
   explained, 1470
   form and content of, 706
   Greek article with personal names, 1551
   Hebrew background, 246
   independence of, and Luke's travel narra-
     tive, 1689
   introduction to, 166, 1358, 1677
   introduction to methods and issues in the
     study of, 173
   Jesus Christ in, 798
   language style, 1651
   literary characteristics, 639
   medieval illustration of documentary the-
     ory of origin of, 1205
   new attempt to explain their development,
     571
   new research on their relationships (1844),
     1419B
   origin, 746, 981, 1499
     and composition, 412, 831, 1048
     and mutual dependence, 1239
     and mutual relation of, 1718
     and relations, 248, 249
   parables in, 174, 866
   reflections on the special design of, 1055
   relationship between, 1705

New Gospel Studies
A Monograph Series for Gospel Research

Series General Editor
William R. Farmer
Perkins School of Theology
Southern Methodist University

Series Associate Editor	MUP Advisory Editor
David B. Peabody	*Edd Rowell*
Nebraska Wesleyan University	Mercer University Press

New Gospel Studies
Editorial Advisory Board

Samuel Oyinloye Abogunrin	*Thomas R. W. Longstaff*
University of Ibadan	Colby College
Harold W. Attridge	*Gerd Lüdemann*
University of Notre Dame	University of Göttingen
Arthur J. Bellinzoni	*Bruce M. Metzger*
Wells College	Princeton Theological Seminary
George Wesley Buchanan	*David P. Moessner*
Wesley Theological Seminary	Columbia Theological Seminary
John Drury	*Pierson Parker*
Kings College, Cambridge	Claremont, California
David L. Dungan	*Ellis Rivkin*
University of Tennessee	Hebrew Union College
Cain Hope Felder	*Philip L. Shuler*
Howard University Divinity School	McMurry College
Martin Hengel	*Joseph B. Tyson*
University of Tübingen	Southern Methodist University

William O. Walker, Jr.
Trinity University